COALITION POLITICS IN INDIA
Problems and Prospects

COALITION POLITICS IN INDIA

Problems and Prospects

Edited by

MAHENDRA PRASAD SINGH
ANIL MISHRA

Foreword by

BIMAL PRASAD

Under the auspices of the
Rajendra Prasad Academy
New Delhi

MANOHAR
2004

First published 2004

ISBN 81-7304-573-9

Published by
Ajay Kumar Jain for
Manohar Publishers & Distributors
4753/23 Ansari Road, Daryaganj
New Delhi 110002

Typeset by
A J Software Publishing Co. Pvt. Ltd.
New Delhi 110005

Printed at
Lordson Publishers Pvt. Ltd.
Delhi 110007

Contents

Foreword 7

PART I: PROLOGUE

1. Introduction
   MAHENDRA PRASAD SINGH AND ANIL MISHRA 11
2. Theorizing and Reforming Coalitional Governance in India
   MAHENDRA PRASAD SINGH 21

PART II: COALITION GOVERNMENTS AT UNION AND STATE LEVELS

3. Unstable Parties and Unstable Alliances: Births, Splits, Mergers and Deaths of Parties, 1952-2000
   E. SRIDHARAN 43
4. The National Front and United Front Coalition Governments: A Phase in Federalized Governance
   MAHENDRA PRASAD SINGH 75
5. Coalition Politics in India: The NDA Experiment
   KAMALA PRASAD 101
6. Coalitional Experiments: The Marriage of Inconvenience
   C.P. BHAMBHRI 123
7. Party Systems and Coalition Politics in Indian States
   HIMANSHU ROY 137
8. The 1999 Lok Sabha Elections and the Left Front in West Bengal
   BIDYUT CHAKRABARTY 155

9. Coalition Politics in Uttar Pradesh
S.K. JHA 187

PART III: DEEPER STRUCTURES AND COALITION GOVERNMENTS

10. Reviewing the Federal Constitution: States' Rights and National Coalitions
BALVEER ARORA 217

11. Coalition Governments and Constitutional Reforms
REKHA SAXENA 233

12. Consequences of Electoral Systems on Coalition Governments
RAVI P. BHATIA 251

13. Pyramids of Coalitions: The Base *versus* the Apex
AJIT KUMAR JHA 273

PART IV: COALITION GOVERNMENT AND PUBLIC POLICIES

14. Coalition Politics and Economic Decision-making
PREM SHANKAR JHA 285

15. Coalition Governments and India's Foreign Policy
NALINI KANT JHA 293

Contributors 327

Index 329

Foreword

Coalition Governments have become a regular feature in India both at the Centre as also in some states. Keeping this in view the Rajendra Prasad Academy organized two seminars consecutively in 1999 and 2000 on this subject. The panelists for the two seminars were more or less common. So they had an opportunity to think through their arguments in a sustained way twice, and then again at the time of revising their papers in the light of the discussions in the Academy and of editorial comments. Most of the authors availed this third opportunity of revising and embellishing their papers.

I am thankful to the contributors for responding to our request for papers and participating in the deliberations. They included Sri Baliram Bhagat, Sri T.N. Chaturvedi, Professor Muchkund Dubey, Sri Prakash Karat and late Sri Arvind Narain Das. Although they made only oral presentations and could not contribute papers, the Academy is thankful to them both for sparing time for the two seminars and for making valuable contributions to their deliberations.

I must especially thank those scholars who were able to contribute valuable papers, which are included in this volume: Dr E. Sridharan, Professor M.P. Singh, Sri Kamala Prasad, Professor C.P. Bhambhri, Sri Himanshu Roy, Professor Bidyut Chakrabarty, Professor S.K. Jha, Professor Balveer Arora, Dr Rekha Saxena, Dr Ravi P. Bhatia, Dr Ajit Kumar Jha, Sri Prem Shankar Jha and Professor Nalini Kant Jha.

Last but not the least, my sincere thanks are due to Professor M.P. Singh and Sri Anil Mishra for shouldering the responsibility of editing this volume. Sri Anil Mishra is my colleague at the Academy as Honorary Deputy Director and was more or less duty-bound to take this responsibility. I am, therefore, especially beholden to Professor M.P. Singh, who readily agreed to my request to take on the major responsibility in editing this volume. His acceptance of this responsibility was especially valuable as he has written and edited several volumes relating to contemporary politics in India and also dealt with aspects of coalition politics in some of his works.

I must also thank the staff of the Rajendra Prasad Academy for their unstinted cooperation in the holding of the seminar.

Director BIMAL PRASAD
Rajendra Prasad Academy
New Delhi

PART I: PROLOGUE

CHAPTER 1

Introduction

Mahendra Prasad Singh
Anil Mishra

The papers edited and compiled in this volume were presented at a national seminar on coalition politics in India organized in New Delhi by the Rajendra Prasad Academy in the spring of 2000. All the papers, except that of Prem Shankar Jha, have been revised and updated for this publication. Timed with the presentation of Union Budget 2000, Jha's paper is a period analytical sketch and therefor best left un-retouched.

Democratic politics in multicultural societies is essentially an exercise in coalition. India got its first coalition government in 1946 when Jawaharlal Nehru formed the Indian National Congress (INC)–Muslim League interim government in New Delhi under the shadow of the last British Governor-General of India, Lord Mountbatten, with the imperial Partition of India hovering overhead. This was a bitter exercise in coalition governance, mainly due to a deliberate and determined impasse occasioned by the control of the purse strings by the Muslim League Finance Minister. It was obviously a purely provisional wedlock before a pre-determined divorce, bereft of the normal features of a parliamentary system with a collective cabinet responsibility under the prime ministerial authority.

Following Independence, recourse to coalition governments were not necessary at Union as well as state levels due to the clear political dominance of the INC. This dominance was buttressed by the departure of the Muslim League from the Indian political scene and the pattern of other ethnic cleavages by the strong surge of nationalist fervour that carried on from the anti-colonial freedom struggle. Class differentiation and routinized electoral politicization of the mass public was also at a lower ebb. Yet coalition governments did surface in at least some states like Kerala even in the first decade after Independence, came with a rush by the late 1960s in most northern Indian states, and by the late 1970s in the north-eastern states.

After a period of Congress restoration under Indira Gandhi in the early 1970s, the last years of the decade witnessed the formation of the first non-Congress government in New Delhi by Janata Party in the wake of the Jayaprakash Narayan or JP movement and the internal Emergency. Although formally a one-party government, the Morarji Desai–Janata dispensation was, for all practical purposes, a coalition arrangement. Its constituents—Bharatiya Jana Sangh (BJS), Bharatiya Lok Dal (BLD), Congress (Organization or Opposition), and Socialists, later to be joined by Congress for Democracy—who hurriedly merged to form a common party on the eve of the post-Emergency election, did not carry the process of integration to culmination before they splintered between 1979 and the early years of the 1980s. And, finally, the recurrent occurrence of coalition governments in states like Kerala and West Bengal since the late 1970s came to be replicated at the centre and in several other states from 1989.

In a society marked by plurality, federality, and hierarchy of status and wealth, a multiparty system and coalition governence ought to be expected, especially when the social cleavages are not bridged by a mass movement or polarized by a class differentiation typical of advanced industrial societies. In exceptional circumstances marked by serious economic crisis and charismatic leadership, bi-polar or multi-polar political configurations may, additionally, be submerged by a one party-dominant system as it was in the post-Independence Nehru and post-Congress split (1969) Indira Gandhi eras.

This volume is divided into four major parts. In Part I, Mahendra Prasad Singh and Anil Mishra introduce the theme of the volume and the seminar at which these papers were first presented. In the chapter that follows, M.P. Singh analyses the conditions, causes, and consequence of coalitional governance in India. In Singh's theorization, the coalition phase of Indian politics may be explained in terms of the relationship between India's social and regional diversities and electoral and constitutional systems, intermediated by the factor of party system transformation since the late 1980s. Briefly, plurality or first-past, the post-electoral system and the federal nature of the Constitution (albeit in combination with parliamentarism) encourage plural and federal political dynamics in the political system, reinforced by the additional factors of multi-party system, judicial activism, and independent constitutional and statutory regulatory authorities.

Part II deals with the working of coalition governments at the Union and state levels. In Chapter 3, E. Sridharan delineates five phases of inter-party electoral alliances and coalitions in Indian politics: (a) anti-Congress Samyukta Vidhayak Dals between 'highly personalized clientelistic parties with extremely weak organizational structures, if any, by disgruntled ex-Congressmen', (b) confederation of Janata Party constituents in the late 1970s that 'never developed unified organizational structures and processes of functioning worth the name, the original constituents, especially the BJS, largely retaining their identities, and hence, remaining extremely vulnerable to splits and defections', (c) post-Janata Left Front (LF) and Left Democratic Front (LDF) in West Bengal, Kerala, and Tripura and All India Anna Dravida Munnetra Kazhagam (AIADMK)–Congress alliance in Tamil Nadu, (d) Janata Dal (JD)-led National and United Fronts consisting additionally of some regional and leftist parties in the late 1990s and early and (e) Bharatiya Janata Party (BJP)-led National Democratic Alliance (NDA) since the late 1990s at the centre and intra-state alliances of smaller parties in Tamil Nadu, Haryana, Maharashtra, Bihar, Himacal Pradesh, etc. Some generalizations about stability or instability of these categories of coalitions at national and state levels are also offered.

In Chapter 4, M.P. Singh takes a close look at National Front (NF) and United Front (UF) governments of New Delhi, the first comprehensive all-India phase of federalized parliamentary governments in New Delhi in which prominent regional parties from major parts of the country effectively participated. Both these regimes were quite diverse in ideological tendencies, but a degree of compatibility was managed to be brought about by stratifying the process of coalescing at two levels in the Parliament, namely, cabinet participation as well as parliamentary support, and support to the coalition limited only to the parliamentary floor. In both the NF and UF, coalition at the cabinet or coordination committee levels was limited only to some regional parties and the communist parties, while Congress and BJP, whose options were limited by mild waves of 'non-Congressism' and 'non-BJPism' in the party system, were reluctant supporters from the floor in the case of the NF. By the time UF governments came to be formed, the Somnath to Ayodhya *rathayatra* and, subsequently, the demolition of Babri Masjid in 1992 had marginalized BJP in the political class, and it fell to the lot of the Congress alone to be a reluctant floor ally of the ruling coalition. Both NF and UF managed to reconcile their internal conflicts of interest reasonably well, much better than the Janata Party *de facto* coalition of the late 1970s. It was due to the withdrawal of the floor support by the external allies—by BJP in the case of NF, and by Congress in cases of both the Deve Gowda and the Gujral UF governments that these coalitions prematurely collapsed.

In Chapter 5, Kamala Prasad traces the growth of coalition idea/practice in the backdrop of political developments and ideological rationalizations of Dr Ram Manohar Lohia and Jayaprakash Narayan (JP) in the late 1960s and 1970s respectively. This phase of coalition politics in the country has seen the divisive politics of competitive populism, casteism, and religious fundamentalism. Governmental instability associated with coalition governments in earlier phases is compounded in the more recent decades by a more comprensive political instability, communal strife and violence, and nauseating corruption and criminality in the political class. The empirical thrust of the paper is on the NDA. Prasad muses: 'the federal objective has been the real strength behind national coalition politics. The BJP has postponed its decision on this issue by ignoring the Sarkaria Commission report and instituting another constitutional review to overcome it. BJP is following a long-term politics of gaining as much strength in the company of regional parties as it did in the company of centrist parties in the north in the Janata Party phase (1977–80).'

In Chapter 6, C.P. Bhambhri takes a generally critical stance to coalition governments, terming them as an unfortunate and destructive 'marriage of inconvenience'. To him, the main villain of the piece is the BJP-led coalition government, which 'has extended very successfully the agenda of aggressive *Hindutva*'. The leading parties and its so-called secular/communal allies are, he believes, 'fully responsible for the communalization of the Indian state and society'.

In Chapter 7, Himanshu Roy examines party systems and coalition politics in Indian states and his analysis suggests that patterns of state party systems have climaxed, from the earlier more or less uniform one-party dominance under Congress or a regional party, into a variegated framework of state party systems, especially over the last two decades or so: (a) two-party systems in Andhra Pradesh (Telugu

Desam Party or TDP and Congress), Orissa (Biju Janata Dal or BJD and Congress), Gujarat (BJP and Congress), Madhya Pradesh (Congress and BJP), Chhattisgarh (Congress and BJP), Rajasthan (Congress and BJP), Mizoram (Congress and Mizo National Front or MNF), Tripura (Congress and CPI-M); (b) one major party against a coalition of parties: Punjab (Congress and Akali Dal–BJP coalition), Karnataka (Congress and Janata Dal (United) or JD(U)–BJP coalition), Jharkhand (BJP and Jharkhand Mukti Morcha or JMM plus allies), Manipur (Congress and Manipur People's Party or MPP), Sikkim (Sikkim Sangram Parishad and Congress); (c) stable bi-coalitional multiparty system: Kerala (United Democrative Front or UDF and LDF), West Bengal (LF and Trinamool Congress–BJP alliance), Tamil Nadu (AIADMK-led alliance and Dravida Munnetra Kazhagan or DMK-led alliance), Bihar (Rashtriya Janata Dal or RJD-led alliance and BJP-led alliance); (d) shifting bi-coalitional multiparty system: UP (Bahujan Samaj Party or BSP and allies and Samajwadi Party or SP and allies), Goa (BJP and allies and Congress and allies), Meghalaya (competing group of regional and national parties, Haryana (competing group of state-based parties in alliance with national parties); and (e) one-party dominant system: Jammu & Kashmir (National Conference or JKNC,) and Arunachal Pradesh (Congress or INC that went over to BJP in 2003 in a legislative realignment).

It is difficult to offer, as Himanshu Roy goes on to suggest, any clear-cut sociological or economic explanation for the various patterns of party system configuration in Indian states. In attempting to offer 'only some plausible arguments' as explanation, Roy associates early anti-Congress stance of Other Backward Classes (OBCs) in *ryotwari* south India, especially in Tamil Nadu and Kerala. On the other hand, in the *zamindari* areas of north India, especially Bihar and UP, the rise of OBCs came to pass much later, a post-*zamindari* abolition phenomenon of 1950s and later. The political consequence of their rise was the weakening and later decimation of the Congress party in these states. We may add, to what Roy observes in this context, that the geographical distribution of state party systems across the country defy any definite regional concentration of a specific pattern in different parts of the country. Nor are the state party systems explainable in terms of linguistic Indo-European, Dravidian, and tribal regions; nor, for that matter, in terms of the Hindi heartland and non-Hindi rimlands. One cannot also attribute these differences in state party systems to divisions such as pre-Independence British Indian provinces and Indian princely states, at least by now, making some allowance for such political differentials in earlier periods.

The state party systems differentials may be explained rather tautologically by saying that the Congress is still the most frequently occurring party factor across all the three categories of state party systems, especially those classified as two-party system and one party *versus* a coalition of parties. The next most frequently happening party factor is BJP, again especially in two-party states. Regional or rather state parties are almost equal in frequency as the BJP in two-party states. State parties are most numerous—ahead of both Congress and BJP—in bi-coalitional states. In one party *versus* a coalition, Congress and regional parties are more or less evenly matched. Finally, there is no clear and consistent relationship of any particular type of state party systems with the presence or absence of a decisively dominant caste or OBC or ST cluster. Nor is there any discernible association between state party system(s) and size (big or small) of state(s).

In Chapters 8 and 9, Bidyut Chakrabarty and S.K. Jha respectively present case studies of coalition governments in two major states of India—West Bengal and Uttar Pradesh. The former presents the most successful instance of coalition governance since 1977 with successive back-to-back majority under the LF dominated by Communist Party of India (Marxist) [CPI-(M)]. An earlier phase of omnibus coalition governance in the state from 1967 to early 1970s was very fractious and unstable. But 1977 marked a watershed and West Bengal stands out as a beacon of purposive and stable coalition governance. However, the incumbency factor seems to be lately dogging the fortunes of the LF in the state. Commenting on the 1999 West Bengal polls, Chakrabarty observes that despite confirmation of 'the popularity of the left coalition at the grassroots', the available straws in the wind suggest that 'what decided the election was not a positive vote for the Trinamool Congress–BJP combination but a negative one against the state government. The formation of the Trinamool Congress and its electoral pact with the BJP provided a forum for those opposed to the Left Front. The forum became apparently strong probably because of the charisma that had built around Mamata Banerjee. This sustains, if not strengthens, the possibility that the CPI(M)-led Front can rebuild its urban support base by paying adequate attention to the grievances of city dwellers.'

Contrariwise, coalition governance in UP, both in the intermittent phase (1967-70 and 1977-9) and in the more enduring phase (from 1989 onwards) has been issuelessly fractious and a byword for malgovernance. S.K. Jha concedes that compared to governments in the one-party Congress dominance phase, a wider process of social churning has been possible in the coalition era, making the political system more widely representative of society, yet he rightly adds: 'But this sociological gain in representativeness cannot be sustained too long at the cost of good governance and economic development tempered by rule of law and equity.'

Part III of the volume is devoted to the deeper structures of the polity and society and their relationship with coalition governments. In Chapter 10, Balveer Arora addresses the problem of states' rights in the context of 'national coalitions' and the review of the Constitution. He remarks that the issue of constitutional review 'arose in the specific situation arising from a series of hung parliaments and the repeated experience of coalitional instability'. He is inclined to question the blank assertion that one-party governments are inherently more effective and imbued with public purpose while coalition governments are necessarily weak and ineffectual. The experience in India based particularly on the 'stable eighties' as against the 'unstable nineties' instead shows otherwise: 'The assertiveness of state parties and their often aggressive articulation of states' rights has contributed in no small measure to the transformation that we witness today in many sectors. Coalitions of the present and the future will therefore need to constructively harness this energy by adapting the Constitution to the imperatives of more federal governance.'

In Chapter 11, Rekha Saxena reviews the debate stirred up in 1970s and 1980s by proposals for a presidential system in India (presumably with a federal dimension), and, earlier than the National Commission to Review the Working of the Constitution (NCRWC), whose report she also comments on, came to the conclusion that reforms rather than a restructuring of the system is required. About the NCRWC report, her assessment is that unless the constitutional amendments and legal reforms recommended by it are introduced as a package, they would not have the desired effect, as the various elements of reforms in party and electoral systems and the internal functional dynamics of government institutions are system-wise interdependent.

In Chapter 12, Ravi Bhatia maintains that political expression of social structures are intermediated by constitutional and electoral systems. He explores the relationship between social structure and electoral system, on the one hand, and party system and coalition governments, on the other. He says that given India's social diversity and the use of plurality electoral system, multiparty system and coalition governments would appear to be an expected outcome, especially with the diminishing effects of the nationalist movement, the passing away of the tall leadership of the Gandhi–Nehru era, and the growing politicization of the masses, classes, communities, and regions.

In Chapter 13, Ajit Kumar Jha maintains that the political structure of coalition politics, which first stemmed from the states in 1967, now sprawls at the Union level as well. Hence, 'unlike the one-party dominant system that followed a top-down chain of command, coalition politics demands a bottom-up style of functioning'. His empirical evidence is mainly drawn from Bihar. He also underlines the importance of a new thrust in study of coalition politics: 'It must move beyond the level of institutions (political parties) and enter the realm of structures (classes, castes, and other fundamental groupings). The relationship between political sociology and political institutions should be the new direction of research in this area.'

The importance of this emphasis can hardy be gainsaid. Social ubiquity of caste/ethnicity, along with class, is the *summum bonum* of structural functionalism of Indian politics. If we add to this the notions of individual-based liberal rights, culture-based minority rights, and corporate states' rights in a parliamentary-federal system of government, and corporate business rights of the market, we have before us the entire spectrum of deeper structures of the society, polity, and economy that coalition-building endeavours in Indian politics must contend with. This vast social and political matrix is sought to be animated by 'we, the people of India . . .' invoked in the ringing declaration of the Preamble to the Indian Constitution, the legatee of a legal transfer of power from the colonial to the national elites at the culmination of an anti-colonial mass movement of long duration and sociological depth with a composite ideological texture and a militant non-violent core. The nationalist elites were further made more representative and complex by democratic elections based on universal adult franchise beginning in 1952. Pre-1950 enfranchisement in the British Raj was to the extent of 25 per cent adult population, premised on property ownership and education under the Government of India Act, 1935, passed by the British Parliament.

It is a truism to say that policy-making under coalition governments is significantly different in both procedure and substance from that under a majority party government. Two chapters (14 and 15) in Part IV in this volume, by Prem Shankar Jha and Nalini Kant Jha, deal with this dimension of coalitional governance. The former outlines the factors that gradually but steadily ushered India into the phase of federal coalition governments: (a) delinking of Lok Sabha and Vidhan Sabha elections since 1971, (b) the failure of plurality voting system to prevent proliferation of small but stable political parties at the national level; and (c) the transformation of the dominant party system to a multiparty system. The author laments the declining economic rationality of federal decision-making on professed policy objectives of the Vajpayee government for reduction in subsidies, government expenditure, postponement of oil price rises, and the like. The story is not much different from economic decision-making by state governments. To quote N.K. Jha: 'There is not a single year in which at least three important states do not go to the polls. As a result there is not a single year in which the central government is not under severe pressure to postpone decisions that extract short-term costs for the people, no matter how beneficial these might prove in the medium and longer term.'

N.K. Jha explains implications of coalition governments for conduct of foreign policy. There is a change from centralized decision-making under one-party regimes to a more decentralized formulation of foreign policy that reflects a greater influence of regional or state-specific interests on foreign policy in the coalition era. He perceives a greater role for the bureaucracy in the new context but often coupled with a lack of political direction. We also note a greater demand for participation of state governments in federal treaty-making power in matters that have implications for areas of exclusive and concurrent legislative jurisdictions of states under the Constitution. Two cases are presently pending before the Supreme Court precisely in this context with special reference to the signing of the World Trade Organization (WTO) treaty by the Union government that entails obligations for state governments or restricts their policy option in areas such as agriculture, an exclusive State List subject.

CHAPTER 2

Theorizing and Reforming Coalitional Governance in India

Mahendra Prasad Singh

Theorizing politics of coalition in a polity of India's size, diversity, and complexity is a daunting task. Yet it must be attempted to make theoretical sense of Indian politics, especially since the 1990s. Beginning as a one-party dominant system under the INC after Independence, it was expected to develop into a parliamentary-federal two-party system of the old British Commonwealth variety. In 1977, it indeed showed some tendency towards that pattern, when only two parties—INC and Janata Party—accounted for over two-thirds of votes and seats.[1] But this tendency could not become a long-term trend. After a decade of regressive and apparent return of the Congress in 1980, India gradually slipped, by the end of the decade, into a multi-party system of coalitional and/or minority governance. It has not looked back since.

The post-colonial structures of state, market, and civil society all variously reflect variegated and shifting coalitions of parties, *varnas* and *jatis*, interest groups and classes, institutions, and regions. Coalitions at the level of political arenas and institutions are often buoyed by coalitions at deeper cultural and social structural planes. Federal coalitions often only cap those originating in the regions or localities, or they respond to political moves from above. Industrial and agrarian capitalists, professional middle classes, and working classes are differentially constructed regionally and nationally as well as at the levels of supranational, regional, and global integration. The political, bureaucratic, economic, and cultural elites and classes form visible and invisible coalition networks that allow relative rather than absolute autonomy to the federal and regional states for economic and cultural reproduction. The ruling elites and classes in India are in essence a coalitional construction. Depending upon the perspective from which it is seen, this kaleidoscopic coalitional panorama evokes the often divergent images of a ruling class coalition managing a 'relatively autonomous' state (Bardhan, 1984), a state as 'a third actor' between labour and capital with 'strained autonomy' (Rudolphs, 1987) and a state with a potentially balanced constitution (Singh, 1990).[2]

The emergence of multiparty system at the national level since 1989 has accelerated the process of federalization of India's parliamentary-federal system that functioned with a parliamentary tilt during the period of Congress dominance. This new trend has been further accentuated by two new factors, neo-liberal economic reforms introduced in a more comprehensive sense since 1991, and a pro-state autonomy shift in judicial behaviour, particularly since the Supreme Court judgement in the Bommai case (1994), bringing central intervention in state administration under Article 356 of the Constitution (President's rule) under judicial review.

Economic liberalization and political federalization since the 1990s have opened up the Indian economy and polity to greater competition. These trends have allowed a certain degree of leeway to autonomy-seeking state governments and institutions of the market and the civil society from the dead weight of an overly centralized federal State.

Incremental democratization of the polity, especially since 1952 when the first general elections based on universal adult franchise were held, has created a new political ferment and transformed the social and psychological base of politics. Political democratization at home, and global and regional integration of the economy, have revealed the dialectical contradictions and complementarities at various levels between the state and the civil society, between the political market of voters' sovereignty, among the agrarian/industrial/service sectors of the economy, and among various components of ruling elites and classes and between their governing and oppositional coalitions. Politics, in any case, and its discourses are a continuous process of competition and coalition-building. In a fast changing political scenario, rules of the game are still in a process of evolution and settlement.

It is not coincidental that economic reforms as well as greater autonomy to state governments are both developments that have occurred in the era of coalition/minority governments in New Delhi. Party system is, of course, the major intervening factor that seeks to integrate the diverse political variables impinging on coalition politics at electoral, legislative, and cabinet levels. In a large federal polity of subcontinental dimensions there is, expectedly, no complete concordance and coherence among coalitions at electoral, state, and federal levels. Unavoidable political compulsions at one level make allies and at another, adversaries. The hangover of habits of parliamentary mode of behaviour stand in the way of a smooth transition to a federal mode of behaviour that is more tolerant of unencumbered and autonomous action in conformity with arena or area-specific demands and imperatives. Regional parties in alliance with national parties in federal coalitions cannot easily shed the pulls and pressures of secular and communal interests in state politics, nor can the national parties and their regional allies fully ignore the compulsions of federal or national politics. Parties to the game are still learning by trial and error. This partly accounts for the instability of coalition governments in New Delhi since 1989, and for that matter in most of the states under coalition governments.

Only the CPI(M)-led LF governments in West Bengal, Kerala, and Tripura, and Congress-led United Democratic Front (UDF) governments in Kerala have settled down to a stable pattern of coalitional governance.[3] The stability of these coalitions may be largely explained in terms of their ideological and programmatic compatibility, and the presence of a larger party that contributes a sizeable stable core of disciplined legislators and voters. These state-level coalitions stand out in sharp contrast to the extremely unstable omnibus coalition governments formed in north Indian states between 1967 and early 1970s by parties ranging from the right through the centre to the left (e.g. BJS, Jana Congress parties formed by those deserting the INC in various states, and socialist and communist parties).[4] Even during that phase, the coalition government formed by like-minded right wing parties in Orissa was relatively more stable than others.

In retrospect, the delinking of Lok Sabha and Vidhan Sabha elections in 1971 for the first time by Prime Minister Indira Gandhi was, at that point in time, done in an effort to bypass the intermediary levers of power controlled by her old guard, mainly right wing opponents who fell apart in the great Congress split of 1969. In the short run, Indira

Gandhi was successful in making direct appeal to the people and thus 'nationalize' or centralize politics that was showing tendency towards regionalization or 'federalization'. But in the longer run, the delinking of the general elections with the regional or state elections had the effect of creating differentiated arenas of federal and state politics with their own sets of issues and campaign strategies. National issues could not now override over regional/local issues in a mixed campaign and constituency. This factor obviously facilitated the eventual advent of coalition politics at the federal level.

There are, of course, economic factors, besides the political ones, involved in this denouement. The mushrooming of regional or state parties since 1990s is, for example, inextricably linked with the rise of regional bourgeoisie in agriculture and industry, including commerce and culture industry. It is also related to the political and economic rise of peasant communities and classes in their various regional manifestations. Decline as well as residual hold of all-India parties like INC and JD and the failure of BJP and other national parties to cross the threshold of the majority status are also reflective of the growing conflict of economic interests among various classes, ethnic groups, and regions as well as national and global bourgeoisie. The INC and BJP between them bag the largest share in financing of political parties by the big corporate business houses,[5] while some regional parties are the favourites of regional bourgeoisie (e.g. TDP has close links with the Kamma community's spectacular success in business and industrial ventures in Andhra Pradesh, including the Telugu film industry,[6] and Samajwadi Party in Uttar Pradesh has a cosy relationship with Sahara Group of industries). Big farming interests like the Shetkari Sangathan in Maharashtra led by Sharad Joshi supported the Dunkal draft proposals and India's signing of the WTO Treaty in 1995, but the Bharatiya Kisan Union representing the interests of the peasant proprietors in western UP and Haryana opposed this move.

Organized interests in agriculture, trade and commerce, and small-scale industries must court the state governments due to their high economic stakes there. Big industrial, service sector, business, and agrarian interests are more affected by national and global economic policies and trends, which, at least partly, influence their political connections.

Hindu and Sikh community organizations active in cultural and political fields draw on community resources for funds and personnel, including temple establishments like Tirupati Devasthanam Trust and Shiromani Gurudwara Prabandhak Committee.

The federal and provincial states, especially the former despite economic reforms, continue to be important actors in the economy. Finance capital is still largely controlled by public financial institutions of the federal State. Central public sector enterprises are still a larger sector of the economy, and, what is more important, they have improved their economic performance.[7] Foreign Direct Investment (FDI) is growing but not yet substantial. The Enron fiasco indicates that Indian economy may not be an easily tractable terrain for Fordist global capital used to a different economic and cultural milieu in the West. Federal nature of the Indian polity and the growing global and regional integration of the Indian economy necessitate different patterns and strategies of coalition-building for the various interest groups and political parties in different arenas of politics and economy.

The degeneration of electoral and legislative politics has given rise to a variety of *new* social movements of ecological and gender justice alongside those based on primordial identities and interests, and extra-legal organizations of radical class and ethnic violence. Established parties are losing control/influence over peasant and trade union movements that now tend to seek autonomous routes of political participation fuelled by alienation and anomie. The big strike by workers of public sector, banking and insurance sectors, ports and transport sectors, etc., in the summer of 2002 was joined by all major trade unions, including those affiliated with the BJP at the head of the ruling NDA.

The bursting forth of coalition governance in the Lok Sabha elected in 1989 was first seen as an aberration produced by the failure of the party system to throw up an one-party government to take over the reigns of administration in New Delhi for the first time under the 1950 Constitution. In fact, the first Prime Minister to head a minority coalition government, V.P. Singh (JD), tended to act much like a majority party leader (e.g. in his dealing with his Deputy Prime Minister, Devi Lal of the same party, and his reactive and impulsive implementation of the Mandal Commission recommendation for OBCs without consulting his cabinet or coordination committee of the coalition on the plea that the matter was included in the NF election manifesto). Then, again, when the 1991 Lok Sabha election resulted in a hung Parliament, the political class balked at the idea of forming another coalition government and instead gave a nod to a minority Congress government fabricated by the largest single party short of a clear majority under P.V. Narasimha Rao, which roughly halfway through its mandate managed to put together a one-party majority in the existing House. It was only since the 1996 Lok Sabha election that the political class reconciled to the imperative of coalition governance and has not looked back since.[8] The UF, led again by JD, formed two unstable coalition governments led respectively by H.D. Deve Gowda and I.K. Gujral between the 1996 and 1998 elections. The NDA headed by BJP has been in office since the 1999 mid-term polls.[9]

In a rather short span of just over a decade, India has witnessed coalition governments of three important heraldic hues—counting only those to have completed a period of about a year or more—(a) a centrist Congress minority government that significantly moderated its previous socialist–populist idiom to usher in a paradigm shift to neo-liberal economic reforms in 1991 in the midst of a severe balance of payment crisis with the tacit approval of the mixed multiparty oppositional majority in the Lok Sabha, (b) three left-of-centre minority coalition governments under the NF and UF, both consisting of over half a dozen national and regional parties and led by JD, and (c) two right-of-centre coalition governments, the former a minority one and the latter a majority one, both led by BJP and comprising national and regional parties ranging between 18 and 24 in number. These coalition governments since 1989 have come in the wake of the end of the dominance of the multi-ethnic, multi-class, multi-regional Congress party precipitated by three major ideological turning points in Indian politics, namely, economic liberalization and globalization, 'Mandalization' of the OBC identity politics, and the advent of strong currents of Hindu, Sikh, and Islamic revivalism and fundamentalism partly moderated by the imperatives of electoral and legislative coalition-building in national and state politics. By now there is a growing realization that coalition governments are perhaps an inevitable outcome in a multi-ethnic and multi-class society and a federal polity like India, where the homogenizing effects of political institutions may be often insufficient to organize social pluralities into two major parties in electoral and legislative arenas as in Anglo-American democracies and Australia (excepting Canada since 1993). Hence the task of ordering the linguistic, religious, caste, tribal, class, and regional pluralities into two or more governing and oppositional blocs is carried over from the electoral arena to the portals of parliamentary arenas in India since 1990s. Thus India is now increasingly coming to resemble continental Europe where coalition governments are a common occurrence. It may therefore be deduced that the first-past-the-post or plurality electoral system in single-member parliamentary constituencies (as against the majority and proportional electoral systems) are effective in producing a two-party system and one-party majority governments only in relatively homogeneous societies. In heterogeneous societies, especially those with a pattern of multi-polar politicization, the same electoral system is more likely than not to produce a multiparty system and coalitional mode of governance. Thus India is having the supposed effects of proportional representation even under the plurality electoral system, which may be explained largely in terms of India's considerable social pluralities and federal system of government.[10]

A recent study of party system evolution in India divides the period between 1952-99 into three distinctive phases: (a) one-party dominance (1952-67), (b) one-party salience, not absolute dominance (1967-89), especially if the arenas of electoral-legislative politics as well as the dimensions of extra-parliamentary opposition in the mass movement and trade union politics are aggregated, and (c) 'a competitive multi-party system with fluid, fragmented political formations and unstable coalition governments' (Koh, 2000: 141-6, 192).[11] The degree of party system fragmentation in this study is measured by calculating the *F* value, an index of fractionalization of party system developed by Rae (1971), and the *N* value, an index of effective number of parties in a system devised by Laakso and Taagepera (1999). Both these indices measure party system transformation on the bases of *number* and *power* of parties. The *F* value ranges from zero to one, while the *N* value gives the number of effective parties in the system. The higher are the values of these indices, the greater the probability that the total votes and seats are more equally divided among a larger number of parties in the system. The study reports that the mean *F* value stands below 0.45 and the mean *N* at 1.8 in the phase of Congress dominance. In the phase of Congress salience, the two indices fluctuatingly moved marginally up over and above the average trend in the first phase. The mean *F* in the second phase amounts to 0.56 and mean *N* to 2.40. It is in the post-1989 phase of multiparty system and federal coalitions that the mean *F* value rises to 0.8 and the mean *N* value averages at 5.

Making allowance for less than absolute mathematical precision in things political, Singh (2001: 8)[12] conceptualizes and theorizes the structural contours of the post-1989 Indian party system as follows:

> Until the 1996 Lok Sabha elections, there were three pivot parties at the core of the system: besides the Congress and the BJP, there was Janata Dal. The Janata Dal, however, has been so decimated through regional fragmentation and electoral reverses that the party that appeared to be a historic alternative to the Congress in 1977 remains only a pale shadow of its past and potential glory. The party has suffered a precipitous decline over the years.

There took place a major electoral realignment in the Indian party system around Lok Sabha mid-term elections in 1998 and soon thereafter in 1999. As a result of these perturbations, there emerged four notable federal coalition groupings of parties in the Lok Sabha elections in 1999:

> There was the BJP-led NDA consisting of 16 parties together accounting for 300 seats. It included the BJP, BJD, DMK, TDP, HVC, INLD, JD(U), Loktantrik Congress, MDMK, MSCP, PMK, Shiromani Akali Dal, Shiv Sena, National Conference, Trinamool Congress, and MGDK. For the first time in years the NDA grew out of the travails of minority coalition governments and formed a majority coalition government. It faced two opposition groups in the electoral and parliamentary arenas: the Congress and allies consisting of 134 MPs and the Left Front comprising 42 MPs. The Congress-led opposition included the AIADMK, KECM, Muslim League, RJD, and RLD. Finally, there were the unattached parties: the BSP, SP, non-party independents, and others with a tally of 61 seats. (Singh, 2001: 94)[13]

In sum, 'political alignments among parties since 1989 have broadly crystallized into a tripartite configuration: the two largest parties—the BJP and the Congress—and their respective allies represent the two poles, while the middle ground is held by the third force comprising the Janata Dal(s), the Left Front, and some regional parties' (Singh, 2001: 84).[14]

The fragmentation of the national party system and variegation of the state party systems have turned India into a chequered federal and coalitional chessboard. The gradual chipping away of Congress dominance by the end of the 1960s, 1970s, and 1980s was recurrent. But by the beginning of the 1970s, and then again the 1980s, non-Congressional coalition-building efforts were stemmed. This was partly due to the ability of Congress to recoup anyhow by aggressive populist electoral mass mobilization, and partly on account of the difficulty of building non-Congress parties into viable state-level coalition governments in north Indian states (1967-71) or maintaining the cohesion of a hurried merger of non-Congress/non-Communist opposition into Janata Party (1977-9). National Front was formed in the run-up to the 1989 parliamentary election largely through the initiative and drive of V.P. Singh, who resigned from the Rajiv Gandhi Congress government in 1987 in righteous indignation at the Bofors scandal to lead the non-Congress and non-BJP coalitional consolidation aiming to put together a front of Janata Party ('Dal' since 1988 after V.P. Singh's Jan Morcha merged with it), some regional parties, and Communist parties. Stung by the failure of a federal aggregation of non-Congress and non-Communist parties into a single federal Janata Party in the late 1970s, opposition unity in the late 1980s preferred a multi-party confederal coalition formation, first, in the NF, and later, on its failure in 1990, the UF in 1996 in the wake of the electoral defeat of the Rao Congress government that year. The constituents of the NF and UF were broadly the birds of the same feather: the Mandal OBC 'bullock capitalist'-dominated JD, some lingo-religious or regional/ state parties, and Communist parties championing lingo-regional and class protest. The minority UF ruled in New Delhi between 1996 and 1998 in legislative (not cabinet) coalition with Congress, initially under H.D. Deve Gowda and subsequently under I.K. Gujral (both JD), a premiership change dictated by the piqued Congress.

An alternate strategy was adopted by the Hindu right BJP, which aimed at 'the revival of a single dominant all-India party, propagating a powerful ideology, that could cut across caste and ethnic divides and reunite the entire country' against the Congress government (Jha, 1993: xi).[15] The rise of militant Hindu nationalism in the early 1990s was the outcome. While it rode to power on its own steam in UP, Madhya Pradesh, Rajasthan, Gujarat, and Maharashtra (as a junior partner with nativist Hindu Shiv Sena), it came to power in New Delhi (and Haryana) by the end of the 1990s in a pragmatic, non-ideological coalition, subsequently calling itself National Democratic Alliance. It happens to be a confederal political formation comprising militant Hindu *Sangh Parivar* ('unionist family' after Rashtriya Swayamsevak Sangh, presiding over multiple Hindu political organizations like Vishwa Hindu Parishad (VHP), Shiv Sena, Bajrang Dal, Rashtriya

Jagran Manch (RJM) propagating economic nationalism, Bharatiya Mazdoor Sangh, etc.), on the one hand, and an assortment of pragmatic regional or state parties and a militant socialist–OBC-becalmed Lohiaite formation, Samata Party, on the other hand. In the hung Lok Sabha verdict of 1998 without any clear majority for any coalition, TDP facilitated a transition from the left-of-centre UF to a right-of-centre BJP-led coalition. Earlier TDP was part of the UF, but with the decimation of the leading party of this front, JD, it offered outside support to the right-leaning coalition (without joining the cabinet) to enable it to form a government. The new coalition started off with the usual paraphernalia of a multiparty coordination committee, much like the one in the preceding UF. Before too long, however, it became apparent that the BJP-led coalition tended to use the forum of the Cabinet to the gradual abandonment of the coordination committee. Behind-the-scene deciding by the top leadership of the heavy-weight parties gained ground, often resulting in rolling back of cabinet decisions, especially concerning economic issues, when the smaller parties and backbench MPs mounted pressure. Yet the top leadership of BJP/*Sangh Parivar*, who were in a more dominating position in the coalition than the JD ever was in the UF, carried on with their close, cohesive, and elitist way of decision-making. Not that the rolling back of cabinet decisions were unknown in the UF, but they were far less frequent. The role of the coordination committee was, for all intents and purposes, handed over to George Fernandes as the convener of the NDA general body, which obviously was more cumbersome to convene than the Committee.

The BJP-led coalition ruled in New Delhi between 1998-9 in the first instance. It was forced to go for a mid-term poll by its mercurial ally from Tamil Nadu, the AIADMK supremo Jayalalitha. Failing to pressurize the Vajpayee government into dismissing her adversary DMK government in Tamil Nadu, slowing down her prosecution in corruption-related cases, and reinstating the dismissed Navy Chief, Admiral Vishnu Bhagwat, Jayalalitha withdrew her party's support to the NDA. Replacing AIADMK by DMK, the BJP-led NDA won a coalition majority in 1999 in the trail of the Kargil war with Pakistan.

It might have been expected that in the aftermath of the 1999 mid-term polls, the BJP and its NDA allies would be able to register a mighty comeback, riding on the crest of national resurgence set in motion by the second nuclear explosion with an objective of weaponization in May 1998 and the Kargil war in 1999. This expectation was belied; partly due to the common man being more concerned with problems of livelihood, and partly to the federal contours of Indian nationalism with attendant regionalization of political and electoral mobilization since the early 1990s. The BJP itself could only marginally improve its electoral performance, because it had cared more for consolidation of the solidarity of the allies than its lone wolf operation. Yet the NDA, with its parliamentary and cabinet allies, was able to win a coalition majority without having to rely on opposition support as a minority government. Speakers of the Lok Sabha since the onset of coalition/minority governments had generally come from opposition parties by consensus. In 1999, the NDA manged to get G.M. Balayogi, a TDP MP (part of the coalition flock), elected to the office, and, after his death in a plane crash, Manohar Joshi of Shiv Sena, a more 'natural' ally of BJP, succeed him. This may be taken as an indicator of a greater acceptance of the *Hindutva* forces by their secular allies in the NDA. The BJP found itself in a more comfortable position and the Prime Minister's office was able to regain its lost authority and the executive edge, at least to an extent.

The NDA found itself in the eye of a political storm in the spring and summer of 2002. This happened in the wake of the Hindu–Muslim communal carnage triggered by the burning of two coaches of the Sabarmati Express at the Godhra railway station in Gujarat carrying Hindu *karsevaks* returning from Ayodhya, the temple town supposed to be Ram's birthplace and the location of the Babri Masjid demolished in December 1992.

The opposition parties in Parliament led by INC agitated for the dismissal of the Narendra Modi government in the burning state, where police forces were alleged to be either unable or partisan in controlling the recurrent chain riots, forcing the centre and state government to deploy the army. Since the BJP happened to be ruling in Gujarat (only state with a majority of its own) as well as governing at the head of the NDA in New Delhi, dismissal of the Modi government did not appear to be in the realm of practical politics. This was also made unlikely in view of the sanctification of the federal principle in the context of the President's rule in a state since the Bommai judgement of the Supreme Court in 1994. Additionally, there was also the precedent of the fiasco of presidential proclamation in Bihar by the NDA government in New Delhi between 1998-9. Then, the dismissed RJD government led by Rabri Devi had to be reinstated because the centre's intervention was approved by the Lok Sabha but not ratified by the Rajya Sabha, in which the INC, RJD's coalition partner in the Bihar government, held the key to majority. Now, as then, the balance of political forces in the two Houses of Parliament remain unchanged, by and large.

In the present crisis, the opposition parties led by INC, nonetheless, agitated for the head of Modi and stalled the proceedings of Parliament for weeks in a row. Some of the NDA allies like TDP, Trinamool Congress, and JD(U), besides the erstwhile deserter AIADMK now veering back, also put pressure on NDA for change of leadership of the Gujarat government. The People's United Front of Communist parties and Samajwadi Party (SP), as well as AIADMK in its individual capacity, also joined the chorus for the departure of Modi. The BJP National Executive Committee (NEC) meeting in Goa decided to ask the Modi government to go for a mid-term poll instead. But sensing that the Election Commission of India was inclined to the view that elections could be held only after a cooling off period, the Modi government decided not to opt for fresh mandate and dissolution of the Assembly.[16]

In any case, the Gujarat tragedy receded in the background as tension mounted between India and Pakistan on the Line of Control in Jammu & Kashmir with the rising summer heat in the subcontinent. It developed into a nuclear standoff of fearsome proportions. By June end (2002), the NDA was able to forge a consensus with the opposition (minus the left parties) on the candidate for the Presidentship of the republic, the missile scientist Bharataratna A.P.J. Abdul Kalam, in succession to K.R. Narayanan. The LF fielded the veteran freedom fighter Lakshmi Sehgal of Netaji Subhas Chandra Bose's Indian National Army. With the break of monsoon in Delhi and the onset of a wet July, Prime Minister Vajpayee effected the eighth reshuffle in the NDA council of ministers since 1999, as much in pursuit of unity in the coalition as for efficiency, as much with elation as with trepidation. The BJP, 'which leads Vajpayee's multiparty coalition [has seen] a string of electoral failures that have forced it out of power in seven states in four years, including UP, one of the largest and most populous in the Union. The party now rules in only four states, Gujarat being only one where it does so on its own steam. Vajpayee also elevated Home Minister Lal Krishna Advani to the position of Deputy Prime Minister and replaced the ageing party president by a younger incumbent, who along with several others renounced cabinet ministership to take on organizational work, in preparation for the next elections two years hence.'[17]

II

There has been a perceptible shift from politics of mass mobilization that reached its peak in the 1970s and 1980s. In the 1970s, populist politics and mass movements were on the macro scale, across the nation more or less. In the 1980s populism and agitational politics manifested themselves at the level of state politics with limited or micro regional agendas. This happened at both state and sub-state levels. With the overarching Congress dominance gone by the end of the 1980s, the process of federalization (with accent on regionalization) gained ground. With greater degree of power sharing in states as well as within the organs of the federal State itself, the tense political atmospherics, believe it or not, cooled off considerably. This allowed a shift to institutional politics, with accent on decentralization.

It is worth noting that political federalization, economic liberalization, and constitutional entrenchment of local self-governing institutions (localization) have all occurred more or less around the same time (since early 1990s). These three dimensions of change in Indian polity and economy are interactional and mutually reinforcing. In fact, the rise of the Mandal elite, the SC/ST reservation aristocracy (bouyed by Harijan/Adivasi welfare policies and politics and Dalit assertiveness), and the aggressive Hindu Right also reached a critical threshold at around the same time. All these factors and forces transformed Indian politics beyond recognition.

The deepening of federal and coalitional imperatives and features of Indian politics have significantly impacted the working of political institutions. The major consequences may be broadly sketched as follows:

- There has been an increase in the discretionary manoeuvrability of the constitutional heads of the federal and provincial states in coalition situations in formation of governments and dissolution of the popular legislative chambers for fresh mandate. Their moral authority has grown enormously, especially if they are willing and able to judiciously exercise it.

- The executive leadership of the Prime Minister/Chief Minister(s) has become subject to greater constraints by cabinet and the legislature. While collective responsibility of the cabinet to the Lok Sabha/Vidhan Sabha has tended to be strengthened, it has at times also become fragmented. This fragmentation has occurred due to remote-controlling of ministers by national or regional leadership of constituent parties in the ruling coalitions. This has weakened the authority of the Prime Minister, a cornerstone of parliamentary federal executive. The complex network of institutions integrating the state, civil society, and market may suffer swampy suspension of animation and concerted action in the absence of an effective federal executive responsive to the President, Rajya Sabha, and Inter-State Council and collectively responsible to the Lok Sabha. The authority of the Prime Minister at the federal centre has a dynamic role to play here. Despite the failed, uninstitutionalized 'presidential'—in the US sense—prime ministership of Indira Gandhi in the 1970s, there is a lingering nostalgia for her leadership not only in India but in the whole of Asia, Africa, and Eurasia, amply documented by observers and opinion polls. This failed experiment in uninstitutionalized populist mass leadership needs to be replaced by an institutionalized federal executive leadership.
- The control of Rajya Sabha, Lok Sabha, and state legislatures by different sets of parties at any given moment now means that legislations and constitutional amendments must be passed through inter-House multiparty coalitional consensus. In case of constitutional amendments relating to parliamentary and federal components of the government, such consensual agreements must be extended to include at least half of the state legislatures.
- With different sets of parties in majority in Lok Sabha, Rajya Sabha, and Vidhan Sabhas, the Speaker of Lok Sabha and Chairman of Rajya Sabha and their deputies are more likely than not to come from a wider spectrum of parties than the ones in governments at the centre and the states.
- The need as well as scope of judicial review has shown enormous expansion. Besides Fundamental Rights and union-state juris-

dictional reviews, judicial activism has expanded the scope of courts' review to new areas such as, for example, President's rule in constitutional emergency in a state under Article 356 since the Bommai judgement of the Supreme Court in 1994.

- Economic liberalization has necessitated the replacement of direct bureaucratic control of the economy by an interventionist state with a new pattern of more autonomous mechanisms of a federal and provincial regulatory state through independent regulatory authorities such as Security and Exchange Board of India (SEBI), Telecom Regulatory Authority of India (TRAI), Electricity Regulatory Authority of India (ERAI) and State Regulatory Authorities, and so on and so forth. These authorities are created under parliamentary or state statutes with autonomous and semi-judicial powers.
- In a country of great cultural and economic disparities and growing spiral of violence and corruption, developments since 1990s have seen the growing need and assertiveness of National Human Rights Commission (NHRC), National Commission for Minorities (NCM), National Women and Child Welfare Commissions, Central Vigilance Commission (CVC), Lokayuktas (ombudsmen) created under statutes at federal and state levels.
- In a society of great plural and federal diversities like India coalition governments have underlined as well as facilitated consensual policy making on controversial and contentious cultural and economic issues. Coalition situation has increased the leverage of the bureaucracy, media, and interest groups.
- Governmental instability and delays and deadlocks are the main negative effects of coalition governments.
- Coalition politics, coupled with economic liberalization/globalization, have reduced the autonomy of the federal/national state and increased the autonomy of state and local governments, private sector, and institutions of civil society, including voluntary associations and social movements.
- Coalition politics have tended to aggravate political opportunism and corruption in the political class evident in politics of defection, oversize ministries and an extensive spoils system in chairmanships of public corporations with politico-economic perks and perquisites.

In sum, the net effect of federal coalition governments has been a departure from a strongly centralized parliamentary government, articulation of the federal features of the constitutionally mandated parliamentary federal system in India, and a shift from majoritarian parliamentary temper to a consensus system of multiple and concurrent majorities. Reformist thought building up over the years, evident in the reports of Administrative Reforms Commission (1969), the Sarkaria Commission on centre-state relations (1987-8), and the Venkatachelliah Constitution Review Commission (2002), have been consistently stressing the desirability of a move towards such a consensual political system. Judicial interpretations of the Constitution over the 1970s to date have created a corpus of constitutional law to enable concrete first steps in this direction. A consensual coalition culture in India is yet to mature. Democracy, said Dr B.R. Ambedkar, the Chairman of the drafting committee, in the Constituent Assembly, was 'a top-dressing on the Indian soil'. In his final address to the constitutional convention on 25 November 1949, he offered three wise counsels to the newly constituted republic, born in law as well as a revolution in restraint,[18] on how to 'maintain democracy not merely in form, but also in fact': (a) people of India must 'hold fast to constitutional methods of achieving our social and economic objectives'; (b) must avoid 'hero-worship' and surrendering our trust to anyone who may 'subvert their institutions' (*a la* John Stuart Mill); and (c) 'make our political democracy a social democracy as well'. He also stoutly defended the federal character of the draft constitution despite the textual use of the term 'Union of States'.[19] Political developments since the 1990s bear Dr Ambedkar's contention out. The Constitution will probably bear up the mighty tumult of disharmony that we witness today. We must bear with them and continue our 'tryst with destiny' to which Pandit Nehru ruefully alluded to at the painful birth of the independent Indian nation in the midst of a bloody inter-religious ethnic cleansing, precipitated by the imperial partition of India.

Yet coalition politics in Indian union since 1989 and in several states over the years intermittently since 1967 have brought to the fore the pressing problem of governmental instability and oversize cabinets to stave off defective floor-crossing on the part of legislators. Politics of defection makes a mockery of fiscal prudence and administrative efficiency and unstable governments find it difficult to seriously address the problems of governance. In the prevailing context of cumulative crises in Indian development, security, and democracy, any lack of decisiveness can be an extremely costly proposition. The task of balanced governance in this complex setting is made doubly difficult on account of two imperatives. First, the missed developmental opportunities of history and the prevailing contemporary ideological atmospherics (conditioned simultaneously by sensibilities of modernity as well as post-modernity, materiality as well as identity), it is difficult to discriminate between the three competing values of democracy, security, and development. Second, given the denouement in India of something reminiscent of the system of separation of powers and checks and balances even within the bedrock of the Westminster parliamentary system moderated by the federal principle, the political class must learn to outgrow the feudal as well as bureaucratic mindset and give a participative collective decision-making in a democratic institutional matrix a chance. Otherwise, the projects of democracy and development in India would run into a dead end.

The Report of the National Commission for Review of the Working of the Constitution (NCRWC) submitted in the spring of 2002 has taken a comprehensive and close look at the state of the art of governance in the country. Its thinking is not retrogressive and its recommendations, if implemented as a package, can go a long way in stabilizing the system without robbing it of its dynamism for change and development through democratic means. First, it has recommended constitutional amendments to textualize the expansion of legal, political, and economic rights and federalization of the predominantly parliamentary mode of governance already accomplished by judicial interpretations and ruling. Second, it seeks to ensure judicial accountability by suggesting the appointment of a National Judicial Commission under the Constitution to provide 'for the effective participation of both the executive and judicial wings of the state as an integrated scheme for appointment of judges'. Third, it favours a more powerful and well-informed committee system in the Parliament and state legislatures as alternative (though not necessarily contradictory) sites for scrutiny of proposals for economic policies, legislation, and constitutional amendments and for parliamentary control of the executive. Fourth, it proposes a ceiling of the size of the council of ministers at 10 per cent of the strength of the popular house of the legislature and of a blanket legal ban on defection of legislators from parties/coalitions between two elections—as individuals and small or large groups (the 1985 anti-defection Act allowed groups comprising one-third or above of the total membership of a party) and admission of a 'constructive' vote of non-confidence in a ministry as in Germany (i.e. only when withdrawal of trust in an incumbent government is accompanied by trust in an alternative administration). Fifth, the NCRWC recommends a comprehensive law governing the organization and the working and financing of political parties to help build a responsible and democratically disciplined party system in the country. It also encourages parties to take initiative at their own levels to introduce the Canadian system of national party conventions for electing party leaders, who in turn lead the party in the campaign and the newly elected Parliament.[20]

NOTES

1. M.V. Pylee, *Crisis, Conscience and the Constitution,* Bombay: Asia Publishing House, 1982, p. 140, remarks: 'The results of the elections of 1977 were hailed as a silent revolution through which democracy was re-established in all its pristine majesty. And it appeared that India was well on the road to establishing a two-party system, like some of the mature democracies of the West.'
2. See Pranab Bardhan, *Political Economy of Development in India*, Delhi: Oxford University Press, 1984; Lloyd and Susanne Rudolph, *In Pursuit of Lakshmi: Political Economy of the Indian State*, New Delhi: Orient Longman, 1987; and M.P. Singh, 'The Crisis of the Indian State: From Quiet Developmentalism to Noisy Democracy', *Asian Survey*, vol. XXX, no. 8, August 1990.
3. For Left Front governments, see T.J. Nossiter, *Marxist State Governments in India: Politics, Economics and Society*, London: Pinter Publishers, 1988; and Ross Mallick, *Indian Communism: Opposition, Collaboration and Institutionalization*, Delhi: Oxford University Press, 1994.
4. See Paul Brass, *Caste, Faction and Party in Indian Politics,* vol. I, *Faction and Party*, Delhi: Chanakya Publications, 1984.
5. See M.P. Singh and Rekha Saxena, *India at Polls: Parliamentary Elections in Federal Phase*, New Delhi: Orient Longman, 2003, Chapter 9.
6. Author's interview with Professor Mudhusudan Reddy of the Osmania University, Political Science Department, Hyderabad, in Pune, Autumn 2001.
7. The *Economic Times, ET 500: The Changing Face of India Inc.*, March 2002, p. 12.
8. See M.P. Singh, 'The Dilemma of the New Indian Party System: To Govern or Not to Govern?' *Asian Survey*, vol. XXXII, no. 4, April 1992; and his 'India's National Front and United Front Coalition Governments: A Phase in Federalized Governance', *Asian Survey*, vol. XLI, no. 2, March/April 2001 (revised version).

9. On 1996, 1998, and 1999 Lok Sabha elections, see M.P. Singh and Rekha Saxena, *India at Polls: Parliamentary Elections in Federal Phase*, New Delhi: Orient Longman, 2003.
10. The Indian experience in this context is not really at variance with theories of comparative politics regarding political consequences of electoral laws. In a cross-national study of 27 democracies around the world spanning the period of 1945-90, Lijphart (1994: 9) observes: 'My main conclusion will be that of the five dependent variables, disproportionality is the one that can be explained best in terms of the electoral system characteristics, and that the strongest explanation of the various dependent variables is provided by what I shall call the 'effective threshold', a combination of district magnitude and electoral thresholds. The effect of the electoral system on multipartism is more modest but still very important, and the explanatory power of the electoral system variables—the electoral formula, assembly size, *apparentement*, ballot structure, and presidentialism—is also more modest but, again, not at all negligible.' Of course, this study is wider both in terms of number of cases and multi-factorial conceptualization and operationalizam than a single case study can be. But the effect of electoral system is not very strong to warrant unqualified assertion. The effect is subject to complex multifactor determination verging on fictional ambiguity. But my hunch is that a majoritarian electoral system in single-member parliamentary constituencies (with double balloting if necessary), combined with rigorous registration criteria and financial incentives for federal parties, further supplemented with national leadership conventions to elect party leadership as in Canada, is more likely than not to discourage the multiplication of parties in India.
11. Kyoung-Hee Koh, 'The Transformation of Political Party System in India: 1952-1999', Ph.D. thesis, Department of Politics and Diplomacy, Hankuk University of Foreign Studies, Seoul, Korea, 2000. The text of the thesis is in Korean, though the abstract, figures, and tables are in English. Read with the help of the author in the summer of 2002. See also, Douglas W. Rae, *The Political Consequences of Electoral Law*, New Haven: Yale University Press, 1971; and M. Laakso and Rein Taagepera, 'Effective Number of Parties: A measure with Application to West Europe', *Comparative Political Studies*, vol. 12, 1979.
12. M.P. Singh, 'Whither Indian Party System? The Electoral and Legislative Dimensions', *Indian Social Science Review*, vol. 3, no.1, January-June 2001.
13. Ibid.
14. Ibid.
15. Prem Shankar Jha, *In the Eye of the Cyclone: The Crisis in Indian Democracy*, New Delhi: Viking/Penguin Books India, 1993.
16. The *Hindu* and *The Times of India*, both 18 April 2002, New Delhi editions.
17. 'The Political Factor', The *Economic Times* (New Delhi), 1 July 2002, p.2. In about half a decade, the BJP has changed its party president thrice: from

Kushabhai Thakaray (Madhya Pradesh) to Bangaru Lakshman (an Andhra Pradesh Dalit) to Jana Krishnamoorthy (Tamil Nadu), and to M. Venkaiya Naidu (Andhra Pradesh). While the first change may be related to the desire to have a more active Dalit leader to replace his ageing predecessor, Lakshman resigned in the trail of Tehelka expose concerning his and other NDA leaders' acceptance of party funds from journalists posing as arms dealers (now subject of inquiry by the Venkataswamy Commission). The latest change appears to be primarily motivated by the impending elections. Naidu and Arun Jaitly resigned as cabinet ministers in the Vajpayee government to strengthen the party organization.

18. For this interpretation, see M.P. Singh, 'Interpreting Indian Constitutionalism', *Think India*, vol. 4, no. 3, October-December 2001.
19. *Constituent Assembly Debates,* Book 5, 1999, 3rd reprint, pp. 976-7 and 978-9.
20. Government of India, *Review of the Working of the Constitution: Report of the National Commission to Review the Working of the Constitution*, Ministry of Law, 2002, Chapter 11, para 122, pp. 29-30.

PART II: COALITION GOVERNMENTS IN UNION AND STATE LEVELS

CHAPTER 3

Unstable Parties and Unstable Alliances: Births, Splits, Mergers and Deaths of Parties, 1952-2000

E. Sridharan

The last five general elections (1989, 1991, 1996, 1998, 1999) have resulted in hung parliaments and hence, coalition and/or minority governments. Coalition politics is the order of the day and looks as if it will remain so in the foreseeable future, given the improbability of either the Congress or the BJP achieving a majority on its own. Underlying this situation is the decline of the formerly dominant Congress party with its declining plurality of the vote, failing since 1989 to translate into a seat majority, or even, since 1996, into giving it the status of the single largest party. Parallel to this decline have been two phenomena: first, the rise of the BJP but not anywhere near sufficient to replace the Congress as a party achieving a seat majority on the basis of a vote plurality; second, the rise of state-based parties, that is, parties with a base mostly in a single state, or at the most two or three states, whether or not with an explicitly articulated regional ethno-linguo-cultural character. Taken together, these two phenomena are the foundation of coalition politics in India at the turn of the millennium.

Where did this multitude of non-Congress parties, relatively large, small, and smaller still, come from? What are their origins, history and evolution? Have they evolved gradually or in discrete jumps? Have they evolved as stable formations? The answer to this last question is a clear negative. The multitude of non-Congress parties that have played an increasingly important role nationally in the hung parliaments of the post-1989 period have a fractured and tortuous history of births, deaths, splits, and mergers. Their genealogy needs to be understood in historical context, if we are to understand the evolution of alliances and coalition politics of the past decade. For, unlike parties in Europe, parties in India are not stable formations. Nor do they neatly fit the social cleavage theory of party systems, each having a well-defined support base based on cleavages of class, religion, language and other ascriptive criteria.[1] While many, especially regional and ideological parties, do partly fit social cleavage theories, a great many of the non-Congress formations are weakly institutionalized and have a catch-all, clientelistic character, splitting or merging vertically on the basis of the feuds or deals of leaders. Understanding coalition politics in India today requires a background in the evolution of the major and important minor parties that play an important role today, especially splits and mergers, since *an important part of the coalition game in India is not just the forging of alliances between existing parties but the breaking of parties into splinter groups to facilitate alliances.*[2]

All major parties in India have undergone splits in the half-century of electoral politics since Independence, with not even cadre-based ideological parties proving immune. The major landmark development that has affected party splits and mergers has been the anti-defection law (the fifty-second constitutional amendment of February 1985, which introduced the Tenth Schedule of the Constitution). This made splits of legislature parties in Parliament and the State Assemblies unlawful, and legislators liable to disqualification from membership of the house, in the event of party splits, unless the breakaway faction formed one-third or more of the legislature party. It also legalized mergers between parties if two-thirds or more legislators formed the merging faction. These rules, introduced just after the top-down Congress party had won a four-fifths majority in the 1984 general elections, made defections and splits of the kind that were common in the 1967-84 more difficult, but not impossible. It merely required that a critical mass of one-third had to be mustered before a split was feasible. Nevertheless, this measure did impart a measure of stability to legislature parties.

This paper traces the genealogy of today's principal national and state parties in India as the necessary background to understanding coalition politics and looks at electoral alliances and coalition governments in terms of the split-proneness of parties.

The Congress Party

Despite its encompassing character inherited from the independence movement and near-total hegemony both at the centre and in almost all states in the first two decades of independence, the Congress party has undergone significant splits by the 1990s at the state level.[3] Initially, there were minor state-level splits. The most important of these was the formation of the Bangla Congress in West Bengal in 1967, which won 9.4 per cent of the vote and 5 seats (1967) and 4.0 per cent votes and 1 seat (1971) in the state in general elections, and actually ruled briefly as part of a coalition in the late 1960s and early 1970s, winning 10.2 per cent votes and 34 (out of 280) seats (1967), 8.2 per cent votes and 33 seats (1969) and 5.4 per cent votes and 5 seats (1971) in state Assembly elections. The Utkal Congress in Orissa was a significant opposition party in 1971 (23.6 per cent of the vote in Orissa and 1 seat in the Lok Sabha, 24.0 per cent votes in the Assembly) and 1974 (26.4 per cent votes in the Assembly). The breakaway Kerala Congress has been a small party in the state since 1965, its post-1984 faction, the Kerala Congress (Mani) having a base in one constituency and polling 2-3 per cent of the state vote in Lok Sabha elections.

The first major Congress split was that of 1969, which took place at the national level in what was essentially an intra-leadership struggle cast as a battle of ideological and policy positions, as well between the parliamentary and organizational wings.[4] The victorious Indira Gandhi-led Congress (I) that emerged as the main faction took most of the Congress vote with it to emerge with a two-thirds majority in the 1971 elections (43.7 per cent and 352 seats versus 10.4 per cent and 16 seats for the losing Congress Organization). The much more centralized, top-down Congress (I) suspended organizational elections within the party from 1972, and depended on state patronage, plebiscitary appeals and Indira Gandhi's charisma. They were next held only in 1992.

The contradiction between the party's encompassing character and lack of internal democracy was probably one of the major underlying factors behind subsequent splits and defections.[5] On the eve of the post-Emergency 1977 elections, the Congress split again, with veteran Scheduled Caste leader Jagjivan Ram leading a faction called Congress for Democracy into a merger with the newly-formed Janata Party.

The next major split took place in February 1978 when the Congress was in the opposition with only 154 MPs after its defeat in 1977. The

Congress (Indira) that emerged had only 78 MPs. The breakaway faction led by K. Brahmananda Reddi and Karnataka Chief Minister, Devaraj Urs, called itself the Congress (Urs), received only 5.3 per cent votes and 13 seats in the 1980 elections, split again to merge with the Congress leaving a rump which became the Congress (Socialist) in 1981, confined to a pocket in Kerala. However, the Congress (U) faction formed the government in Karnataka and, in coalition, in Maharashtra in the 1978-80 period.

The next significant splits in the Congress took place during the Narasimha Rao government as the 1996 elections neared. Former UP Chief Minister, Narain Dutt Tiwari, left the Congress to float a party called the All India Indira Congress (AIIC), or Congress (Tiwari), which cut into the Congress vote in a small way (3-4 per cent) in MP, UP, Assam, and Rajasthan, winning four seats in 1996 and one in 1998. Former Cabinet Minister Madhavrao Scindia floated a faction called the Madhya Pradesh Vikas Congress (MPVC) which won one seat in MP in 1996. However, these factions soon rejoined the Congress, the MPVC before the 1998 elections and the Congress (Tiwari) after Sonia Gandhi's taking over the leadership of the Congress after the 1998 elections.

Also, in Haryana, former Congress leader Bansi Lal broke away before the 1996 elections to form the Haryana Vikas Party (HVP), which fought the Lok Sabha and Assembly elections allied to the BJP. It won 3 seats and 15.2 per cent votes while the BJP won 4 seats and 19.8 per cent votes, and in the Assembly 33 seats and 22.7 per cent votes, and formed the government with the BJP as its junior partner with 11 seats and 8.8 per cent votes. In the 1998 elections, the HVP won 11.6 per cent votes and 1 seat. In July 1999, just before the general elections, the BJP withdrew support from the HVP government, and struck an alliance with Om Prakash Chautala's INLD, whereby Chautala became the Chief Minister.

The most significant and damaging split, however, was in the Tamil Nadu unit of the Congress just before the 1996 elections, in revolt against the decision to ally with the AIADMK, leaving a rump affiliated to the Congress. The major faction formed a new party, the Tamil Maanila Congress (TMC). This split cost the Congress dearly, as the TMC won 27 per cent votes (against the official Congress' 18.3 per cent) in Tamil Nadu and 20 seats in alliance with the DMK

(25.6 per cent and 17 seats) while the official Congress' AIADMK ally got none and 7.8 per cent votes. An indication of the damage caused by the split and how different history could have been, is the fact that *with the TMC's 20 seats, and those of the Tiwari Congress (4) and the MPVC (1), the Congress could have emerged as the single largest party in 1996, ahead of the BJP*, which could possibly have led to a minority and/or coalition government of a type very different from the United Front!

Another important state-level split took place in the UP unit of the Congress, when nineteen out of thirty-seven MLAs broke away to form the Loktantrik Congress Party (LCP) in October 1997 and allied with the BJP to form a coalition government.

Three other significant splits took place just before the 1998 elections as the Congress appeared to be disintegrating under the presidency of Sitaram Kesri, between the fall of the UF (Gujral) government in November 1997 and the February 1998 elections. The major one was the breakaway in West Bengal of the faction led by Mamata Banerjee to form the Trinamool Congress, which then proceeded to ally itself with the BJP in the state and won 7 seats and 24.4 per cent votes in 1998 while the official Congress won only one and 15.2 per cent votes. The provocation for the split was an intense conflict in the state unit of the Congress in which the central leadership of the Congress backed the less popular formal leadership of the state unit against Mamata Banerjee. In Arunachal Pradesh, again just prior to the 1998 elections, the Chief Minister, Gegong Apang, broke away to form a new party, the Arunachal Congress, which won both seats in the state and 52.5 per cent votes against 23.9 per cent for the Congress. The Arunachal Congress split again in 1999, the major faction merging with the Congress.

The most damaging recent split in Congress was in May 1999, led by the Maharashtra political heavyweight Sharad Pawar, former Lok Sabha Speaker P.A. Sangma, and Bihar leader Tariq Anwar. Ostensibly against Sonia Gandhi's fitness to be projected as the Congress Prime Minister in the event of victory in the 1999 elections on account of her foreign birth, the trio called for a constitutional amendment to bar foreign-born citizens from high political office. The move was triggered off by Congress president Sonia Gandhi's implied claim to prime ministership in the event of the Congress forming a government in the aftermath of the BJP-led government's resignation in April 1999, without due consultations within the Congress Working Committee. A split was inevitable once the issue was posed, not in terms of intra-party democracy or of Sonia Gandhi's merits, but in terms of constitutional bars on the grounds of foreign birth. The trio were expelled and went on to form the Nationalist Congress Party (NCP). The NCP immediately provoked splits in Maharashtra and Meghalaya. In Maharashtra, where the party had won 33 (37 with its allies) out of 48 seats in the 1998 elections, in 1999 it won only 10 seats, the NCP winning 6 seats, though their combined vote was 51 per cent compared to the combined vote of the Shiv Sena and BJP fetching them 28 seats together! Indeed, it prompted the ruling Shiv Sena-BJP coalition to dissolve the Assembly prematurely so that simultaneous elections were held for the Lok Sabha and the state Assembly. In the latter, however, the Congress and NCP did better contesting separately than the Shiv Sena-BJP combine and patched up to form a coalition government in the state.

The Bharatiya Janata Party

The BJP, like the left parties, being an ideological, cadre-based party, based essentially on the cadre of its parent organization, the RSS, has been less split-prone than most other parties. With its electoral rise since 1989, however, and the vast expansion of its social and geographical base to include castes other than the traditional upper castes, and regions other than the north and west, it has become internally much less homogeneous and cohesive than it once was.[6] There have been two significant splits in the BJP in recent years—one in Gujarat in 1995 and one in UP in 1999. In Gujarat, a group led by Shankarsinh Vaghela, presenting itself as representing the OBCs, broke away over what was essentially a no-holds-barred power struggle, with a Congress hand in the background. Vaghela was expelled. However, the BJP remained in the saddle before being brought down by the imposition of President's rule in September 1996. A minority government of Vaghela's Rashtriya Janata Party, supported by the Congress was sworn in in October and continued in office to the end of 1997. The March 1998 Assembly elections returned the BJP to power, the Vaghela faction merging with the Congress.

In UP, in November 1997, Chief Minister Kalyan Singh was expelled from the party and replaced by Ram Prakash Gupta, after a prolonged internal power struggle with strong caste overtones, in the state BJP and the ruling BJP-led coalition government. The Kalyan Singh faction represented the increasingly assertive OBCs in the party while the faction supported by the BJP national leadership represented the entrenched upper castes. Kalyan Singh failed to engineer a split and take away the required minimum one-third of the party to his newly-formed Rashtriya Kranti Party, but appears to have caused OBCs in the electorate to drift away from the BJP.

Despite infighting in the party on a caste basis and over the spoils of office in several state units, these have been the only actual splits in the BJP. *What is significant is that they have taken place in two of the party's stronghold states and when the party was in power.*

The Janata Family of Parties

The Janata family of parties is collectively the next largest to the Congress in terms of vote share for the period 1977-89, losing that position to the BJP in the 1991, 1996, and 1998 elections. The Janata family is not an alliance but a disparate group of parties that can be said to have originated in the Janata Party.[7] Hence the term Janata family (*parivar*) of parties. However, its roots go back well before 1977, to the late 1960s, and can be stretched back to the Congress Socialist Party of the 1930s. The latter was a pro-land reform, socialist grouping whose base was UP and Bihar and the poor peasantry, mostly of intermediate and lower castes.

After independence, some of the socialists split from the Congress to form the Socialist, later Praja Socialist and Samyukta Socialist parties, at various times in the 1950s and 1960s. The Socialist and Praja Socialist parties were the leading opposition parties in terms of votes in the 1952 and 1957 elections with 10.6 per cent and 10.4 per cent respectively, and totalled 9.5 per cent in 1962, and 8 per cent in 1967. They won 12, 19, 18, and 26 seats together in the first four general elections. The ideology of anti-Congressism propagated by Ram Manohar Lohia, the leading ideologue of the Socialist parties, advocated the coming together of all non-Congress parties in a broad anti-Congress alliance to avoid splitting of the non-Congress majority vote, which repeatedly gave the Congress a plurality vote and a seat majority.

These developments led to the formation of non-Congress coalition governments in several major Indian states in the period 1967-71, when the Congress won a bare majority in the 1967 general election and lost eight major states to such alliances in the state Assembly elections held simultaneously. A former Congressman, Charan Singh, became Chief Minister of such a coalition government in UP, and in 1969, formed the Bharatiya Kranti Dal (BKD), a party based on intermediate castes (mainly Jats), small landowning peasants of western UP. In 1974, the BKD merged with the Samyukta Socialist Party (Raj Narain faction), Swatantra, Utkal Congress, and three minor parties to form the Bharatiya Lok Dal (BLD). The ideology of the BKD/BLD, was a vague agrarian socialism, based on Charan Singh's ideas of peasant proprietor self-sufficiency and labour-intensive small-scale industry. It was based mainly on the intermediate-caste small farmers, centred in western UP, who were experiencing the prosperity of the Green Revolution, and becoming politically assertive independently of a Congress party they found dominated by upper castes (mainly Brahmins and Rajputs in UP).

In 1977, the BLD merged with three other parties—the right wing (but secular), big business-landowner Swatantra Party, the right wing, (then assertively) Hindu-chauvinist BJS, the ancestor of the BJP, and two breakaway Congress factions—Congress O (Organization or Opposition) and the Jagjivan Ram-led Congress for Democracy—to form the Janata Party and confront the Congress with a grand alliance of almost the entire opposition, in the general elections held after the lifting of the 1975-7 Emergency in which democratic freedoms and civil liberties were suspended. The elections were a virtual referendum on the Emergency and were tailor-made for such an alliance. The Janata Party won a thumping victory with 41.3 per cent of the vote and 295 seats. Its main bases were in northern and western India, winning 219 out of 225 seats in the main Hindi-belt states of UP, Bihar, Madhya Pradesh, Rajasthan, Haryana, Himachal Pradesh, and Delhi, besides performing well in Gujarat, Maharashtra, and Orissa.

However, the Janata Party was a fractious party composed of incompatible elements ranging from the Hindu nationalist right to the socialist left. It failed to evolve an organization or conduct party elections. In July 1979, it split into two factions, one led by the then just-ousted Prime Minister, Morarji Desai, and party president, Chandrashekhar, and the other by Charan Singh. The latter became Prime Minister with Congress support but resigned in three weeks and continued in a caretaker capacity for a few months before the Janata Party was defeated in the January 1980 elections in which the Indira Gandhi-led Congress returned to power with a majority. However, the two factions of the Janata party won 19.0 per cent (31 seats) and 9.4 per cent (41 seats) respectively, as against the Congress' 42.7 per cent and 353 seats.

After this defeat the Janata Party disintegrated, as the BJP split off from the Morarji Desai–Chandrashekhar faction, reasserting its Hindu nationalist identity in 1980. Subsequently, the Charan Singh faction underwent a split after his death in 1987, the emergent factions being led by his son, Ajit Singh, and an ex-Congressman from UP, H.N. Bahuguna, the latter faction dying with its leader's death. In 1989, the Ajit Singh faction, as well as the collateral Chandrashekhar faction, merged with the group of Congressmen opposed to Rajiv Gandhi's leadership of the Congress, led by former Finance Minister (and later Prime Minister, 1989-90), V.P. Singh. Thus the Janata Dal, a descendant of the Janata family of parties was born in October 1988.

In the 1989 elections, JD, the leading party of the NF coalition of regional and minor parties, after making pre-election 'seat adjustments' to avoid vote-splitting, with the BJP and the Left Front parties in various states, got 17.7 per cent of the vote and 142 seats (54 in UP, 31 in Bihar, 16 in Orissa, 11 each in Rajasthan and Gujarat).

In 1991, reduced by a split, mainly affecting its UP unit, it received 11.8 per cent of the vote and 59 seats (31 in Bihar, 22 in UP, 6 in Orissa). Its strength was regionally concentrated, receiving 34.6 per cent of the vote in Orissa, 34.1 per cent in Bihar, 21.3 per cent in UP, 18.5 per cent in Karnataka and 12.5 per cent in Haryana. Its offshoot, the Samajwadi Janata Party received 3.4 per cent, primarily consisting of 10.5 per cent of the vote in UP and 25.4 per cent in Haryana. The major part of this splinter eventually became the Samajwadi Party led by Mulayam Singh Yadav while the rump remained the Samajwadi Janata Party, (SJP) led by former Prime Minister, Chandrashekhar, based mainly in Haryana. The Haryana unit broke away after the 1996 elections to form the Haryana Lok Dal (Rashtriya), later the INLD led by former Chief Minister, Om Prakash Chautala. Another regional splinter (which eventually merged with the Congress), the JD (Gujarat) received 13.1 per cent of the vote in Gujarat.

In the 1996 elections, JD received 8.1 per cent of the vote and 46 seats, its major areas of strength being Bihar (31.8 per cent of the vote, 22 seats), Karnataka (34.9 per cent, 16 seats), and Orissa (30.1 per cent, 4 seats). The Samajwadi Party, the major UP offshoot, received 20.9 per cent of the vote and 16 seats in UP. Another offshoot (of the Bihar unit of JD, mainly based on a particular backward caste, the Kurmis), the Samata Party received 14.4 per cent of the vote and 6 seats in Bihar, 8 seats nationally. In May 1997, JD's major state unit in Bihar split again under the leadership of the former Chief Minister, Laloo Prasad Yadav, and formed the Rashtriya Janata Dal, taking away 18 of JD's 46 MPs.

In the 1998 elections, JD was decimated, winning only 6 seats and 3.25 per cent of the vote, and virtually wiped out in its three stronghold states. In Orissa, this was because its state unit split in late 1997, with the winning faction, the Biju Janata Dal (BJD), aligning with the BJP. The BJD won 9 out of 21 seats and 27.5 per cent of the vote in the state. Five other Janata family descendants also did fairly well in the 1998 elections. The Samata Party, allied to the BJP, won 12 seats—10 in Bihar and 16 per cent of the state vote. The SP won 20 seats, all in UP and 28.7 per cent of the state vote. The RJD won 17 seats in Bihar and 26.3 per cent of the state vote. The Lok Shakti, a JD splinter group in Karnataka led by expelled leader Ramakrishna Hegde, allied with the BJP as a junior partner in the 1998 elections, won 3 seats and 11.5 per cent votes in Karnataka (as against the BJP's 13 seats and 27.0 per cent votes). Its principal base was in northern Karnataka and among the Lingayats, a landowning numerically large caste, and one of the dominant castes in the state. Finally, the Haryana Lok Dal (Rashtriya) won 25.9 per cent votes in Haryana and 4 seats in alliance with the BSP (7.7 per cent votes and 1 seat) in a triangular contest against the Congress and the BJP-HVP combine.

The latest split and merger in the Janata Party took place just before the 1999 general elections when JD in Bihar and Karnataka split into two splinter groups, the original faction led by former Prime Minister Deve Gowda calling itself the Janata Dal (Secular) and the larger faction led by JD president Sharad Yadav merging with the Samata Party in Bihar and the Lok Shakti in Karnataka to form the JD(U) and allying itself with the BJP in the BJP-led NDA. The split was over the issue of secularism and alliance with the BJP, and was provoked by the decision of the JD's Karnataka Chief Minister, J.H. Patel, to ally with the BJP, to improve what was otherwise seen as a hopeless electoral situation for the party. The JD(U) contested on a common symbol and won 21 seats in 1999. However, in January 2000, just before the Bihar State Assembly elections, the Samata Party component of the JD(U) decided not to effect the merger. The JD(U) reverted to two of its original constituents, the Samata Party with eleven MPs, and the JD(U) with ten MPs (including the original Lok Shakti component that accounted for three MPs).

Thus, one can see that over the past two, even three decades and more, the Janata family of parties and their progenitors have played a significant anti-Congress oppositional role in the national and most northern state party systems, and in Karnataka and Orissa. In general, it can be said that the support base of the Janata family of parties consists of small peasant proprietors of the intermediate and lower castes in the northern belt, primarily UP, Bihar, and Haryana, whose interests were not adequately represented in the caste coalitions that underpinned the Congress in these states. Since the late 1980s, the social coalition has extended to Muslims disenchanted with the Congress, especially for the SP in UP. In Bihar, in the 1990s, the JD coalition is much broader, encompassing a large mass of lower backward castes and the rural poor, including Scheduled Castes. In Orissa and Karnataka, as in Gujarat and Rajasthan, the party consisted of disgruntled ex-Congressmen based on dominant peasant castes.

Ideologically, the Janata family of parties is, in the post-1990 environment of politicization of religion and caste, not only broadly agrarian but also more explicitly lower caste in orientation, specifically in terms of job reservation for the caste-defined OBCs, and less uniformly and importantly, more explicitly secular (though the BJD and the Samata Party were, out of electoral calculation, allied with the BJP from 1998 and 1996 respectively, while distancing themselves from its ideology). This has changed with the virtual collapse of the JD with the splitting off of the main Sharad Yadav-led faction and its merger with the Samata Party and Lok Shakti to form the JD(U), and its alliance with the BJP, a merger that was again reversed in early 2000. This can only be understood in the context of JD's perceived principal threat being the Congress in Karnataka, and then-current caste alignments in Bihar, where a section of the non-Yadav backward castes and even Scheduled Castes are disenchanted with the RJD government and aligned with the BJP–Samata Party out of electoral compulsions. The Janata family's attitude to economic liberalization is ambivalent, being essentially populist and in favour of government intervention and spending on welfare programmes, but pragmatic in practice.

However, the main weakness of the Janata family of parties is and has always been organizational. They have always been the most weakly organized of the major political parties in India, certainly compared to the cadre-based left parties and the BJP, but even compared to the mass-based Congress at its worst periods of organizational decrepitude. The Janata family parties never managed to evolve even state-level organizational structures in their stronghold states, let alone nationally, that went beyond being a loose coalition of state and local-level leaders linked to their followers by a combination of clientelist and primordial, primarily caste, ties. They have never had credible organizational elections.

This is linked to the kind of social base they have. The Janata family parties have been based largely on rich peasant proprietors belonging to relatively numerically large (in their stronghold states) intermediate and 'backward' castes, relying largely on the mobilizational pull of already existing and, in recent years, politically heightened caste identities overlapping with class interests.[8] This is further reinforced by preferential patronage when the parties are in power at the state level, a crucial mobilizational factor in an economy, including the agrarian economy, where the depth and scope of state regulation makes private opportunities and fortunes a matter of government decisions and political power. As part and parcel of being less institutionalized, the Janata family parties are even less allied to formal civil society organizations.

It is premature to talk of the decline of some Janata family parties, despite their current alliance with the BJP. Parties belonging to this family, as well as those closely related in social base and politics like the Scheduled Caste-based, pro-reservation BSP, can be said to represent a gradually awakening, countrywide, broad, if inchoate, social constituency, which finds it extremely difficult to unite in the form of a cohesive organized party due to variations in agrarian relations and caste structures between states, and particularistic leaderships based on these, but is not going to fade away.

The Left Parties

The left parties have historically played an important role in some regions of India. The Communist Party of India (CPI), founded in 1920, grew steadily in the years up to India's Independence, acquiring localized bases among industrial workers and peasants in a few areas, and remained ideologically close to the Soviet Union. After leading an unsuccessful uprising in the Telangana region of Andhra Pradesh, immediately after Independence, the CPI turned to parliamentary politics and contested elections. The CPI emerged as the single largest opposition party in the Lower House in the 1952, 1957, and 1962 elections, with 16, 27, and 29 seats (i.e. only 3-6 per cent of the seats) due to its relatively concentrated vote share of 3.3 per cent, 8.9 per cent and 9.9 per cent respectively, despite it being only third in vote share in the first two elections behind two Socialist parties. Its principal regional bases were in the states of Kerala, Tripura, West Bengal, Andhra Pradesh, and Bihar. The first three states, continue to be the principal strongholds of the left parties, and have seen the left alternating in power with Congress-led governments in Kerala and Tripura, with the LF ruling West Bengal continuously since 1977.

In 1964, the CPI split into two parties, the CPI(M) and the original CPI. This was a result of both domestic and international factors, principally the Sino–Soviet split, which was reflected in domestic politics because of the post-1956 Soviet line of peaceful coexistence with the West and improvement of relations with the Congress government in India, and because of the Indo–China border war of 1962. The domestic factors were centred around tensions over the stance to be maintained towards the ruling Congress party.

As a result of the split, the pro-Soviet CPI emerged as a smaller faction nationally and in all its major stronghold states—except in Bihar and Andhra Pradesh, eventually only in Bihar by the 1990s—than the initially more radical and more pro-Chinese CPI(M). The latter underwent further splits in 1967, as insurrectionary Communist factions formed the CPI (Marxist-Leninist), or CPI(ML) in turn splintering into several factions. The CPI tended to back the Congress, at least its left-leaning factions, as a bulwark of anti-imperialism and representing the national bourgeoisie against US-led transnational capital, while the CPI(M) tended to be more strongly anti-Congress, to a large extent due to it being the principal left party intermittently in power in West Bengal, Kerala, and Tripura, with the Congress as its immediate adversary. However, the CPI(M) assumed a posture of equidistance between the Soviet Union and China. Since the late 1970s, the CPI and CPI(M) began to cooperate in left coalitions, along with some minor left parties, like the Revolutionary Socialist Party (RSP) and the All India Forward Bloc (AIFB), initially in West Bengal, then in Kerala, and then nationally.

The left's electoral record since the split has been as follows: In 1967, the immediate post-split CPI still remained the larger party in votes and seats, but has yielded that position to the CPI(M) in every election since. The combined seats of the CPI(M) and CPI, have been in the range of 28 (1984) to 49 (1991), currently 36 in 2000 (41 with minor left parties) or about 5-10 per cent of the seats with minor leftist parties. The combined votes have ranged from 6.9 per cent (1998) to 9.8 per cent (1971), or about 7-10 per cent with minor leftist parties. Seats contested, and consequently, both seats and votes have been overwhelmingly concentrated in West Bengal, Kerala and Tripura. The social base of the left parties has been fairly stable and mainly in the rural areas and among the middle and small peasantry and agricultural labour in its stronghold states.

Since 1989, the left parties have followed a broad, multi-class, social-democratic reformist strategy, striking electoral alliances with the JD-led NF, supporting its short-lived government in 1989-90, and its successor UF coalitions in the 1996 and 1998 elections, with the CPI participating in the UF government of 1996-8. Hung parliaments and coalition politics have magnified their clout in government formation and policy in certain situations, depending on the specific numbers, despite a stagnant social base and vote share, and the marginalization of class issues in election campaigns.

The Regional Parties

The period since 1967 has seen the birth, steady growth, and consolidation of a host of major and minor regional parties. There are six major regional parties, or groups of parties if offshoots are treated as a single family for genealogical purposes, and if the definition is limited to parties that are not only based in a single state but also have an explicitly ethno-linguistic/cultural, nationalist/regional, autonomist ideology. These are the Dravidian parties of Tamil Nadu (originally the

DMK, now the AIADMK, MDMK, and PMK), the SAD of Punjab, the JKNC of Jammu & Kashmir, the TDP of Andhra Pradesh, the Asom Gana Parishad (AGP) of Assam, and the Shiv Sena of Maharashtra.

The most significant have been the Tamil parties, as they have been the only parties to have displaced the Congress from both first and second places in state Assembly elections, as well as have eliminated Congress rule in a state continuously since 1967.[9] Originating in the non-Brahmin movement beginning with the South Indian Liberal Federation, which became the Justice Party in the early part of the century, the DMK was formed as a breakaway from the Dravida Kazhagam in 1949 and grew to come to power in the state Assembly elections of 1967, winning 138 (out of 234) seats and 40.8 per cent votes, after hugely swelling its base in the anti-Hindi agitation of the mid-1960s. The DMK formally dropped the secessionist agenda in 1963. The DMK won 25 out of 39 seats, and 35.8 per cent votes in the 1967 general elections. After the death of its first Chief Minister, C.N. Annadurai, in 1968, the DMK split into two, with the emergence of the AIADMK led by film actor M.G. Ramachandran (MGR) from 1972. In the 1971 elections, the post-split Congress lost disastrously despite the DMK not putting up candidates against it in many constituencies, leading to a change of strategy in 1977. The dominant Congress (I) allied in 1977 to the MGR-led AIADMK winning 14 out of 15 contested seats with 22.3 per cent votes, while the AIADMK won 18 out of 20 with 30.5 per cent beating the DMK (1 seat and 18 per cent votes) and the separately contesting Congress (O) (3 seats, 17.7 per cent votes). This alliance was based on trading Lok Sabha seats for state Assembly seats, with the Congress getting a large or majority share of the former while the AIADMK got a majority share of the latter, enabling it to capture the Assembly and state power. This arrangement lasted until the AIADMK dumped the Congress in 1998. It was successful for both the Congress and the AIADMK in 1977, 1980, 1984, 1989, and 1991 in general elections, and likewise in Assembly elections, failing only in the 1989 Assembly elections due to the split in the AIADMK after MGR's death.

Since 1996, however, the party system in Tamil Nadu has become more complex and is fragmenting along factional and caste lines. The main Tamil parties have splintered, with the emergence of MDMK from the parent DMK in 1993, led by V. Gopalaswamy, and the PMK, a party based on the lower OBC Vanniyar caste centred in northern

Tamil Nadu, and the emergence in the southern districts of a new Dalit party, Pudhiya Tamizhagam. The Congress in Tamil Nadu split in 1996 over the high command's decision to ally with the AIADMK, the bulk of the Congress joining the newly formed Tamil Maanila Congress (TMC), which allied with the DMK, and together won 37 out of 39 seats, with the DMK winning the state Assembly elections. In 1998, the AIADMK dumped the Congress and allied with the MDMK, PMK, and BJP, and won 30 out of 39 seats. However, alliance partners switched again in 1999, with the Congress allying with the AIADMK, while the DMK allied with the BJP and the smaller MDMK and PMK, and won 26 out of 39 seats, the TMC contesting alone and drawing a blank. Towards the end of 2003 a realignment is again in the offing, with DMK and MDMK leaving the BJP-led NDA and aligning with Congress, while the AIADMK moving closer to NDA. The Tamil parties are in a state of flux, with caste assertions splintering what was formerly a broad, anti-Brahmin, 'Dravidian' unity against the centre and the Hindi-speaking north, and a virtual abandonment of 'Dravidian' ideology, signified by the alliance with the BJP.

The JKNC and the SAD of Punjab have a long history pre-dating Independence and Partition. The JKNC, principally based on the Kashmiri Muslims of the Valley, is however, a secular party in principle, and does draw some support from non-Muslims in both the Valley and other parts of the state. It has been the principal party of the Kashmir Valley, and since 1977 of the Jammu & Kashmir state, while the Congress traditionally dominated Jammu and Ladakh until the 1990s. Elections in J&K from the arrest of Sheikh Abdullah in 1953 to the end of the Emergency in 1977 are widely accepted to have been less than free and fair. The Congress won over 50 per cent votes and 5 (out of 6) seats in the state in 1967 and 1971, and similar majorities in the Assembly, despite JKNC having won 70 (out of 75) seats and 67 per cent votes in the Assembly in 1962. In 1977, after the release of Sheikh Abdullah, the JKNC bounced back with majorities in the Assembly based on pluralities of the vote in 1977, 1983 and 1987, the last year being in alliance with the Congress. In the general elections, JKNC, won the three Kashmir Valley seats in 1980, 1984, and 1989, and in certain years was a runner-up in the three Ladakh and Jammu constituencies. After the restoration of elections since 1996, JKNC won the Assembly elections (57 of 87 seats, 34.8 per cent votes) and formed the government in October 1996, and in the general elections, won the three Kashmir Valley seats in 1998 and the same plus the Ladakh seat in 1999. However, it must be emphasized that since 1989, due to the ongoing insurgency, turnouts were extremely low, touching a new low in 1999. However, under the shadow of cross border terrorism, the state went to the polls in 2003, considered largely free and fair by independent national and international observers.

Assembly elections in 2003 have brought a turning point, dislodging the Abdullah dynasty-led JKNC, and voting in power a Congress–People's Democratic Party coalition headed by Mufti Mohammad Sayeed.

The SAD, a confessional party of the Sikh community, its primary base being among the landowning Jat Sikhs, emerged as a major party in Punjab after Independence and Partition, especially after the successful agitation led by it to form a Punjabi-speaking, Sikh-majority state of Punjab in 1966. The Akali Dal has gone through a few splits over the decades, but has remained basically intact and has consolidated itself as the main party of the Sikh community in Punjab and one of the two main parties in the state. Since 1967, it or its principal faction (SAD–Sant Fateh Singh in 1967, SAD–Mann in 1989) have won the second largest share of votes next to the Congress in Punjab in general elections, winning more in 1977 when allied with the Janata Party, and following essentially the same pattern in Assembly elections. The insurgency in Punjab in the 1980s tended to marginalize the Akali Dal, leading it to boycott the Assembly elections of 1992. However, it bounced back by winning 8 seats each in the 1996 and 1998 general elections, and 75 out of 126 seats in the Assembly elections in 1997, the last two elections in alliance with the BJP, and forming a coalition government in the state with the BJP. In 1999, however, the SAD–BJP alliance (3 seats) lost to the Congress (8 seats). The Akali Dal has always been pressurized by the political demography of the state to look for coalition partners and has been successful only because of them. This is because, as a Sikh confessional party in a state where the Sikh–Hindu ratio is roughly 60 : 40, it receives most of the votes of the Sikhs but few Hindu votes, thus finding it very difficult to win on its own. In 1967, it formed a coalition of the extremes with the BJS and CPI, in 1977 an alliance with the Janata Party, and in 1996 with the BSP for general elections, and since the 1997 Assembly elections, with the

BJP, thus contributing to the tendency toward bipolarity at the state level for both Vidhan Sabha and Lok Sabha elections.

The TDP of Andhra Pradesh, is a major new regional party, that has been and is playing a role in successive coalition governments at the centre since 1989. The TDP was formed in 1983 by the late film actor, N.T. Rama Rao (NTR), as a regional nationalist response to a perceived slight to the then chief minister of the state by the Congress high command. It swept the Assembly elections of 1983 and 1985 with an almost identical 46 per cent votes and just over 200 (of 294) seats both times. In 1989, it lost to the Congress both in the general (2 to 39 seats) and state Assembly elections (74 to 181 seats out of 294), but performed slightly better in 1991, though still losing. It, however, won both the 1994 (217 seats) and 1999 Assembly elections (179 seats) handsomely. In 1996 and 1998, it lost again to the Congress, but won a thumping victory in 1999 (29 seats), simultaneously with its victory in the Assembly. The TDP is, like the Congress, a catch-all party at the state level, and unlike the Tamil parties, does not have an articulated regional nationalist ideology but is vaguely federalist, autonomist, and coalitional. It underwent one major split in 1995, just before the death of NTR, when his son-in-law, Chandrababu Naidu, took over the reigns of the party and the great majority of its MLAs, and became the Chief Minister. The TDP has played a prominent role in coalition politics at the centre, being part of the NF coalition of 1989-90, the UF coalition of 1996-8, and a key external supporter of the BJP-led coalitions since 1998. It appears to have consolidated itself as one of the two principal parties in the state, although the BJP has been rising as a third force in the state since 1998.

The AGP, of Assam is a major new regional party that could be on the verge of eclipse at the turn of the century. A product of the Assam agitation since 1979-80 against illegal immigration from Bangladesh that was perceived to threaten the demographic supremacy of the Assamese in their home state, the AGP was an outgrowth of the All Assam Students Union, which spearheaded the movement. It first contested elections in 1985 for both the Assembly and the Lok Sabha (the delayed 1984 election), boycotting the 1983 Assembly elections, winning seven out of fourteen Lok Sabha (33.4 per cent votes) and 65 out of 126 Assembly seats (35 per cent votes). Elections were not held in 1989 due to disturbed conditions, but in 1991, the AGP lost to the

Congress in both the Assembly and the Lok Sabha. In 1996, the AGP and the Congress won 4 Lok Sabha seats each, while the AGP won 59 out of 126 Assembly seats and formed a coalition government with the Left and small state-based parties, while being part of the UF coalition at the centre. In 1998 and 1999, the AGP fared disastrously in the general elections, losing to the Congress both times, winning no seats, and being pushed to third place in vote share behind both the Congress and the BJP. The AGP and Congress governments have failed to contain the extremist and separatist United Liberation Front of Assam (ULFA) insurgency in the state and it remains to be seen whether the AGP will survive as a party if it loses state power, or gets marginalized by the ULFA, as the Akali Dal nearly did during the height of the Punjab insurgency, or as the JKNC was threatened with in Kashmir.

The Shiv Sena is a regional party with a difference, in that while it began as a Maharashtrian-chauvinist sons-of-the-soil movement in Bombay (now Mumbai) city in 1966, directed primarily at south Indian migrants, it evolved into an anti-Communist force in the 1970s and 1980s, and since the late 1980s, into a virulently anti-Muslim party that positions itself to the ideological right of the BJP, while toning down its Maharashtrian chauvinism. Its growth as an electoral force began from Bombay, contesting elections only sporadically, the key event being the capture of the Bombay Municipal Corporation in 1985, and spread to the rest of Maharashtra in the 1990s. The Sena first contested Lok Sabha elections in 1971, winning 1.6 per cent votes in the state and none of the 5 Bombay seats contested, and Assembly elections in 1972, winning 1.8 per cent votes and 1 of 26 seats contested. It skipped the 1977 general elections but contested the 1978 Assembly elections, again winning 1.8 per cent votes but none of the 35 seats contested. In the 1980 general elections, it got 0.6 per cent votes and neither of the two seats contested. The Sena did not contest the 1980 and 1985 Assembly elections and the 1984 general election. During this decade, however, it grew steadily in Bombay and in the second half of the decade more widely in Maharashtra, on the basis of anti-Communist and anti-Muslim mobilization.

In the 1989 general elections the Sena won only 1 out 3 seats contested and 1.2 per cent votes in the state. In the 1990 Assembly elections, however, contested in alliance with the BJP, the Sena won 52 seats and 15.9 per cent votes. This rose to 4 seats and 9.5 per cent votes in the state in the 1991 general elections, and in the 1995 state Assembly elections, the Sena came to power in Maharashtra for the first time, in alliance with the BJP. It won 73 seats and 16.5 per cent votes and formed a minority coalition government with the support of independents who were later inducted into the coalition to secure a majority. However, this was due to a large number of rebel contestants in the Congress camp, and even so the Congress vote share was fractionally larger than that of the Sena–BJP combine. In the 1996 general elections, the Sena won 15 seats (out of 48) and 16.8 per cent votes in alliance with the BJP. The tables were turned in 1998 when the Congress won 33 seats, the Sena crashing to 6 seats but with 19.7 per cent votes despite the alliance with the BJP, which got 4 seats. In 1999, the Sena–BJP alliance benefited from the split in the Maharashtra Congress, the Sena winning 15 seats. However, the alliance lost the state Assembly elections (combined 123 seats) to the Congress (76) and the breakaway Sharad Pawar-led NCP (59), who despite contesting independently, formed a post-election coalition government with the support of smaller parties and independents. It is interesting to note that the Sena's charismatic and authoritarian leader, Bal Thackeray, has never contested an election in his life. Also noteworthy is the fact that the Sena has sustained an alliance with the BJP since 1990, and has suffered only one significant split, when in December 1991, a group of MLAs led by a major leader, now with the NCP, Chhagan Bhujbal, joined the then ruling Congress and enabled it to secure a majority in the Assembly.

Other minor regional parties include the Maharashtrawadi Gomantak Party of Goa, the Sikkim Democratic Front and Sikkim Sangram Parishad of Sikkim, the MNF of Mizoram, and less stable formations in Nagaland, Manipur, Meghalaya, and Arunachal Pradesh, and the decades-old sub-regional, tribal-based Jharkhand Party and its off-shoot, the JMM, and their various splinter groups in south Bihar now, Jharkhand, and adjoining parts of Orissa and West Bengal.

The overall picture, however, is of state-based parties, whether with an explicitly regional nationalist ideology or not, consolidating themselves as one of the two major parties in a number of important states containing a large number (162) of Lok Sabha seats, even if we count only the fairly long-established and stable regional parties—the DMK and AIADMK, TDP, JKNC, SAD, AGP, and Shiv Sena.

The Bahujan Samaj Party

The BSP had its origins in the formation by its founder-leader Kanshi Ram, of the Backward and Minority Communities Employees Federation (BAMCEF) in 1978. The BSP, formed in 1984, is a party of the Scheduled Castes, now over 16 per cent of the population with 15 per cent of public sector jobs reserved for them under the Constitution. However, the BSP's philosophy and its concept of what constitutes the *Bahujan Samaj* has never been limited to the Scheduled Castes alone. *The Bahujan Samaj* concept includes all non-*dvija* (twice-born) Hindus, that is, all those not belonging to the three *dvija varnas* (caste groupings) as well as religious and ethnic minorities. All these peoples have, according to this preception, been at the receiving end of institutionalized discrimination at the hands of the upper caste-dominated Hindu social order. The Scheduled Castes, who have historically been at the bottom of the caste heap, are its core base from which political and social mobilization is to move outward in additive steps. The BSP thus seeks to build a political majority from the bottom. Its focus and major success has been states like UP and Punjab, and to a lesser extent MP, Haryana, Delhi, and the Jammu region of J&K, where the Scheduled Castes are both numerically large and most excluded from the power structure of the dominant Congress party, even while constituting a key component of the Congress vote. It is this denial of due share of power in party power structures that has induced them to gravitate to the BSP as an alternative. In other words, a clear case of the logic of exit, voice, and loyalty to use Hirschman's pithy phrase.[10]

The BSP emerged as a significant party only in the 1990s, winning 1.6 per cent votes and 2 seats in 1991, 3.6 per cent votes and 11 seats in 1996, 4 seats and 4.7 per cent votes in 1998, 14 seats and 4.2 per cent votes in 1999. This made it the fourth largest party nationally by vote share in 1998—a meteoric rise in ten years. These votes are highly concentrated in a few states, primarily UP, Punjab, MP, Haryana, and J&K, but within these states, are spread over constituencies in a way that does not translate proportionately into seats, reflecting the distribution of its core voters, the Scheduled Castes, as a minority of the electorate everywhere, even in the reserved seats. In Lok Sabha elections in UP, the BSP got as much as 20.6 per cent votes in 1996 but only 6 out of 85 seats, 20.9 per cent votes in 1998 but only 4 seats, and 22.1 per cent votes and 14 seats in 1999. Likewise in Punjab, it got 19.3 per cent votes in 1991 but only 1 out of 13 seats, 9.4 per cent (in alliance) in 1997 (deferred 1996 election) and 3 seats, 12.7 per cent in 1998 and no seats, 3.8 per cent votes and no seats in 1999. However, the BJP does pose a significant threat to the prospects of the party that was the erstwhile beneficiary of the bulk of the Scheduled Caste vote, in UP, Punjab, and MP, viz., the Congress, and hence indirectly helps the Congress' principal opponent in these states, viz., the BJP in UP and MP, and the SAD-BJP alliance in Punjab. It is therefore positioned to ally tactically with either the Congress or with the BJP or Akali Dal, and being perceived as pivotal for the prospects of victory, extract disproportionate concessions both at the electoral alliance stage and in government formation, and has done so at various times, most importantly in forming a tail-wags-the-dog coalition government with a much larger BJP in UP in 1995 after the SP–BSP coalition's breakup, and in 1997, both experiments being short-lived.

THE SOCIAL BASES AND IMPACT OF COALITIONS

The social bases of political coalitions depend on the social bases of the parties comprising the coalition. To answer the question of whether political coalitions represent underlying social coalitions, one needs to examine the social bases of the parties in the coalition, and whether the coalition is a durable one or a temporary marriage of convenience. Here we can usefully distinguish between catch-all parties and 'ethnic' or class parties. Catch-all parties are parties that have a political programme that cuts across 'ethnic'—including religious, linguistic, caste, tribal and other ascriptive—identities, as well as socio-economic and geographic boundaries, or at least the former but within the boundaries of a state or region. 'Ethnic' parties are those whose support base is, either explicitly or implicitly, but overwhelmingly, of particular religious, linguistic, regional, cultural, caste or tribal groups. This definition includes regional parties based on an explicitly regional-cultural identity. Class parties are those that have a definite socio-economic class character in their support base and ideology.[11]

'Ethnic' parties include regional-linguistic-cultural parties such as the Dravidian parties, the Akali Dal, the AGP, and the Shiv Sena. They also include implicitly or explicitly caste-based parties such as the SP, the BSP, or within states, the PMK in Tamil Nadu. Class parties are the left parties. Implicitly or explicitly communal parties such as the BJP and the Shiv Sena, and the various Muslim Leagues and the SAD, are also 'ethnic' parties, though the character of large parties like the BJP may also vary from state to state, being an upper-caste-oriented party in states such as UP and Bihar, where the upper castes form its core base despite projecting itself as a broad catch-all party at least of the Hindu majority. Political coalitions can be said to reflect social coalitions when the parties constituting the political coalition are 'ethnic' and/ or class parties that are seen to be representing, indirectly, distinct segments of society, and when such coalitions prove themselves to be lasting, at least in the context of particular states. Thus, one can say that the LF coalitions in West Bengal, Tripura, and Kerala are not only political but also to some extent social coalitions, whereas the UF coalition at the centre and the two BJP-led coalitions at the centre, are essentially opportunistic coalitions, both being at least partly post-election coalitions cobbled together to form governments and not on the basis of a clearly united socio-political or economic programme and ideology. One can further observe that intra-state coalitions are more likely, though not necessarily so, to represent social coalitions since the socio-cultural configuration of each state varies, particularly its caste structure, and therefore, the social cleavages that define party bases and social coalitions do not easily cross state boundaries. Inter-state coalitions at the national level tend to be, for the same reason, opportunistic power-seeking coalitions.

Coming to the related question of the impact of coalitions, it must be first stated that it is too early to tell, as coalition politics in India has been in continuous existence only from 1996. Political and social coalitions are still evolving. One can, however, usefully look at two questions: Has coalition politics led to more consensual as against more confrontational politics? And has coalition politics led to the strengthening of federalism? The answers to both questions is a qualified yes.

Governments are becoming more consensual, willy-nilly, because, in the first instance, even the formation of the BJP-led coalitions after the general elections of 1998 and 1999 required the shelving of the BJP's controversial *Hindutva* agenda for most of its pre- and post-election coalition partners to be able to join it in government. Second, no party enjoys a majority in the Lok Sabha since 1996 and the passage of legislation requires taking along one's coalition partners. Third, the passage of ordinary legislation requires passage in both houses of Parliament. The BJP-led coalitions have not enjoyed a majority in the Rajya Sabha and therefore, depend on at least minimal cooperation from the principal opposition party, the Congress. Fourth, the kinds of coalitions that have ruled India since 1996 has been, by comparative experiences worldwide, very large coalitions. The UF coalition consisted of thirteen parties, including both those participating in government and those supporting it from outside. Similarly, the BJP-led NDA coalition consists of twenty-four parties, again including supporting parties, not participating in government. This implies that the coalition as a whole is socially and geographically encompassing and has to satisfy the demands of a wide range of social groups and regions, forcing it to act in at least a minimally consensual manner. Last, the UF and first BJP-led coalition were minority coalitions dependent on the support from outside of parties that were not a part of the coalition, a fact that further constrained them to act relatively consensually.

Similarly, coalition governments since 1996 have been relatively more federal in functioning. Examples of this are the greater difficulty in using Art. 356, for example, in the case of Bihar in 1999, due to the fact that the NDA coalition lacked a majority in the Rajya Sabha. Basically, the coalitions at the centre have been more federal because they are critically dependent on state-based parties like the TDP, the DMK and AIADMK, the Trinamool Congress, Akali Dal and BJD. However, this works both ways. The AIADMK and the Trinamool Congress made demands on the centre to actually misuse Art. 356 to dismiss rival party governments in their states, viz., the DMK and LF governments in Tamil Nadu and West Bengal respectively for essentially partisan political reasons. That is, they made anti-federalist demands.

The reason why we qualify our statement that that the coalition governments have been more consensual and more federal is that this has been evidently so *under constraint and not due to a change in political culture* towards one of greater accommodativeness. In fact, the BJP has shelved its *Hindutva* agenda with utmost reluctance and has employed all sorts of devices to raise issues not on the common agenda of its coalition, including by having its affiliated organizations in the broader *Sangh Parivar*, such as the VHP, Bajrang Dal, and others, raise such issues, to private members bills, to stealthy moves by ministries controlled by it, such as Human Resource Development, and so forth. Also, unlike in coalitions in European States, there is a lack of a basic acceptance of other parties as they are, indicated most strongly by continual attempts on the part of not only the major parties like the BJP but also almost all parties at the state level, to split their opponents and absorb splinter groups. This is not consensual behaviour or acceptance of political diversity.

ELECTORAL ALLIANCES AND COALITION GOVERNMENTS IN THE CONTEXT OF SPLIT-PRONE PARTIES

The foregoing account of births, deaths, splits, and mergers of the currently important large and small parties in India brings out the unstable and weakly institutionalized character of most Indian parties. In this final section, we look at the evolution of electoral alliances and where such alliances are victorious, coalition governments, and relate these alliances and the behaviour of coalitions to the fact of many important parties being highly prone to splits and mergers, all in the pursuit of power. *The one important factor, though not the sole one, in the instability of coalitions in India, is the split-proneness or unstable character of most parties.* The underlying logic of this, not explored here, is the fact that politics in India is overwhelmingly about capturing state power to redirect resources towards one's social constituency, the state as owner, regulator, and financier, directly or indirectly, of much of economic activity, playing an overwhelmingly important role in the 'life chances' of people in a developing country with a still largely agrarian population and electorate where primordial religious, caste, and linguistic ties are able to mobilize voters.

Electoral alliances and coalition governments in India, at the central and state levels, have gone through several phases since the 1960s. The first phase of coalition politics was the formation of broad, anti-Congress electoral alliances in the 1960s, with ideology and policy taking a back seat. Ram Manohar Lohia was the chief ideologue of anti-Congressism. The driving force of these inchoate alliances was the fact of electoral arithmetic that the Congress won a majority of seats on the basis of a plurality of the vote. Therefore, an electoral alliance offering one-on-one contests to the Congress had good prospects of success. Pre-election coalitions were formed in several states in 1967, including UP, Bihar, West Bengal, and Orissa, centred around splinter groups that broke away from the Congress just prior to the February 1967 elections to form short-lived parties. The SVD coalition governments formed with these short-lived parties by the Charan Singh-led Bharatiya Kranti Dal (BKD), BJS, Swatantra and the Socialist parties, ideologically ranging from right to left, in a number of northern states in the 1967-74 period, however, proved unstable, foundering on the extreme instability of parties. Five of these SVD governments collapsed due to splits and defections by 1969, resulting in mid-term Assembly elections that year in five states. This period saw a number of splits in both the opposition parties and in the Congress. It saw an extraordinarily large number of defections with legislators leaving or joining parties in even ones and twos, something that was possible until the anti-defection legislation of 1985. Most splits and defections were motivated not by ideology or policy considerations but by conflicts over sharing the spoils of office.

The next round of electoral alliance building was the 1974-7 period, interrupted by the Emergency, in which several of the parties, which formed the failed SVD coalition governments in the 1967-74 period, merged to form larger entities and eventually the Janata Party. Thus, after defeat in the 1972 and 1974 state Assembly elections in the northern states and Orissa, the BKD, Samyukta Socialist Party (Raj Narain), Swatantra, Utkal Congress, and three minor parties merged to form the BLD. After the post-Emergency elections of 1977, the BLD, Congress (O), Socialist Party, BJS, and the Jagjivan Ram-led Congress for Democracy merged to form the Janata Party. However, the Janata Party, a hastily put-together coalition of factions without a unified organization, collapsed due to a split in July 1979, essentially over a power struggle between the Morarji Desai and Charan Singh factions.

The return of the Congress to power from 1980-9 interrupted the process of coalition formation, which resumed when V.P. Singh, after his expulsion from the Congress in 1987, brought together, with his ex-Congress followers, the Lok Dal (Ajit Singh), Lok Dal (Devi Lal), and the Janata Party (Hegde) and formed the JD in October 1988. However, unlike in 1977, there were several influential regional parties on the scene in 1989. The JD allied formally with several regional parties, including the DMK, TDP, and AGP, which were in power in their respective states so as to offer one-on-one contests to the Congress, without entering one another's turf. It also struck, at another level, informal alliances through seat adjustments with the BJP in the northern states and Gujarat, and with the LF in the latter's stronghold states, all to avoid splitting the anti-Congress vote.

The NF minority coalition government formed, however, with the external support of the BJP and the Left Front, proved unstable and short-lived. Although this was primarily due to the conflict between the NF, principally the JD and the BJP, it was crucially due to the internal conflicts within the JD, between V.P. Singh and Devi Lal. The trigger was the 'Mandal' decision on reservations in government jobs and education for the OBCs in August 1990, a political blow aimed at both the non-OBC, Jat-based Devi Lal faction of the JD and at the BJP. The government collapsed following the BJP's decision to withdraw support in October 1990, and JD immediately split into the V.P. Singh and Chandrashekhar–Devi Lal factions. A key factor underlying the instability of the coalition was the internal conflict and split-proneness of the JD itself.

Following the collapse of the short-lived Chandrashekhar government, the Congress returned to power as a minority government with external support from the AIADMK and some minor Kerala parties in mid-1991, which still left it short of a majority. It was dependent on the divisions in the opposition between the BJP and the rest. It capitalized on the split-proneness of other parties, engineering splits, and eating up splinter groups, from the TDP and the Lok Dal (Ajit Singh) particularly, to acquire a majority by the end of 1993.

The replacement of Prime Minister Deve Gowda in April 1997, and the resignation of Prime Minister I.K. Gujral, bringing about the fall of the UF government in November 1997, was not due to splits in any of the constituent parties in the coalition but due to withdrawal of support by the Congress party. However, in the immediate aftermath of Gujral's resignation, there was a strong attempt by the BJP to split the Congress Parliamentary Party as well as several other parties to effect a realignment in the existing house so that the BJP could form a government. An appeal was made to the first-timer MPs who were presumed to have a major stake in the life of the existing Lok Sabha. L.K. Advani boasted that forty Congress MPs, just eight short of the required one-third, were ready to break away from the party. More significantly, the Congress split in West Bengal leading to the emergence of the Trinamool Congress which allied with the BJP, and the JD split in Orissa, leading to the emergence of the BJD as its major faction, which also allied with the BJP. Both developments helped the BJP significantly in the 1998 elections.

While the fall of the first BJP-led coalition government in April 1999 was not caused by any split in existing parties, an important split in the JD in Karnataka just prior to the 1999 elections, leading to the emergence of its major faction led by Chief Minister J.H. Patel, and the merger of this faction with the Lok Shakti, and their alliance with the BJP, led to the decimation of the JD in Karnataka. The merger of the JD in Bihar and Karnataka, and the Lok Shakti and the Samata Party in Bihar just before the elections, to form the JD(U) helped to unify the votes of these splinters and helped the NDA, including the BJP, in Bihar. While the formation of the BJP-led NDA coalition has lost some allies, it has gained servel others.

The pattern of evolution of electoral alliances and coalitions with respect to party splits and mergers can be summarized as follows:

In the first phase of coalition politics in the 1960s and early 1970s, *intra-state* SVD alliances between highly personalized clientelistic parties with extremely weak organizational structures, if any, led largely by disgruntled ex-Congressmen, and based purely on anti-Congressism, were the order of the day. These were extremely prone to splits, defections, and mergers as would be expected.

In the second or Janata Party phase, again based on anti-Congressism, but this time based more calculatedly on avoiding splits in the non-Congress vote, coalitions were *both of an intra-state and inter-state character*. For example, in UP and Bihar, the Janata Party was constituted of intra-state mergers of BKD/BLD, Socialists, BJS, and Congress defectors, while the Janata Party at the national level unified these parties across states. However, the Janata Party never developed unified organizational structures and processes of functioning worth the name, the original constituents, especially the BJS, largely retaining their identities, and hence, remained extremely vulnerable to splits and defections.

The post-Janata phase saw the emergence and/or consolidation of two types of electoral alliances. First, the consolidation of the LF and

LDF alliances in West Bengal and Kerala respectively, following the alliance of the CPI and the CPI(M)-led Left Fronts. Thus, CPM-dominated Left Fronts including the CPI and smaller left parties consolidated themselves in the party systems of West Bengal, Kerala, and Tripura. Second, the AIADMK–Congress alliance in Tamil Nadu from 1980-96, emerged as a possible form of accommodation of regional parties, in which the AIADMK took the majority of state Assembly seats in exchange for giving the Congress the majority of Lok Sabha seats in the state, thus not cutting into each other's turf. However, this did not survive the relative decline of national parties and the relative rise of state-based parties since 1996.

The JD-led NF coalition marked a departure from the earlier Janata Party in that it learnt from the experience of the breakup of the artificially unified Janata Party, and did not try to unify its very different constituent parties. Rather, it merely adopted a common manifesto and went in for seat adjustments to give the Congress one-to-one contests in as many seats as possible. It also marked a departure in that it included explicitly regional parties like the DMK, TDP, and AGP and included the LF, unlike the SVD and Janata experiments. In the process, it also *marked the beginning of cross-state alliances of state-based parties, which did not compete on each other's turf, i.e. spatially compatible even if ideologically heterogeneous alliances.* The UF was another alliance of this type.

Three other types of alliances can be observed in the post-1991 period. First, *intra-state ideological alliances*, viz., the BJP–Shiv Sena, similar to the LF alliances but limited to one state. Second, *intra-state alliances*, which are a reverse of the Congress–AIADMK type, i.e. those in which the regional party contests the majority of both Lok Sabha and Assembly seats. Examples are AIADMK–smaller parties–BJP in 1998, DMK–smaller parties–BJP in 1999, TDP–BJP in 1999, BJD–BJP in 1998 and 1999, HVP–BJP in 1996 and 1998, and BJP–INLD (Chautala) in 1999. Shiv Sena–BJP also fits this to an extent, except that it is also ideological in content. Third, *intra-state alliances* between a national party and a minor state party in which the former contests the majority of both Lok Sabha and Assembly seats, e.g. BJP–Lok Shakti in 1998 and 1999, BJP–Samata Party in 1996-9, BJP–HVC in HP.

Relating the stability of different types of alliances to the split- and merger-proneness of parties, the following major points can be made.

First, parties are not reconciled to what would be considered 'normal' coalition politics in the European sense, i.e. to acceptance of the coalition partner's existence, ideology, and social base as a permanent feature over the long term, and hence, having to make compromises with this reality. To the contrary, Indian parties typically try their best to engineer defections, splits and mergers with themselves of the emergent splinter groups or defectors to acquire a majority on their own. Coalitions are typically seen as an unstable stop-gap arrangement by the parties themselves. The only possible exceptions are the Left Front parties since 1977.

Second, ideological alliances have been the most stable, the most noteworthy being the LF alliances in West Bengal, Kerala, and Tripura, and the stability of the LF's functioning at the national level in wider alliances with the NF or as part of the UF, since 1989 and 1996 respectively. The Shiv Sena–BJP alliance has also been stable since 1991.

Third, spatial alliances where parties divide territory among themselves and do not compete on each other's turf, or have a trade-off arrangement between Lok Sabha and Assembly seats, have been the next most stable. The AIADMK–Congress example of 1980-96 is an example of the latter type. The loose 'third force' represented by the NF and later, UF coalitions, consisting to a large extent of state-based parties that did not compete on each other's turf, are the best example of spatially compatible coalitions. These fell not so much because of the splitting of parties but because of the withdrawal of outside support; splits took place only subsequently. Their instability is not so much due to the split-proneness of parties but due to the propensity of state-based parties to switch partners such as when several former UF parties, such as the TDP and the Tamil parties switched to the BJP-led coalition in 1998.

Fourth, the most unstable alliances, and those whose instability is due to the split-proneness of parties, are intra-state alliances of non-ideological parties. These were precisely the kinds of alliances that typified the SVD governments of 1967-74, and which underpinned the Janata Party in the Hindi-belt and Gujarat in 1977-9 where the various BKD, Socialists, and Congress splinters, each to a large extent congruent with particular caste and class combinations, unified to form the Janata Party. The splits, mergers, and realignments that characterize intra-state caste politics are reflected in the split-proneness of such parties and instability of such alliances. The JD of the post-1989 period is a prime example of such split-proneness, having fragmented in every state where it was once a force, being essentially a loose combination in every state of various intra-state caste and class alliances.

One can conclude, perhaps, optimistically, that with the long-term tendency, observable since as far back as 1967, but gathering strength in the 1980s and 1990s, towards the bipolarization of state party systems into either two-party or two-alliance or one-party-*versus*-alliance systems,[12] one may expect coalitions at the national level will increasingly be like the UF coalition, or the BJP-led coalitions, consisting of spatially compatible state-based parties rather than of the SVD/Janata Party/JD type of unification of intra-state parties and splinter groups. In which case, while one can expect coalitions in India to continue to be unstable for reasons outlined elsewhere, the split-proneness of Indian parties will become a decreasingly important factor. At the same time, the proneness of state-based parties to switch partners at the national level to alternative coalitions will become an increasingly important factor in coalition instability.[13]

NOTES

1. For a classic statement of the social cleavage theory of party systems, see Seymour Martin Lipset and Stein Rokkan, *Party Systems and Voter Alignments*, New York: Free Press, 1967. For a modified version, perhaps more relevant to post-1990 India, that argues that social cleavages do not translate automatically into party systems but offer easy mobilization opportunities, see Stefano Bartolini and Peter Mair, *Identity, Competition and Electoral Availability: The Stabilisation of European Electorates, 1885-1985*, Cambridge: Cambridge University Press, 1990.
2. Coalition theory in the European politics literature tends to implicitly assume stable parties with well-defined social bases, rather than clientelistic parties centred around individual leaders, which split easily.
3. See Richard Sisson and Ramashray Roy, eds., *Diversity and Dominance in Indian Politics*, vols. I and II, New Delhi: Sage, 1990.
4. For a detailed account of the split see Francine R. Frankel, *India's Political Economy 1947-1977: The Gradual Revolution*, New Delhi: Oxford University Press, Chapters 9-10.
5. This has been one of the main themes of the literature on deinstitutionalization of the Congress party and of Indian politics generally in the 1980s; see, for example, Atul Kohli, *Democracy and Discontent: India's Crisis of Governability*, New York: Cambridge University Press, 1991.

6. For an excellent account of the geographical, caste and class expansion of the BJP see Oliver Heath, 'Anatomy of the BJP's Rise to Power', *Economic and Political Weekly*, vol. 34, nos. 34-5, 21-8 August 1999.
7. This account of the Janata family of parties draws heavily on statewise accounts in Sisson and Roy (1990); Francine R. Frankel, 'Middle Castes and Classes', in Atul Kohli, ed., *India's Democracy*, Princeton: Princeton University Press, 1988, and Francine Frankel and M.S.A. Rao, eds., *Dominance and State Power in Modern India*, vols. I and II, New Delhi: Oxford University Press, 1989; Paul Brass, 'The Politicisation of the Peasantry in a North Indian State', in Sudipta Kaviraj, ed., *Politics in India*, New Delhi: Oxford University Press, 1997, besides others.
8. See Subrata K. Mitra and V.B. Singh, *Democracy and Social Change in India*, New Delhi: Sage, 1999,
9. For a detailed study of the Dravidian parties, see Narendra Subramanian, *Ethnicity and Populist Mobilisation: Political Parties, Citizens and Democracy in South India*, New Delhi: Oxford University Press, 1999.
10. Albert O. Hirschman, *Exit, Voice and Loyalty*, Cambridge, MA: Harvard University Press, 1970. See Kanchan Chandra, 'Mobilizing the Excluded', *Seminar*, 480, August 1999, for an outline of this argument.
11. For survey data on the social bases of political parties and coalitions (National Front, United Front, BJP-led), see Subrata Mitra and V.B. Singh, *Democracy and Social Change in India: A Cross-sectional Analysis of the National Electorate*, New Delhi: Sage, 1999, pp. 132-40.
12. See E. Sridharan, 'Duverger's Law, its Reformulations and the Evolution of the Indian Party System', Centre for Policy Research, May 1997; and *IRIS India Working Paper*, no. 35 (February 1997), IRIS Center, University of Maryland, for a detailed version of the argument on bipolarization of state party systems.
13. See E. Sridharan, 'Coalition Politics', *Seminar*, 437, Annual Number, January 1996, for an outline of reasons why coalition politics can be expected to be unstable in first-past-the-post electoral systems, particularly in India.

CHAPTER 4

The National Front and United Front Coalition Governments: A Phase in Federalized Governance

Mahendra Prasad Singh

After decades of Congress-dominance, India today must be governed by coalition or minority governments. However, neither coalition politics nor governments of this kind are new to India. For politics and government of the democratic variety, especially in a country of India's size and diversity, have to be necessarily a coalition exercise, whether at the electoral or governmental level. The legacy of the freedom struggle bequeathed to the INC, an essentially coalitional framework until around the end of the 1960s when Indira Gandhi stamped out its plurality and gradually turned it into an authoritarian pack of personal loyalists, first to herself and then to the dynasty. At a narrower semantic plane, the present phase of coalition governments at the national and state levels since the 1989 Lok Sabha elections was preceded by at least four phases of coalition governments in the past: (1) the interim government formed by Congress and Muslim League and headed by Jawaharlal Nehru under the British Cabinet Mission proposals in 1946 on the way to Independence; (2) the non-Congress catch-all coalition governments in most north Indian states after the 1967 general elections until 1971-2 when Indira Gandhi brought the Congress back to power in New Delhi and in a majority of states moulded in her own image; (3) the Janata Party governments at the centre and most north Indian states in the wake of the 1977 and 1978 elections (for these governments were really coalitional as the five constituent parties, which hurriedly merged in 1977 under the shadow of the Emergency authoritarianism, practically continued to function as separate parties); and (4) the CPI(M)–LF coalition governments in West Bengal since 1977 and intermittently since in Kerala and Tripura.

Coalition governments in Kerala go back to the late 1950s when Praja Socialist Party–Congress coalition governments were formed in the wake of the Presidential dismissal of the first democratically elected Communist government in the state, indeed probably anywhere in the world. There were also the Congress–CPI coalition governments there in the 1970s. Besides, there have been the Congress-led UDF in the state later (April-May 1996) unseated by the LDF, which in turn yielded to the UDF in the next elections. Governments in many other states in the 1990s have been actually coalitional or minority, often both, though the relatively large size of the main party in the government has often rendered the smaller partners invisible. Moreover, most governments in New Delhi since 1989 have been both coalition and minority. The Chandrashekhar and the P.V. Narasimha Rao governments formed in 1990 and 1991 respectively were one-party minority governments, but they were based on legislative coalitions. The former was supported by the Congress and the latter by the unspecified 'opposition' majority until, half-way through its tenure, it managed to become a one-party majority government by accretion of parliamentary support, stemming from elections in Punjab in the meantime and merger of opposition-splinters with it. It also survived a confidence vote allegedly through bribing JMM MPs subsequently leading to judicial action and CBI investigations.

In view of the fact that India in the 1990s seems to have got stuck with the compulsions of coalition and/or minority governments, it would appear that the long spell of Congress dominance until 1989, with only occasional or partial breaches in 1967 and 1977, merely served to conceal the essentially fragmented and coalitional nature of the Indian society and culture. Historically, too, India experienced long periods of political fragmentation and internecine conflicts among regional states, but with recurrent interventions of major subcontinental states—Maurya, Mughal, and British Raj—that imposed an overarching imperial unity under centralized bureaucratic state structures. Indian history also offers examples of *ganasanghas* (incipient republican federations) in ancient India, segmentary Chola and Vijayanagara states in early medieval south India with regional *nattars/nayakas* wielding the real power under the ritual sovereignty of the monarch, and the nominal monarchy of the post-Shivaji Maratha state with real power exercised by the hereditary prime ministers, *Peshwas*.[1]

II

In the wake of the Congress split of 1969, the Indira Gandhi government was reduced to a parliamentary minority but it survived being voted out with the strategy of forming a *legislative* coalition with some regional and left parties, who supported her government without entering into a *cabinet* coalition with it. But this brief experiment with a minority government was soon overtaken by the return of the Congress led by Mrs Gandhi with a comfortable majority in the 1971 mid-term Lok Sabha elections.

Although coalition government at the centre formally began in 1989 and has continued since, the Janata Party government in New Delhi was also a *de facto* coalition as the merger of the constituent parties that went into its making was never carried through its logical conclusion. In the five elections spanning the decade 1989-99, no single party won a majority in the Lok Sabha. In these classic coalition contexts recourse to a coalition or minority government—often both—became a necessity. The decade has seen a series of unstable coalition and/or minority governments following each other like a game of musical chairs: the NF government headed by V.P. Singh of JD, the Congress-backed Samajwadi Janata Party minority government led by Chandrashekhar, the Congress minority government formed by P.V. Narasimha Rao, the two UF governments in the same Lok Sabha under the Prime Ministership of H.D. Deve Gowda and I.K. Gujral respectively preceded by the 13-day BJP minority government, and the two BJP coalition governments, both with Atal Behari Vajpayee as the Premier. Among these, only the Congress minority government headed by P.V. Narasimha Rao eventually turned into a single-party majority government as a result of internal parliamentary realignments and elections in the Punjab. It also lasted its full mandate, though it came under the clouds for haggling its survival in a vote of no-confidence through dubious deals. The NDA government of Vajpayee is still in office.

IIi

Outside West Bengal and Kerala, coalition experiments in India of any appreciable magnitude have been half-hearted and casual. They seldom display long-term pre-election parleys and organization, and very rarely extend to all levels of the political system—local, regional, state, and national—and to all arenas of politics—electoral, legislative, and executive. West Bengal and Kerala have been exceptions to this rule, where the Left Fronts led, with decisive dominance, by CPI(M). These two states have over the years produced fairly purposive and effective governments known for economic and political recovery, communal harmony, and land reforms. These governments have also been relatively less corrupt and their leaders more inclined to austere life and civic orientations. The Congress-led UDF in Kerala has also alternated in power and provided reasonably good governance. The Congress party in West Bengal has displayed a remarkable persistence in perpetual opposition since 1977, though this experience has lent it some cynicism and flamboyance, deepened also by the absence of parties in the state willing to coalesce with it. Despite a groundswell of support for it in the panchayat and municipal elections in the mid-1990s, the Congress was unable to make it to governmental power at the state-level.

Most frequently the cementing bond of coalitions in India has often been negative rather than positive. 'Non-Congressism' kept building up over the years of Congress predominance and was brought to rather fickle climaxes in 1967 in north Indian states and, in 1977, at the national level and in north Indian states.[2] The ideologue of these ephemeral moments of non-Congress power were, respectively, Ram Manohar Lohia, the former Congress Socialist and the founder of the Samyukta Socialist Party, and Jayaprakash Narayan, the Congress Socialist-turned Gandhian who emerged from virtual political retirement to lead the anti-corruption movement against the Indira Gandhi regime in the 1970s and became the ideological grey eminence of the Janata Party. Politics of non-Congressism until 1989 brought together the centrist Janata Party (Janata Dal since 1988), the leftwing Socialist and Communist parties [shedding the earlier leanings of sections of the left such as Praja Socialist Party (PSP) and CPI for progressives in Congress], and the right wing BJS/BJP (especially after the Indira Gandhi Emergency's onslaughts on the opposition parties). The Left conveniently rationalized this comprehensive non-Congress combination as 'democratic and secular forces'. The merger of the BJS in the Janata Party in 1977 was seen as heralding the secularization of this main Hindu communal party in the same way as the merger of the communist elements with Nehru's and Indira's Congress was construed as political liberalization of Marxists. As Kothari (1982: 23) observed: 'The real challenge before Janata was to bring the Jana Sangh within the democratic framework just as the Communists had been under Nehru.' However, when the Janata Party government prematurely fell in 1979 in New Delhi, the precipitating factor, among other background reasons, was the question of 'double' membership of Janata leaders in the party as well as in Hindu communal Rashtriya Swayamsevak Sangh, aggravated by Desai–Charan Singh personality clashes. The BJS constituents in the Janata Party split off and formed the BJP, hitched on *Hindutva*, in 1980. The Sikh-communal SAD was also catholically accepted as a part of the non-Congress front by its protagonists; it was indeed a coalition partner of the Janata Party government in New Delhi (1977-9).

By the early 1990s, when non-Congressism waned a bit, another negative factor in coalition endeavours, i.e. 'anti-BJPism', appeared on the scene as a spur bringing parties together. It would be perhaps more accurate to say that while non-Congressism persisted in an attenuated way, anti-BJPism reached a feverish pitch. The political 'untouchability' of communists evident in the early post-Independence days, of course, became a thing of the past. This happened in the wake of liberalization and 'nationalization' of the Communist movement (meaning their taking to the parliamentary path and patriation to India from their ideological Meccas in the international Communist movement) and their growing electoral clout and political institutionalization in at least some states (Mallick, 1994; Nossiter, 1988). Even at the national level, the CPI held the portfolio of the Home Ministry in a UF government in the 1990s. Indrajit Gupta was the first Communist Home Minister occupying the same Chair once held by Sardar Patel!

The antipathy to BJP is rooted in Gandhi's assassin Godse being an RSS activist and its negative perception among the sizeable Muslim electorate. This antipathy sharpened noticeably when BJP from a low of two seats in the Lok Sabha in 1984 shot up to being the third largest party after Congress and Janata parties in 1989 and to the second position in 1991. Despite disclaimers to the contrary, it is widely perceived to have acquiesced in the demolition of the Babri Masjid in Ayodhya on 6 December 1992, by a frenzied mob of Hindu *karsevaks*, following which its government in Uttar Pradesh (where Ayodhya is located) hurriedly resigned and those in Madhya Pradesh, Rajasthan, and Himachal Pradesh were promptly dismissed by the Congress government in New Delhi under Article 356 of the Constitution on the plea, among others, that the chief ministers and ministers in these states being RSS activists, the centre could not count on their active cooperation in implementing the ban on RSS and some other Hindu (and Muslim) communal organizations. A tribunal later ruled that the ban on the RSS was unwarranted and the Madhya Pradesh High Court declared the dismissal of the BJP state government there unconstitutional, which was subsequently reversed by the Supreme Court, which found the sacking of the BJP government(s) in order. In the re-elections that followed, the BJP could retain only one (Rajasthan) of the four states previously ruled by it. The BJP displayed an inclination to go it alone and was less than serious in electoral adjustments with any other party (excepting Shiv Sena in Maharashtra) in the 1993 Assembly elections in its upbeat mood (*aj char pradesh, kal sara desh*). Its mood was much mellowed in the run-up to the 1996 Lok Sabha elections when it joined forces with Samata Party in Haryana (though not in Bihar, but later there as well). Shiv Sena–BJP and Samata Party–BJP coalitions won in Maharashtra and Haryana, adding two more states besides Gujarat and Rajasthan to the category of BJP-ruled states at that time. Political isolation of the BJP was, however, embarrassingly demonstrated to the whole nation and the world at large when its minority government in New Delhi formed by Atal Behari Vajpayee in the wake of the 1996 elections, given two weeks to demonstrate its coalitional majority by the President, failed in the confidence vote in May as no additional parties could be won over by it. Moreover, BJP's stocks had gone down also because its reputation of being the most cohesive party in India had been dented by the 1994 revolt of the Shankarsinh Vaghela faction against the Keshubhai Patel government in Gujarat resulting in its replacement by a new BJP government headed by Suresh Chandra Mehta.

Among centrist parties, coalitionability of Janata Party/JD had been greater than the Congress, but the latter both in power and opposition generally proved to be relatively less fractious than the former. This may be because of a number of reasons. For one thing, Congress, being the ruling party for so long after Independence, has been a party of governing temperament, to say nothing of its glorious nationalist past going back to the freedom struggle and tall national leaders as also its nation-wide organizational presence and vested stake in power, both assets of diminishing efficacy now. There has also been the unifying effect of the Nehru–Gandhi dynasty. Besides, the party was exposed to be the most corrupt among all by scandals and scams; only the reputations of Communist parties and some regional formations stayed unsullied this way. The Bofors and Hawala scandals bursting forth on the political scene in 1987 and 1995 respectively were only the flag-symbols among the now recurrent scams indicating cancerous corruption and corruptibility of the political, administrative, and managerial classes in the country. The nation was a mute witness to the shocking deluge of media reports of judicial proceedings and investigations of the Lakhubhai Pathak cheating case against the political godman Chandraswami and co-accused P.V. Narasimha Rao (earlier Minister of External Affairs in the Rajiv Gandhi government); the JMM MPs' bribing case against the then Prime Minister Rao's bid to survive in a confidence vote in 1993.

The Congress did not initially take easily to the idea of coalescing with other parties due to the psychological hang-ups of its unique predominant role in Indian politics. However, in phases and regions of its decline, it was/has been compelled to cultivate coalitional support, e.g. its coalition with PSP and Muslim League in Kerala in the Nehru era, dependence of the minority Indira Gandhi government briefly in the wake of the 1969 Congress split on the parliamentary support of Communist and regional parties, its alliance with regional parties in the north-eastern states over the years, its long-term alliances with AIADMK in Tamil Nadu and National Conference in Jammu & Kashmir that (both) ran into rough weather in the 1990s, and its alliance with BSP in UP in mid-1990s, following the latter's disillusionment with Samajwadi Party of Mulayam Singh Yadav in UP bringing down the SP–BSP coalition government in the state in 1995 and the fall of the BSP minority government in the same state propped up by the legislative support of BJP that pulled the rug from under its feet, barely four months after its formation, in the wake of the fall of the SP–BSP coalition government. The misuse of constitutional provisions of President's rule in states under Article 356 of the Constitution during the Indira and Rajiv eras worked as a repellant reducing the coalitionability of the Congress, but the use or threat of use of this power at least partly explained the willingness of the AIADMK and JKNC to ally with Congress in order to bargain reprieve from dismissal of their state governments by the Congress-controlled centre under Indira and Rajiv Gandhi. During the Rao Congress government in New Delhi, M.G. Ramachandran's successor, Jayalalitha, snapped the alliance. Its renewal by Rao and the lady from the Poes Gate in April 1996 in opposition to Congress leaders from the state led to a major split in the Tamil Nadu unit of the Congress and the formation of the regional TMC that fought the 1996 general elections as an ally of DMK and practically wiped out both AIADMK and Congress in the state. The Congress–National Conference alliance in Jammu & Kashmir remained in the limbo during the insurgency in the state. The JKNC later also boycotted the 1996 Lok Sabha elections in the state but joined the fray in the Assembly elections a few months later. It was subsequently drawn into the orbit of the Congress or BJP coalitions at the centre.

Janata Party/JD saw itself as the historic focal point of non-Congress coalitional alternative at the centre since 1977 when Congress (O) (forced out of Congress led by Indira Gandhi in 1969), BJP, Bharatiya Lok Dal, Socialist Party, and Congress for Democracy merged with it under the shadow of the Emergency just before the Lok Sabha elections that unseated Indira Gandhi.[3] The *de facto* Janata Party coalition government, formed by the non-Communist opposition parties baptised by the Janata Party movement on the one side and Emergency repressions on the other, started out well and purposively completed half of its term. It dismantled the authoritarian amendments to the Constitution by the Emergency regime. Its economic performance too was not unimpressive. But its regime was marked by the onset of atrocities against Scheduled Caste agricultural workers by dominant peasant castes in the countryside, and its leaders in the government kept constantly quarrelling among themselves along the lines of the pre-merger five constituent parties and bitter personality clashes between the Prime Minister and the Deputy Prime Minister, Morarji Desai and Chaudhary Charan Singh. Both former Congressmen, Desai represented the Congress (O) and was supposed to be close to the big business lobby and Singh led the BLD, primarily a party of Jats and other middle caste peasant proprietors. The BJS controlling the largest number of parliamentary seats and Janata state governments played the mediator but failed to keep peace. The Janata government fell victim to factional feuds in July 1979 on the issue of 'double' membership of the BJS faction in the Janata Party overlapping with RSS, raised critically by the BLD faction. A less domineering personality than Desai with the Prime Minister's own party controlling the largest number of seats may probably have provided a more reconciliatory setting. But that was not to be. On the fall of the Janata government, the Janata Party defectors led by Charan Singh of the BLD faction formed a minority government with legislative support of the Congress led by Indira Gandhi. Within three weeks, the Congress pulled the rug from under the feet of Charan Singh, just before the first vote of confidence, leading to the unceremonious resignation of Singh without facing the Lok Sabha. The Janata Party fell apart and all its major constituents, except Congress (O) and Socialists, split off to revive themselves.

The JD-led NF government, comprising JP, TDP, DMK, AGP, and Congress (Socialist), was as much fractious as the Janata Party government and even less durable. It lasted barely eleven months from November/December 1989 to November 1990. It was marked by weak coordination and fragmented collective responsibility of the cabinet. Neither the Prime Minister nor the Coordination Committee of constituent parties of the coalition, chaired by N.T. Ramarao (the TDP Chief Minister of Andhra Pradesh) and convened by Prime Minister V.P. Singh himself, could bridge the tendencies of 'empire-building' by major factions and divided ministerial responsibilities and factionalized overseeing of state governments. The feuding between the Prime Minister—a Congress dissenter who resigned from the Rajiv Gandhi government in 1987 on the Bofors scandal and led the Jana Morcha including other Congress deserters until its merger in 1988 with Janata Party to form JD—and Deputy Prime Minister, Devi Lal, of the Janata Party background would have probably sealed the fate of the NF government in due course. It was this factional feud that propelled V.P. Singh to suddenly implement the Mandal Commission's recommendation for reservation of 27 per cent central government jobs for OBCs besides the pre-existing reservations for SCs/STs in a huff without reference to the coordination committee or the Cabinet (even though the matter was part of the NF election manifesto). This triggered a veritable caste war in north Indian cities and towns among students. In the meantime, the immediate reason for its fall turned out to be the failure of legislative coalition between UF and Left parties and BJP. The Communist parties and BJP were supporting the NF government from the parliamentary floor without joining it. Both organized bandhs and mass mobilizations against the NF government they were selectively supporting issue-wise in the Parliament. BJP's Somnath to Ayodhya *rathayatra*, in disregard of the government's plea to call it off in the interest of communal harmony, was finally stopped with the arrest of the BJP President, L.K. Advani, in Samastipur in Bihar. The withdrawal of BJP's support to the government forced it out. A less cocksure Prime Minister than V.P. Singh and a more effective coordination committee, comprising only parties in the government but also those extending parliamentary support to it, would have ensured a more stable and programmatic coalition government. Moreover, even though the JD, the party of the Prime Minister, was the one with the largest number of parliamentary seats, it was a house divided. Chandrashekhar, a senior JD leader with long innings in the party, with former Congress background and socialist leanings, and the courage of conviction to oppose Indira Gandhi's Emergency from within the Congress and jailed for this reason, was passed over for V.P. Singh, a Sanjay Gandhi loyalist during the Emergency but riding on the crest of public euphoria in the wake of his resignation from the Rajiv Gandhi government over the Bofors scandal. With the fall of the NF government, the JD splintered into Samajwadi Janata Party led by Chandrashekhar and the Devi Lal clan in Haryana and SP in Uttar Pradesh led by Mulayam Singh Yadav. The Congress again played the 'Charan Singh card' in propping up the SJP minority government headed by Chandrashekhar.

Chandrashekhar demonstrated a more earthy common sense and earnestness than his predecessor but the Congress, in extending support to it from the parliamentary floor (without formally joining it), kept it in office only for four months. Protesting against surveillance of Congress president Rajiv Gandhi's residence by two Haryana constables, the party withdrew its support and brought the Chandrashekhar government down. A larger SJP representation in the Parliament would have probably helped develop a more balanced relationship between the party in government and its legislative ally. A joint governmental responsibility undertaken by both would have been even a better recipe for stability. But then imperatives of electoral mobilization overrode those of governance.

IV

The JD-led UF government was formed following the 1996 Lok Sabha elections. Being the third party in the Lok Sabha after BJP and Congress, the JD got its chance after the failure of the BJP government headed by Atal Behari Vajpayee to muster majority in the hung Parliament and the decline of the presidential invitation to form the government by the Congress. The structure of party competition in the House and state-wise distribution of seats are given in Table 4.1 and 4.2. The fragmented and uncertain verdict of the electorate is evident from Table 4.1, especially in view of the absence of any pre-election overarching coalition among the three major party-clusters or groupings, neither of which was alone mandated to power by the electorate. Table 4.2 underlines the growing regionalization of the party system such that the nation-wide spread of the Congress considerably shrank and the national pretensions of BJP were contradicted by its continued failure to outgrow its support-base mainly limited to Hindi-speaking states plus Maharashtra, Gujarat, and Karnataka. Its strong identification with *Hindutva* was another limitation in the context of pluralist and composite Indian nationalism, although its ideologues have been at pains to clarify that its notion of Hindu nationalism is not based on the religious connotation of the term Hindu, rather it is premised on the original territorial extension of it whereby all Indians irrespective of religions are Hindus (residents of Sindhu–Hindu–Inde–India, etc.). Needless to say, such philological fineries are remote from the realities of communal politics (Savarkar, 1989).

The JD too, including SP as a Janata *parivar* (family) party, was basically limited to Bihar, Karnataka, and Orissa. Its formal or informal understanding with regional parties and the left wing, however, did give it a wider spread, though still short of a majority. To stake its claim to form the government, it had to shed its non-Congressism and depend on a legislative coalition with Congress without the latter joining its government. Congress itself appeared divided and generally reluctant to join the government, and the CPI, a UF partner, went on record opposing the idea of a coalition government in which Congress was also present.

TABLE 4.1: PARTY POSITION LOK SABHA, 1996

Parties	Seats
BJP and Allies	
BJP	160
Shiv Sena	15
Samata Party	8
Akali Dal	8
HVP	8
Congress and Allies	
INC	136
JMM(S)	1
IUML	2
KC(M)	1
SDF	1
JD and Allies	
JD	43
SP	17
TDP (Naidu)	16
DMK	17
AGP	5
ASDC	1
CPI(M)	32
CPI	11
RSP	5
AIFB	3
Uncommitted	
TMC*	20
BSP	10
Congress (Tiwari)*	4
MIM	1
MPVC	2
MGP	1
UGDP	1
KCP	1
Independents	7

Note: At the time of government formation, TMC and Congress (T) joined the United Front Council of Ministers.

Sources: *The Times of India*, New Delhi, 14 May 1996, p.1; and *Indian Recorder*, New Delhi, 17-23 June 1996, p. 2050. The total elected seats were 543 and elections were held for 537. There is some discrepancy between seats of some parties in the two sources, e.g. the *Indian Recorder* gives 8 seats for HVP, 161 for BJP, 10 for BSP, 12 for CPI, and 7 for Independents. I have preferred *The Times of India* figures. However, its classification of BSP as a regional party is problematic, as it is a multi-state party with sizeable presence in UP, Punjab and MP and a national party since 1996 in terms of Election Commission of India classification.

TABLE 4.2: STATE-WISE BREAKUP OF MAJOR PARTIES IN LOK SABHA 1996

Parties	Seats Won	Total Seats
BJP		
Assam	1	14
Bihar	18	54
Delhi	5	7
Gujarat	16	26
Haryana	4	10
Karnataka	6	28
Madhya Pradesh	27	40
Maharashtra	18	48
Rajasthan	12	25
UP	52	85
Congress		
Andhra Pradesh	22	42
Assam	5	14
Bihar	2	54
Delhi	2	7
Gujarat	10	26
Haryana	2	10
Himachal Pradesh	4	4
Karnataka	5	28
Kerala	7	20
Madhya Pradesh	8	40
Maharashtra	15	48
Manipur	2	2
Meghalaya	1	2
Mizoram	1	1
Nagaland	1	1
Orissa	16	21
Punjab	2	18
Rajasthan	12	25
UP	5	85
West Bengal	9	42
Janata Dal		
Bihar	22	54
Karnataka	15	28
Orissa	4	21
Regional Parties		
AGP (Assam)	5	14
HVP (Haryana)	3	10
Shiv Sena (Maharashtra)	15	48
Akali Dal-Badal (Punjab)	8	13
TMC (Tamil Nadu)	20	39
DMK (Tamil Nadu)	17	39
TDP and Allies (AP)	18	42
SP and Allies (UP)	26	85

Source: *The Indian Recorder*, 17-23 June 1996, pp. 2052-3.

V

A coalition-situation inevitably raises questions about the limits and desirable directions of presidential discretion in inviting a leader (party or person?) to form the government. In the context of government-formation in May-June 1996, the President obviously could not go by the non-controversial course of a purely nominal role in inviting the leader of the party with absolute majority in the newly elected House for there was none. In the ongoing political discourse he was offered varieties of suggestions: to invite the largest single party; the largest coalition, preferably the one that was of pre- rather than post-election origin, the one with not only the largest number of seats but also votes and wider national spread, the one likely to be most stable, the one likely to ensure constitutional values and social justice; and, finally, a national government inclusive of all or at least major political formations. He was also suggested to wait until the old House was dissolved and the new one constituted with newly elected MPs already having taken the oath of membership, as the anti-defection law did not go into effect until then. There was also the suggestion to allow enough time to all combinations to fairly settle into a discursively negotiated partnership. As it happened, President Shankar Dayal Sharma adopted a more pedestrian, if somewhat hurried, approach in extending invitation to the largest single parties through a process of elimination by the test of confidence vote or self-denial, a course followed by President R. Venkataraman in 1989, though not by President Neelam Sanjeeva Reddy in 1979.[4]

The BJP failed in producing a majority, with Vajpayee resigning just before confidence vote after a valiant, if essentially a campaign, speech in the Lok Sabha. The speech was nationally televised by changing the rule to this effect by Sushma Swaraj, the Minister of Information and Broadcasting in the BJP government that lasted barely two weeks. The practice was continued by the successor UF government and the debate on confidence motion for the H.D. Deve Gowda government was also similarly televised. The nearly two weeks of the BJP in government showed considerable relenting on a number of issues, e.g. recommissioning the Srikrishna Commission that was appointed by the Congress government in Maharashtra to inquire into Bombay blasts and riots but was disbanded by the successor Shiv Sena–BJP government, not insisting on Articles 370 and 44 of the

Constitution relating respectively to Jammu & Kashmir and Common Civil Code, etc.

After Vajpayee's exit, the President offered the chance to the Congress, and on its decision not to take it, to the UF, an assortment of over a dozen parties that came together after the elections. This strictly constitutional, nominal, and mechanical role of the President does not go well with protagonists of an activist presidency. The activist construction of presidential power in India going beyond the British monarchy is premised on: (a) election of the President by a federal electoral college consisting of elected members of the Parliament and state legislatures (unlike the hereditary British monarchy); (b) constitutional provision of impeachment of the President (unlike the British monarchs who can do no wrong due to transference of Crown's responsibility on his ministers on whose advice it is generally expected to invariably act); (c) expectations of President's intervention, or at least moral pressure, in the affairs of his government indicated by recurrent appeals to him by the opposition. However, there should be no doubt that an activist presidency is inconsistent with the Indian constitutional design and practice. Article 74 read with Article 75 makes it clear that the council of ministers provided for in the Constitution must be collectively responsible to the Lok Sabha. The fact that the Constituent Assembly initially contemplated but subsequently dispensed with the idea of incorporating an Instrument of Instructions for the President cannot be construed to mean unfettered discretion for the President. The decision about which government rules the country is ideally exercised by the electorate. Failing this, the President must leave the matter to be decided by the balance of party forces in the Parliament. Any departure from this norm would go against the grain of the basic principles of parliamentary government, one of the two axial coordinates of Indian constitutional system, the supplementary and subsidiary being federalism. Both must cohabit and one cannot be allowed to destroy the other. Any activist role for the President in government formation must be restricted to genuine constitutional and national emergencies.

VI

To come back to the role of parliamentary parties in government formation in 1996, the formation of the UF was by and large a post-election development. This was a clear contrast to the formation of the Janata Party in 1977 and the NF in 1989, formed prior to the elections. Moreover, Janata Party and NF were marked by joint manifestos, comprehensive seat-adjustments to avoid mutual contests, and common campaigning. To be sure, in 1996 there was some residue of bonhomie between some partners of the NF–LF combine of the yore, but, with gradual exits of AGP, TDP-Naidu, and DMK at various points in time on various issues, the NF by 1996 pre-election days practically meant only JD. Communist parties and their favourite Janata *parivar* maverick, Mulayam Singh Yadav, who deserted the Janata Party in the wake of the NF government's fall in 1990 to float his own Samajwadi Party with its strength mainly limited to UP, provided the other angles of the emerging new axis of the parties of the Janata Party and *vam paksha* (left wing) *parivars*. These groups had, even before the 1996 elections, kept some informal contacts and talks going rather casually about the inter-party equations in and after the polls. Janata Dal leaders like V.P. Singh had also kept personal contacts with TDP splinters in the wake of the split in the latter party and the subsequent death of NTR, and admonished NTR's widow Lakshmi Parvathi and son-in-law Chandrababu Naidu to avoid parting of ways in vain. The NF was practically defunct and disparate since the fall of the V.P. Singh government. The national press, however, generally and generously continued to use the terms UF–LF combine. But this was more because of journalistic habit and euphemism.

During the electioneering, Congress and the BJP had shown the proclivity of going alone, except for their minor and regional allies. Both had publicly tried to distance each other, turning their back to the covert or overt coming closer during the last phase of Indira Gandhi, Rajiv Gandhi rule, and the pre-Babri Masjid demotion of the Rao regime. In the process, the Congress had drummed derisively about BJP's communalism and the latter decried the former as corrupt and subservient to the IMF-World Bank. The so-called third force had government, 'unconditionally' (for President's consumption) and 'without eyes closed' (in pursuit of real politics), but staying out of both the government and the steering committee. The Congress dilemma in supporting the UF government was also deepened by the exasperation of its state units in Kerala (where the Congress-led UDF was ranged against CPI(M)-led LDF), in Andhra Pradesh (where the Congress must oppose TDP), in West Bengal (where the Congress must cross swords with the LF), in Bihar and Uttar Pradesh (where the Congress must challenge the JD and SP in order to rehabilitate itself), in Tamil Nadu and Madhya Pradesh (where the Congress must oppose DMK and TMC and MPVC respectively in order to regain the lost ground). These objectives spelled conflicts with major and minor parties in the UF. But that the national leadership of the party was driven by the death-wish was clear from the way it happened to be bent upon ruffling the feathers of the MP Chief Minister, Digvijay Singh, and his supporters for alleged 'anti-party' activities in favour of Madhavrao Scindia and his cohorts who rebelled against the central Congress leadership to float the MPVC when denied party tickets in 1996. Vociferously condemned both Congress and BJP as scourges of Indian politics, but had done little to project a cohesive image and strategy. To neutral observers, the third force was more a residual category than anything else. If anything, it appeared visibly failing as a coalitional endeavour in bringing together Naidu and Parvathi in Andhra Pradesh or resolving the reservations of DMK over bringing in AIADMK during Jayalalitha's flirtations with the NF rump. Her new flirtations proved to be as ephemeral as her flirtations with BJP earlier. She finally clinched a deal with Rao, to the virtual elimination of both Congress and AIADMK in Tamil Nadu at the hands of the DMK–TMC combine in the elections that followed.

The UF government actually emerged in the complicated post-election negotiations among parties. As it happened, before H.D. Deve Gowda, JD Chief Minister of Karnataka, emerged as the third front's choice for the Prime Minister's office, the political scene witnessed the canvassing of the candidatures of Rao in sections of Congress and JD (e.g. Ramakrishna Hegde and Laloo Yadav), V.P. Singh in sections of JD and DMK, and Jyoti Basu in sections of CPI(M) and Congress. Laloo Yadav had on his own (without a formal decision by JD national leadership) campaigned in Bihar as a possible future Prime Minister, but his name did not figure in the post-election parleys of the hierarchs of the kindered parties. Vajpayee and Rao were the only ones who had campaigned as the possible Prime Ministers in the event of their respective parties winning. In public opinion polls before the elections, Rao had a clear edge over others as the most favoured candidate for being the Prime Minister, while in those during the post-election parleys, when Vajpayee became the Prime Minister for two weeks, the

BJP leader had elbowed the others out with a plurality of 50 per cent mark in a sample from the eight metropolitan cities.[5] Rao was hamstrung by dissidence within his own party rising against him in the wake of electoral reverses and by reservations against him in the communist and regional parties (e.g. TDP-Naidu, Akali Dal, etc.) and sections of JD. V.P. Singh firmly announced political *sanyas* until 1999 for mysterious reasons. CPI(M) finally decided not to join any government in which it was not a dominant partner for its long-term electoral strategy, but was willing to extend legislative support to the UF government and also joined the steering or coordination committee of the Front. With its options shrinking, the Congress found itself in an unenviable position of extending legislative support to the UF government, 'unconditionally' (for President's consumption) and 'without eyes closed' (in pursuit of real politik), but staying out of both the government and the steering committee. The Congress dilemma in supporting the UF government was also deepened by the exasperation of its state units in Kerala (where the Congress-led UDF was ranged against CPI(M)-led LDF), in Andhra Pradesh (where the Congress must oppose TDP), in West Bengal (where the Congress must cross swords with the LF), in Bihar and Uttar Pradesh (where the Congress must challenge the JD and SP in order to rehabilitate itself), in Tamil Nadu and Madhya Pradesh (where the Congress must oppose DMK and TMC and MPVC respectively in order to regain the lost ground). These objectives spelled conflicts with major and minor parties in the UF. But that the national leadership of the party was driven by the death-wish was clear from the way it happened to be bent upon ruffling the feathers of the MP Chief Minister, Digvijay Singh, and his supporters for alleged 'anti-party' activities in favour of Madhavrao Scindia and his cohorts who rebelled against the central Congress leadership to float the MPVC when denied party tickets in 1996.

The JD, with its rather meagre parliamentary presence, found itself under layers of political pressures: from the left partners generally unfavourably disposed towards economic reforms, from the regional parties in the coalition (DMK, TDP, AGP) that promptly formed a 'Federal Front' within the UF, from the Congress favouring economic reforms and keen to seek favours due and undue. The extended circle of the formal opposition to the government came from the BJP and its allies, then also including the Akali Dal that deserted the third force during BJP's search for allies in the post-election parleys, to the exasperation of its ally, the BSP that now joined hands with Rao, demonstrating simultaneously that it was not averse to electoral understanding with JD too, provided the latter ditched Mulayam Singh Yadav.

The tragic–comic interlude of the Vajpayee government highlighted some ideological and institutional dilemmas of Indian politics. It revealed the growing secular-communal divide in Indian politics, even though it must be pointed out that it is superficial and unfair to say that only parties usually branded 'communal' are communal. The so-called secular parties also partake in covert communalism. The BJP's charge of 'minority communalism' practised by the 'pseudo-secular' parties does not appear to be entirely unjustified. BJP's *Hindutva* revivalism is a reversal of its political liberalization (one may even say secularization) over the 1960s and 1970s, culminating in the Janata Party experiment (that included BJP's predecessor BJS). However, BJP's two-week stint in government in 1996 demonstrated that in Vajpayee's broadcast to the nation as the Prime Minister and in President's address to the joint session of Parliament outlining the BJP government's policies, the party was willing to soft-pedal its insistence on the deletion of Article 370 and on Common Civil Code, concentrating mainly on measures such as a Lokpal Bill, curbing the centre's misuse of Article 356 against state governments, electoral reforms, and the like.

The institutional dilemma brought to the fore by the Vajpayee government related to the anomaly of the presidential invitation to a party or coalition to form the government that did not *prima facie* enjoy the majority. Could the President have waited longer to allow time to the three fronts to negotiate and settle down to a *prima facie* majority? Could this be done without violating the legality of convening the Parliament sooner and without running the risk of facilitating horse-trading among parliamentary parties simply by giving them more time? The RSS leadership indeed expressed publicly their anxiety lest the BJP leadership compromised on ideology and the means through which parliamentary support was secured for the party's minority government.

Even before the motion of confidence in the BJP government could be taken up, the process of electing the Speaker made it clear that the fate of the BJP government was sealed. The BJP made an offer of selecting the Speaker by consensus, hoping that other parties will involve it in the process. Left to itself, it would have probably preferred G.G. Swell for the office, a north-eastern Christian who had been a Deputy Speaker. But it offered a bait to the Congress by indicating that it was willing to support Shivraj Patil, a Congressman and the Speaker of the outgoing House. The Congress and the third front, however, quickly moved to a consensus whereby a north-eastern Congressman, P.A. Sangma, was put forward as their common candidate. BJP opted not to oppose and let Sangma be elected unanimously to avoid a showdown even before the motion of confidence was taken up for discussion. For technical reasons, the motion of thanks to the President for his address to the constitutionally mandated joint session of the Parliament after an election and motion of confidence in the government could not be mixed. Hence the anomaly of the President outlining the policies of the BJP government followed by two confidence motions—one in the short-lived BJP government and one in its successor, the UF government that had to unceremoniously begin without the luxury of another presidential address to another joint session.

With speed and alacrity, the UF forged a Common Approach and Minimum Programme (CAMP) among its partners that reflected a fine balance between social democratic and working class preferences of the left wing, agrarianism with OBC bias of Janata Dal, and regionalism with augmented federalism articulated by the regional parties in the UF. There was also a measure of consensus not to undermine, only modify, the policy of economic liberalization stepped up by the Rao minority government in 1991 and carried out with a broad consensus in the party system, until half-way through his term, Rao fabricated a majority for the Congress party. Evidently, policy innovations are better initiated and carried out by minority and coalition governments, even though political leaders themselves, the civil servants, and the business circles are generally averse to coalition governments.

VII

The two UF governments in the eleventh Lok Sabha headed by H.D. Deve Gowda and I.K. Gujral respectively—both from JD with a Congress past—were essentially an exercise in governance by the third force in Indian politics between Congress and BJP. The two polar forces represented the two variants of the emergent right in Indian politics—the Hindu nationalist BJP and the Congress moving away from Indian variants of Nehruvian socialism and Indira Gandhi's populism to neo-classical economic liberalization and globalization. With these two largest single parties hamstrung on the margins owing to communal or corruption charges, the third force parties managed to put together a heterogeneous coalition of JD, the left wing, and regional parties. All these three categories of parties also happened to be the ruling political forces in some states: JD in Bihar and Karnataka, the Communists in West Bengal and Kerala, and TDP, AGP, and DMK in Andhra Pradesh, Assam, and Tamil Nadu respectively.

Beyond this assortment of parties in the cabinet coalition, the UF also roped in the support of Congress from the parliamentary floor. Unwelcome by the UF as a cabinet partner and divided by an unbridgeable gap between itself and BJP, the options of Congress were rather limited to tactically helping the UF governments to cross the threshold of the majority mark in the Lok Sabha with a veto on government formation and maintenance. Using this veto, Congress forced the UF to change its Prime Minister—from Deve Gowda to Gujral—in April 1997 and finally ditched and doomed its government in November the same year. The fall of the UF governments was due more to the role of the Congress than the parties internal to it. Despite their myriad differences, the UF parties managed to reconcile their differences with a fair degree of success. This must be considered a remarkable achievement especially in view of the fact that the coalition included three distinct groupings of parties from the centrist, leftist, and regional sectors of the party system. Moreover, the government had to steer its way through the new terrains that were fast changing in terms of growing economic liberalization and political federalization of the governance system. Internal policy and personality differences of the coalition were more or less publicly resolved by a steering or coordination committee of parties in the government plus the CPI(M), which was part of the coordination committee but not of the government. The Front's relations with its external ally, Congress, were handled directly by the Prime Minister(s) and the Congress president. A proposed coordination committee with the Congress was never formed. P.V. Narasimha Rao, the Congress president, and Prime Minister,

Deve Gowda, got along reasonably well. But after Rao was charge-sheeted in the JMM bribery and some other cases, Sitaram Kesri took over as Congress president. By available accounts, the government, especially the judiciary and the CBI under judicial supervision, did not go soft in pursuing the corruption charges against Rao and Kesri and others in the political class. The issue on which the Congress finally withdrew its support to the two UF governments was the alleged insensivity of the government to its Congress ally. The UF first yielded to the Congress demand for changing the Prime Minister. But on the second occasion, when on the release of the Jain Commission Report on Rajiv Gandhi's murder, the Congress demanded that the government drop its DMK ministers for the implied indictment of the DMK government in Tamil Nadu for its handling of Rajiv Gandhi's security, the UF refused to comply and bowed out of office.

The UF experiment passed into history. But not coalition governments *per se*. India's quest for a workable federal coalition government is still on, with the second BJP-led coalition government, the NDA, in office since 1999.

VIII

Where one-party majority governments in competitive party systems are not forthcoming, coalition governments become the second best option. The experience with coalition and minority governments in India appears to be negative. But a decade of India's experience at the centre is a rather short period to make any definitive conclusion. Besides, apart from the fact that at least a few coalition governments in Indian states (e.g. West Bengal, Kerala, and Tripura) can be rated as fairly successful in terms of stability and performance, such governments may well be more likely to pursue and promote liberal democratic values of consensus and wider representation. Hence a plea can be made for a greater receptivity to the coalition idea among the political class and analysts in India. This will bring about a desirable change in elite political behaviour and culture in the country. The political leadership must respond to the current compulsions of mass political behaviour and the social structure in the country. Without ruling out reformative politics, constitutional engineering must contend with the imperatives of the social and regional realities. The contemporary spate of judicial activism in India prompted by the failings or disfunctionalities of the political and representative structures and processes is not a panacea for the political problems the country is menaced with. Eventually the political process must provide the answer. The first step in this direction is electoral and party reforms. The party system is the indispensable key to a successful representative democracy. The decay and decomposition of the party system and consequently of the political system at large in India is universally stressed by all political analysts. There are only three ways of ideological and organizational renewal of parties: (1) alternation in power, forcing ruling parties into opposition *vanvas* and vice versa, (2) intervention by social and grassroots movements, and (3) baptism by fire of parliamentary parties by their respective fundamental classes and cultural mainsprings. For as the cliché attributed to Lord Acton goes, power corrupts and absolute power corrupts absolutely. Gandhi's last will and testament in 1948, written days before his assassination, admonishing the dissolution of the Congress after attainment of Independence and its replacement by a Lok Sevak Sangh,[6] is the ultimate political metaphor in this context. But I do not think a Gandhi or a JP or an M.N. Roy would be a mute witness to the ruination of the nation by a party or parties. They would plunge in oppositional mass movements, begetting parties so long as they are needed, pending perfection of human nature.

NOTES

1. See Thapar (1984), Stein (1980), Fukazawa (1982), Kulke, ed. (1995) and Singh (1995).
2. A participant's account of politics of non-Congressism may be found in Limaye (1984). The author was a former socialist and subsequently a Janata Party leader.
3. An insider's view of the formation of Janata Party and its politics is available in Limaye (1994).
4. See Venkataraman (1994) and Reddy (1989).
5. The Times-MODE poll on the question 'Who should be PM?' showed 50 per cent preferring Vajpayee, 31 per cent Rao, 11 per cent V.P. Singh, and 8 per cent Jyoti Basu, *The Times of India* (New Delhi), 15 May 1996, p.1.
6. See Gandhi (1970: 290).

REFERENCES

Austin, Granville, *The Indian Constitution: Cornerstone of a Nation*, Bombay: Oxford University Press, 1996.

———, *Working a Democratic Constitution: The Indian Experience*, New Delhi: Oxford University Press, 1999.

Bhambhari, C.P., 'Coalition Politics: Mixed Experiences', *The Hindu Magazine* (New Delhi), 16 June 1996.

Brass, Paul R., 'Coalition Politics in North India', *Faction and Party*, vol. 1 of *Caste, Faction and Party in Indian Politics*, New Delhi: Chanakya Publications, 1984.

de Swaan, Abraham, 'An Empirical Model of Coalition Formation as an N-person Game of Policy Distance Minimization', in *The Study of Coalition Behaviour*, ed. Sven Groenings et al., New York: Holt, Rineheart, and Winston, 1970.

———, *Coalition Theories and Cabinet Formations*, Amsterdam: Elsevier, 1973.

Dodd, L.C., *Coalition in Parliamentary Government*, Princeton: Princeton University Press, 1976.

Fukazawa, H., 'Maharashtra and the Deccan', in *The Cambridge Economic History of India*, ed. Tapan Raychaudhuri and Irfan Habib, New Delhi: Orient Longman in association with Cambridge University Press, 1982.

Gamson, William A., 'A Theory of Coalition Formation', *American Sociological Review*, 26, August 1961.

Gandhi, M.K. *Gandhi: Essential Writings*, selected and edited by V.V. Ramana Murti, New Delhi: Gandhi Peace Foundation, 1970.

Karunakaran, K.P., ed., *Coalition Governments in India*, Simla: Indian Institute of Advanced Study, 1975.

Kothari, Rajni. 'Towards Intervention', *Seminar*, January 1982.

Kulke, Hermann, ed., *The State in India 1000-1700*, New Delhi: Oxford University Press, 1995.

Leiserson, Michael, 'Factions and Coalitions in One-Party Japan: An Explanation Based on the Theory of Games', *American Political Science Review*, LXII, September 1968.

Limaye, Madhu, *Janata Party Experiment: An Insider's Account of Opposition Politics*, vol. I, 1975-7; vol. II, 1977-80, New Delhi: B.R. Publishing Corporation, 1994.

Limaye, Madhu, *Birth of Non-Congressism: Opposition Politics 1947-1975*, New Delhi: B.R. Publishing Corporation, 1984.

Mallick, Ross, *Indian Communism*, New Delhi: Oxford University Press, 1994.

Mehra, Ajay K., 'The Cabinet System: Conflict Resolution in Coalition Situation', *Politics India*, vol. 1, no. 1, July 1996.

Nossiter, T.J., *Marxist State Governments in India*, London: Pinter, 1988.

Reddy, Neelam Sanjiva, *Without Fear or Favour: Reminiscences and Reflections of a President*, New Delhi: Allied Publishers, 1989.

Riker, William H., *The Theory of Political Coalitions*, New Haven: Yale University Press, 1962.

Savarkar, V.D., *Hindutva*, Bombay: Veer Savarkar Prakashan, 1989, rpt.

Singh, Mahendra Prasad, 'Constitution and Consensus', in *The India-Canada Relationship: Exploring the Political, Economic and Cultural Dimensions*, ed. J.S. Grewal and Hugh Johnston, New Delhi: Sage, 1994.

———, 'Evolution of the State', in *Indian Political System: Structure, Policies, Development*, ed. M.P. Singh and Himanshu Roy, New Delhi: Jnanada, 1998, 2nd edn.

———, 'Union Executive', in *Indian Political System: Structure, Policies, Development*, eds., M.P. Singh and Himanshu Roy, New Delhi: Jnanada, 1998, 2nd edn.

Sridharan, E., 'Coalition Politics', *Seminar* (India 1995), no. 137, January 1996.

———, 'Coalition Politics in India: Lessons From Theory, Comparison and Recent History', *Occasional Papers*, New Delhi: Centre for Policy Research, May 1997.

Stein, Burton, *Peasant State and Society in Medieval South India*, New Delhi: Oxford University Press, 1980.

Thapar, Romila, *From Lineage to State: Social Formations in the Mid-First Millennium B.C.*, Bombay: Oxford University Press, 1984.

Venkataraman, R., *My Presidential Years*, New Delhi: Indus—An Imprint of Harper Collins Publishers India, 1994.

CHAPTER 5

Coalition Politics in India: The NDA Experiment

Kamala Prasad

India's democratic politics has undergone remarkable change in the last fifty years. There are more than 150 political parties competing for representation, recognition, and share in power. This has surpassed the vision of the founding fathers. Internal and external security environment had led them to a flexible though centralized governing structure. Comparative balance between the union and the states was left to be shaped by convention to address emerging problems. A heavy responsibility was assumed by the leadership. This was clear, for instance, in Sardar Patel's defence of the All India Services, an element for stability and centralization. The possibility of major structural shift was left until after the polity stabilized. There was confidence that the Congress party with a range of factions was a capable instrument to respond to signals for change in the right direction. Democratic politics had to settle for progressive adjustment to meet the changes in the context.

This approach fitted the social composition of the Congress party then. The people in general trusted the leaders of the freedom movement who assumed power. The promises held out in the Constitution and its working released new political and social impulses and forces for change. There was scope for well-meaning dissent but also the hope that the legitimate concerns will be addressed. In any case the country saw a new dawn and had no doubt that common man's aspirations would be honestly heeded. This translated in due course of time into politics of entitlement, politics of identity, politics of assertion—

regional and social. 'The real diversity of India, often socially proclaimed, is now becoming increasingly manifest politically.'[1] Coalition politics is the latest political manifestation of this impulse.

Indian polity was conceived to be representative as well as responsible. Adult suffrage was one manifestation of representation; the social content was expressed in reservation for SCs/STs. Article 46 of the Constitution left the definition of 'weaker sections' vague. This ambiguity led to the competitive populist politics. Political paternalism became standard political policy as well as stratagem for party politics in the country, from Congress, Janata Party, BJP, down to Communists, Socialists, SP, BSP and the rest of the parties. However, India's stagnant society generated struggles for justice on a broad front. Deprived sections in the inequitable Indian social order craved recognition. Their voice became louder as time passed. These 'layer upon layer of deprived communities, hitherto submerged in the political substratum at the bottom of the Indian pyramid' managed progressively to become players in the political game. With the passage of time they could not but fight for a share in state power. Indian democracy has facilitated their assertion.

The multiparty political system admits of wider representation. The absence of an effective opposition party brought a suggestion during the 1950s that the Congress party should help promote a two-party system. It remained unanswered. Instead, the Congress engaged in poaching on other parties to further its power game. The party tended to drive our ideological dissenters from early on, especially after 1947. But later on there was an attempt to rope in Socialist leaders in the government. But Nehru's dialogue with Jayaprakash Narayan was effectively closed once he gave a fourteen-point programme for party level collaboration with the government.[2] Since then multiplicity of parties has enormously increased. This reflects the surge of geographical, cultural, social, economic, and political identities. The identity brings in its train new concerns, unfulfilled demands, aspirations scorned. This reflects the failure of a single ruling party to restructure itself to empower this baffling array of interests. The multiparty system is asserting this urge in its extreme manifestation.

The root of a coalition politics is inherent in this development. Coalition has brought in its train new problems and unfamiliar situations. The task of managing or coordinating multiplicity of parties and egos of their leaders has challenged the inefficient overseeing of multiple concerns by a single party. Representation has to result in better polity and good governance; there is no sign of it yet. Responsible government demands responsible grassroots organizations for signals of manageable demands. The task is more arduous than appears at the surface. Coalition system can be wrecked by irresponsibility in parties and their leaders. Since it is an alternative to the experience in a majority party rule, it must reflect matching responsibility in governance. The way this challenge is met remains an open question.

Indian politics has entered a new era. Political leaders are being called upon to govern under unfamiliar conditions. Political players are being forced into compromises beyond their expectations. Leaders, if not parties, are expressing frustration with the limitations the new environment imposes. Limitation is the hallmark of responsibility but the lesson has to be relearned. A whole range of governing concepts in the country's politics seems to convey irrelevant message. In this new era achieving a balance in what the people and the political players desire and what political ability and ingenuity can achieve is difficult. The adjustment to a new paradigm of politics is bound to be slow and incremental progress frustrating. This leaves greater sense of dissatisfaction compared to the past. The UF phase encountered it in ample measure. The answer was sought in evolving a culture of coalition. The NDA leader and Prime Minister finds solace in affirming: 'We are convinced that maturing of coalition politics is what India needs at the present juncture.'[3] He calls for 'coalition *dharma*' without explaining what its implications are. Coalition has opened up a new phase of learning about how to do politics.

GROWTH OF COALITION IDEA

The coalition system was inherent in the development of politics since Independence. The Congress party ceased to be a broad-based platform by 1950. The process started soon after Congress came to power. All the eminent national leaders joined the government. The tussle for separation of the leadership of the party and that of the government ended with the resignation of J.B. Kripalani as Congress president in 1946. The Socialist Party was given the option either to dissolve itself with the Congress or to leave it. It parted company. Then Kripalani formed the Kisan Mazdoor Praja Party (KMPP). This party and the Socialist Party merged to form the Praja Socialist Party. The party split into two and the Samyukta Socialist Party came into existence. The CPI also developed ideological and personality cleavage and ultimately split in the early 1960s. The Bharatiya Jan Sangh was formed in 1952 as a moderate modernist party of the Hindu majority and it refused to have any merger with the neo-traditional Hindu Maha Sabha or the Ram Rajya Parishad. Swatantra Party appeared in 1959 as a conservative alternative to counter the Congress brand of socialism or state capitalism. The first twenty years, thus, saw the gathering momemtum towards a multiplicity of parties. The Congress hegemony was founded on this fractured foundation.

This multiparty configuration produced inequitable consequences for a country steeped in politics. Some people were permanently in power, while others were effectively excluded. The electoral statistics disclosed another reality. Despite claims of monopoly in winning Independence and the control over government at the centre and in the states, the Congress could not mange more than half the votes polled and much less of those registered. The electoral victory had infirm foundations. Lack of numbers implied the absence of marginalized groups in the electoral process. Their assertion came with greater awakening. There was benefit from launching of massive programmes of development initially. As time passed, corruption crept in at the political level and fostered it in administration. The ideological edge was getting blunted with departures from the Congress party, the Socialists, and the Swatantra leadership alike. The Congress was also becoming far too dependent on the one-person leadership of Pandit Nehru. This created the opportunity for taking it on.

The difficulty was in the extreme position of the opposition parties in their ambition to be the alternative to the Congress. They were more virulent in attacking one another than the Congress failures. There was the regional factor. The Congress culture brought frustrating level of centralization. Centralization in the party was its internal concern; that in the government was not. The state Congress leaders were resentful. Regional demand had been met by creating linguistic states. The regional parties in their present incarnation were slow to emerge. There was the strong projection of the division within the Congress between the conservatives and the progressives. This ideological assertion ignored another reality of growing resentment from denial of adequate share in power to the deprived groups. The Congress was vulnerable. Weakness of the opposition due to disunity concealed this vulnerability.

Ram Manohar Lohia in his thesis on 'The consolidation of opposition parties' in early 1966, explained this phenomenon.[4] The context was that Indian politics was plagued by a fatalism that Congress as a ruling party could not be defeated through the democratic electoral process. This was a dangerous feeling that could result in recourse to removal by other, non-democratic means. Defeat of the Congress was necessary for the growth of democratic process. There was another cause too. The Congress rule had infected the polity with undesirable traits. Dynasticism, casteism, money power, corruption, and cult of continuity and stability was weakening the democratic and social urges of the people.[5] Opportunity was also within striking distance. This needed an appreciation of the game of numbers. The consolidation of popular votes of Swatantra Party, BJS, SSP, the Communists, and the regional parties like the DMK, and the Janata Party in Bihar would be more than the Congress party. Singly no party other than the Congress had even the 'strength to make a powerful demand for proportional representation'. It was necessary to work out an agreed strategy to take advantage of this opportunity to strengthen democratic processes. This philosophy of coalition was in defence of constitutionalism.

The strategy suggested was three-fold. First, a choice had to be made from four alternatives available for consolidation: (1) mergers, (2) joint front, (3) limited front, and (4) electoral adjustments. A fundamental problem in consolidation was confusion between the four. It resulted in failure of action. Second, (1) one seat–one joint candidate, (2) allotment of seat on the basis of comparative performance in the earlier poll, (3) irrelevance of prior consensus on incompatible ideas, and (4) the prospect of change to relieve the voter of fatalism were adequate to inspire optism. Finally, a 'spearhead' party and its leader could wait till after the results were known. Similarly, rather than a minimum programme, joint fronts on agreed issues could be devised individually. When the division between parties was so great, the first necessity is to bring them together. The basis was the clubbing of all parties that were not in government as 'opposition' with seats for them on the same side in Parliament. Therefore, rather than imitating the Congress, 'expending as much energy fighting inside as they do fighting the

Congress' was inescapable if they were to graduate from being mere 'opposition' parties.

An election-eve electoral and legislative adjustment among the opposition parties in 1967 was enough to unseat Congress in the northern states as well as Tamil Nadu and demonstrated that the public was ready for change. A mere seat adjustment produced the result. The Samyukta Vidhayak Dals assembled to form ministries in north Indian states, were not a success; they fell prey to their infighting and pressures and inducements of the Congress controlling the central government. But the faith in change in government by the established democratic process had been restored. Dr Lohia underlined the failure of the alternative governments. 'Given the coalition talk in seven or eight voices', he lamented, 'it is not a child's play to convey one meaning out of these so many voices.' He proceeded: 'When someone becomes a minister, he forgets the urgency of change. He clings to his post and worries about stability. The party leaders and executive members also tread on the same slippery ground when they get mixed up with ministerial dealings and government paraphernalia.'[6] Finally, the control of the central government increased the numerical strength substantially. 'The main reason why the non-Congress governments in the states were barren and stunted is the existence of the Congress government at the Centre. The *Patwari* has changed but the Collector is the same as before.'[7] Control of the central government was necessary to improve longevity of coalitions at the state level. 'The superstition that the Congress cannot be dislodged from the Centre needed to be smashed so that the road would be clear for alternative moves and strategies.'[8] The problem was in a sharp division of views between the Communists and the BJS on foreign policy in particular. Lohia found their differences to be phoney. 'Political parties of India', stated Lohia, 'live on borrowed experience. Some borrow from America, others from Soviet Union, or China, or Britain or even from a number of countries in a hotchpotch.' We should take into account the experience of the country and analysis of the implications. The need in the country was more urgent for a policy of equality, austerity, and reconstruction to enrich that experience. 'Our need today is not so much of able administrators, as of men, who can see what requires to be changed, where, and in what manner, and who have the will to bring about that change.'[9] The opposition disunity at the national level persisted. Indira

Gandhi used it to her advantage. The maladies wrought by Congress rule multiplied. Populism and pseudo issues received spotlight. Despite the West Bengal troubles and travails in repeated central rule in the 1960s, the two Communist parties went their separate ways. Dangers to democratic processes were increasing. The Congress party promoted another political trend, that of the game of defection of legislators. The phenomenon of *Aya Ram Gaya Ram* implied the floor crossing of members elected from one party to another for considerations of a post or money. The move was largely one-sided and it helped Congress more than other parties. Its more pernicious impact was to devalue ideology and the credibility of elected representatives. Government patronage replaced ideology. Central government had much more patronage than any state government. Authoritarianism grew out of such patronage. Lack of direction in the opposition parties, expansion of patronage, role of money power, and the game of defection combined to pave the way for the Emergency of 1975. Democracy was derailed. The then opposition parties cannot disclaim their share of the guilt simply because their leaders were jailed.

The Emergency did not make any distinction between parties. Their members had interacted in legislatures earlier. Now they shared company in the jails. This was a greater leveller. Anti-authoritarian/corruption movements in Gujarat and Bihar were the immediate context for the imposition of the emergency. Jayaprakash Narayan assumed leadership of the movement against Congress misrule. Another dialogue for consolidation of opposition forces at the national level was overdue. The dialogue was initiated in the jails. This led to the announcement on 25 May 1976 of the formation of a new party, Janata Party, with the merger of Socialist, BJS, BLD, and Congress (O), which was joined by the Congress for Democracy of Jagjivan Ram later. From seat adjustment to merger was a dramatic improvement even if the Communists did not join the new party. But seat adjustment with others including regional parties was not excluded. When elections were called in early 1977, Jayaprakash Narayan took extensive campaigning despite distressing health conditions. The Janata Party later swept the polls to gain absolute majority. The Congress (I) was dislodged from power at the centre.

Politics in the intervening ten years between 1967 and 1977 had been further devalued. The 'dynamic decade' did not strengthen democracy. The progress on the development front was questionable. The coercive powers of the state were misused. The machinery of government became more inefficient. Jayaprakash Narayan was indicated in his assessment that 'people as a whole were fed up with the Congress party and wanted change'.[10] The formation of a new party reflected JP's view: 'I have always believed that if we have to run parliamentary democracy successfully in this country, it is absolutely essential to have a strong opposition party.'[11] Jayaprakash Narayan might have been convinced of the necessity of a two-party system but the reality of multiple parties could not be overlooked either. His belief that other parties could join the newly formed party did not come true. Instead, the Janata Party showed all the symptoms of a coalition of practically independent parties. The election of the leader itself showed schism and democratic processes were not convincingly honoured. The seeds of the breakup of the new party lay in these developments. Application of the principle of merger was perhaps premature.

The significance of this change can now be summed up. The credit that Congress claimed from the freedom movement had almost been dissipated. The trend of displacement that started in 1967 was confirmed in 1977. India started on a more balanced democratic path where prospects of an alternative could not be discounted. The pattern at the state level stabilized sooner with either a single party or a coalition alternating in power. The problem of an alternative at the central level has been more difficult. It is possible to trace the troubles to the factors enumerated by Lohia, to which a stronger social dynamics has been added since. But a coalition system remains the only alternative. Lohia had foreseen this: 'Someday the people of this country will accept one of the opposition parties as their own but that may take a long time.... The opposition parties should, therefore, try to find a way out without compromising their ideas and programmes, which may help the people in performing their task.'[12] That time is still awaited.

THE NATIONAL DEMOCRATIC ALLIANCE

When elections were held in 1996, however, the Congress party lost heavily. The Congress was losing its support in segments that were its strength. Bhagalpur riots in 1989 contributed to its defeat in Bihar; the Ayodhya demolition in 1992 led to its loss of UP. Secularism and social justice had emerged as important issues of appeal to the voters. The BJP as the single largest party in the new House survived for just thirteen days in government. The demolition of the Babri Masjid by its supporters in the presence of its national leaders made it a pariah. A centrist-regional party coalition with participation by the CPI replaced it. The CPI(M) supported it from outside. The numbers were still inadequate. The Congress, left with no options, provided that support in the name of secularism. One more step in the march of coalition had been taken. Two alternatives to the Congress had appeared on the political scene. Both played on primordial sentiments of caste and community: the UF on caste and BJP on Hindu communalism.

The Congress remains out of power since then. Three elections have been held in these four years and coalitions have assumed power. The 1996 UF coalition was a 'secular' alliance. Federalism, secularism, and social justice were its ideological anchor. The UF of thirteen parties, with Congress and CPI(M) support, ruled for little less than two years. The Congress politics plunged further into chaos. The Congress ditched the coalition on untenable ground. The parties to the coalition neglected the party and wasted their energy fighting among them. The BJP took advantage of the animosity of leaders of all parties. The party was alerted to the prospect of early poll but was unsure of a majority. Vajpayee speculated on the possibility of a NDA after the poll, if required. The party did not expressedly endorse it. Instead, a scramble to reach out and persuade leaders from the Congress proved more rewarding. The BJP showed great flexibility in diluting its extremist position by all possible means. Some centrist parties split to join it. There was still no clear verdict in favour of the NDA. It succeeded finally in securing the support of the TDP, the past convenor of the UF. The NDA of eighteen parties ruled for thirteen months and won in a mid-term poll in 1999. It has twenty-three parties in the coalition at present. Even though gaining in states, Congress strength has been further reduced in the Lok Sabha. It is the first time that three coalition governments have occupied office, one after the other. What is more, the NDA has been voted back to power in 1999; a positive endorsement of the coalition system.

The UF coalition counted on an inheritance, howsoever deficient. The NDA, despite some of its constituents being elements in the earlier coalitions, started on a clean slate. The UF was a post-election venture in 1996; the NDA was equally a post-election enterprise in 1998. The UF had to work under the constant threat of the Congress support being withdrawn; 1998 marked a dramatic break from the past in dispensing with such role for the Congress as NDA could do without it. The UF had to contend with the contest between single party rule and a coalition of diverse parties; the NDA settled that in favour of the latter. Both the NDA and the UF were forced to admit the reality of the numerical strength of parties outside the unitary Congress and the BJP and their capacity jointly to make or unmake governments at the national level. The smaller parties have lent their weight to coalition system in Indian politics. As noted in an earlier section, this is more representative of the Indian geographical, social, cultural reality. Its dynamics as disclosed in experience is what is important for the future.

The UF emerged as a Front of fronts—the Left Front, the hurriedly conceived Federal Front of the Left, and the rest. The collegiate working was conditioned accordingly, both at the party and the government levels, in the reality of powerful compatible parties with commitments of their constituency. The partnership of equality made for a realistic consensus making. The UF pursued political consensus to great lengths, sounding public opinion in the process, and faced the charge of internal contradiction. The strategy was feasible but its defence from opposition attack could have been more effective at the party political level. The UF era exposed this political weakness. Its weakness was in leadership. It is possible to discern six elements of significance in the new scenario:

- *The Consultation Process Leading to the Front*: The UF lacked a spearhead-party in the absence of pre-election agreement. The task was taken up by leaders post-election and wrapped up at the end. The partners were keen to have all parties participate in the ministry. They succeeded in persuading the CPI but failed with the CPI(M). The West Bengal Chief Minister, Jyoti Basu, was not permitted by his party to agree to be Prime Minister; he called it a 'historic blunder' later. The party nonetheless participated in the coordination committee designed for political monitoring.
- *Nomination of the Leader*: The failure to get Basu made the UF leaders and chief ministers settle for Karnataka Chief Minister, Deve Gowda, to head the coalition. He was from Janata Party, the largest constituent participating in the government. He was acceptable

to the rest. The leadership choice was smooth and without rancour since it had gone through the widest possible consultation.

- *Common Approach and Minimum Programme* (*CAMP*): Unlike in the past the UF settled on a document for the government to be made accountable. It was titled 'an approach to major policy matters and a minimum programme'. The Congress party extended formal support from outside only after this document was finalised.
- *Ministry Making*: The strategy to leave the choice of nominees to the participating parties was followed. The emphasis was on party and its integrity. The numbers, by and large, reflected the numerical strength of the participating parties. The distribution of portfolio was left to the Prime Minister, but the influence of the Congress, apart from the UF parties, was clear in the distribution of economic portfolios.
- *Monitoring Mechanism*: A coordination committee of all participating and supporting parties, except the Congress, was constituted. It developed into a clearing body for important policy matters, progress of implementation, exchange of political intelligence and guidance on matters agitating public mind. A secretariat was established and a spokesperson was also named. While each party had strong voice in the committee, the consensus was aired by the spokesperson. The absence of Congress from the committee and neglect of a formal consultation mechanism became, in due course, a great handicap.
- *Conflict Resolution*: Formal mechanism is important for resolving conflict of formal policies and programmes. The coalition faced conflict from the 'prime ministerial' mindset of the past, as also ego clashes between colleagues. This could not be totally provided for. The parties assumed the role of restraining their members, in keeping watch over their functioning, and disciplining them on occasions. Essentially, the area of demarcation between the leading party and the government, with the party being assigned the role to intercede with the Prime Minister, tended to gradually develop into practice.

The NDA in 1998 had the advantage of this past practice for working a coalition system. It took advantage of it but only partially. The composition of the NDA, compared to the UF, adversely influenced the process of future growth.[13] The President followed the earlier practice of taking consent from the parties who joined the coalition after the election in examining the stake of the leader to form a government. In ministry making, the UF precedent was followed. A coordination committee constituted as a routine but without a secretariat or a spokesperson, and later without much use. The dominant BJP assigned that role to its own party machinery and the leader of a major ally, George Fernandes of Samata Party. A 'National Agenda of Governance' was proclaimed. This was unlike any agenda with details of policies or a timeframe of implementation. It was a kind of a long-term wishlist. The meetings of the coordination committee were rarely held and had to be forced upon the Prime Minister by aggrieved partners. Conflict resolution tactic has followed the Congress practice of dispatching emissaries who had the confidence of the Prime Minister. The breach with Jayalalitha was as much from her mercurial temper as from the BJP's big-brother, single-party approach. It was an alliance of satellites with their own compulsions. They were products of party split or faced the Congress as the dominant opposition in the states involved. In a way, NDA further pushed regionalization of Indian politics.

Is the pattern at the state level being adopted at the centre? The UF did not articulate on any of these things. The BJP, on the other hand, pondered over the Kerala and the West Bengal patterns of coalition internally. Its preference was for the former, but the lot of the latter. The LF in West Bengal represents an ideological and geographical homogeneity. There is a material difference where the country as a whole is involved and policy diversity has to address contending interests. Serious differences were being exposed. The impression of BJP bossing over and ignoring the concerns of partners individually and jointly surfaced. The worry about the price revision of grains for the poor was repeatedly aired by a number of allies. The exhortation of the allies to get the differences resolved in the coordination committee, which hardly met prior to decisions, was a ritual. The committee's convener was George Fernandes and the Chair, the Prime Minister.

The NDA had faced withdrawal of support from AIADMK, which led to the mid-term poll of 1999. The BJP had all the trump cards by the time the poll took place. The manner of its defeat in Lok Sabha by ditching was presented as an institutional hurt. A long 'caretaker' government phase gave it the Kargil war to be encashed for getting votes. The UF had disintegrated and JD splits added strength to NDA. The BJP faced an opposition weaker than in 1998. The NDA converted the National Agenda into a virtual manifesto so as to keep the controversial items of the BJP manifesto out of public debate. The outcome was salutary though not as spectacular as expected. The NDA return was a dramatic break from the past. The trend towards coalition was further confirmed in the Congress party losing further ground to be a decisive factor in government making. It paid a price for its politics of going it alone. The BJP and the Congress were together in attack on the non-aligned parties of the old UF, but could not stem the tide of strong preference for regional and caste-oriented parties. The BJP faced stagnation and the Congress decline in electoral terms.

To conclude, four years and three quick parliamentary polls continued the coalitional trend. The Congress remains the principal opposition. A coalition threatens the dynastic principle of Congress leadership to the detriment of the current structure in the party. The issue of foreign origin of its leader keeps coming up. Its declining electoral fortune forced it to accept the pressure of state leaders to enter into local level coalitions. The BJP preferred the Congress to stay mired this way. The centrist and the regional parties, barring some exceptions, were indifferent to sound political development.

The present stage of coalition has brought chaos to the structure of politics, political integrity, and culture.[14] The increasing imbalance between parliamentary and organizational wings made parties withdrawn from public concerns and alienated from the grass-roots. Electoral punishment for the sitting members of the two major parties in 1999 poll was a most visible demonstration of this influence.

The coalitions failed to evolve a pattern of discipline for their units in state governments to adjust to the overall limitation of national coalition. The UF failed the test in Bihar in firmly handling corruption; in UP, it indulged in the use of the Governor for partisan political ends. BJP has failed this test in Gujarat and in UP, in safeguarding minority interests and in keeping administration insulated from communal taint. There are visible signs of intolerable strain in working out programmatic consensus. The UF surmounted problems on administered prices but failed to put across a people-friendly alternative economic reform agenda; the BJP-alliance abandoned *swadeshi* to show commitment to the Congress-sponsored globalization before pragmatic liberalization delivered promised competition. The NDA has failed to sharpen instruments of implementation of policy in preference to grand design of their intents. The administrative reforms deliberated upon during the UF period have not been attended to and accountability remains at a discount. The autonomy of higher educational institutions has been further breached. Despite the increased presence of regional parties, devolution of authority and finances remain a distant dream. There is failure of will to craft a culture of a multi-party coalition. The NDA is more culpable since its partners do not present any threat as seen in the summary disposal of their grievances.

A NEW PHASE IN COALITION POLITICS

The new phase provides opportunity to rethink about alternatives to single-party political games. The BJP is a reluctant convert to the strategy of coalition politics as a reflection of India's diversity. There is an undercurrent about the BJP that it does not consider that coalition has come to stay. The federal objective has been the real strength behind national coalition politics. The BJP has postponed its decision on this issue by ignoring the Sarkaria Commission report and instituting another constitutional review to overcome it. BJP is following a long-term politics of gaining as much in strength in the company of regional parties as it did in the company of centrist parties in north India in the Janata Party phase (1977-80). It has failed so far to appreciate the lessons of 1999 when it lost heavily in UP to remain stuck at the former numerical level nationally. BJP's persistence will, in this manner, provide the opportunity for another alternative front to challenge the NDA. The smaller parties have shown that they are not averse to alternating their choice between contending fronts. Future electoral contests will be between fronts and not individual parties believing in monopoly of power.

Coalition does not signify the end of ideology. Pragmatism in the post-cold war era has produced some confusion. An analysis by Rao (1999) has concluded that 'neither of the two major parties, Congress and BJP, is capable of rising to the occasion to confront the interrelated evils of communalism and casteism. Both the parties are drifting together in a groove of obsolete ideas; they can at best tinker at the margins. Under the circumstances a virtual two-party system with the Congress and the BJP at the forefront will only worsen the situation.'[15] The NDA has already travelled some way to adopt Mandal in its present phase. Greater clarity about ideology in a period of transition confirms the reality of its position as a powerful anchor. What is under challenge is attachment to the past as unchangeable. The Congress is losing out in the hope that failure of others will benefit it. The BJP pragmatism is also skin deep only as it becomes clear from time to time. The Indian reality in the era of coalition has Congress cosmopolitanism, BJP's *Hindutva*, pragmatic communism, cooperative federalism, secularism, and social justice struggling to enlarge their social constituency. Coalition of non-compatible parties has failed so far to prove its potential for creative reinterpretation of ideology. The longer the transition takes, the greater the danger to the polity. Compatible coalition fronts are, however, not in sight in the near future.

India's diversity, an ideology in itself, is now asserting itself in multiple forms. The thirty-five parties in the present Lok Sabha (1999), and more outside, indicate the roots of segmented electoral outcomes. Even one vote counts in the present phase of unstable coalitions with marginal majorities. The 'people's movements and NGOs are helping in identifying marginalized interests and deprived sections of the population. Their impact on relative appeal of parties is increasing. The NGO movement at some stage turns into what we may call 'loyal but critical people's movements'. They are not expressions of fissiperous tendencies but mechanisms of mediation between the government agencies, elected representatives, and the people. They remind the parties between elections of the pledges made and want them to account for what they have done about them. The coalition system and instability of governments are furthering democratic accountability. The assertion by regional parties is challenging the distortions in federal relations in the last half century that has derailed the scheme of the Constitution. The Constitution provides for a strong union but it does not prescribe weak state governments, except in genuine emergencies. States have, in fact, larger responsibility for welfare. If the performance is unsatisfactory the cause lies in the distortions and in misuse of the enabling powers of Parliament to legislate on subjects in the concurrent list as also by use of central financial powers. Judicial review has gone the same way. The vertical integration of judiciary presents a contrast to the effective separation of executive and the legislature at the union and state levels. The judiciary has interpreted the Constitution to expand its discretion manifold. It has failed, however, to correct the imbalances in the working of the Constitution.

A wholesome alternative package is within the realm of politics alone, politics not just of power but of good governance. India is a federal and a parliamentary system. That is the means of change that people desire. Ideology is what people willingly approve. The failure is not of politics but of the narrow elite dominating the political scene.

There are lessons to be learnt from the USA where the federal relations have contributed to the policy for globalization. The background to the clash there between bilateralism and multilateralism reflects federal relations in a wider context. That is the proven ground in political management. It facilitates approaches, pace, and direction for globalization in relation to regionalization, and localization.[16] Coalition politics in its early phase introduced elements of negotiation and arbitration between interest groups with which politics is not familiar. India needed active political engagement at all critical layers of politics to make more relevant policies, national and international. Coalition provides it more competently than a single party in the present stage of political development. The significance of this transition is yet to dawn on leadership. To this end, the stage for rethinking the prevailing idioms of politics shaped during the last fifty years and to assign contemporary values to them has arrived.

IDIOMS IN NEW POLITICS

Politics is prisoner to the confusion of realpolitik; jostling for distinguished positions, leadership clashes, display of inflated egos, and exposure of improprieties. Getting back to rooting for the past it is necessary to re-examine the changed meaning of popular concepts in electoral and governmental politics. Since the list is rather large a selective enumeration will convey the essence of inherent direction of rethinking politics.

Politics is the essence of democracy. Democracy is about rights and duties of citizens and the institutions to which they subscribe. Our democracy is a multi-level enterprise. The voters reflect popular democracy. Legislators are the showcase of representational democracy. Government institutions must be built on responsibility and accountability in democracy. The pride in our 'functioning democracy' must be tempered with the realization of deficiency for each one of our political institutions. We merely have procedural democracy. When a Chief Minister thinks he is the 'State' and a Prime Minister is permitted 'presidential'(in the US American sense) powers; when Parliament does not transact any business for days together; when voters are prevented from exercising their franchise, then politics loses its radical character. Extra-constitutional, unconstitutional, and violent reaction is the result. The whole business of democracy is a sham at present, a monument to its continuing defilement. Coalition era may be an opportunity for making it better. Equality and justice is the cornerstone of the Constitution. Parties must reflect that ideology is above all. The controversy on electoral reform, women representation, structure of probity at the political level, insularity of administration from politics, and scheme of accountability in the system only shows that political maturity remains distant. This area needs greater attention.

Mandate theory is being wrongly applied. The British concept is inappropriate in a multi-party system. The European model is inapplicable in the absence of proportional representation. Mandate for a leader of a single party or of a coalition is even more inappropriate in the express denials of an election being a referendum. The Indian context improvises mandate only for the legislatures to devise modalities for survival for full term. The freedom for them to frame rules without undue interference by the judiciary provides a basis of creative politics. The growing rigidity in constitutional amendment holds the risk of breakdown and may open up undemocratic alternatives. Constitutional provision is required to discipline the members in the exercise of mandate by institutions.[17] The present tendency to claim mandate for pet projects on the basis of uncertain verdicts is a grave danger to federal politics.

Mandatory consensus politics via coalition/minority governments has entered the political process for a decade now. Its implications and limitations are being overlooked. Consensus displays a process, an outcome, and a mindset. Coalition forces a multi-stage process. Each party has two sets of agenda: one that of unit parties and another that of the coalition. The NDA has disclosed serious difficulties in reconciling the two on crucial occasions. It is bad enough for domestic agenda but dangerous in the sphere of foreign policy. India's Sri Lanka policy shows the dilemma. BJP's hidden agenda is hard to be disputed. The Communist parties' economic agenda posed similar problems for the UF. The second stage is a broad agreement within the coalition. The coordination mechanism provides a viable forum. Its effectiveness depends on the leader for genuine consensus. The final stage is informal and formal dialogue with the opposition. Government works under a time squeeze at times. The partners and the opposition co-operate on such occasions. Problem arises when governments try to be clever. The more outstanding current cases are economic reforms agenda, foreign and nuclear policies, and the minorities problem. Outcomes have been questionable. The problem is the mindset of rulers. The Congress brought this vocabulary to prominence in its minority phase; the UF achieved some measure of success; the NDA is failing. The BJP mindset is to blame. Brinkmanship and consensus within coalition cannot pull together.

Stability is an over-used slogan in Indian politics. It was a Congress trade-mark. Multiparty coalition is a system of dynamic stability. Dynamic stability can be displayed in the politics of overlapping consensus. It enjoys politics of political bargaining and accommodation. This will bring into play the nature and the content of the agenda of the coalition. Where a coalition worries about the stability of the government, discussion on programmes accommodation and patronage distribution is possible. The critical factor is the leader and the parties in the government. Overemphasis on stability overlooks the managerial content of the executive domain. Dynamic stability focuses on it. Leadership failure should not be covered up as lack of stability. The single dominant party system under a charismatic leader also bears a constant prospect of instability.[18] The difference is only of degree.

Integrity of institutions needs restoration and renewal after charismatic leaders have battered them. Coalition is a better guarantee for it than a single party. First, there are constitutional bodies. Then there come statutory bodies created by Parliament. Finally, the institutions under executive order make the grade. This hierarchy of constitutional and representative virtue must be maintained. There is regrettable exposure of the presidency and even confidential communications have become public. The UF was graceful, for instance, in quietly dropping the proposal for central rule in UP in the late 1990s after the President returned it for reconsideration.[19] The BJP government in New Delhi tried to do the same with the RJD government led by Rabri Devi in Bihar in 1998. The President, K.R. Narayanan, sought some additional information in the matter. Senior union ministers of the Vajpayee government threatened to reiterate the proposal, in which case the President would have to sign on the dotted line. Arun Shourie wrote an article in a newspaper using confidential reports from the

Governor. It is a poor coalition culture to bring constitutional authority of the highest order into controversies. In most such cases, BJP ministers in NDA are involved, indicating the party is not comfortable in running a coalition. Renewal of integrity involves respecting the autonomy accorded and honouring the scheme of accountability flowing from it.[20]

Accountability is a frequently talked about necessity. In practice it is least visible. Administrative accountability suffers without effective political accountability. One positive step in respect of ministers representing regional party quota is that they account for what they are doing to the party leader in the state capital. In the UF phase, the ministers had to accommodate the nominees of the party leaders as private secretaries to that end. The BJP follows it partly in suggesting names for final selection by the minister concerned but the purpose is not clear. A number of recent decisions, such as on *Sankhya Vahini*, disclose reluctance to enforce a new code of accountability. Transparency is lacking as a result. Coalition has yet to make a departure from single party rule in this respect.

Prerogatives and privileges of the Prime Minister are used as shields for politics of manipulation and of authoritarianism. The coalition shows no difference in legal terms from the single party rule of the past. The role of coteries has also appeared. Ministerial grading and power follows from this phenomenon. The NDA is showing greater inclination towards majoritarian intolerance than was the case during the UF rule. The collegiate system of functioning of coalition as a rule is on trial.

The coalition working so far does not disclose forward-looking politics. The coalition parties have not displayed inventiveness and commitment to institutional reforms that strengthen coalitional governance. The present stage of the major concepts crucial in the discourse on politics of coalition indicates as much. The emerging areas of concern point to the need for further adjustments.

NATURE AND STRUCTURE OF THE SYSTEM

The system has outgrown the ideological anchor suggested by Lohia and JP. They had foreseen the consolidation of parties in the opposition in Parliament to end Congress monopoly of power and dangers to democratic politics flowing from it. The vision of choice in alternatives in government was the core of coalition. Its urgency at that point of time was the essence. This phase effectively ended in 1979. The second phase in planned coalition mobilization through the NF was born in the decade of the late 1980s. Congress remained the target of attack. The possibility of a different target appeared only in 1992 after the Babri Masjid demolition. Politics of power had shown BJP as dangerous in its potentials as the Congress was so far. The UF heralded in 1996 the beginning of a new phase. It supported a coalition of parties other than the BJP. Ideological clash of secularism *versus* communalism made a strong appearance. Opposition to BJP became the target of major mobilization. The BJP-led coalition that came to power in the wake of the failure of the UF in 1998 heralded the current phase that renewed its mandate in 1999 in a snap poll and is carrying on in the NDA experiment with two dozen parties on board. There is no immediate prospect of moves for eventual consolidation into manageable number of partners in governments. Ideologically there is growing heterogeneity. Some parties have shared power in all coalition governments during the 1990s. Their views on the three critical forces of regionalism, communalism, and casteism differ widely. Politics of coalition government at the federal level is still maturing.

NOTES

1. B.G. Verghese, 'Shedding Stability for Change', *Mainstream*, 15 June 1996.
2. Bimla Prasad (ed.), *Socialism, Sarvodaya and Democracy: Selected Works of Jayaprakash Narayan* (Bombay: Asia Publishing House, 1964), pp. 79–90.
3. Atal Behari Vajpayee, 'Speech at Asia Society', *Mainstream*, New York, 17 October 1998.
4. Ram Manohar Lohia, *Notes and Comments*, vol. II, pp. 36-47.
5. Ibid., 'General Election 1967 and After', pp. 174-81.
6. Ibid., 'Urgency of Change', p. 259.
7. Ibid., p. 254.
8. Ibid.
9. Ibid., 'General Election 1967 and After', p. 178.
10. Jayaprakash Narayan, *A Revolutionary's Quest: Selected Writings of Jayaprakash Narayan*, ed. Bimal Prasad, New Delhi: Oxford University Press, 1980, p. 375.
11. Ibid., p. 372.
12. Kamala Prasad, 'Political Verdict of the Lok Sabha Poll', *Mainstream*, 28 March 1998.
13. Kamala Prasad, 'Electoral Verdict at the Millennium End', *Mainstream* 30 October 1999.

14. Kamala Prasad, 'Democracy, Political Parties, and their Culture', *Mainstream*, Annual Number, 1977.
15. Ranjit Sao, 'The Two-Party Syndrome: Conservative versus Liberal?' *Economic and Political Weekly*, 14 August 1999.
16. Lawrence H. Summers, 'Distinguished Lecture on Economics in Government: Reflections on Managing Global Integration', *Journal of Economic Perspectives*, vol. 13, no. 2, Spring 1999.
17. Kamala Prasad's article in *Mainstream*, 8 February 1997, and 3 May 1997.
18. Nikhil Chakravarty, 'Meaning of "Instability"', *Mainstream*, Annual Number, 1997.
19. Reference is to the proposal of United Front Government of I.K. Gujral to dismiss the BJP government of Kalyan Singh in U.P. in the mid-1990s.
20. Kamala Prasad, 'Bihar Crisis and the Union Cabinet', *Mainstream*, 17 October 1998.

CHAPTER 6

Coalitional Experiments: The Marriage of Inconvenience

C.P. Bhambhri

It is essential to contextualize the phenomenon of coalition politics as coalitions have emerged on the political scene because of the continuing decline of the one-party dominance regime of the Congress. It may be mentioned that wherever Congress party vacated the political space because of electoral defeats, the alternative governments were mostly coalition of parties. During the last fifty years, fragmented political groups and fractions were dominated either by a single all-India national party or by coalitions of multiple political groups. What is the explanation for the replacement of an all-India national party? Further, politics and society have a very complex dialectical relationship for determining the directions of political development in a transitional society. Politics is a mirror reflection of society, but it also actively provides direction of change in society. Thus the essence of the politics–society relationship lies in this 'duality' where the superstructure of politics and material base of society are always involved in a dynamic inter-connection and inter-relationship. In the light of this formulation, it is essential to focus attention on significant developments in the Indian society that have given birth to the fragmentation of parties and political groups. Why are fractions and strata of the dominant-exploiting classes not able to operate on the basis of dominant class–caste based political formation? Why are different fractions of the dominant classes floating and supporting multiple political groups to protect their specific class interests? Further, the 1990s have witnessed the emergence of the phenomenon of *Hindutva*. The rise of

Hindutva and its capacity to capture the Indian state with the help of coalition should compel us to look at the phenomenon of coalition and the real social essence of these coalitions in a critical manner. If V.P. Singh or Chandrashekhar or H.D. Deve Gowda or I.K Gujral or the leaders of *Hindutva* maintain that 'India has entered the era of Coalitions Politic', we have to ask a question: What is the social essence of a coalition government?

It is essential to briefly describe the story of Indian politics or the post-Independence phase before a critical evaluation of coalition governments is undertaken. India launched her grand democratic experiment on the basis of universal adult franchise in 1952 and political freedoms and the electoral political process has revolutionized the levels of consciousness of an 'Unchanging India'. The Lok Sabha and state Assembly elections of 1952, 1957, and 1962 were contested by many political parties, but the Congress party maintained its electoral dominance by winning a majority of seats in the Lok Sabha and in almost all the states of India. The elections of 1967 are a kind of watershed because the Congress party was defeated in Vidhan Sabha elections in major states of India, and in the Lok Sabha elections, though it could retain its majority, its number of seats declined as compared to 1952, 1957 and 1962. Indians experienced a system of an absolutely unstable coalition governments in all the major states. For the first time, India witnessed individual MLAs or small groups breaking one coalitional arrangement and replacing it by another unstable formation. The most important special feature of the post-1967 state Assembly elections was that legislators began walking out or walking in different so-called parties on the basis of 'money power' to form short-lived coalition governments. This new feature of coalitional experiment is still operative in Kerala, but a negative feature of this arrangement has been an 'institutionalization of communalism' in Kerala. The Indian Union Muslim League was able to successfully bargain either with the Left or the Congress for seat adjustments during elections and it emerged as a permanent feature in coalitional politics of Kerala. It was only in the 1980s that CPI(M) decided to keep away the communal Muslim League from its Left Front, but the Congress party still has an alliance with it. Besides the communal Muslim League, sectarian Christian and Hindu groups are also involved as partners in the governance of Kerala, either as a part of the Congress-led UDF or the Communist-led LDF. Many governmental decisions are taken by these two coalitional group in Kerala to satisfy the demands of sectarian and narrowly communal Hindu, Christian, and Muslim communities.

The phase of the revival of the Congress party domination over Indian politics at the end of the Nehru era was initiated by Mrs Indira Gandhi in 1971. It came to an end in 1977, when the electoral verdict of Lok Sabha elections was decisively against the Emergency regime of Mrs Gandhi and her extra-constitutional coterie of individuals who practised illegality in governance. The Janata Party experiment of 1977 came to an end in 1979. Indira Gandhi who had again split the Congress in 1978, came back to power with a majority of seats in the Lok Sabha and, in 1980, she also brought the Congress party back to power in some states as well. During the phase of 1977-9, Indian politics was neither an honest coalition nor a majority party rule. The Janata Party government was a conglomerate consisting of Congress (O), Congress for Democracy, BJS, JP-inspired leaders who came under the umbrella of a movement that included socialists and the Bharatiya Kranti/Lok Dal of Charan Singh. This Janata Party experiment dismantled the authoritarian Emergency regime and after plenty of internal quarrelling, it disappeared from the political scene in 1979. The main feature of this short-lived coalition of 1977-9 experiment was again a repetition of the 1967-9 phase of Indian politics, i.e. dissimilar groups assembled together to exercise political power, and fought with one another on purely non-policy issues. The only binding factor among the leaders like Morarji Desai, Charan Singh, Jagjivan Ram, Atal Behari Vajpayee, George Fernandes, Madhu Limaye, and Chandrashekhar was a desire for the governance of India without any programmatic or policy consensus. Every group and leader was busy in pulling down one another and they collectively collapsed. The 1977-9 experiment of governance clearly reveals that desperate groups and individuals enter into a marriage of strange bed fellows for the sake of power only, and their individual desire to maximize the benefits of power creates schisms and conflicts among themselves and these arrangements for governance collapse like a house of cards. The logic of raw power becomes dominant among the cooperating groups to govern, but it has become clear that such a logic is self-destructive and leads to instability.

The ninth Lok Sabha elections again brought a strange arrangement for governance in India because fragmented groups emerged in place of the simple majority party like the Congress. The V.P. Singh's JD government manufactured a parliamentary majority on the basis of an outside support of the BJP, on the one hand, and the Communist parties, on the other. This arrangement of 1989 was based on absolute 'contradictions' because the Communists, the BJP, and the JD were ideologically opposed to each other. Such opposition among the three major political formations was not on marginal issues, it was fundamental ideological opposition. V.P. Singh, as the leader of this political arrangement, described himself as an expert in the 'art of management of political contradictions' and this tall claim ended in a disaster within eleven months.

The tenth Lok Sabha elections were held in 1991 and the Congress party formed a government under the leadership of P.V. Narasimha Rao because it was the single largest minority political group in the Lok Sabha. The Narasimha Rao government began with a minority support in the Lok Sabha and used legal loopholes of the Anti-Defection Act to convert its minority into a majority in the Lok Sabha. The eleventh Lok Sabha elections of 1996 repeated the story of ninth Lok Sabha elections of 1989 with a comic situation. With the outside support from the Congress and CPI(M), H.D. Deve Gowda of the JD constituted a working majority consisting of thirteen political groups in Parliament. If Moraji Desai could not manage the conflicting goals of five partners and if V.P. Singh could not deal with the contradictions of two major supporters from outside, the Deve Gowda government was an extremely inconvenient arrangement of thirteen partners who claimed to agree on a Common Minimum Programme for governance of India.

A comparison of party-wise position in the Lok Sabha can throw some more light on the nature of H.D. Deve Gowda coalitional arrangement in 1996 (Table 6.1).

POLITICS OF TRANSITIONS

India has experienced both stable and unstable parliamentary regimes. It is maintained that India is witnessing a clear transition from the system of clear parliamentary majority and minority syndromes to a non-majority and multiple party milieu.

David Butler, Ashok Kumar Lahiri, and Prannoy Roy, who published on important study in the middle of the 1990s, brought out a few facts about the voters' verdict on the basis of which some explanation may

TABLE 6.1: PARTY POSITION IN THE TENTH AND ELEVENTH LOK SABHAS

Name of Party/Group	Tenth Lok Sabha	Eleventh Lok Sabha
Congress (I)	227	140
BJP	119	161
Janata Dal	56	43
CPI(M)	35	32
CPI	14	12
JD (Gujarat)	1	0
MPVC	0	2
AIADMK	11	0
Samajwadi Party (Mulayam)	0	17
Revolutionary Socialist Party	4	5
MGP	0	1
UGP	0	1
Shiv Sena	4	15
Samata Party	0	8
Samajwadi Janata Party	5	0
Bahujan Samaj Party	1	10
Jharkhand Mukti Morcha	6	1
Telugu Desam Party	13	16
Muslim League	2	2
Forward Block	3	3
MPP	1	0
ASDP	1	1
NPC	1	1
AIMIM	1	1
Kerala Congress (M)	1	1
SSP	1	0
SDF	0	1
Haryana Vikas Party	1	3
Akali Dal	0	8
Assam Gana Parishad	1	5
Tamil Manila Congress	0	20
KCP	0	1
DMK	0	17
JKNC	0	0
Congress (Tiwari)	0	4
Independents	1	7
Vacancies	32	0
Total seats	542	539

Sources: *Lok Sabha Poll 1991* (New Delhi: News Services Division, All India Radio, 1991), p. 2; Election Commission of India, *Statistical Report on General Elections, 1996, The Eleventh Lok Sabha*, vol. 1 (New Delhi: ECI, 1996).

emerge to grapple with the ongoing process of parties and groups that divide among themselves the Lok Sabha seats without anyone of them receiving a clear majority of seats/votes.

The Congress vote has ranged from 35 per cent to 49 per cent. It provided large majorities in the Lok Sabha for the Congress party except in the elections of 1967, 1989, and thereafter and witnessed many 'close contests'. It has been suggested that the first-past-the-post electoral system helped the Congress to achieve majority of the Lok Sabha seats with the minority of votes polled by the party. Whatever be the relationship between the system of voting and party performance, the Congress party vote has been fluctuating since the 1980s and David Butler et al. describe it as a growing volatility of the Indian voters.

Another important finding of Butler and his colleagues was that except for the two Communist parties, other parties did not contest all the national elections. Among these 'others', 'those that have contested two or more elections . . . have seen their votes at least doubled or solved'.

Two important facts emerge from election studies of India. First, the Indian voter has become very politically conscious. India began its democratic journey from a relatively low level of political participation, and the voter's turnout has increased quite considerably. Second, Table 6.2 clearly reveals that the Indian voters' turnout increased when the country was gripped with special situations. The Congress had to be punished in 1967 and the voters turnout was 61.3 per cent. The 1977 elections were a 'referendum' on the Emergency and 60.5 per cent voters participated to punish the party that had committed a great assault against democracy. The 1984 elections were highly 'emotive' because Indians had witnessed, for the first time, political assassination of a democratically elected Prime Minister and the voters, turnout was 64.1 per cent, the highest in the history of post-Independence period in India. In the Lok Sabha elections of 1989, the teeming millions of India, who had a living experience of dealing with corrupt public functionaries,

TABLE 6.2: TURNOUT IN LOK SABHA ELECTIONS (PERCENTAGE)

1.	1952 (45.7)	5.	1971 (55.3)	9.	1989 (62.0)	12.	1998 (61.97)
2.	1957 (47.7)	6.	1977 (60.5)	10.	1991 (56.7)	13.	1999 (59.99)
3.	1962 (55.4)	7.	1980 (57.0)	11.	1996 (65.82)		
4.	1967 (61.3)	8.	1984 (64.1)				

voted in strength against the then Prime Minister Rajiv Gandhi, who was accused of taking bribes in public office in the Bofors scandal.

The decline of the Congress has seen the emergence of many groups and political factions that are competing for power and also the strengthening of the state-based political parties like the TDP of Andhra Pradesh, DMK/AIADMK of Tamil Nadu, AGP of Assam, the Akali Dal of Punjab. Not only this. The Congress is and will be the only all-India national party in the real sense of the term. All other political groups are either regional or claim to be an all-India formation in their social perspective but have a political base limited to only a few states of India. This is the meaning of Indian political transition and it has been acclaimed that India's real federal character is now emerging because Parliament should be a mirror reflection of the continental diversity of the country. It will be worthwhile to highlight some of the experiences of the previous unstable, politically weak, central governments, which did not have a clear majority support in the Lok Sabha. The V.P. Singh government felt highly insecure and, as dissidence emerged within his own JD, he abruptly and unilaterally announced on 7 August 1990, the implementation of the Mandal Commission report on reservations for OBCs in government jobs. As if it was not enough, he suddenly announced on 7 August 1990, a public holiday for the birthday of Prophet Mohammad. It was also felt that V.P. Singh had done this to win over the support of a social constituency to extend his political base. The Chandrashekhar government with a support of miniscule fifty-six MPs, took a critical decision to hold elections in Punjab at the peak of terrorist violence in that state. Thus ill-thought out, ad-hoc responses of unstable and insecure governments have been inflicted on the Indians from 1989-91. It does not mean that the stable party-led government do not indulge in political adventurism. But the unseemly craze of securing a place in history is a more likely lust of temporary alliance governments because they are haunted by the fear of losing power without warning. Further, corruption in public life in India has assumed dangerous proportions, but the possibility of its greater growth exists more in unstable coalitional governments than in stable arrangements. Not only this. The political groups that are part of a ruling alliance indulge separately and independently in public corruption because they have a separate political identity and separate personal and family goals. A law of jungle can emerge in public life where many political groups get busy in abusing public office because they happen to strike gold by fluke.

It has also been suggested that the Congress party had done great harm to the cause of federalism in India by over-centralizing the Indian political system, a coalition of parties including state-based parties in the central government will be very sensitive to the problems of the various states in India. The experiments of 1989, 1996 and 1998 central governments proved otherwise. Disparate groups constituting the central government apparently cannot resolve the centre-state or inter-state or intra-state complex problems of India miraculously. The V.P. Singh government did not show any exceptional capacities in dealing with the ongoing crises in the states of Jammu & Kashmir and Punjab. On the contrary, it has been suggested that the V.P. Singh government aggravated terrorist militancy in Jammu & Kashmir because the militants perceived that the Union Government of India was weak and internally divided to deal with the situation. The Deve Gowda government was always saddled with inter-state water disputes among the southern states. The AGP government of Assam with its own representatives in the Deve Gowda's Council of Ministers had hardly anything new to offer to the ongoing problems of ULFA or Bodoland conflicts of Assam.

COALITION LED BY THE *HINDUTVA*

It has been suggested that the emergence of the phenomenon of coalitional system of governance in the 1990s has facilitated in the creation of a new political milieu for the smooth functioning of centre-state relations because regional parties have become active participants in the Union Government of India. The argument has been further extended by maintaining that the BJP as a partner in coalition has become moderate and party leaders have openly stated that they have abandoned 'contentious issues' like the building of Ram Temple or Common Personal Law or special status of Jammu & Kashmir. During the Lok Sabha elections of September/October 1999, L.K. Advani maintained that the BJP has shown its immense capacity to work with coalitional partners while managing the cental government under the leadership of Atal Behari Vajapayee. It has been a very important electoral plank of the BJP that regional formations have joined the BJP-led NDA because they firmly believe that Vajpayee is essentially an accommodative leader who can effectively manage the culturally pluralist federal polity of India. After all, the NDA consists of BJP and twenty-three groups and parties representing every state and region of India, and it can be possible only if the regional leaders have confidence over the catholicity of approach of the BJP leadership. How far can such tall claims of the apologists or aggressive defenders of cultural plural federalism be taken on face value? The regional parties and leaders that have decided to join the NDA should have some things in common to make them work together. The *raison d'être* of regional formations like the TDP, DMK, JKNC, & BJD and others lies in their firm belief that in a multicultural country, the central government should be controlled by a party that agrees with the basic philosophy of respect for diverse and plural cultures of India. Have the regional parties strengthened the forces of cultural pluralism and democratic federalism by forming a genuine alliance with the BJP? It deserves to be emphasized that the BJP does not agree with the definition of multiculturalism, very dear to regionalists from J&K to Tamil Nadu to the north-east. The cornerstone store of BJP philosophy is summed up in semitization of Hindu India. 'One people, one culture, one country, and one nation' which in concrete terms means hegemonic homogeneous society in India. A few facts may be mentioned to substantiate the argument that the regional supporters of the NDA have strengthened the BJP and in the process they have helped in the consolidation of the forces that are opposed to the essential belief system of the regionalists.

The BJP has succeeded in extending its area of influence on the support base provided by its so-called secular regional allies. Lok Sabha elections in Bihar were held for fifty out of fifty-four seats and a break-up of the voters' support for the RJD, its break-away group, the JD(U), and the BJP gives us an interesting insight into the success of the BJP because of the split between the secular forces represented by Laloo Prasad Yadav and Samata Party leaders like George Fernandes, Nitish Kumar, Ram Vilas Paswan and Sharad Yadav. The RJD of Laloo Prasad Yadav on its own secured 29.6 per cent votes and the BJP and JD(U) polled 22.2 per cent and 21.4 per cent of votes respectively. It is also worth mentioning that the RJD increased its support base in 1998 when it had secured 26.5 per cent of the votes. Bihar would have witnessed a marginalization of the BJP if the regional secularists represented by the RJD, JD(U), and Samata Party had formed a united front of their own. The regional political leaders of Bihar have contributed to the growing strength of the BJP by splintering among themselves and also providing legitimacy to the BJP by alligning with it during the Lok Sabha elections. While BJP gained in strength in a major state in north India because an important section of regionalists decided to form an alliance with it, in south India, the BJP was carried on the shoulders by M. Karunanidhi of DMK, N. Chandrababu Naidu of the TDP and J.H. Patel and Ramakrishna Hedge of JD(U). In Andhra Pradesh, the TDP–BJP alliance secured thirty-six of the forty-two Lok Sabha seats. A further analysis of voting pattern in Andhra Pradesh shows that the BJP established its foothold only because of an alliance with the TDP. In the 1998 Lok Sabha elections, the Congress, the TDP, and the BJP secured 22, 12, and 4 seats in Andhra Pradesh. In 1999, the Congress, the TDP and the BJP secured 5, 29 and 7 seats and while the Congress and the TDP got 42.8 per cent and 40.7 per cent votes, BJP had only 9.1 per cent. It is the generosity of Chandrababu Naidu and other regionalists that has helped the BJP to lead a government at the centre in 1999.

A little more deserves to be mentioned about the regional formations to substantiate the argument that the regionalists are supporting a political party that stands against all cherished values of the regionalists. The late N.T. Rama Rao had floated the TDP on the slogan of 'self-respect of the Telugus' because Rajiv Gandhi as Congress leader had humiliated in public the Congress Chief Minister of Andhra Pradesh. Rama Rao championed the cause of 'true federalism to safeguard multiple identities of India'. Is TDP today committed to cultural pluralism as cherished by its founders?

While Rajiv Gandhi and Congress have always believed and practised the politics or cultural pluralism in a federal polity, and it was a lapse on his part to show discourtesy to the Andhra Pradesh Chief Minister T. Anjaiya, but the TDP is supporting a political party that believes in the concept of Hindu culture and Hindu identity for every Indian. C.N. Annadurai, a tall leader of the DMK, fought for cultural and linguistic autonomy for Tamilians and a flashpoint emerged in 1965 when self-immolations took place during powerful anti-Hindi agitations and the whole country was perturbed at the turn of events in Tamil Nadu. Mrs Indira Gandhi who was Information and Broadcasting Minister

TABLE 6.3: PARTY ALIGNMENTS IN THE THIRTEENTH LOK SABHA, 1999

NDA		Cong+Allies		Left Front		Others	
BJP	182	Cong	114	CPI	4	BSP	14
BJD	10	AIADMK	10	CPI(M)	33	SP	26
DMK	12	KC(M)	1	AIFB	2	NCP	8
HVC	1	MUL	2	KC	1	SAD(SSM)	1
INLD	5	RJD	7	RSP	3	JD(S)	1
JD(U)	21					IND	6
Lok Tantrik	1					AIMIM	1
MDMK	4					CPML	1
MGRADMK	1					MLKSC	2
PMK	5					BBM	1
SAD	2					ABLTC	2
Shiv Sena	15					SJP (R)	1
AITC	8						
TDP	29						
PWP	1						
SDF	1						
JKNC	4						

in the Lal Bahadur Shastri Council of Ministers then reached Madras to provide a healing touch to the angry Tamilians who were agitating against the imposition of Hindi. Indira's credentials as a believer of pluralism were impeccable because she was Nehru's daughter and the emotionally surcharged people of Tamil Nadu responded positively towards her. Congress party has always followed a very cautious language policy for a multi-lingual federal India, and BJS and the *Sangh Parivar* have always believed that the Indian nation should have one language, i.e. Hindi. The *Sangh Parivar* maintains that India cannot be a 'Nation' without an all-India language of its own.

The upshot of this is that the BJP has a specific definition of India and the regionalists have their own vision of a multicultural, multi-lingual country, and the 'marriage' between these two contradictory brands of politics is based on the logic of politics of opportunism. What is the natural linkage between the promoters of Hindi as *lingua franca* for the whole of India, and the DMK's legitimate championship of Tamil language and culture? Futher, the BJP and the *Sangh Parivar* have aggressively and openly targeted the Muslim and Christian minorities of multi-religious India, and its alliance partners have not been able to prevent the ongoing hate campaign launched by the *Sangh Parivar* against marginal and cultural minority groups. The BJP has not abandoned its essential ideology of *Hindutva* and its own government in Gujarat has not been able to protect the life and property of Christian and Muslim communities. The anti-pope campaign is going on with full speed and the protective umbrella provided by Vajpayee-led government has encouraged the RSS, the VHP, the Bajrang Dal, and others to terrorize the minorities in India. It is worth mentioning that out of thirty-one Muslim MPs who have been elected in 1999, only one MP of the BJP is a Muslim. It is secularist Farooq Abdullah who has contributed four Muslim MPs to legitimize BJP-led NDA. Do we need any other evidence to prove that the secularists and the regionalists have entered into a marriage of convenience with the BJP whom Muslims and Christians perceive enemy. The BJP has gained legitimacy by practising the politics of alliances and in the process, the forces of *Hindutva* are marching forward because their own Hindu leaders are in control of the central government. The 'regionalists' are supporting a central government led by a leader and a party whom the cultural minorities perceive a threat to their very existence. The 'regional' parties by supporting the BJP have abandoned their own rationale of creating a 'true' federal India. Hence, NDA is built around a logic of pure political opportunism in which the real power resides with the votaries of *Hindutva* who are successfully exploiting the opportunistic provincial leaders like N. Chandrababu Naidu, Naveen Patnaik, or Farooq Abdullah, M. Karunanidhi, Mamata Banerjee and others like them.

The moral of this discussion is that the essence of Indian politics lies in contest/conflict/contradiction and any assumption that a so-called coalition government of India can arrive at a consensus, even minimal on national or global, is quite off the mark. Social reality of the country does not support the claims made in fervour of unstable coalition governments. It is essential to contextualize the ongoing process of birth and death of parties in the country. Indian politics has been communalized and sectarianized on the basis of religion and caste. The BJP and its many organizations like the RSS, Bajrang Dal, VHP, etc., are softer Hindu variants of fascism. As if religion *versus* religion polities was not enough, caste *versus* caste is the raw politics of the self-appointed. V.P. Singh, Sharad Yadav, Mulayam Singh Yadav, Laloo Prasad Yadav, Ram Vilas Paswan, Kanshi Ram, and Mayawati are the practitioners or new messiahs of spurious social justice for the backward classes. All of them have one *mantra*—reservations in public services and institutions. It started with Mandal Commission and does not seem to be ending because religion-based reservations for the so-called Christian Dalits and the Muslim OBCs is the next item on the agenda. What Sita Ram Kesari was doing covertly inside the Congress, V.P. Singh-trained Janata Dals are doing openly, aggressively, and fractiously. Different leaders and multiple party groups are identifying assured 'social constituencies' to succeed in the politics of power and pelf. Laloo Prasad Yadav has always maintained that Muslims and Yadavs are his 'safe' supporters but they are unleashing criminal violence against others that breeds retaliatory spirals of violence and gang wars. This politics of 'electoral pocket boroughs' is responsible for casteism and the communalization of Indian society and politics. The logic of raw political power has dictated fractions and political groups to fragment the already fractured society by identifying separate sections for electoral battles. If the central government is not in the driver's seat, regionalists, casteists, and communalists will have a field day in politics of petty maneouvering, aided and abetted by the buccaneer globalizers and their crony liberalizers and privateers. Politics of transition is never smooth. It is full of up and downs. Societies move forward and backward to grapple with the emerging problems of social and political transition. The destination or outcome of transition cannot be predicted, but the processes of ongoing transition can be analysed dialectically, and its negative and positive features can be identified. The BJP-led NDA has extended very successfully the agenda of aggressive *Hindutva* and supporters of coalition politics are fully responsible for the communalization of Indian State and fragmentation of Indian society.

REFERENCES

David Butler, Ashok Lahiri, Prannoy Roy, *India Decides*: *Elections 1952-95*, New Delhi: Books and Things, 1995, 3rd edn., pp. 3-4.

Bhambhri, C.P., *Elections 1991: An Analysis*, New Delhi: D.K. Publishers, 1991.

CHAPTER 7

Party Systems and Coalition Politics in Indian States

Himanshu Roy

The dominant trend in the contemporary party systems in different states of India has not been adequately analysed. This interprets the electoral and the political processes in the existing polity as well as the factors that influence voting behaviour of the electorate. Most of the political formations that have been analysed here pursue, by and large, parliamentary route to power and believe in the existing constitutional ideology. The focus of the study is on broad patterns under which comes the functioning of party systems of each state. The specifics of each state are not delved into separately. Finally, the analysis of pre- and post-poll alliances, the nature of government formation, changing electoral base of parties, and trends of development towards political polarization are essential prerequisites of judging the nature of party systems. Like the Owl of Minerva, to use the Hegelian metaphor, this paper only theorizes the actual functioning of the party systems in the states of India.

I

In the electoral history of independent India, 1967, 1977 and 1989 are the turning points in the nature of the party system.[1] In 1967, the 'Congress system' faced its first major crisis particularly at the centre. It lost in eight of the then sixteen states, but retained the centre with a reduced majority. Since then the Congress began to gradually lose its electoral base in the states to be replaced by the non-Congress parties either purely regional in character or nominally national. In 1977, the Congress lost power at the centre (gaining only 154 seats) and in many states of north India. But it retained or won Karnataka, Andhra Pradesh, Kerala (UDF), Punjab, Tamil Nadu (AIADMK-led alliance), etc., when Assembly elections were conducted in 1977-8. In 1989, the Congress party lost and no single party got majority at the centre. This incremental change of ringing out the old and ringing in the new, is still continuing. However, the developments were not unilinear. There were ups and downs.

In the last ten years (1989 and after), in the electoral war of position, the BJP has acquired a vantage position *vis-à-vis* the Congress. From being confined to a few pockets of north India in the aftermath of Mahatma Gandhi's assassination by a Hindu fanatic, it expanded into most states of India, though it did not win seats in legislative assemblies or the Lok Sabha in every state. Further, in coalition with other non-Congress parties or singly, it has managed to form governments in several states and in New Delhi.

In the two decades from 1967, changes in the party systems, both at centre and in states, may be described as a part of resolutive-compositive process. The old party system got dissolved and on its ruins emerged a new one. Of the old system certain elements of the Nehruvian project like greater democratization of social structure, secularism, unity in diversity, focus on universalization of health and education, etc:, were retained. The discrepancies that had crept into the old body politic during the Indira–Rajiv regimes are being discarded either as part of self-purificatory measures or under the pressure of competitive politics. Issues like centralization of power at the administrative level, or the monopolization of power by top leaders *vis-à-vis* cadres and grass-roots workers at party levels, are now on active political agenda. Willy-nilly, there is a greater decentralization of power and governance to the states in their routine functioning. Democracy within parties is now a question being discussed as it was during the Nehruvian period with additional items like party funding, accounting and auditing, and the like. The directives from the Election Commission have played an affirmative role in such developments. And the parties that are not adapting to the changing situation are either facing internal revolts or are breaking up. As a result, the resolutive-compositive process has led to four types of party systems in the states, which may be described as:

(a) Bi-party system, (b) Bi-coalitional system, (c) Shifting multiparty coalitional system, and (d) One party *vs* alliance or coalitional system.

In the bi-party system, as it is operational in states like Gujarat, Delhi, Rajasthan, Himachal Pradesh, Madhya Pradesh, Andhra Pradesh, Assam, Orissa, Karnataka, Jammu & Kashmir, etc., it is mainly two parties that have dominated the political and electoral proceedings and formed the government. One of them is the Congress. The second party in the respective states is BJP, or TDP, or AGP, or JD, or BJD, or JKNC (see Table 7.1). The dominance of two parties in different states as stated above, however, does not preclude the existence of other parties, either in the legislative assemblies or as electoral contestants. In Himachal Pradesh, for example, the BJP in recent elections formed a pre-poll alliance with HVC. Similarly, in Madhya Pradesh, the BSP have had pre-poll alliances / 'friendly' contests / electoral understanding without any formal declaration, either with the BJP or the Congress, and it maintained a presence in the Assembly as well. But, in both the states, the HVC and the BSP are only fringe parties either as electoral partners or as partners in the government. In Gujarat, the attempt of Shankarsinh Vaghela to break the BJP and emerge as the third political force (Rashtriya Janata Party) too did not last long. In Delhi, the Assembly/parliamentary elections witnessed similar operation of bi-party system reducing the non-Congress, non-BJP parties to the fringes. In these states, a marked feature of the party system is the electoral, organizational, and political stability of the two predominant parties, either as the governing or the main opposition party, irrespective of revolts, factional quarrels, and breakups. The change in the nomenclature of the local unit of the predominant parties does not essentially change the character of the party system as it happened during Chief Minister Chimanbhai Patel's tenure in Gujarat. He broke away from the parent party (JD), converted its state unit into a new party mainly basing on the strength of the MLAs, Gujarat Janata Dal. The change in the power configuration at the centre had compelled Chimanbhai to act in such a way. Thus such states have virtually become bi-party systems.

In the second kind of party system operational in the states like Kerala, West Bengal, Maharashtra, Tamil Nadu, etc., a bi-coalitional pattern may be observed (Table 7.2). The essential features of it are the existence of (a) two polarized political formations, each being led by

TABLE 7.1: STATES HAVING BI-PARTY SYSTEM: PARTIES IN POWER OVER THE YEARS, PERCENTAGE VOTE (SEATS)

State & Assembly seats	1985	1987	1989	1990	1991	1992	1993	1994	1995	1996	1997	1998	1999	2000	2001
Andhra Pradesh (294)			Congress 47.7 % (181)				TDP 43 % (213)					TDP (180)			
Assam (126)	AGP 35 % (65)				Congress 29.2% (66)					AGP (59)					Congress
Delhi (70)							BJP 42.8 % (49)					Congress 47.76 % (52)			
Gujarat (182)	Congress 55 % (149)		Janata Dal	29.4 % (70)					BJP 42.5 % (121)			BJP 44.81 % (117)			
Himachal Pradesh (68)				BJP 41.8 % (46)			Congress 49.1 % (52)					BJP 39.02% (31)			
Jammu & Kashmir (76)		JKNC 33 % (40)								JKNC 37.08 % (57)					
Karnataka (224)	Janata Party 43.9 % (137)			Congress 43.8 % (178)			JD 3	8.5 % (115)				Congress	(132)		
Madhya Pradesh (320)				BJP 39.1 % (220)			Congress 40.8 % (174)				Congress	49.59 % (172)			
Orissa (147)	Congress 51.1 % (117)		JD	53.7 % (123)				Congress	39.3 % (88)			BJD (68)			
Punjab (117)			SAD 38.0 %			Congress				SAD	37.64 %				

TABLE 7.2: STATES HAVING BI-COALITIONAL PARTY SYSTEM: COALITION IN POWER OVER THE YEARS

States with their assembly seats	1987	1989	1991	1995	1996	1999	2001
Kerala (140)	LDF, CPM led the coalition with 22.8 % vote (38)		UDF, Cong. led the coalition with 32.1 % vote (55)		LDF, CPM led the coalition with 21.5 % vote (40)		UDF
Maharashtra (286)				BJP Shiv Sena with12.6% vote (64) 6.5% vote (73)		Democratic Front: Cong.+ 27.20% (75) Nationalist Congress+ 22.60% (58) others (157)	
Tamil Nadu (234)		DMK led an alliance with 33.3 % vote (151)	AIADMK led an alliance with 44.40 % vote (164)		DMK led alliance 42.07% vote (173)		AIADMK 31.44 % vote (132)
West Bengal (294)	LF led by CPI(M) (187)		LF led by CPI(M)		LF led by CPI(M) (157)		

two different and dominant parties, (b) constituents of each political formation having electoral understanding / jointly contesting elections/ sharing seats and forming alternate coalition governments, and (c) each of the two coalition groups working on the basis of common action and minimum programme (CAMP) irrespective of different ideological strands. In Kerala, for example, LDF and UDF are led and dominated by the CPI(M) and the Congress respectively. In Tamil Nadu, it is the DMK and the AIADMK which lead their coalition partners. In West Bengal, it is the CPI(M) and the Trinamool Congress. And, in Maharashtra, it is the Congress and the Shiv Sena which respectively lead and dominate the two coalitions, their main partners being the NCP and the BJP respectively. About West Bengal, a point must be specified here. Till recent years, the party system here was essentially one coalitional dominant system with Congress being gradually reduced to a minor party. In recent parliamentary and assembly elections, however, the coalition of Trinamool Congress along with the BJP, or the Congress and other smaller parties attempted to pose a serious electoral challenge to the LF. The Trinamool Congress proposed a *mahajot* (a grand electoral coalition) of non-LF parties, which the central Congress leadership, did not approve thus providing a needed breather to the LF. It is believed that if the *mahajot* becomes operational, the LF, which wins because of the fragmented votes of the opposition, may lose elections. Unless the *mahajot* becomes feasible and wins alternative space for itself, which remains vacant, West Bengal today cannot be called a state with a real bi-coalitional system, where smaller parties may shift their allegiance from one coalitions to another but this does not affect the functioning of the system. A case in point (around 1999 Lok Sabha polls) is Tamil Nadu, where the BJP, Tamil Rajiv Congress, etc., which were earlier in the coalition led by the AIADMK, shifted to the coalition led by the DMK. Or in West Bengal (around the 2001 Assembly election), where the Trinamool Congress formed an alliance with the Congress and dumped the BJP with which it had earlier formed an alliance for the parliamentary elections. Governance in such system is smoothened through a coordination committee of the coalition partners, which resolves the internal contradictions among the parties that arise in spite of a common minimum programme.

A third category of party system, operational in states like Manipur, Mizoram, Bihar, and UP, is the shifting coalitions of multiple parties, major and minor, contesting Assembly and parliamentary elections. Table 7.3 portrays such a system. There is no fixed number of coalitions and there are many parties contesting elections independently. These parties, without joining any coalitions, may or may not enter into limited electoral 'adjustments', 'friendly' contests, or constituency-specific understandings. In brief, every possible political gamesmanship occurs in this system. For example, in Manipur, for the Assembly election 2000, there were three alliances: (1) United Front consisting of MSCP and Federal Party, (2) Secular Democratic Front consisting of Congress, MPP, CPI, CPI(M), JD(S), RPS, and (3) Manipur Democratic alliance consisting of BJP, Samata Party, Kuki National Assembly. Besides these three alliances, there were parties like Nationalist Congress Party (NCP) which contested the elections on its own. Similarly, in Bihar Assembly election 2000, there were three alliances: (1) RJD alliance consisting of CPI(M), JD(S), SJP, (2) CPI, CPI(M-L) alliance, and (3) NDA alliance of JD(U), Samata Party, and BJP. Further, there were other parties like Congress that contested the election alone. Earlier, in 1995, JD and CPI were in alliance but contested the election alone. In Uttar Pradesh, in 1993, SP and BSP had formed alliance whereas BJP, Congress, and JD had contested the Assembly election independently. In Mizoram, in the 1998 elections, there were two coalitions that contested the Assembly election, namely, (1) MNF + Mizo People's Conference and (2) MNF (Nationalist) + Citizens Common Forum. Thus, the Congress contested alone. Besides, due to electoral compulsion, parties keep on forming. Another feature of this system is that even electoral opponents may join hands in government formation. (A case in point is the role of the Congress and RJD in Bihar.) Or the parties split with a faction joining the government against the earlier electoral stand of their parent parties. Splits in the BSP and Congress in UP are cases in point. Bihar is galore with such examples. Recently, in March 2000, Congress supported the RJD and CPI(M-L) abstained, which contradicts their earlier electoral stands. But even in such a political flux, one characteristic can be noted—irrespective of changing number of coalitions and number of parties contesting the elections, there are broad but sharp polarizations either in favour of or against the single largest party. In UP, for example, there is polarization in favour of or against the BJP. Similarly, in Bihar, the polarization is between those in favour of or against the RJD. In such

TABLE 7.3: CHANGING NUMBER OF MULTIPLE COALITION AND MULTIPARTY SYSTEM: PARTIES IN POWER

States with Assembly seats	1987	1989	1990	1991	1993	1995	1996	1998	2000
Bihar (324)			JD alliance, 25.7% (123) (JD + BJP) Congress contested alone)			JD alliance 28.7% (167) (JD + Left, BJP, Samata, Congress) (124)			RJD alliance. (124) (CPI+ CPIML), NDA, Cong. (23) (122)
Manipur (60)			Congress			Congress (22)			United Front alliance (29) 29 MSCP+FPM 23+06
Mizoram) (40)	MNF	Cong. 32.8% (23)			Congress alliance (Cong. 16 + Mizo Janata Dal 8)		(21 +12=33)	MNF alliance MNF+MPC 21+12	
Uttar Pradesh (425)				BJP 31.5% (221)	SP +BJP alliance (109) +(67)18% + 11% BJP, Cong. and JD contested alone		BJP alliance (174) 32.5%		

systems, parties/coalitions are evenly balanced and no political formation is in a decisively dominant position. Survival, therefore, is the guiding principle of praxis resulting in frequent bickerings, even in the matter of governance that is adversely affected it, as there does not exists any coordination committee of parties in power. Instead of using institutionalized mechanism, contentious issues are resolved through ad hoc decisions taken by the top leadership of the largest parties in power in consultation with the leadership of the smaller parties sharing power.

Finally, there is one party *vs.* an alliance system operational in states like Haryana where Congress single-handedly contests elections against the combines of BJP + INLD (NDA)/HVP. In states like Assam, Orissa, Karnataka, and Andhra Pradesh too the Congress has single-handedly contested against the combines of AGP + CPI + CPI(M) + UPPA, BJP + BJD, Lokshakti + BJP, TDP + BJP respectively. But a closer look of the strength of the BJP in Andhra Pradesh, Karnataka, and Orissa, or that of CPI + CPI(M) + UPP in Assam brings forth the fact that they are only minor political formations in such states. JP + JD + BJD in Orissa, TDP in Andhra, AGP in Assam, or JP + JD + Lok Shakti in Karnataka are formidable enough to form governments on their own strength. They form alliances to check the splitting of votes that may benefit the Congress. In this system, the alliance partners may not necessarily join the government, they may not even share each other's ideologies, but work together on the basis of a common minimum programme. Further, the single largest party contestant may make minor, formal/informal electoral adjustments with parties having limited electoral influence in order to check splitting of votes. But this does not alter the nature of the system. And the trend is either towards the bi-party system or bi-coalitional system. If either of the alliance partners is electorally marginalized, then there is a likelihood of a bi-party system. Marginalization of the single largest party may lead to a bi-coalitional system as well, because, in order to check splitting of votes, it may enter into major alliances as well. Some of these states cited had, earlier, bi-party system with the Congress being at one pole. In any case, there exists a sharp polarization, and the trend of development indicates towards such existence in future as well, albeit may be in a different format.

Like the third category of the party system, this category too lacks institutionalized mechanism to resolve the contentious issues that arise despite the common minimum programme. Conflict management takes place at the top level of the parties concerned, with the state-based parties having the dominant say.

Overall, this survey of the party systems in different states of India points out that there is a development towards political polarization that may make the third and fourth categories of party systems, as discussed, vacuous. Moreover, in the age of globalization and growing centralization of capital, the party system cannot remain undented. The mounting electoral expenses with only a few seats won by a party may not be viable in future. With the scale of economies tilting against such parties, they may become politically obsolete in course of time, and in the changed social context and competitive political milieu, where accountability and auditing by the people are in vogue, only the fittest may survive on the electoral firmament. Thus, except for an aberration in Arunachal Pradesh, which still clings to the one-party dominant system with all its features, except for the caste being replaced by the tribe, the party systems in different states may have either bi-coalitional or bi-party system in future. Or, at least, irrespective of number of parties, polarization among them may become sharper.

II

It is difficult to explain as to why some states have bi-party or bi-coalitional systems while others have other kinds of party systems. There are no definite reasons in such a diverse society and for such systemic variations. Only some plausible arguments may be posited. One such important factor may be the political emergence of OBCs, as a force to be reckoned with, a force that has been generally considered as hostile to Congress.[2] In the *ryotwari* areas of mainly south India, e.g. Tamil Nadu, Kerala, etc., the OBCs arrived on the political horizon relatively earlier. Their individual political mobility was propelled by capitalism from below in agriculture through new revenue settlement in the early years of the nineteenth century in colonial India, which was a caricature of the 1789 French model of development. It may be noted here that in France during the bourgeois revolutionary period of 1789, the peasants had seized the lands of the estates and appropriated them as their private property that was later legalized. The landed intermediary strata ceased to exist thenceforth. It was a self-emancipatory process. The peasants were brought into direct relation with the state. In colonial south India, neither the British as the lead party nor the peasantry played the role as the peasants did in France. Nonetheless, the new land settlement initiated a limited break from the past. Modern education further helped the peasants to compete for new spaces provided by colonial capitalism. In the *zamindari* areas of mainly north India, e.g. Bihar, UP, etc., the emergence of OBCs was facilitated by the land reform measures initiated in the 1950s, which were formulated in instalments and implemented after years of court ranglings and administrative circumvention.

Actually, it was the sheer raw power that decided the fate of land reforms in villages, at least, in the initial years. Later on, the economics of market and numerical power of OBCs tilted the possession of land in their favour. Being in majority as OBCs, but not cohesive and united, they formed a number of parties in the electoral fray that challenged the Congress, but could not keep it out of power for long because of the lack of opposition unity factor. The OBCs, therefore, took many years to dethrone the Congress through painful forging of opposition unity. The rise of the OBCs in the *ryotwari* areas in combination with the power of their brethren in the post-*zamindari* areas led to the undermining of the electoral base of the Congress.

The states undergoing such social transformation felt the change in the nature of party system only in the post-*zamindari* period. The change being gradual and the *zamindari* areas, comprising approximately 60 per cent of the territory in the country, being too vast, it took almost two to three decades, depending upon regions, for the OBCs to catapult not only the non-Congress parties to power on a sustained basis but also their caste brethren in the hierarchies of these parties. Such socio-political transition as per the history of India's growth rate was relatively fast temporaily stayed Indira Gandhi, and for a brief period by Rajiv Gandhi, through their deft electoral handling. The gradual demise of landlords, particularly of the absentee variety, and the rise of bullock capitalists[3] along with the rich farmers disjointed the class coalition of the bourgeoisie and the landlords that was reflected in the nature of the state during the Nehruvian period. It was replaced by the absolute dominance of the bourgeoisie, which was lacking on their part till 1960s, after which Indira's authoritarianism facilitated their absolute dominance. Her economic policies, such as nationalization of major private banks, marginalizing the party private banks, was to facilitate the availability of large amount of capital, using the resources of the state at the disposal of a weak bourgeoisie that was devoid of such benefit in the absence of big banks. Indira–Rajiv charisma or her deft electoral handling could not withhold the social transformation underway for long. Once the splitting of OBC votes was checked through some semblance of opposition unity in our plurality of first-past-the-post system of elections, the Congress system, which was already undermined, collapsed. The weakening of the Congress system also led to another interesting change—the legal demise of the *zamindari* system, already corroded by the market and electoral system, which in turn led to the change in the roles that political parties had, hitherto, played. Now onwards, they confined themselves, gradually, to contesting elections and forming governments. Their social development commitments and roles atrophied clearing the way for NGOs.

It may be apt to point out here that the areas having *ryotwari* system like Madras and Bombay presidencies or the areas having *zamindari* system but with effective land reforms (Bengal Presidency) were the weakest links in the chain of Congress system and were broken first giving rise to alternative party systems.

Further, with the expansion of industrial economy to hinterlands, and mechanization of agriculture and growth of agro-based industries, there is an increasing differentiation among the peasantry. And the more the differentiation, which has been facilitated by economic liberalization beginning in small measures during Rajiv Gandhi's premiership, the greater the desperation among the peasantry to cling to old systems and values. BJP and other non-Congress parties used this opportunity to catapult themselves to power.

Muslims did not remain aloof from all these developments. Mainly residing in rural areas, particularly in rice growing belts that are situated in river basins,[4] some of them did benefit from the commoditification process but a large section was displaced and remained marginalized. Still quagmired in poverty (the benefits of green revolution, which had occurred in wheat growing areas first, did not percolate to them much) and illiteracy (Muslim women are much below the Dalits in literacy), the Muslims are electorally appropriated by different parties in different states. Though not voting enbloc, they do influence considerable number of seats by their religious perceptions. Lack of modern education and rural economic development have placed them in a blind alley. Majority of Muslims being converts from the poor economic and caste strata, they mainly perform their traditional professional chores, which have been hit hardest by economic liberalization. In the economic milieu of searching for alternative livelihoods, a section of them are attracted towards religious revivalism and fundamentalism.

Apart from these socio-economic factors, the role of contemporary problems like river water disputes, religion, language, region-specific problems, caste, cultural identities, etc., do play important role in electoral and party politics. In the last ten years their importance has increased. Further, the constituency-specific problems and the number of candidates contesting in a particular constituency ultimately decide the victory of a candidate. Increase in the percentage of votes of a candidate may not be the winning factor. A candidate with a less percentage of vote may win the election, depending upon the splitting of opponents votes. Thus there are innumerable factors responsible for the victory of candidates of different political parties that determine the nature of party systems in Indian states.

III

It is believed that there has been growth of regionalism in the past thirty years, which has moved in fast track in the last decade.[5] Arguments are posited, to substantiate it, that state-based parties have recently proliferated in large numbers and they have successfully positioned themselves in governmental power replacing national parties, mainly the Congress.[6] Even the BJP, which has emerged as a national party in the last ten years eclipsing the Congress, has been halted by the phenomenon of regionalism, which focuses on sons of the soil, local issues, and greater autonomy to the states.[7] At the surface, such arguments may seem plausible. But deeper probe makes them unsustainable. A brief explanation to refute such beliefs is required here.

With the expansion of capitalism in agriculture and benefits of land reforms reaching the OBCs, SCs, and STs, and there realizing the importance of electoral politics and given the kind of numerical strength they command, the pre-capitalist dominance of the upper castes, which had lingered on till the 1960s, gradually declined. The new sets of political power holders (now known as Mandal elites along with Dalits), backed by their constituencies, dismantled the Congress system dominated by the upper castes. The fall out of *zamindari* abolition combined with the benefits of *ryotwari* system hastened its decline. The neglect of emerging social aspirations by the Congress played an equally important role in its gradual demise. The new rulers' political survival depended on nurturing local/rural aspirations. Away from Congress, they formed parties that mainly survived at regional levels. Thus, what has been termed as growth of regionalism is essentially: (1) an electoral protest of new social forces, mainly OBCs against the Congress system for its failure to cater to their local requirements, and (2) decentralization of power reflected through the growth of mainly single state-based parties that are accessible at district and *taluqa* levels catering to their local needs. The grass-roots perception never differentiated between the 'regional' or 'national' parties. But people definitely vote for the parties that perform. Mainly belonging to the profession of cultivation and possessing a traditional rural outlook, these castes, now dominant, required parties that were locally rooted like them and would work for them. Unconscious of or indifferent to the image of regionalism, as created and sustained by the parties and leaders for their own political ambitions, the local population faces similar problems that are encountered by the populace of other regions and constituencies all over India. They, simultaneously, face problems that are region, and constituency-specific. Solution of their problems, and not the dominance over others, therefore, is desideratum of the people. Behind voting regional parties into power or providing primacy to the issue of separation, the intention is the solution of their problems of everyday existence. Recognition of identity meant a desire to participate in their development in democratic governance. Separation just for its sake and false prestige have not been the part of their psyche. They have voted Congress or other 'national' parties back into power time and again, and they have rejected their 'regional' parties when the parties of the regions have failed to perform. Regionalism, thus in contemporary period, is only a electoral verbiage for the state-based parties and leaders bereft of any serious popular support, or used by such leaders and parties use the to keep their electoral support intact or conceal their failure of performance by blaming others. Growth of state-based parties reflect only the local problems. Indirectly, it creates pressure on the 'national' parties to take into account seriously the local needs of the people and their solution. In an economy, which has still to acquire developed capitalist structure, the competition for distribution of resources to different regions and segments of society is reflected in different images. Many of such images are false and deliberately created to pressurize the distributing agencies. Regionalism is one such false image used for appropriating resources by a regional party from among the competing sections. The desire of a state government for an autonomous administrative functioning, away from the clutches of the central government, need not be confused for regionalism. The proliferation of state-based parties have no serious link with regionalism today. It is only a desire for autonomous administrative funtioning. The growth of regionalism takes place when democratic government and welfare measures elude a society. In India's flexible Constitution, liberal democracy and expanding capitalism provide enough space for social mobility that acts as countervailing force to regionalism.

IV

The incremental change in the nature of party systems in different states of India in the last thirty-five years have resulted into coalition politics both at the centre and in states. The years 1967 and 1989 are marked as watersides in such changes that heralded and culminated into the breaking of the hegemony of the Congress and one-party dominant system, and substituted it with either bi-party system, bi-coalitional system, or polarized pluralism. There were many factors responsible for such changes. Growth of OBCs as bullock capitalists in the post-*zamindari* period, breakdown of the class coalition between bourgeoisie and landlords and its replacement by absolute dominance of the bourgeoisie, expansion of civil society, etc., were such factors that affected the process of change. More importantly, the Congress represented a period of transition from political dominance of upper castes to their decline, from their land dominance in rural India to their urban-orientation. It was the dominance, both actual and residual, that had lingered on from the pre-capitalist society. The beginning of the end of Congress system was also the end of vestiges of feudalism and expansion of rural capitalism at a faster pace. *Ryotwari* areas had witnessed such socio-economic changes earlier; hence anti-Congressism in such states in the South arrived earlier. When the benefits of *zamindari* abolition coalesced with the benefits of *ryotwari* system the Congress system was dismantled. It heralded the arrival of rural capitalism all over India at grass-roots level, which politically energized the majority of rural population against the Congress system that was dismantled for ever.

The dismantling of the Congress system affected different regions and segments of population in different proportions. The non-fulfilment of the aspirations of the people under the Congress system threw up many local parties and leaders who promised a better life to their constituencies in the post-Congress system. It resulted in open display of caste, communal, and regional cards for vote mobilization. Suiting the local requirements of the rural population who felt the sense of power, it became a necessity for the non-Congress parties to identify with the idioms of the rural world and competitively prove themselves in verbiage more faithful to the sons of the soil. Most parties, however, got trapped in political cocoons of being regional and local, creations of their own, and could not expand beyond a limited vote bank. This proved detrimental to their expansion and graduation to governance on their own steam. They were consequently compelled to form coalitions for government formation and electoral contests resulting in the coalition politics of the day and polarization of political forces. Apart from acquiring the image of being regional, secular, religious, or casteist, which suited these parties in the initial stage in the aftermath of the Congress system, such features are now turning into their fetters. Economic liberalization has posed another problem for their survival. It has hastened the process of differentiation and uprooting among the rural population thereby eroding and changing the vote banks of different parties. It has also extended the law of market to the realm of political competition with more intensity. With larger number of competitors for votes targeting the same voters and voters migrating to towns every year in a different socio-economic mileu, a number of parties may become extinct or marginalized due to splitting of votes among large number of candidates. The rising electoral expenses with lesser probability of electoral success shall deter parties from making bad ventures. Thus the economy, acting as catalyst, may, in future, help in further polarizing the political forces into blocks.

The diverse factors acting against various political parties, and the contemporary political trend already existing towards polarized existence, may cause the nature of party systems in different states of India to move towards bi-coalitional or bi-party systems.

NOTES

1. The data presented in Tables 7.1, 7.2 and 7.3 have been compiled from David Butler et al., *India Decides*, New Delhi: Books & Things, 1995; Election Commission of India, *Elections in India: Major Events, New Initiatives 1996-2000,* New Delhi, 2000; M.S. Rana, *India Votes*, New Delhi: B.R. Publishing Corporation, 2000.
2. Himanshu Roy, 'Mandal Elite vs. Indian Democracy', in *Political Science Annual*, 1997; M.P. Singh and Rekha Saxena, eds., New Delhi: Deep and Deep Publication, 1998.
3. For the economic and political emergence of OBCs, see L.I. Rudolph and S.H. Rudolph, *In Pursuit of Lakshmi, Political Economy of The Indian State,* New Delhi: Orient Longman, 1987, pp. 49-55.
4. This information was given by Professor Imtiaz Ahmed in a lecture at Academic Staff College, Jawaharlal Nehru University, New Delhi in 1999.
5. For such a view, see Yogendra Yadav et al., 'Regional Parties to the Fore', *Frontline*, 17 March 2000, pp. 127-30.
6. See Balveer Arora's arguements in Francine Frankel et al., eds., *Transforming India: Social and Political Dymamics of Democracy*, New Delhi: Oxford University Press, 2000.
7. For arguments on increasing federalization of Indian democracy mainly in matters of administrative governance, see Mahendra Prasad Singh, 'Political Parties and Political Economy of Federalism: A Paradigin shift in Indian Politics', *Indian Journal of Social Science*, vol. 7, Delhi, 1994.

CHAPTER 8

The 1999 Lok Sabha Elections and the Left Front in West Bengal

Bidyut Chakrabarty

Given the defeat of the Left Front candidates in as many as thirteen West Bengal parliamentary constituencies in the thirteenth national poll, held in 1999, its performance is perhaps illustrative of its apparent decline. Not only had the leading partner of the Front, CPI(M), lost one-fourth of the total seats contested, its share of votes had also declined. In the light of such an outcome, the idea gains ground that '. . . the left (is likely to) get marginalized in Indian politics as has already happened in the USA, the Scandinavian countries, Mexico and, to a certain extent, in Britain and West Germany'.[1] Although the Left parties have national forms, they are basically regional and the CPI(M) with its numerical majority is effectively running the government in West Bengal, Kerala, and Tripura though under the constraint of a not-so-friendly federal government. Given the general apprehension of the prospect of the Left and a remarkable Right Wing consolidation in West Bengal, the question—has the Left dwindled?—assumes unprecedented significance. The aim of the paper is thus two-fold: (a) to examine whether the process of decline has already started in view of the reduction of the Left votes; and (b) to assess whether the coalition that sustains the Left consolidation continues to remain viable.

THE POST-POLL SCENARIO

The winners in the 1999 elections are 'coalition politics', 'leadership', and 'economic liberalization'. The future, while it will revolve around the two major parties, the Congress and the BJP, does not belong to them. With increasing importance in national politics, the regional parties are playing a larger role than before in the Indian political system, which is multipolar, coalitional, and marked by immense complexity, divergence, and heterogeneity.[2] Never was this articulated as clearly as in the 1999 national poll. As compared with its tally in 1998, the Congress' strength in the Lok Sabha was reduced drastically despite the euphoria among its rank and file following Sonia Gandhi's decision to lead the party in the 1999 elections. Similar to the Congress, the JD also suffered significant losses primarily due to factionalism within the party that even failed to put up candidates in a large number of constituencies. As shown in Table 8.1, the BJP and its allies enhanced both its share of popular votes and its parliamentary seats.

Despite increasing their numerical strength in the Lok Sabha, it was not possible for either the BJP or the Congress to form the government without support from their electoral partners. This reconfirms the trend, ushered in following the 1996 national poll. As Table 8.2 shows, a large number of regional parties that have, with a strong base in one

TABLE 8.1: ELECTORAL PERFORMANCE OF MAJOR POLITICAL PARTIES AND THEIR ALLIES: 1996, 1998 AND 1999 ELECTIONS

Major Parties	Seats Won (% vote), 1996	Seats Won (% vote), 1998	Seats Won, (% vote), 1999
BJP	161 (20.3)	179 (25.4)	182 (33.5)
Allies of BJP +	26 (4.0)	72 (10.8)	123 (22.7)
Congress	141 (28.8)	141 (25.8)	114 (21.0)
Allies of Congress*	–	26 (-)	22 (-)
United Front**	174 (28.6)	98 (20.9)	–
Others	41 (19.3)	24 (17.5)	21 (17.7)

Notes: Though the table is not exhaustive it nonetheless exemplifies the trend. Figures in the parenthesis indicate the percentage of votes secured.

\+ Major allies of the BJP include the AIDMK of Tamil Nadu with eighteen seats and the Samata Party with nine seats.

* Congress' major ally is the Laloo Prasad-led RJD with seventeen seats.

** The United Front was a loose coalition of ten parties with two major partners, namely the LF and SP that won thirty-three and twenty parliamentary seats respectively.

Source: Computed from *West Bengal: a special number on the 12th Lok Sabha Elections, 1998*, Department of Information and Cultural Affairs, Government of West Bengal, 1998, pp. 89, 93-112.

TABLE 8.2: PERFORMANCE OF SINGLE-STATE AND MULTI-STATE PARTIES IN NATIONAL POLLS: 1996, 1998 AND 1999

Party	1996	1998	1999
*National Parties**			
CPI(M)	32	32	33
CPI	12	09	04
JP	46	06	–
Samata Party and JD(U)	08	12	21
BSP	11	04	14
State Parties			
RJD	–	17	07
BJD	–	09	10
SP	17	20	26
SAD	08	02	02
Trinamool Congress	–	07	08
NCP	–	–	08
TDP	16	12	29
Shiv Sena	15	06	15
AIDMK	00	18	11
DMK	17	06	12
TMC	20	03	00
Total	203 (37.5)**	172 (31.8)**	200 (36.9)**

Notes: * The classification of parties follows the principles, enunciated in the *Symbol Order* of 1968. According to para 7(1) of this Order, if a political party is treated as a recognized political party in accordance with the paragraph 6 in four or more states, it shall be known as, and shall have and enjoy the status of a 'National party' throughout India. Parties that do not fulfil this criterion shall be known as 'state parties'.

** Figures in the parenthesis show the percentage of the seats, obtained by these parties.

Sources: Election Commission of India, *General Elections, 1996, 1998, 1999: seats won by parties in states and union territories.*

state, played a crucial role in the formation of the national government.

The poll outcome clearly shows the growing importance of the regional parties in the contemporary political arithmetic. What is less evident but nonetheless significant is the dwindling of the Left, which is probably the only cohesive group with more or less well-articulated views. Of the LF partners, the Forward Block, and Revolutionary Socialist Party suffered loss of both parliamentary and popular seats. The trend is not different in regard to either CPI(M) or CPI; while

CPI(M)'s aggregate vote decreased from 6.12 per cent in 1998 to 5.18 per cent in 1999, CPI's came down from 1.97 to merely 1.75. Not only is this decline alarming, it has failed to capture even a single seat in the 'Hindi heartland'.[3] The CPI(M) is confined to West Bengal, Kerala, and Tripura, while the strength of CPI in Lok Sabha has been reduced from nine MPs in 1999 to four in 1999.

In West Bengal, the LF[4] maintained its hegemony by capturing 29 of 42 parliamentary seats, which is remarkable given its decline elsewhere in the country.[5] What disturbed the leadership[6] is the decrease of 2 per cent of popular votes in the Left bastion like West Bengal, which is being ruled uninterruptedly by the CPI(M)-led coalition. Despite its continuity in the state for more than twenty years, the Left accounted for only 47 per cent of popular votes, which does not appear to be significant since the aggregate vote for them was only marginally higher than the Trinamool–BJP's 30 per cent and the Congress' 16.2 per cent put together. Even in Kerala, the situation is not radically different with the LF winning 8 out of 20 parliamentary seats in the state. By winning 2 out of 2 parliamentary seats in Tripura, the CPI(M) reinforced the strength of a political outfit drawing sustenance from and backed by an organization with a well-defined ideology.[7]

The 1999 election is unique in another way. Whereas national politics is being articulated in terms of a coalition of a variety of political parties, sometime even with conflicting interests, at the state level, the signal is clearly for 'a two-party system' in most states with notable exceptions of UP and Bihar. Except West Bengal, the principal contenders in elections are primarily the Congress and the BJP. The situation in West Bengal is different since the newly emerged Trinamool Congress[8]–BJP combination, led by Mamata Banerjee posed a formidable challenge to the CPI(M)-led coalition in a majority of constituencies. With no ideological affinity, the alliance appeared fragile from the outset since both the BJP and Trinamool Congress fought the poll without a well-defined political agenda. Neither party sought to articulate those local issues that would have given them political dividends; instead of projecting a positive image by offering viable socio-political and economic programmes, their campaign during the election revolved around what the LF failed to do in the state. The outcome of the poll, as Table 8.3 shows, illustrates the extent to

TABLE 8.3: COMPARATIVE PERFORMANCE OF POLITICAL PARTIES IN TERMS OF SEATS, WON IN 1991, 1996, 1998 AND 1999 LOK SABHA POLL IN WEST BENGAL

Name of the Political Parties	Seats Won			
	1991	1996	1998	1999
INC	05	09	01	03
CPI	03	03	03	03
CPI(M)	27	23	24	21
RSP	04	04	04	03
FB	03	03	02	02
BJP	–	–	01	02
Trinamool Congress	–	–	07	08

Note: The leading partner of the LF coalition, CPI(M), contested thirty-two Lok Sabha seats winning twenty-one. An interesting outcome of the thirteenth national poll in West Bengal is the meteoric rise of the BJP, which had won the Dum Dum and Krishnanagar seats and came second in as many as ten Lok Sabha constituencies. The other remarkable feature is the success of the newly emerged Mamata Banerjee-led Trinamool Congress, which captured eight seats and held second position in terms of number of votes in its favour.

Source: Computed from the figures in *West Bengal: a special number on the 12th Lok Sabha General Elections, 1998*, Department of Information and Cultural Affairs, Government of West Bengal, 1998, pp. 92-5; for the 1999 figures, see the compilation of the Chief Electoral Officer, Government of West Bengal.

which the strategy paid off in as many as nine parliamentary constituencies in the state.

Similarly, the share of votes, secured by those parties in the electoral fray, clearly shows the trend of a sudden spurt of support for non-Left political consolidation. The Congress' loss is certainly gains for the Trinamool Congress. In fact, the anti-Left votes swung toward the Trinamool Congress whose vote-share shot up. Although the BJP, which never had a substantial following in the state, succeeded in winning two parliamentary seats, the consistent rise of its votes, as compared with 1996 figures, is nonetheless significant. Barring CPI(M), other constituents of the Left coalition, as shown in Table 8.5, had also suffered marginal losses in terms of votes.

Both Tables 8.4 and 8.5 are self-explanatory. In absolute terms, the CPI(M), the Front leader, is far ahead of its partners (CPI, Forward

TABLE 8.4: COMPARATIVE PERFORMANCE OF VARIOUS POLITICAL PARTIES IN TERMS OF % OF VOTES, CAPTURED IN 1991, 1996, 1998 AND 1999 LOK SABHA POLLS

Year	CPI(M)	Trinamool Congress	INC	BJP	CPI	Forward Bloc	RSP
1991	35.2	–	36.2	11.7	3.7	3.7	4.5
1996	36.7 (+1.5)	–	40.1	6.1	3.8	3.4	4.8
1998	35.4 (-1.3)	24.4 (+24.4)	15.2 (-24.9)	10.2 (+4.1)	3.6 (-0.2)	3.3 (-0.1)	4.5 (-0.3)
1999	35.5 (+0.1)	26.0 (+1.6)	13.3 (-1.9)	11.1 (+1.1)	3.4 (-0.2)	3.4 (+0.1)	4.2 (-0.3)

Note: Figures in the parenthesis show the percentage of growth/decline of various political parties in West Bengal.

Sources: *West Bengal: a special number on 12th Lok Sabha General Elections, 1998*, Department of Information and Cultural Affairs, Government of West Bengal, 1998, p. 88; For the 1999 figures, see the compilation of the Chief Electoral Officer, Government of West Bengal.

Bloc, and RSP) and its rivals (the Congress, Trinamool Congress, and the BJP). Despite retaining 29 Lok Sabha seats, however, the reduction of Front's share of votes is alarming in a state with 70 per cent turnout of voters. The major loser is, however, the Congress, which suffered a setback as result of a sharp decline of almost 25 per cent of votes within a span of two years. Perhaps the winner in the thirteenth Lok Sabha elections was the BJP, which not only succeeded in defeating the CPI(M) candidate in the CPI(M) stronghold areas like Dum Dum and Krishnanagar, it also enhanced its share of votes in these two constituencies. The BJP has thus been able to take advantage of gradual growth in West Bengal by positioning itself as a viable electoral opposition at the state level. This has been partly achieved through a localized electoral strategy and a concurrent use of the BJP's national leader, electoral themes, and political prominence within a specific state context.[9] The CPI(M)'s failure to retain the Contai seat also indicates its gradual decline in a constituency where the LF candidates always won since 1977. With a massive reduction of votes—from 13.2 per cent in 1998 to a mere 4.1 per cent in 1999 elections, the Congress appears to be the worst-hit due largely to its failure to arrive at a consensus regarding the selection of the candidate for Contai. What

TABLE 8.5: SHARE OF VOTES (IN PERCENTAGE) IN DUM DUM, KRISHNANAGAR, CONTAI, NABADWIP, BERSHANPUR, AND RAIGANJ CONSTITUENCIES (ASSEMBLY SEGMENT-WISE) IN THE THIRTEENTH LOK SABHA POLL.

Dum Dum (*in per cent*)

Assemblies	CPI(M)	Congress	BJP
Bhagabanpur	-1.1	-11.1	+11.7
Rajarhat	-1.2	-4.5	+5.4
Khardah	+2.3	-2.2	+4.0
Panihati	+1.1	-0.5	+1.3
Kamarhati	-0.5	+1.4	+1.4
Baranagar	+3.2	-2.1	-0.5
Dum Dum	+1.4	-1.1	-0.1
East Belgachia	+0.2	-1.1	+2.1
Total	+1.2	-1.6	+1.4

Krishnanagar

Assemblies	CPI(M)	Congress	BJP
Palashpara	+0.2	-5.5	+4.3
Nakashipara	-1.7	-8.1	+11.5
Kaliganj	-0.8	-6.5	+4.2
Chapra	-0.1	-2.1	+3.3
Krishnaganj	-0.7	-3.3	+5.4
Krishnanagar (East)	-0.4	- 4.1	+6.1
Krishnanagar (West)	-0.4	-5.2	+8.1
Total	-0.3	-5.1	+7.1

Contai

Assemblies	CPI(M)	Congress	Trinamool Congress
Bhagabanpur	-1.1	-11.1	+11.7
Khajuri	+1.7	-2.2	+1.3
Contai (North)	+1.4	-15.1	+13.9
Contai (South)	+1.2	-15.6	+15.4
Ramnagar	-3.5	-5.1	+9.0
Egra	-1.1	-9.2	+10.6
Mugberia	-1.7	-6.1	+9.2
Total	-0.8	-9.5	+9.9

contd.

TABLE 8.5 (contd.)

Nabadwip

Assemblies	CPI(M)	Congress	Trinamool Congress
Nabadwip	+2.7	-5.7	+3.5
Shantipur	+1.0	-6.1	+6.1
Hanskhali	-2.5	-8.5	+11.6
Ranaghat (East)	-3.2	-6.6	+9.8
Ranaghat (West)	-0.3	-3.7	+5.3
Chakdah	+1.2	- 4.7	+4.6
Haringhata	-2.6	-3.8	+6.8
Total	-1.4	-5.4	+7.1

Berhampur

Assemblies	RSP	BJP	Congress
Nadia	-8.0	-10.3	+17.8
Berhampur	-8.3	-27..6	+37.5
Beldanga	-4.1	-10.3	+28.5
Kandi	-5.5	-13.1	+23.1
Barwan	-9.7	-16.1	+25.8
Bharatpur	-9.3	-13.4	+22.1
Ketugram	-6.6	-12.1	+26.8
Total	-6.9	-15.3	+25.4

Raiganj

Assemblies	CPI(M)	Trinamool Congress	Congress
Goalpukhur	+4.1	10.8	+5.1
Karandighi	+3.8	15.6	+6.8
Raiganj	-0.7	20.1	+11.4
Itahar	-2.4	8.9	+4.5
Kharba	-6.0	9.3	+11.4
Harishchandrapur	-0.8	12.1	+6.5
Ratua	-5.5	8.7	+10.2
Total	-0.9	12.6	+8.4

Note: * In the twelfth Lok Sabha elections, the BJP contested on behalf of the Trinamool Congress–BJP combine and captured 17.8 per cent of the total votes, polled.

Sources: Computed from figures available in *West Bengal: a special number on 12th Lok Sabha General Elections, 1998*, Department of Information and Cultural Affairs, Government of West Bengal, 1998. For 1999 figures, see the compilation of the Chief Electoral Officer, Government of West Bengal.

enabled the Trinamool Congress to ensure a majority was the decline of Congress votes, which went in its favour and the outcome was the victory of Nitish Sengupta who contributed to the development of the subdivision during his stint as the Government of India's Finance Secretary. Sengupta won the seat by capturing 48.4 per cent, while his predecessor got only 38.2 per cent in the twelfth elections. The CPI(M) lost the seat only by a margin of 0.4 per cent votes. As evident from Table 8.6, the CPI (M) failed to capture these Lok Sabha seats largely because of the massive swing of the committed Congress, voters for the Mamata Banerjee-led Trinamool Congress, which is gradually emerging as 'a party capable of bringing together the disgruntled Congressmen in West Bengal'.[10]

The LF appears to have lost its grip in some of the urban/semi-urban constituencies, as the tables demonstrate. While the Trinamool Congress–BJP influence was more pronounced in the south Bengal, the Congress performed relatively better in some pockets in north Bengal. However, the trend is slightly reversed in case of Howrah, an industrial town—where the CPI(M) candidate comfortably wrested the seat, captured by the Trinamool Congress in the 1998 elections.[11] Not only did the CPI(M) nominee, Swadesh Chakraborty, win the elections by a comfortable margin, he had also polled 49.9 per cent votes in his favour, which is more than the share of votes of both the Trinamool Congrees and the Congress candidates. The Howrah outcome is also remarkable because, unlike the 1998 elections in which the CPI(M) lost in all the Assembly constituencies, the 1999 figures show

TABLE 8.6: HOWRAH

Assemblies	CPI(M)	Congress	Trinamool Congress
Bally	+10.0	-4.0	-6.8
Howrah (North)	+17.5	-5.5	-11.1
Howrah (Central)	+3.1	-2.4	+0.6
Howrah (South)	+11.4	-8.6	-2.0
Shibpur	+5.3	-2.8	-2.2
Domjur	+4.1	-3.8	+1.0
Sankrail	+0.1	-2.6	+4.6
Total	+8.1	-3.8	-3.1

Source: Computed from the figures compiled by the Chief Electoral Officer, Government of West Bengal.

a clear victory in all including the Howrah Central Assembly constituency, which was considered to be the stronghold of Trinamool Congress. As the Table 8.6 indicates, both the major rivals, Congress and Trinamool Congress suffered a setback, showing probably the CPI(M) success in retaining its traditional support base among the workers.

Table 8.6 is illustrative of the phenomenal growth of CPI(M), particularly in the urban areas, at the cost of both the Congress and Trinamool Congress. One of the probable explanations lies in the consistent effort of the CPI(M) local leadership to win back its supporters by streamlining the party organization in those areas within the Howrah municipality where industrial workers constitute a sizeable section of local population. The sudden CPI(M) popularity is also due to the failure of the Trinamool Congress to sustain its newly acquired base in the district. The former MP was blamed for being 'an absentee MP' who was not only unavailable to the district population during his term but was also blamed for his inability to bring back the glory of Howrah as an industrial centre.[12] The CPI(M) certainly had an edge over the Trinamool Congress at the outset since its candidate is a Howrah domicile, while Kakali Ghosh Dastidar of the Trinamool Congress, was 'an elite politician belonging to Calcutta's upper strata' who was 'trying to reach the hinterland'. Her nomination for such a prestigious parliamentary constituency was attributed to her proximity with the Trinamool Congress supremo, Mamata Banerjee, despite vehement opposition from the local activists.[13]

THE LEFT FRONT AND THE POLL OUTCOME

Election results and governmental performance are not the only indicators of the success of a LF government in West Bengal; but they are nonetheless central to any viable strategy. Whereas 'the anti-incumbency' factor drastically reduced the numerical strength of the party in power in Rajasthan and Madhya Pradesh, it hardly had any noticeable impact in West Bengal. Hence, it is hard to resist the conclusion that the LF has successfully geared 'the bourgeois state power' to its advantage by undertaking plans and programmes for the benefit of the majority.[14] Disillusioned with the LF, the urban voters in the state articulated their opposition clearly by ensuring an almost complete wash-out of the Front in Calcutta and its vicinity. What irks and disheartens ordinary people is the steady decline of urban services, including electricity and transport. The most disturbing factor that decisively swung the verdict against the Front is the nexus between 'ruling party leaders, big and small, and those out to make a fast buck by bending the power of the government and the party in their own direction (and) . . . the growing realization that those in power are too busy to reap the fruits of their own dominance to care for what happens to others'.[15] Whatever the consequence of the growing resentment of the urban populace, the fact remains that 'the LF government [is] providing a service to the status quo by handling a problematic state better than the Congress could have done'.[16] Hence, the LF experiment is a failure, either from the point of view of a transition to socialism or the development of a specific type of capitalism drawing upon liberalization.[17]

The situation is not as extreme or dismal as some of the political commentators seem to think. Its achievement in the rural areas in particular—its land reform measures, the registration of sharecroppers (operation *barga*), the panchayati system—has ushered in a significant process of radical changes in the political layout of the state.[18] Much of the economic change in rural West Bengal since 1977 has been made possible because of a significant political process, initiated and carried forward by the LF government. Important here has been the devolution of power—including considerable financial powers—to the elected panchayats. This step, together with a strong political commitment to implementing land reforms, has ensured a process of genuine democratic participation by the rural poor in the remaking of their lives and their socio-economic environment. Although the enactment of the Seventy-third Amendment Act is a significant step towards revamping the panchayati institutions in the country, the LF initiated the process as early as 1977-80 by giving pachanyats substantial power for local development.[19] Since the programmes for poverty alleviation, sponsored by New Delhi or other agencies, have been closely supervised through the party hierarchy, they are better implemented in West Bengal than in any other states. Such a supervisory role has developed and sustained a constant interaction with the people at the grassroots which, *inter alia*, accounts for the consolidation of the LF in rural Bengal. Furthermore, with its long tradition of political mass mobilization and struggles—in championing the cause of the working class, urban and rural workers, the poor peasants, and the middle-class employees—the

LF has not only sustained but also gradually expanded its organizational network within the state.[20]

Apart from its land reform programmes, the LF appears to have created a permanent base in both urban and rural areas by drawing upon the federal arrangement, which is tilted in favour of the centre. As the states have to depend largely on financial grants from the centre for most of their developmental plans, they are reduced to mere structural units of a union 'that cannot be federal simply because it is rooted in the imperial 1935 Government of India Act'.[21] There are constitutionally-approved agencies that add to the process of concentration of power in the central government. For instance, the Planning Commission is a centralizing agency with hegemonic control over the finances. The Governor is another, acting largely on behalf of the central government. Seeking to review the centre-state relations, the LF government undertook a campaign when it came to power in 1977. One of the outcomes of this campaign was certainly the appointment of the Sarkaria Commission in 1980. The issue of the centre-state relations has however gradually lost its significance in the LF poll campaign presumably because none of the post-1989 central governments had the numercial strength in the Lok Sabha to completely ignore the state governments. The situation appears to be favouable for a thorough review of the centre-state relations with the installation of a coalition government at the centre following the 1999 Lok Sabha poll in which the support of the constituent regional parties is crucial for its survival.

Furthermore, the success of the LF parties in elections is also attributed to a well-tuned election machinery. During the election campaign, the structure elaborately shown in Table 8.7 is created to effectively mobilize voters for the LF, which is probably unmatched in any other electoral democracy in the world. Managed by the full-time party cadres, these committees play crucial roles both in the selection of the candidates for the Assembly segments as well as in the campaign during the elction. Operating within sepecified geographical boundaries, the activities of these committees are coordinated by the district committee, the apex body in the district, which is put under the state-level committee, located in Kolkata. Although during the elections their activities are geared towards the elections, they continue to function even in the aftermath of elections as permanent local units of the LF parties, involved in day-to-day life of the people living in

TABLE 8.7: ELECTION COMMITTEE FOR ASSEMBLY SEGMENT

Urban Areas	Rural Areas
Ward Committees	Area Committee
Booth Committees	*Anchal* Committee
Station or Sub-Station	Branch Committee
Street-in-Charge	Booth Committee
Campaign Workers	Campaign Units for groups of households

Source: Available from District Committee, south Kolkata.

particular localities. In other words, they continue to remain as the link between the localities and the provincial party machinery, which provides the basic input to the LF government in adopting the appropriate policies.

The CPI (M)'s reformist orientation has enabled it to pursue some 'redistributive programmes'[22] without fundamentally alienating property-owning productive groups. As a system of governance, panchayats have radically altered the structure of power in rural West Bengal where 70 per cent of the state's population live. With the presence of the LF activists in every key institutions at the grassroots—ranging from the governing bodies of credit societies to the primary schools—the government has been able to build and sustain a well-entrenched network among the rural population. This has led to the consolidation of what is identified as 'governmental locality' that signifies 'the presence of government in a locality as an institution (and also) locality's presence in government as a process'. Such governmetalization of rural localities has 'generated a new and innovative corespondence within and between village representative bodies and tied them with the Assembly House and the Writers' Buildings'.[23] In such a symbiotic network between the villagers and the Front activists[24] lies the explanation as to why the LF retains its grip in rural West Bengal without any substantial dents.

A TENTATIVE EXPLANATION OF POLL RESULTS

The uninterrupted rule for 23 years by a popularly elected LF coalition led by CPI(M) within the broader socio-economic constraint of a transitional society and India's federal structure has few parallels even today. As a political arrangement, the coalition continues to remain viable though the loss of nine parliamentary seats is too significant to wish it away. One general explanation draws upon 'the anti-incumbency' factor that largely accounts for the massive reversal in Rajasthan, Madhya Pradesh, Tamil Nadu, and Maharastra.[25] Only 2 per cent loss of popular votes may not prove the contention when something as substantial as 47 per cent votes are clearly for the Left coalition. What it demonstrates, however, is the failure of the ruling parties in power to effectively project its sincerity and commitment to those in urban areas. This is well-demonstrated in voting figures from Kolkata and its vicinity. In fact, the drastic reduction of Congress votes (almost by two-thirds) is what largely explains the dramatic performance of the Trinamool Congress in the poll. By harping on a rather unacceptable treatment, meted out by the national leadership of the Congress towards the most popular Congress leader in the state, Mamata Banerjee, the new political formation succeeded in translating the vindictiveness of the central leadership (which upheld the views of those provincial Congress leaders without effective support base[26]) into votes. The scene was not very different in 1999 when 'the Mamata wave'[27] continued to be decisive in the poll outcome and the Trinamool Congress captured more seats than the Congress tally. Whereas CPI(M) got 2 per cent less votes in comparison with its share of 47 per cent votes in 1998, the share of its other coalition partners, CPI, Forward Bloc and Revolutionary Socialist Party, diminished to the tune of approximately 3 per cent within a span of one year. A constituency-wise analysis of the data in Table 8.8 offers a better grasp of the situation by underlining 'the swing factor' that determined the poll outcome.

As is evident, the reverses came mainly in the Kolkata urban area and its outskirts. Out of forty-two seats, the LF coalition gained, in terms of votes, only in eight constituencies, which are primarily rural. Not only were the three Kolkata seats lost to the Trinamool Congress, the rout of CPI(M) in the 'heartland' of urban industrial centres, Dum Dum, Jadavpur, and Srirampur, suggested that the working class seemed to have withdrawn their support as well. Furthermore, the decline of LF votes in Contai, Berhampur, and Nabadwip clearly demonstrated substantial dents in the Front's rural base. How does one account for this pattern in the poll outcome? Several tentative explanations can be offered.

TABLE 8.8: COMPARATIVE PERFORMANCE OF THE LEFT FRONT CONSTITUENTS IN 1998 AND 1999 LOK SABHA POLLS

Predominantly Urban Constituencies	% of Votes 1998 & 1999	% of Swing	Won (W) or Lost (L)	Name of the political party (LF Constituents)
Asansol	46.38, 41.09	-1.52	W	CPI(M)
Barrackpur	49.54, 46.01	-0.76	W	CPI(M)
Kolkata (north-east)	41.93, 37.26	-0.88	L	CPI(M)
Kolkata (north-west)	33.55, 33.17	-5.13	L	CPI(M)
Kolkata (south)	40.14, 32.95	-7.18	L	CPI(M)
Dum Dum	39.66	+1.20	L	CPI(M)
Durgapur (SC)*	40.29, 55.68	-3.87	W	CPI(M)
	51.81			
Hooghly	49.31, 46.25	-3.05	W	CPI(M)
Howrah	42.54, 49.98	+8.10	W	CPI(M)
Jadavpur	46.17, 41.45	-4.70	L	CPI(M)
Srirampur	45.87, 40.14	-5.74	L	CPI(M)
Predominantly Rural Constituencies				
Alipurduar (ST)*	53.11	-4.07	W	RSP
	51.47	-3.43	W	CPI(M)
Arambag	59.57	-0.10	W	RSP
Balurghat (SC)*	56.15			
	49.02			
	48.90			
Bankura	56.24	-3.57	W	CPI(M)
Barasat	49.42	-3.49	L	Forward Bloc
Bashirhat	46.24	-2.81	W	CPI
Behrampur	40.83	-6.92	L	RSP
	50.63			
	48.85			
	44.46			
	36.55			
Birbhum (SC)*	50.35, 49.06	-0.55	W	CPI(M)
Bolpur	60.55, 59.55	-0.99	W	CPI(M)
Bardhaman	59.92	-1.04	W	CPI(M)
Coochbehar (SC)*	58.88	+2.43	W	FBL[++]
	42.22			
	43.77			
Contai	47.80, 46.95	-0.84	L	CPI(M)
Darjeeling	45.91, 44.75	+4.80	W	CPI(M)
Diamond Harbor	47.37, 45.97	-0.98	W	CPI(M)
Jalpaiguri	48.70, 49.12	-0.54	W	CPI(M)
Jangipur	44.04, 47.94	+3.91	W	CPI(M)
Jhargram (ST)[+]	60.29	-3.50	W	CPI(M)
	56.78	+7.50	W	RSP

(contd.)

TABLE 8.8 (contd.)

Joynagar (SC)*	48.17			
	48.48			
Katwa	50.46, 49.47	-0.99	W	CPI(M)
Krishnanagar	42.03, 41.16	-0.30	L	CPI(M)
Maldah	38.29, 36.52	-1.76	L	CPI(M)
Mathurapur (SC)*	48.10	-0.56	W	RSP
	46.50	-3.61	W	CPI
Midnapur	56.29			
	52.75			
Murshidabad	46.51, 49.96	+3.46	W	CPI(M)
Nabadwip (SC)*	43.04	-1.42	L	CPI(M)
	41.93	+0.06	W	CPI
Panskura	54.82	-1.09	W	Forward Bloc
Purulia	54.82			
	54.88			
	51.02			
	51.27			
Raiganj	39.76, 38.14	-8.60	L	CPI(M)
Tamluk	47.82, 51.24	+3.82	W	CPI(M)
Uluberia	49.07, 47.51	-0.97	W	CPI(M)
Vishnupur (SC)*	58.14, 56.79	+0.53	W	CPI(M)

Notes: * Scheduled Caste, + Scheduled Tribe.

Sources: Computed from the figures available from *West Bengal: a special number on 12th Lok Sabha Elections, 1998*, Department of Information and Cultural Affairs, Government of West Bengal, March-April 1998, pp. 83-7; for the 1999 figures, see the compilation of the Chief Electoral Officer, Government of West Bengal.

First, what probably affected the urban sensibilities most seriously is the irresponsible utterances against Mamata Banerjee as being 'a 420', 'a cheat and a liar', 'a fake doctorate' from an octogenarian patriarch like Joyti Basu.[28] Similarly, the CPI(M) characterization of the BJP as 'barbaric', 'beastly' and 'uncivilized' did not take the Front any further in the absence of a clearly spelt-out political programme to counter the so-called anti-secular bogey. Even the grass-root party workers expressed dismay at the way the leadership conducted the poll campaign. Instead of explaining the BJP as a phenomenon and the probable consequences of a BJP government in Delhi, the strategy of mere verbal castigation was certain to fail in Kolkata and its outskirts where the most articulate and politically aware section of the Bengalis live.[29]

Second, an equally significant factor was the deterioration of civic life in urban areas which seemed to have been aggravated by the rapid decay of transport particularly in Calcutta and severe crisis of electricity and potable water in its outskirts. It is true that the improvement of transport and power generation plants involves costs for which the LF government has to depend on centre's discretion and therefore no drastic change can be made without central government's concurrence. However justified is the blame on the centre, a majority of urban voters seem, as the poll results illustrate, unwilling to attribute this entirely to the central government.

The situation is equally dismal in several other most important aspects of social and political life, namely, health, and education. Despite good doctors and other health workers around, the decay in the basic services is appalling. Moreover, the growing practice of according priority to those with recommendations by the local party activists for treatment in the government hospitals alienated a large number of committed voters, leave alone non-committed ones, who found, in this, a deliberate effort to marginalize those opposed to the Front.[30] Moreover, as confirmed party sources suggested, the LF policy of completely eliminating English up to Standard V in schools contributed to the erosion of its support among the urban middle class.[31] Even as regards recruitment of teachers, from primary to the university level, merit is at a discount and what appears to be decisive in most cases is the approval of the CPI(M) high command in the state.[32]

The gradual decay of civic amenities such as maintenance of roads and regular clearing of street garbage also consolidated the opposition to the Front in urban areas. Neither the Kolkata Municipal Corporation nor other Municipal bodies in the outskirts of Kolkata made any significant impact on the minds of urban voters as significant and effective civic institutions. What alienated the Kolkata voters from the LF was probably the failure of the government to halt the decline of Kolkata as a metropolis. Kolkata ceased to be the centre of activity and its decay is slow but obvious. The process began with the Naxalite movement and the violence introduced in the field of labour by the policy of *gherao* under the two United Front governments (1967-70). The flight of capital ensured that fewer jobs were available and the well-planned design to cripple academic institutions like Presidency College led to the brighter among students and teachers migrating elsewhere, mainly to Delhi. What replaced them, however, was not 'a great sense of proletarian cultural revolution, but a feeling of frustration and bitterness and perhaps a sense of having missed the bus in every respect—the bus of communism and also of capitalism'.[33] Even the decree that English will not be taught till Class VI is seen as a deliberate move to cripple the Bengali middle class, which will be at an disadvantage *vis-à-vis* others, in jobs outside West Bengal.[34] The domestic job market is not very encouraging either. The younger voters in particular have thus become hostile presumably because of rapidly shrinking job opportunities in the state. Since these voters do not have any political memory of state repression, prevalent in the late 1960s and early 1970s, they are not emotionally attached to the LF as an ideological force.

Third, one of the persuasive reasons for the diminishing popularity of the LF government is certainly its failure to accomplish the promised industrial resurgence in the state. Notwithstanding open invitation to the MNCs following the adoption of a highly liberal industrial policy, the inability of the Front government to reverse the industrial decline or even to mitigate the stagnation after more than two decades of being in power has caused serious disenchantment with it among a large section of urban population.[35] The nodal agency for industrial regeneration, West Bengal Industrial Development Corporation (WBIDC), headed by the CPI(M) MP, Somnath Chatterjee, has apparently failed to bring about any noticeable impact on the industrial front. The fanfare with which the WBIDC was hailed was short-lived since, till March 1997, eighteen of the twenty-six projects were shelved after having spent almost Rs. 12 million. During 1996-7, the loss of the Corporation was as much Rs. 120 million, though its chairman did not stop undertaking expensive foreign visits presumably to attract the MNCs to the state.[36] Furthermore, the industrial scene is equally devastated due to reasons connected with mindless crude economism, engineered primarily by the CPI(M) leadership. Far from industrial rejuvenation in the state, frequent closure of factories, and consequently retrenchment of a large number of workers eroded the support base of the left coalition substantially.[37] In such a milieu, the comfortable BJP victory in an industrial suburb like Dum Dum does not seem to be astonishing.

THE PROSPECT OF THE COALITION

Although the overall electoral performance of the LF in the urban areas may have indicated its decline the victory in a majority of the rural constituencies has nonetheless conclusively proved otherwise.[38] Of the two predominantly rural seats, Maldah has traditionally been a Congress stronghold area, while Barasat, which has been held by the Left till the 1996 elections, indicates an erosion of its rural support. But given the number of seats retained by the coalition, the Barasat result is indicative rather than a substantive trend. Whatever the explanation of this particular outcome, the overall results in rural Bengal definitely demonstrated that the majority of rural votes were still with the LF. Here comes the success of the Left agrarian programme[39] emphasizing distribution of ceiling-surplus land to the landless, operation *barga* and supporting agricultural wage movements. Furthermore, the introduction of a new popular institution in the form of the three-tier panchayati system involving participation of political parties led to qualitative changes in the attitudes and self-confidence of the majority of poor, landless, low caste peasants and agricultural workers in their day-to-day interaction with the wealthy and landed gentry. Following the installation of the LF government in 1977, a radical change took place in some of the most critical aspects of relations between classes in rural Bengal.[40] There is no doubt that much of what was accomplished since 1977 was possible mainly because of the political character of the government, which successfully geared the legislative and administrative machinery for the benefit of the largest section of the population.

The defeat of the Front candidates in predominantly urban constituencies was undoubtedly a jolt to the leadership. The CPI(M) West Bengal unit was probably paying the price of remaining in power for such a long stint. Those who wielded public influence and shaped policy were not ideologues or mass leaders, but those in government offices. Furthermore, the government decision, on most occasions, was largely the product of inputs, provided by the solaced Local Committees (LCs) that became parallel centres of power in the localities. These LCs held so much power that the government officer appeared peripheral in the administration.[41] At the grass-roots, this means the panchayat office-holder's ability to dole out favours replaced the local

TABLE 8.9: DISTRIBUTION OF VOTES IN THE 1998 PANCHAYAT ELECTIONS

(*in per cent*)

	Left Front	Congress	Trinamool Congress	BJP
Gram Panchayat	55.9 (64.3)	11.9 (26.7)	20.1 (-)	7.7 (3.9)
Panchayat Samiti	64.9 (72.7)	9.5 (22.9)	18.9 (-)	3.6 (1.9)
Zila Parishad	89.2 (87.3)	4.3 (10.9)	5.4 (-)	0.2 (0.0)

Sources: *The Telegraph*, 2 and 3 June 1998; *Ananda Bazar Patrika*, 1 May and 5 June 1998.

party leader's talent to mobilize people. This bred manipulators and backroom tacticians, not leaders. Given the general trend, it was too early to judge whether this jolt was a significant milestone in coalition politics in West Bengal and also whether the recent victory of CPI(M) in two[42] out of three Assembly seats proved little. But the 1998 panchayat elections ensuring majority of seats for the LF[43] indicate that the red bastion was as strong as before despite the rising consolidation of the opposition parties, as Table 8.9 shows that the Front succeeded in capturing an overwhelming majority reinforced its useful role in making the government resources available for the less privileged in society. This well-organized, reform-oriented ruling coalition has thus undertaken a different kind of project in which the well-being of the people is what is sought. By sincerely following a well-articulated social democratic agenda, the left coalition has created a stable constituency which on the whole has remained in tact despite occasional hicc ups here and there. As a well-organized coalition of parties with a clear electoral mandate, the LF was able to create and sustain a cohesive government that in itself is unique given the failure of other coalition experiments both at the centre and various provinces.

CONCLUDING OBSERVATIONS

Except for eighteen months in 1975-7, India has maintained its democratic institutions ever since it attained freedom in 1947. What has baffled the theorists of democracy is its growing strength despite circumstances, which are not at all congenial for its survival, let alone continuity.[44] What further fascinates the analysts is that 'despite the steady erosion of democratic institutions . . . (India) continues to stand as the most surprising and important case of democratic endurance in the developing world'.[45] Elections are held regularly and peaceful transfers of power between rival political parties have occurred seven times at the central and many more at the state/provincial levels. Since 1967, the party that ruled in New Delhi has not ruled in nearly half of the states. Since 1977, the incumbent governments have repeatedly been defeated in elections. Illustrative of the extent to which democratic practices like elections are well-entrenched, not only is the trend well-set, it has also contributed immensely to the consolidation of democracy at the grass-roots.

The 1999 election was another significant milestone in India's journey as a democracy. What was initiated in West Bengal in 1967 and at the centre in 1977 was further reinforced, if not strengthened, in 1999 with the formation of a coalition government of disparate parties at the national level.[46] There are clear indications that India is heading towards a coalition era.[47] West Bengal is being ruled uninterruptedly for the last twenty-three years by a coalition of Left political parties that is both 'stable and mature'[48] probably because of acceptable plans and programmes. Notwithstanding some kind of loose ideological affinity among the LF constituents, what has primarily sustained the coalition is the numerical majority of CPI(M) which, with almost two-thirds Assembly seats, is able to form the government in West Bengal without the support of other constituents. Table 8.10 clearly shows that since 1977 the CPI(M) has consistently retained an absolute majority in the West Bengal Legislative Assembly.

Despite the loss of as many as thirty seats in comparison with its tally in 1987, the leading partner of the LF, CPI(M), still holds the majority in the Assembly. The withdrawal of support by other coalition partners, including the CPI, Forward Bloc and RSP, shall therefore make no difference to the dominant party within the coalition. This is probably one of the formidable reasons cementing the bond between the CPI(M) and other coalition partners that know that their existence as political forces depends largely on being associated with the leading party of the coalition. For the CPI(M), the decision to lead the coalition government stems from its commitment to champion the left cause,[49] articulated through radical programmes and policies involving people at large.

Despite a clear polarization between urban and rural voters, the 1999 West Bengal poll results reconfirm the popularity of the Left coalition at the grass-roots. On the basis of evidence, it seems likely

TABLE 8.10: NUMBER OF SEATS, WON BY DIFFERENT POLITICAL PARTIES IN THE WEST BENGAL ASSEMBLY ELECTIONS, 1977-96

Parties	1977	1982	1987	1991	1996
CPI(M)	178 (35.4)	174 (38.4)	187 (39.3)	182 (35.3)	157 (37.9)
Forward Bloc	26 (5.3)	28 (6.1)	26 (5.8)	29 (5.2)	21 (5.2)
RSP	20 (3.7)	19 (4.0)	18 (3.9)	18 (3.5)	18 (3.7)
CPI	02 (2.6)	07 (1.80)	11 (1.9)	06 (1.7)	06 (1.7)
Others*	06 (1.8)	10 (1.8)	09 (1.8)	10 (1.8)	10 (1.9)
Congress	20 (23.3)	49 (35.6)	40 (41.6)	47 (35.2)	82 (39.5)

Notes: Figures in the parenthesis show the percentage of votes, polled by the parties.
* Others include those small parties within the Left Front that contested the West Bengal Assembly elections with different symbols and election manifestos.

Sources: Computed from data available in the following documents: For 1977, 1982, 1987 and 1991 figures, see *Election Results in West Bengal: statistics and analysis, 1952-91*, CPI(M), West Bengal State Committee, 1995, pp. 8, 306-8 and for 1996 figures, *Election Commission of India, General Elections, 1996 to the Legislative Assembly of West Bengal, 1997*, p. 14.

that what decided the election was not a positive vote for the Trinamool Congress–BJP combination but a negative one against the state government. The formation of the Trinamool Congress and its electoral pact with the BJP provided a forum for those opposed to the LF. The forum became apparently strong probably because of the charisma that had built around Mamata Banerjee. This sustains, if not strengthens, the possibility that the CPI(M)-led front can rebuild its urban support base by paying adequate attention to the grievances of the city dwellers. Since industrial regeneration depends partly on the central government's discretion in granting industrial licenses and partly on the industrialists'/ or other MNCs, willingness to invest in West Bengal, the LF is practically left with no choice. In an already handicapped situation, the consistently declining industrial employment opportunities and labour retrenchment necessitated by strikes and lockouts, have rendered the LF and CPI (M) trade union, Centre for Indian Trade Union (CITU) in particular, unpopular with the labour. Industrial population in West Bengal comprised one-third of the total urban votes which is not very significant given the massive number of rural votes. The fact that the LF has retained a majority of rural votes despite a wave for the Trinamool Congress–BJP alliance, demonstrates that the rural masses by and large are still with the left. Therefore fears that the coalition is becoming 'marginal' much less 'moribund'[50] political force do not seem to be justified by the evidence.

NOTES

* I am thankful to J. Sirkar, IAS, the Chief Electoral Officer, Government of West Bengal, for having allowed me access to 1999 (parliamentary) elections data concerning West Bengal.

1. Editorial, *The Telegraph*, Calcutta, 17 April 1998.
2. The coalition government that assumed power following the 1999 national poll is not entirely different in its composition from the one that captured power in New Delhi after the 1998 elections. The future of the coalition is as uncertain as before in view of the diverse nature of the partners and the fact that the BJP does not command a parliamentary majority and, more fundamentally, the party itself is trapped between its Hindu-nationalist core and the moderation it must assume to govern peacefully and effectively. While this may not be totally unfounded, the fact that none of the national parties succeeded in winning an absolute majority in three consecutive elections since 1996 shows clearly the direction in which Indian polity is going.
3. For the first time since 1977, the CPI and CPI(M) failed to win a single seat from Bihar, which regularly returned candidates fielded by the communist parties. In terms of votes polled, the two major communist parties polled only 4 per cent of the popular votes in 1998 (while their share in 1996 elections was as much 10 per cent).
4. The history of the coalition of the left parties in West Bengal can be traced back to 1967 when a tenuous coalition of the left parties with breakaway Congress groups formed the government in the state. The coalition government did not last long due to internal squabbles. What followed the 1969 elections was similar since the United Front constituents also failed to provide a stable coalition government in the state. The 1977 elections ushered in an era of stable coalition, led by the CPI(M) with two-third seats in the state assembly. Barring ideological considerations and an endeavour to try a new experiment, one of the reasons for the continuity of the LF since 1977 is probably the numerical majority of the CPI(M) that is capable of forming the government on its own strength. As a well-organized party with a clear electoral mandate, the CPI(M) was able to provide a stable and cohesive government. Organizational discipline also enabled the party to limit elite factionalism and the elite-initiated political conflicts that generally follow. For a subjective assessment of the situation, see Partha Chaterjee, *The Present History of West Bengal: essays in political criticism*, New Delhi: Oxford University Press, 1997, pp. 190-2.
5. As the following table shows, during the period of twenty-two years (1977-99), the 1989 Lok Sabha poll sent a maximum of 27 CPI(M) candidates to the Lok

Sabha, while the thirteenth national poll is probably the LF's worst electoral performance.

Year	Leading party	Seats won	Runner up	Seats won (% vote)
1977	CPI(M)	20 (26.2)	BLD	15 (21.5)
1980	CPI(M)	28 (39.9)	Congress	04 (36.5)
1984	CPI(M)	18 (35.9)	Congress	16 (48.2)
1989	CPI(M)	27 (38.4)	Congress	04 (41.4)
1991	CPI(M)	27 (35.2)	Congress	05 (36.2)
1996	CPI(M)	23 (36.7)	Congress	09 (40.1)
1998	CPI(M)	24 (35.4)	Trinamool Congress	07 (24.4)
1999	CPI(M)	21 (35.5)	Trinamool Congress	08 (26.0)

Sources: *Statistical Handbook: Parliamentary Election in West Bengal, 1991-1998*, Office of the Chief Electoral Officer, West Bengal, 1998. For the 1999 figures, see the compilation of the Chief Electoral Officer, Government of West Bengal, 1999.

6. The decline is attributed to 'organizational failure' apart from the alienation of the new generation of voters. As a senior CPI(M) leader candidly admits, 'the new generation of voters is not supporting the Left Front'. (*The Telegraph*, Calcutta, 9 October 1999). The explanation appears plausible since a generation that has grown up seeing the LF at the helm of the state as long as it can remember is unlikely to be forgiving for its 'neglect' and 'highhandedness'. Equally and naturally, it would want a change.
7. Praful Bidwai has sought a detailed exposition of the phenomenon of the decline of the Left in the 1998 elections. See his 'Through the looking glass, darkly . . .', *Seminar*, no. 465, May 1998, pp. 24-9.
8. The Trinamool Congress came into existence following the rustication of Mamata Banerjee from the Congress (I) for her alleged anti-Congress activities. Drawing upon Mamata's emotional appeal as a firebrand and the most outspoken leader of West Bengal, the party was hailed as an alternative to the LF. The provincial Congress suffered a jolt when, as a result of split, a few of its prominent members including MLAs and MPs joined the Mamata-led political outfit.
9. The BJP adopted as its primary theme the idea of 'a Bengal first' politics rather than promoting any overriding national considerations. As a result, the party placed great emphasis on the issue of illegal Bangladeshi 'infiltration' into West Bengal and the impact of this influx on unemployment, pressure on resources, illegal trade, crime, and social tensions. For a comprehensive discussion on the BJP's style and the issues it harped upon in the context of West Bengal, see Michael Gillan, 'BJP in 1998: Lok Sabha Elections in West Bengal', *Economic and Political Weekly*, 5-12 September 1998, pp. 2391-5.

10. Interviews with the voters in these constituencies during the 1999 election campaign. Furthermore, there was a massive influx of Congressmen, both leaders and those at the grassroots to the Trinamool Congress immediately after its emergence with the hope that its leader, Mamata Banerjee, would galvanize those associated with the 'moribund' Congress into action against the well-entrenched CPI(M) and its partners in the Left Front. For details, see Bidyut Chakrabarty, 'The all time sure bet; Mamata Banerjee', *Women in Politics: knocking at the male bastion*, ed. Suchita Kaushik, New Delhi: National Commission for Women, 1998, pp. 51-66.
11. The CPI(M) candidate lost the Howrah seat by a narrow margin of just 6,535 votes. The poll outcome in 1998 swung in favour of the Trinamool Congress candidate who secured only 0.6 per cent more votes than his CPI(M) rival. See, *Statistical Handbook: Parliamentary Elections in West Bengal*, Office of the Chief Electoral Officer, Government of West Bengal, 1998, p. 24.
12. During the 1998 Lok Sabha poll, the Trinamool Congress election campaign revolved around the pledge of re-establishing Howrah as a leading industrial centre in the east. One of the reasons for denying nomination to the sitting MP, Bikram Sarkar, was the charge that he never visited the constituency after the elections nor did he support the effort of the grass-roots Trinamool Congress workers to build an organization on the basis of the favourable outcome of the 1998 poll.
13. Although she was supported by Mamata Banerjee, the Trinamool Congress candidate did not receive the cooperation of the workers during the 1999 election campaign. Critical of Banerjee's decision of nominating an outsider for the constituency, a large number of newly recruited Trinamool Congress members remained either totally aloof from the campaign or openly supported the CPI(M) candidate presumably because of his local roots. It will therefore not be an exaggeration to argue that 'sabotage' from within the party was one of the major factors for the defeat.
14. Instead of making empty promises, Jyoti Basu, the state Chief Minister and the LF leader, articulated the goal of his government as follows: 'The aim of our programmes is to alleviate the sufferings of the rural and urban people and to improve their conditions to a certain extent. We do not claim anything more, as we are aware that without structural changes in the socio-economic order, it is hardly possible to bring about any basic change in the conditions of the people'. See the foreword by Jyoti Basu in *Left Front Government in West Bengal: eight years,* Department of Information and Cultural Affairs, Government of West Bengal, 1985, pp. i-ii.
15. Partha Chatterjee, *The Present History of West Bengal: essays in political criticism*, New Delhi: Oxford University Press, 1997, p. 136.
16. Ross Mallick, *Indian Communism, Opposition, Collaboration and Institutionalization*, New Delhi: Oxford University Press, 1994, p. 239.
17. Supporting the contention, Ross Mallick strongly argues that '(w)ith neither

socialism nor capitalism developing, West Bengal fell economically behind more dynamic business-oriented states. Communist work methods had undermined socialist and capitalist development, both of which required productivity reforms and efficient allocation of resources, rather than electoral patronage'. See Ross Mallick, *Development Policy of a Communist Government: West Bengal since 1977*, Cambridge: Cambridge University Press, 1993, p. 219.

18. For a sympathetic account of the LF rule, see Atul Kohli, *Democracy and Discontent: India's crisis of governability*, Cambridge: Cambridge University Press, 1991, pp. 267-96.
19. Articulating the views of those who are critical of the West Bengal panchayats, Poromesh Acharya argues that '(n)o doubt, there emerged a new generation of leadership in rural West Bengal but the class and caste background of the new leadership' remain more or less unchanged. 'There developed a new institutional structure, decentralized in form but still dominated by the middle and rich peasants. The agricultural labourers and poor peasants, though not in proportion, have their representatives in the new structure but their participation in the decision making process is still a far cry'. See Poromesh Acharya, 'Panchayats and left politics in West Bengal', *Economic and Political Weekly*, 29 May 1993, p. 1080.
20. Attributing the unparalleled success of the LF in every election in West Bengal since 1977 to an all-pervasive party organization, Partha Chatterjee argues that the consistent performance of the LF 'has a great deal to do with elaborateness, intricacy, and discipline of the CPI(M)'s organization in its campaign to mobilize votes'. Apart from this, the CPI(M) also utilized a parallel structure consisting of units from its mass front organizations, more often the cultural front units. What sustains the party is its discipline, which is reinforced through the electoral process. Thus, even from the perspective of the vote-getting machine, it is not as if campaign issues and political debate are irrelevant. They are 'relevant because without them the machine cannot be fed with the political support which it can convert into votes'. See Partha Chatterjee, *The Present History of West Bengal: essays in political criticism*, New Delhi: Oxford University Press, 1997, pp. 141, 151, and 157.
21. B.T. Randive, 'The Sarkaria Commission Report: empty rhetoric', *The Marxist*, vol. 6, January-March 1988, p. 19.
22. The best though slightly dated account of the redistributive programmes is articulated in Atul Kohli, *The State and Poverty in India: the politics of reform*, Cambridge: Cambridge University Press, 1987.
23. While explaining the success of the LF in rural West Bengal as compared with its performance in urban areas, Dwaipayan Bhattacharyya adopts this line of argument, which is probably plausible given performance of the Front in rural constituencies. See Dwaipayan Bhattacharyya, 'Ominous outcome for left in West Bengal', *Economic and Political Weekly*, 20 November 1999. pp. 3268-9.

24. For an in-depth study of this symbiotic network underlying the agrarian changes in West Bengal in a comparative perspective, see Ben Rogaly et al. (eds.), *Sonar Bangla: agricultural growth and agrarian change in West Bengal and Bangladesh*, New Delhi: Sage, 1999.
25. Seats won by various political parties in 1998 in four states:

	Congress	BJP	AIDMK	DMK	Shiv Sena
Madhya Pradesh	11 (40)	29 (40)			
Rajasthan	09 (25)	16 (25)			
Tamil Nadu	02 (15)	04 (11)	11 (22)	12 (17)	
Maharastra	10 (41)	13 (25)			15 (22)

Note: Figures in the parenthesis show the number of candidates fielded by these parties.

Source: *The Times of India*, New Delhi, 9 October 1999.

26. The decision of the Sitaram Kesari-led Congress High Command to endorse the views of those who held positions in the Bengal Provincial Congress articulated the devastating and obvious consequences of the age-old factionalism within the state unit of the party. Ignoring the views of an effective Congress leader like Mamata Banerjee on a large number of substantial issues, including the preparation of the election manifesto and selection of candidates for the 1998 Lok Sabha poll, the central leadership completely misread the situation in West Bengal in which the party fared well in the 1996 election.
27. The rallying point of political disenchantment in the state has been Mamata Banerjee. The significance is paradoxical for the LF since short on ideology but rather long on symbolism, Mamata Banerjee's persona consistently portrayed the image of a very simple leader whose style of politics is clearly different from the elitist parameters. Through populist imageries she could effectively work herself into the very coalition of the lower and middle strata that the Left had so assiduously built for itself and which, thanks to the Left have come to believe that they are active participants on democracy and the welfare of the state. Furthermore, she deployed the militant modes of protest so favourite with the Left until recently, to combat the Left. In her activist gear, she is none but 'one of us' for millions swayed by the dreams of her Bengal package. Besides the image of an uncompromising anti-establishment leader, she has succeeded in projecting herself as an honest and a leader capable of fighting the 'corruption' and 'high handedness' of the LF leaders and cadres.
28. Even some of the hard-core CPI(M) activists, leave alone sympathizers, condemned the personal vilification of Mamata Banerjee who never indulged in personally attacking her poll opponents. The prominent dailies, *The Telegraph* and *Ananda Bazar Patrika* (Bengali) created a constituency for

Mamata by constantly harping on the 'insult' meted out to a lady, which had seriously harmed 'the *bhadralok*' sensibility.

29. In my personal interview with those Front activists involved in the campaign, this point was constantly hammered. That the leadership did not take the urban voters seriously affected further their sensibilities, which probably was translated into votes against the Front candidates.
30. Even a sympathetic Bengali daily like *Aajkal* warned the Front of the probable serious consequences of politicizing health service in the state. See editorial of *Aajkal* (Kolkata), 16 February and 23 April 1998.
31. *Peoples Democracy*, weekly organ of the CPI(M), 18 April 1998.
32. Expressing disgust and dismay, a large number of academics who are otherwise oriented to the left and left radicalism on condition of anonymity confirmed the extent to which Alimuddin Street, the address of the CPI(M) provincial headquarter, intervenes in every appointment in school, colleges, and even universities. My interview with them (during early September 1999) also reinforces the argument that by deliberately following such a policy, the party aims at creating and consolidating a long-lasting support base in the state. At regular intervals, there are articles and editorials in the leading dailies, like *The Telegraph*, *The Statesman*, *Ananda Bazar Patrika* underlining the devastating consequences of biased appointments in the educational institutions.
33. Amulya Ganguli, 'No Garden of Eden', *The Hindustan Times* (New Delhi), 28 February 1999. While explaining the disturbances in the Calcutta stadium during the February 1999 test match between India and Pakistan, the author further argues that 'it is the frustrated middle class of today, living in a state that is paying a heavy price for the follies of its past and present, which probably tries to rekindle the fires of its revolutionary ardour by challenging the world (and) the end result may be that the world will simply ignore Calcutta'.
34. Since English medium schools are allowed to function in the state, the government policy in this regard is attributed to an elitist design seeking to confine the English education to a few. This is an issue that has brought even the hard-core CPI(M) activists in Kolkata and its vicinity together with those holding views opposed to the Left ideology. In a survey, conducted just before the poll in Kolkata by the *Ananda Bazar Patrika* and *The Telegraph*, the two leading dailies, it was evident that 80 per cent of Calcutta's population are opposed to this decision of restricting English education. See *Ananda Bazar Patrika* and *The Telegraph*, 25, 26, and 27 August 1999.
35. See Ranajit Dasgupta, 'West Bengal: Industrial Development Policy—a critical view', *Economic and Political Weekly*, 29 July 1995.
36. Somnath Chatterjee's frequent foreign visits and signing of Memorandum of Understanding (MOU) earned him the title of, 'MOU Chatterjee' by the local press. For details of the role of WBIDC, see Eesenjit, 'West Bengal:

Grassroots realities confront Left Front', *Economic and Political Weakly*, 21-7 March 1998, p. 633.

37. Of the sixty-seven units that suspended their operation during the period between 1995-7, as many as twenty-nine units were closed in 1997 alone, see ibid, p. 634. For a critical exposition of the role of the LF government in the industrial sector, see Ross Mallick, *Development Policy of a Communist Government: West Bengal since 1977*, Cambridge University Press, 1993, Chapter 5 (pp. 171-212).
38. West Bengal LF seems to have a remarkable record: more than fifteen consecutive victories in Assembly, Parliament, and Panchayat elections and this is because of a steady transformation of West Bengal's rural economy through land reform and the panchayat system; no major corruption scandals despite twenty-three years in office; communal peace; and the arithmetic of an ideologically cohesive coalition, the sincerity of whose senior leaders is not in doubt. This probably explains the failure of the anti-LF movements to ever assume alarming proportions in recent years.
39. While charting-out the agrarian policy, the *People's Democracy* adumbrates the following programmes as most important for rejuvenating the rural masses: 'Vigorous implementation of land reforms; distribution of land to the tiller; breaking of land concentration; cancellation of the debts of agricultural workers and poor peasants; remunerative process for peasants' produce; cheap credit and subsidized inputs for peasants.' See *People's Democracy*, 18 November 1984.
40. Ben Rogaly has shown that 'the dominant class in the villages has shifted from *bhadralok* to *chashi* (middle peasant) and the CPI(M), controlled by this class in the countryside, has continued to operate on the basis of local power equations and above all, local patron-client ties especially between junior and senior party activists. These vertical ties have helped deflect the potential horizontal organization of rural workers'. See Ben Rogaly, 'Containing Conflict and Reaping Votes; management of rural labour relations in West Bengal', *Economic and Political Weekly*, 17-24 October 1998, pp. 2729-39.
41. Since CPI(M) draws upon the Marxist principle of 'democratic centralism', the party think tank justifies the hegemonic role of the LCs in administration as probably the most appropriate in the context of a transitional society. However the LCs firm grip over the affairs of the localities did not allow sufficient space for the articulation of grievances and differences. The disenchantment of the electorate that has been voiced in this election, argues a commentator, 'has more to do with this sense of being left out'. See Surajit C. Mukhopadhyay, 'Nineties Politics II: Irrelevance of secular-communal divide', *The Statesman*, 23 October 1999.
42. The by-election was held in June 1998, in which the CPI(M) candidates won in Chanditala and Bowbazar Assembly constituencies while the Trinamool Congress captured the Rashbehari seat. The Bowbazar seat (a north Kolkata

constituency) was wrested after a gap of sixteen years, but recaptured Chanditala in Hooghly, which it had lost to the Congress in 1996. Mamata's Trinamool Congress had to be content with only one seat—Rashbehari in Kolkata. The Congress was relegated to the third position in all the three Assembly constituencies. Its comfortable victory in Bowbazar and Chanditala in which Muslims constitute about 35 per cent of the population, reconfirms the minority support for the Front government; barring factional squabbles within the Trinamool Congress that largely made the victory of the CPI(M) candidate possible. Its success in this constituency at the heart of Kolkata also roughly indicates the growing acceptance of the Marxists by the city dwellers. See for details, *The Telegraph*, 28 June 1998 and *The Statesman*, 1 July 1998.

43. However the remarkable success of the BJP–Trinamool combine at all levels of panchayat is indicative of a possible decay of the Left support base in the state. Critics of the LF argue 'the land reform movement gradually petered out especially after the beneficiaries of welfarism and economic redistribution began to form a privileged section of the populace'. See Surajit C. Mukhopadhyay, 'Nineties Politics: Irrelevance of secular-communal divide', *The Statesman*, 22 October 1999.
44. According to the dominant trend in democratic theory, poverty, widespread illiteracy and a deeply hierarchical social structure are 'inhospitable' conditions for the functioning of democracy. Yet democracy thrives in India quite consistently. See Barrington Moore, *Social Origins of Dictatorship Democracy: lord and peasant in the making of modern world*, Boston: Beacon Press, 1966; Samuel Huntington, *Political Order in Changing Societies*, New Heaven: Yale University Press, 1969; Atul Kohli, *Democracy and Discontent: India's growing crisis of governability*, Cambridge: Cambridge University Press, 1991; Ayesha Jalal, *Democracy and Authoritarianism in South Asia: a comparative and historical perspective*, Cambridge: Cambridge University Press, 1995.
45. Larry Diamond, et al. (eds.), *Democracy in Developing Countries*, vol. 3 (Asia), Boulder, Colorado: Lynne Reinner, 1989, p. 1.
46. The trend is further reinforced in the recently concluded state Assembly elections in Bihar, Orissa, and Haryana where a coalition of parties with different, if not contradictory, ideologies formed the government in these states. What is however striking is the overwhelming majority of essentially regional parties. The Bihar-based RJD has, for instance, captured 122 seats in an Assembly of 323 members, while the national parties like the Congress and BJP lag far behind with only 54 and 67 seats respectively. The scene is not different in both Haryana and Orissa—where the local parties (INLD in Haryana and BJD in Orissa) secured an absolute majority on their own in the respective state assemblies.
47. V.P. Singh, who headed a coalition government at the centre that lasted for two years (1989-91) pointed out this in an interview with the press expressing

doubts about any single party winning a simple majority in Parliament in the near future. Hence, he hopes that 'political parties will gradually evolve a coalition culture . . . and not the sort of brinkmanship as we see now which reflects a confrontationist era of politics in this country'. See *The Times of India*, New Delhi, 8 September 1998.

48. Appreciating the LF government for being stable and mature, Singh however, warns of the adverse consequences of a situation in which 'the dominant party tends to bulldoze others'. See ibid.
49. While explaining the objective of the coalition—when the CPI(M) itself could have formed the government in the state, *People's Democracy* hailed the coalition government under the CPI(M) stewardship as 'the best example of unity' drawing upon more or less similar kinds of ideological belief. See *People's Democracy*, 11 November 1985.
50. With the victory of the Trinamool Congress and BJP candidates from Kolkata and its outskirts, *The Telegraph* felt that the process of making the CPI(M) and its coalition partners 'marginal' and eventually 'moribund' was initiated. See *The Telegraph*, 30 July 1998.

CHAPTER 9

Coalition Politics in Uttar Pradesh

S.K. Jha

POLITICAL PROFILE OF UTTAR PRADESH

Uttar Pradesh occupies a pre-eminent position in the country for very many reason. It had the privilege of being the centre of India's struggle for freedom. Anand Bhavan, the residence of Nehrus, was the place where the heroes of the nation, especially in the later phase of the freedom struggle, used to assemble, plan their strategies, and take important decisions informally. Moreover, all the Prime Ministers of the country since independence, with exception of Narasimha Rao (for a full term of five years, 1991-6), H.D. Deve Gowda and I.K. Gujral for brief periods during 1996-7 have been from this state.

Till the formation of the Uttarakhand out of it, Uttar Pradesh was the fourth largest and the most populous state in India. On account of its population, it had the largest strength of 85 members in the 545-member Lok Sabha, the lower House of Indian Parliament. This enabled it to have a decisive role in, and influence on, the national politics. Not unnaturally, people jokingly say, 'India, that is Bharat, that is Uttar Pradesh'.

The state has all the ingredients for flowering of various ideologies. Rampant poverty, unemployment, economic disparity, great urban–rural divide, and, above all, an exploitative social structure provide suitable grounds for flourishing of socialist and left ideologies as well as the rightist one. The state is quite suitable for the success of the religion-based politics on account of an overwhelmingly large Hindu population and a sizeable number of Muslims too. It is also fertile for Dalit politics and for politics based on the interest of the peasantry as they constitute the majority population. Nevertheless, for years the Congress subsumed all these considerations and took proper care of various sectional interest. It managed the solid support of the Muslim, Scheduled Castes, and the forward class for a long time since independence and as such, even though the political parties representing some of there interests came into existence, they failed to provide a viable alternative to the Congress rule. The state being traditionally the bastion of the INC, the party had no difficulty in forming stable governments after the first three general elections in 1952, 1957 and 1962 by securing comfortable majorities. The political situation, however, changed by the time of the fourth general elections in 1967. It was a change not typical of UP but of the entire Hindi heartland and also of some other states.

1967 ELECTION SCENARIO

The Chinese debacle in 1962 had shaken the nation's faith in the effectiveness of the Congress rule. Further, the death of Nehru, the charismatic leader, removed the magnetic pull of the people towards it. On the other hand, Ram Manohar Lohia's ceaseless tirade against the Congress and the Nehru family ultimately showed its effectiveness in fomenting anti-Congressism in the Hindi belt, especially in UP and Bihar.

There was a political vacuum in the state on the eve of the fourth general election. There was no single party in the state to take the place of the Congress, which had lost the confidence of the people. Congress leaders who drew huge crowds at the time of the third general election, were now finding it difficult to hold peaceful public meetings. In Lucknow, Congressmen often took off their white 'Gandhi' caps before stirring out. The situation was also not much different in other big cities. The rural areas, however, were still considered safe for the party.

In spite of this, the opposition political parties did not seem to translate the widespread popular dissatisfaction with the Congress into political capital. Initially the Left Opposition parties—the CPI, the Left Communists, the Samyukta Socialist Party, and the Republican Party—began negotiations for electrol adjustment but failed. They failed because their efforts were more in the nature of manoeuvre; these were not born of a desire to beat back the onslaught of reaction and give a progressive lead to the people. Hence they subsequently fought among themselves in at least sixty-four Assembly constituencies.

This gave the BJS and the Swatantra Party a chance to claim that they were the real alternative to the Congress. The Swatantra Party had large financial resources, though politically it was weak. The BJS possessed not only innumerable jeeps, cars, and loudspeakers, but also a large army of well-disciplined RSS volunteers to work for it. It had a considerable following among traders and small businessmen. It was also supported by a section of the *taluqdars* and *zamindars*, who had not joined the Congress. It is notable that most of the BJS members in the 1962 Assembly were elected from Awadh—the heart of the *taluqdari* system. Of its forty-nine members, twenty-nine were elected from the rural areas in Awadh. Their success was due to their feudal influence rather than their party's political prestige. Curiously, the Swatantra Party had come out as a protector of the cow and the Hindu *dharma* and at the same time, it had won the support of the Majlish Mushawarat—a Muslim communal organization.

The Congress candidates in the rural areas banked on the support of the richer sections of the peasantry. These sections also provided the village bullies. A large number of Congressmen who were not given party tickets, however entered the election as independents. All of them were not disgruntled elements; many deserving people had rebelled against the wrong selection of candidates. Nearly 300 Congressmen contested the election as independents and, to a great extent, damaged the prospects of the Congress.

The anti-Congress storm that swept across the state and the internal conflict of the party liquidated the Congress party's absolute majority. Nevertheless, its performance in the election was not so dismal as was expected. It still came out as the largest single party and was short of only sixteen for a majority in a 425-members House required for the formation of a government. The opposition parties failed to convert their support into success presumably because they were at that time not fully conversant with the tricks of the election and also because of the lack of understanding among them to defeat the Congress.

The BJS, which fought the election with the slogan that it would form the new government alone, utilized popular discontent against the Congress and emerged as the second largest group in the Assembly, bagging 98 seats. But the strength of the Swatantra Party was reduced from its position in 1962. The parties of the Left such as the SSP, the CPI, and the Left Communists spent their energy mostly in fighting each other. Their failure to unite and present a progressive alternative to the Congress helped in polarizing the electorate between the Congress and the BJS. Even so, wherever they served the masses and avoided cutting each other's throat, they registered gains. The Socialist Party of India's strength in the Assembly went up from 24 in 1962 to 42. The Communists maintained their earlier position, while the Left Communists who mainly acted as disruptors of Left forces were wiped out from the legislative scene. A large number of Independents won the election. They were mainly those from the Congress who had good public image but were refused tickets on account of fierce factional fights between Kamalapati Tripathi and Chandra Bhan Gupta. Table 9.1 presents the changing party positions in the successive elections since 1952.

Although the result of the 1967 election was not so bad for the

TABLE 9.1: PARTY POSITION IN UP VIDHAN SABHA, 1952-67

Parties	Seats (% votes)			
	1952	1957	1962	1967
INC	390 (47.95)	286 (42.92)	249 (96.3)	199 (32.11)
BJS	02	17	14	98 (21.65)
SSP*	19	-	49	44
CPI+	01	09	02	14 (3.11)
CPI(M)†	02	-	24	01 (1.11)
Swatantra Party	01	-	08	12 (4.0)
Praja Socialist Party	01	44	15	11 (4.71)
Republican Party of India	-	-	38	09 (10.0)
Independent	14	74	31	37 (18.72)
Total	0	430	430	426

Notes: * Socialist Party in 1952.

+ Includes Kisan Majdoor Praja Party in 1952 and Scheduled Castes Federation in 1962.

† Includes UPPP in 1952.

Source: Data obtained from the office of the Chief Electoral Officer, Uttar Pradesh, Lucknow.

Congress in terms of seats, it had a very damaging and demoralising impact on its popularity and prestige. The Congress now came to be identified with anti-social elements, black marketeers and corrupt contractors. The anti-social practices of the Congress MLAs and Zila Parishad chairmen had alienated the people everywhere. In Basti district, where the Congress suffered a heavy loss, no one could be appointed a primary school teacher without giving money to the bigwigs of the Zila Parishad. Not only permits and licences, but fair price shops, ration shops and expansion of education had become sources of income for the Congressmen. This was highlighted during the election.

Moreover, UP became one of the worst administered states since the exit of Dr Sampurnanand. Neither C.B. Gupta nor Kamalapati Tripathi had any time to think of the state's manifold problems born of poverty and backwardness. The Congress election campaign had entirely banked on manipulation of caste and community votes through extensive use of official machinery—a brazenly corrupt practice. Its only election slogan was that the opposition parties would never be able to form a stable government. All this led to the weakening of the support base of the party.

Finally, the prestige of the party in the state slumped beyond redemption during 1967 election. The defeats of UP Congress chief, Kamalapati Tripathi, Law Minister, Ali Zaheer, Finance Minister, Kailash Prakash, Health Minister, Dau Dayal Khanna, Food Minister, Negi, and ex-Governor, A.P. Jain blew to bits the myth of invincibility of the party in the state. Worst of all, the debacle of the Congress in some areas amazed even its opponents. In Rampur, for instance, it lost all the four seats to the Swatantra Party; in Bahraich, it lost all the nine seats and in Haripur all the five seats to the BJS; in Etawah it lost six out of seven seats to the Socialist Party of India and one to the BJS; in Banda, it could get only one seat out of five. Its strongholds in Banaras, Gorakhpur, Bulandshahr, and Meerut were shattered.

FORMATION OF GOVERNMENT

After the results of the election were announced, the non-Congress parties became surcharged with activities to form a government. Representatives of such parties held a meeting to explore the possibilities of forming a coalition government. There was no difference of opinion on the point that they should do their best to form a non-Congress government, but they could not come to an agreement about the nature of the coalition. However, there was lack of clarity on two points: one, whether the BJS and the Communists could share power, considering their earlier declarations about each other; and two, whether a coalition of such disparate groups could evolve a minimum common programme. A suggestion was made at the meeting that a minority single-party, non-Congress, ministry should be formed either by the BJS or the Socialist Party of India, and the other parties should support such a ministry so long as it ran the government to the satisfaction of all the parties concerned. But both the BJS and the Socialist Party of India leaders were reluctant to take on such a responsibility. The meeting thus remained inconclusive. However, with political developments in Bihar, where the BJS and the Communists had agreed to join hands, their coming together here also looked possible and the efforts continued.

A little later, Ram Chandra Vikal, a rebel Congressman, unanimously elected leader of the United Legislators' Party (which was popularly known as SVD, Samyukta Vidhayak Dal). Ram Chandra Vikal was accepted unanimously with acclamation as he had been a consistent critic of the C.B. Gupta and Sucheta Kriplani regimes, and on one occasion had voted with the opposition defying the mandate of the party. Vikal informed the Governor that he had the support of 215 members in the 425-member Assembly, but his claim did not satisfy the Governor. Meanwhile, the BJS as the biggest unit in the opposition camp tried to foist its own leader on the coalition and suggested Atal Behari Vajpayee's name. But the Communists and the Republic Party members made it plain that they would not join any coalition headed by the BJS.

Several other names were mentioned in the committee formed to discuss the possibility of forming a non-Congress government. The suggestion by the Socialist Party of India representatives that their leader Raj Narain, MP, should be invited to lead the government was opposed by Socialist Party of India rebel Chandrabali Singh on the plea that the leader should belong to the UP legislature. Before this point was conceded, Acharya Kripalani's name was also mentioned by somebody. Nobody was, however, accepted as the common candidate for chief ministership of the possible SVD government. A favourable development for the prospect of such a government, however, was that the central command of BJS gave the green signal to its UP unit to join hands with the Communists, if necessary.

Meanwhile the Congress also met to elect its leader of the new legislature party. The party was in a critical situation. Even then its members did not sink their factional differences. In the absence of Kamalapati Tripathi, who was defeated in the election, the members of the anti-Gupta faction started gathering round Charan Singh. C.B. Gupta, the veteran Congress leader, found himself in a very difficult situation because his faction had suffered heavy losses in the election. The Gupta faction in the new Assembly had not more than ninety-four members and the remaining ninety-five formed a solid group against him. Moreover, the Congress Working Committee decision that the party leader should be chosen by those who had been elected on the Congress ticket put Gupta in a tight corner. Many of his supporters had returned to the Assembly as independents but they could not help him. C.B. Gupta, having a superb ability of political manoeuvrings, ultimately managed to become the leader of the Congress Legislature Party on the advice of the Prime Minister and also won over support of a number of independents and some members of the other parties as well. But it was not a welcome choice for the Congress members as a whole.

With Gupta's return to power, began a new phase of dissidence in the Congress and political uncertainty in the state. Charan Singh, who had conceded leadership to Gupta on the Prime Minister's advice, was likely to become a rallying centre for all the anti-Gupta elements. Gupta himself provided the opportunity to hasten this likelihood. The clumsy manner in which he proceeded to form his ministry not only further annoyed Charan but also turned some of his own loyalists into disgruntled elements, if not enemies. He finalized a list of eighteen members of the ministry without consulting Charan Singh and informed the nominees of their good fortune. But when he discovered that Charan Singh was dissatisfied with the proposed composition, he dropped six names from the list. The excluded were informed at the last moment—one of them, Jagan Prasad Rawat, came to know only when his name was not called for swearing-in at the Darbar Hall. Ultimately Charan Singh and his close associate, Jai Ram Verma, who had refused to join the ministry, were anyhow persuaded to do so and the Gupta ministry was sworn in on 14 March 1967.

But the internal crisis and rivalry in the party continued. Gupta did not take seriously the fast that Charan Singh was the leader of a large number of backward peasant caste/class MLAs who felt ignored in the Bania-dominated ministry. Instead his provocative statement on 31 March 1967, that there would be no dissidence so long as Gupta led the party, further annoyed them and Charan Singh interpreted it as a threat to his position.

In a dramatic move on the morning of 1 April 1967, Charan Singh decided to break his 45-year old association with the Congress. He called his supporters one by one asking them to sign the announcement that they were leaving their party and joining a newly formed organization—Jan Congress. He hesitated once again before taking the plunge when, before the crucial voting on the Governor's address, Gupta sent word through Banarasi Das that he would get the voting postponed and in the meantime accept Charan Singh's two nominees in his cabinet. The hesitation was momentary; all the same, Charan Singh moved cautiously. Thrice he sent his couriers to their Assembly Chamber to find out if the opposition members were present in sufficient numbers. This was obviously to ensure that his defection would bring down the Gupta ministry and clear the way for the formation of a non-Congress government.

Charan Singh's famous statement on the 'historic turn in our lives' struck the treasury benches dumb, while the opposition members thumped and cheered. He said:

> Today the people are unable to understand why prices came down in those states where the non-Congress governments were formed and not in this state . . . Public service is the main instrument of a political party. We had cherished certain ideals and principles of political life. We find we cannot work for those ideals if we remain within the Congress and we feel we would be able to follow them by going out.[1]

Following this, the 19-point amendment to the motion of thanks to the Governor moved by CPI's Jharkhande Rai, was passed by 215 votes to 198, and Chief Minister Gupta, announcing the resignation of his 18-day old government in the Assembly itself, immediately left for Raj Bhawan to submit the letter. The very day, Charan Singh was unanimously elected leader of the SVD of the opposition and on 3 April 1967, he was sworn in as Chief Minister of the first coalition government in UP.

While the downfall of the Gupta government came as relief to the people, the SVD government led by Charan Singh, which was formed in its place was widely acclaimed and people had high hopes from it. Even Congressmen expressed their satisfaction at the end of the Congress regime, which had identified their party with black marketing, hoarding of food grains, corruption, callousness towards the needs of the people, bossism, factional intrigues, and lust for power. On the other hand, there was considerable popular jubilation over the formation of the SVD government led by Charan Singh. The high expectations, however, soon turned out to be a great disappointment.

Initially the SVD government did try to wake up the administration from its long slumber. Hence, despite the anti-procurement propaganda carried on by the Congress as well as the BJS, the procurement drive was taken up with modest success. The government also moved vigorously against corrupt and inefficient officials. The government also took effective steps for recovery of huge loans that the Congress government had given mostly to its sympathetic entrepreneurs and industrialists. Finally, unlike the Congress, it took an instant and firm decision for the separation of judicial cadre from the executive in the state. But this positive trend did not continue for long.

The SVD government, which was formed with the sole object of providing a non-Congress government to the people, consisted of eight parties—Jan Congress,[2] BJS, SSP, Swatantra Party, CPI, Left Communists, Republican Party, and Independents. The BJS was by far the biggest party with 98 members followed by the Socialist Party of India with 45, CPI 14, PSP 11, Swatantra 10, Republican Party 7, and Nirdaliya Dal formed by 18 Independents. It was a combination of heterogeneous elements and their ideologies, interests, programmes, and policies were not only different but also conflicting. Hence to hold them together for long was a difficult proposition. Their binding force of anti-Congressism weakened once the Congress was outsted from power.

FAILURE OF THE SVD GOVERNMENT

The leader of the team, Charan Singh, soon found it difficult to implement the policies and programmes of the coalition partners. As such he refused to commit himself to implementing the amendment passed, with his party's support, in the motion of thanks to the Governor. The amendment provided for immediate abolition of land revenue, urban land and house tax and profession tax, increase in the

DA of state government employees; rise in the salaries of school teachers, anti-hoarding and anti-marketing drives, and switchover to Hindi in all government offices.

Hence, the conflicting attitudes, interests, and policies of the SVD partners marred the successful functioning of the government. Not long after the formation of the government, the SSP made it plain to their partners that if land revenue on small holdings was not abolished, they would quit the government or hasten its fall by voting with the opposition on a cut motion. Chief Minister Charan Singh was, therefore, compelled to announce gradual abolition of land revenue. This averted the crisis but did not remove any of its causes.

Soon CPI also resorted to a similar tactics as that of the SSP. The CPI chairman, S.A. Dange, made a sharp criticism of the UP government and threatened that if the government adopted the wage-freeze, harshly treated its employees who had been detained or retrenched, and failed to do justice to the demands of the Kalagarh workers, he would ask his party to quit the government and seek fulfilment of the united front programme through mass movements.

But perhaps more annoying to the other constituents of the coalition was BJS's policy of political infiltration into the departments and institutions looked after by its ministers. Arrogantly ignoring the protests of his colleagues, Minister for Cooperatives, Ganga Bhakt Singh, carried through a virtual blitzkrieg on the district cooperatives societies and district cooperative banks, removing the already nominated members in the middle of their term and replacing them with the BJS and RSS workers. At several places, the minister even removed the secretaries of the cooperatives to find room for his partymen.

The Department of Education under the charge of the BJS leader and the Deputy Chief Minister Ram Prakash Gupta, pursed the partisan policies with greater vigour. Completely ignoring the SVD pledges to the teachers in regard to parity in salaries, the department diverted large sums of money to *Shishu Mandirs*—a chain of educational institutions established by the RSS to train children in its ideology. This money could have been better used to increase the salaries of teachers belonging to other schools. Worst of all, the Education Minister, ignoring protests from SVD parties and also defying all norms, constituted district education committees with RSS men and tried to convert every institution under his control into a BJS *Shakha*.

The Transport Department, which was also under a minister from the BJS, summarily rejected the suggestion for nationalization of some bus routes. The regional transport authorities were packed by RSS men, and bus and truck permits were reportedly given freely to those who could bring chits from the RSS bosses.

The BJS ministers were neither deterred by the criticisms of their colleagues nor the advice of the Chief Minister or even his threat to resign. They were, in fact, bent upon turning the governments departments into their party's preserves. The BJS proceeded on the assumption that it will form a ministry on its own after a mid-term election. Its leaders, therefore, asserted themselves in order to convey to the people that they were the real inheritors of power. Without caring for the sentiments of other SVD partners, the Sangh members in some of their speeches in Assembly made fun of the ideas of socialism, democracy, and secularism. A BJS minister, Vermeshwar Pandey, lauded the virtues of German fascism and described Hitler as a glorious leader of the people.

Although there was a SVD coordination committee as a forum for discussion and solution of differences among the coalition parties, its authority was often undermined and finally its boycott by the SSP reduced it to some kind of a non-entity. The contradiction between the rightist and leftist elements in the government did not allow even minimal unity among the coalition partners for smooth functioning. Their constant pressure on, and defiance of, the Chief Minister forced Charan Singh to submit his request to the SVD to relieve him from the post, especially when the BJS ministers arbitrarily interfered in the promotion and transfer of the government officials. However, a resolution by the parties reiterating their full faith in the Chief Minister averted the crisis for the time being.

Thereafter, the CPI and the SSP adopted an uncompromising stand on the issue of total remission of land revenue on holdings up to one acre. When the Chief Minister refused to accept it, they decided to resign from the ministry. Accordingly SSP ministers, Prabhu Narain Singh, Ram Swarup Verma, Mangal Deo, Roop Nath Yadav, and CPI ministers, Jharkhande Rai and Rustam Satin, resigned. This step of the Left brought the BJS closer to the Chief Minister who asserted his position and refused to resign. However, the BJS too become very much annoyed with the Chief Minister when he changed the portfolios of some of its ministers. Simultaneously, the two successive defeats the SVD suffered on the first day of the winter session of the Assembly showed the symptoms of the declining health of the government. The government lost in a snap vote in the Assembly and the SVD candidate Ramesh Sinha (CPI) was defeated by the Congress nominee Gauri Shankar Rai for a Council seat from the Assembly constituency. This emboldened the Congress to campaign for the resignation of the government, though without tabling a vote of no-confidence because the disgruntled elements in the coalition were in no mood to defect as the Congress had expected. Nevertheless, the coalition did not last long in face of ever-growing crises. The crisis that ultimately brought about the collapse of the Charan Singh regime began on 22 January 1968. The SVD coordination committee on that day adopted a resolution saying the Excise Minister Ram Chandra Vikal would be deemed leader of the SVD in case Charan Singh fails to satisfy the constituents of the SVD. The resolution passed in the absence of the Chief Minister's party, BKD, was drafted by the BJS, which wanted the Chief Minister to knuckle down and restore to the Sangh minister the portfolios taken away from them. This resolution led to the disintegration of the SVD. Charan Singh informed the coordination committee that he would submit his resignation to the Governor on 8 February.

Meanwhile attempts were made to persuade him not to do so and the leaders of all the constituent parties showed keenness to save the SVD coalition. They also knew that the SVD could not be held together unless they agreed to re-elect Charan Singh as the leader. What prevented them from putting understanding into effect was Charan Singh's insistence that his prerogatives as Chief Minister should be unequivocally accepted and that all the constituent parties, including the SSP and the CPI, should join the ministry. This was not acceptable to BJS, CPI, and the SSP. Ultimately, Charan Singh submitted his resignation on 17 February 1968 and recommended the dissolution of the Assembly.

Subsequently, a last attempt was made to save the SVD government. In the morning of 21 February 1968, Charan Singh was unanimously re-elected its leader. A few hours later, he informed everybody concerned that he was not willing to be elected. By afternoon a truncated coordination committee elected Vikal as leader and hurriedly informed the Governor of the decision to avert a fresh election.

The Governor accepted the resignation of Charan Singh and imposed President's rule in the state on 24 February 1968. However, he did not dissolve the Assembly. Instead, he kept it under suspended animation.

The formation of the SVD government wrought havoc with the Left parties. The PSP and the SSP lost several members to Chief Minister Charan Singh's BKD. The SSP not only lost four of its MLAs but was also split into two groups fighting against each other even while the SSP was in the ministry. After the resignation of the SSP ministers, sharp differences arose between the two groups on the question of support to Charan Singh. The revolt of Maharaj Singh Bharti, MP, and the formation of anti-high caste *Arajak Sangh* were the manifestation of deep differences inside the party.

The experience of working with the BJS convinced the Left parties that they could hardly work with rightist parties without sacrificing their cherished ideals. The CPI took a pledge to avoid any adjustment with the BJS and to keep out of any coalition ministry formed with the participation of the BJS.

Moreover, the working of the first coalition government fully exposed the difficulties of governance by heterogeneous elements. The new political culture that emerged in course of the coalition politics led to governmental instability on account of factionalism, defection, casteism, adventurism, and unprincipled and ad hoc alliances.

POST-SVD COALITION

After the resignation of Charan Singh, the state remained under the President's rule. In the beginning, the Assembly was not dissolved in order to explore the possibility of an alternative government. When this could not materialize, the Assembly was dissolved and a fresh election was held in early 1969. In the election, the Congress again emerged as the single largest party, by securing 211 seats, i.e. only 2 short of absolute majority. The BKD of Charan Singh was the second largest by securing 98 seats. The strength of BJS was reduced from 97 in 1967 to 49 and the SSP secured 33 seats. All other parties were almost routed. The strength of the Independents were also reduced from 37 in 1967 to 18 now. Under the circumstances, the deck was cleared from the Congress to form its government. On 26 February 1969, C.B. Gupta was once again sworn in as the Chief Minister of the state. But soon the division of the Congress into Syndicate and 'Indicate' (Indira's Congress) at the centre leading to the formal split created problems for C.B. Gupta. He threw his lot with the Syndicate and was deserted by a large number of his own loyalists and partymen. Nevertheless, as a master strategist, he tried to survive in power by support from other parties. He did his best to win over the BJS, the SSP and also ultimately the BKD—the party of his arch rival, Charan Singh. He could not come to terms to BKD as he refused to accept Charan Singh as Chief Minister. However, in order to have a coalition, the central leaders of the Syndicate Congress were agreeable to it. A sizeable section of the BJS under the leadership of Nanaji Deshmukh and the SSP led by Raj Narain (with whom Gupta had personal rapport) were, however, there to support him in power. Nevertheless, in spite of all this, it became clear that it would be difficult for Gupta to survive against the combined opposition of the Indira Congress [Congress (I)] and the BKD of Charan Singh. A last attempt was made by Gupta and the BJS leaders to win away Charan Singh by offering him chief ministership, but he turned down the offer. Meanwhile, majority of the Congressmen and MLAs in the state shifted their loyalties to the Congress (I) led by Kamlapati Tripathi. The last minute effort by Gupta to bring Nijalingappa, the Syndicate president, to muster up support proved all the more counter-productive and Gupta had ultimately to go. But before that he won away Charan Singh to form a coalition government with SSP, BJS, Swatantra, and Syndicate. Everything was finalized for this coalition but at the last moment, the Congress persuaded Charan Singh to form his BKD ministry supported by it.

BKD–CONGRESS COALITION GOVERNMENT

Thus on 17 February 1970, Charan Singh was once again sworn in as Chief Minister with the support of the Congress. Later, there arose some problems on the inclusion of the Congressmen in the ministry. After the split in the Congress, ten ministers had resigned from the Gupta ministry and demonstrated their loyalties to Indira Gandhi. UP Congress president, Kamlapati Tripathi, now wanted that nine of them (Tripathi himself was not inclined to join) should be included in the ministry. Although Charan Singh was willing to include Congressmen in his ministry, but he wanted a free hand in selecting his colleagues.

He was hesitant in accepting the nominees of the UPCC chief as ministers. Later, he agreed to it on the condition that the distribution of portfolios would be done by him. Congress leaders pressed for some important portfolios and the matter was ultimately settled, though not to its full satisfaction.

The state Congress entered the coalition for two reasons: to strengthen the Congress government at the centre, and to facilitate the merger of the BKD with the Congress. However, Charan Singh had reservation on the merger issue; though it would have been advantageous for him because it would have established his Jat/OBC peasant proprietors' lobby's supremacy over the Congress party in the state. This was also the reason why Kamlapati Tripathi, a Brahman literate, did not favour it internally.

The Congress–BKD differences on the distribution of portfolios, coupled with BKD's opposition to the Indira Gandhi's Privy Pursue Bill in the Parliament, ultimately precipitated a crisis and led to the virtual withdrawal of the Congress from the coalition government. Kamlapati Tripathi asked the Chief Minister to call a session of the Assembly before the end of September and face the House. In a letter to Charan Singh, Tripathi wrote that after the BKD's opposition to the bill for abolition of privy purses in Parliement, 'it is well-nigh impossible for the Congress to support his Ministry'. A copy of the letter was also sent to the Governor. Charan Singh had now only two options. He could either resign and recommend the dissolution of the Assembly or seek the support of the Syndicate and the BJS, which was not so easy to get. Nevertheless, he did try to coerce the parties to come to terms with him or face a mid-term election. The ease with which the BKD chief changed sides had created apprehensions in the minds of even those who admired his political manoeuvres. So, despite their desire to go to the help of the BKD chief, the Syndicate and the BJS were not prepared to give a blank cheque to Charan Singh as the Congress did. Both the Syndicate and the Sangh wanted Singh to resign first and then negotiate the terms of their support. C.B. Gupta, a Congress Bania, reportedly demanded that Charan Singh should not only resign but also accept him as leader. When Charan Singh failed to agree to this condition, Gupta called a meeting of all opposition parties on 18 September 1970 to plan the operation to topple the ministry. There was talk of a motion of no-confidence; but it was deferred on the plea that this might compel Charan Singh to make up with the Congress.

Charan Singh was banking on the interference of the Prime Minister, Indira Gandhi, to ask the Congressmen in UP to continue to support him, for he thought she was so against C.B. Gupta that she would not give him a remote chance to become the Chief Minister. This did not happen. Mrs Gandhi indicated to Singh her inability to help him. Meanwhile, C.B. Gupta manoeuvred to get his little known protégé, T.N. Singh, a Congress Rajput, nominated as leader of the alliance and foist him on the unwilling legislators belonging to these parties. Even before the ministry was formed, in the last week of October 1970, the five parties started pulling in different directions on the question of policies and programmes and distribution of seats in the Council of Ministers and subsequently on the allocation of portfolios. The unusually large ministry of 60, which expanded to 70 by the time the Assembly met, was originally conceived by the Syndicate and BJS leaders for only one purpose—to prepare the ground to oust Prime Minister, Indira Gandhi.

It was to this end that Syndicate and BJS leaders were working from the day of the formation of the Congress–BKD coalition in UP. To them, the first task was to break up the coalition. To achieve their objective, they utilized their personal relations first with UPCC Congress chief, Kamlapati Tripathi, and then with BKD chief, Charan Singh. They were successful. They know that Tripathi was not happy over the formation of a coalition, which did not have him as its leader. Charan Singh, who headed the coalition, did not show a spirit of accommodation towards the leader of the larger party that had placed him at the head of the state government. With the formation of the coalition government, communication channels were snapped and they were estranged from each other.

Gupta's lieutenants in the Syndicate and in the SSP utilized this estrangement between the two leaders to assure Tripathi that he could become Chief Minister if only he pulled down Charan Singh from the high office he occupied. They regularly visited Tripathi assuring him that they would extend unconditional support to him if he formed a ministry. Even SSP leaders met Tripathi to tell him that they were not against the Congress being in power in the state; they only wanted Charan Singh to be removed from chief ministership. If the Congress formed a ministry after toppling Charan Singh, they would be ready to tolerate a ministry headed by Tripathi.

Tripathi was taken in by the glib talk. This, as also the growing estrangement between Tripathi and Charan Singh brought the coalition to the verge of collapse . Meanwhile the resignation of six members of the BKD legislators and their decision to sit in the opposition unnerved Charan Singh. Under the circumstances, he divested 13 of the 26 Congressmen in his 46-members Council of Ministers of their portfolios. Again, only a few hours later he recommended to the Governor to dismiss those thirteen minister. Following this, Tripathi went to the Governor to inform him of his party's withdrawal of support to Charan Singh's government. Next morning, BJS sent a letter to the Governor extending support to the Chief Minister. However, Charan Singh was told that Syndicate support would not be forthcoming unless he abjectly surrendered to C.B. Gupta. This he finally did. He went to Gupta's house and pleaded for help. Gupta agreed to support him on the condition that the leadership question would be decided by Gupta after the first day of the Assembly on 6 October.

Now Gupta went forward to elicit the support of the SSP and found it wavering. Being thus in a minority the Charan Singh government was dismissed in 18 October 1970 and the state was put under President's rule till an alternative government was formed.

RIGHTIST COALITION: T.N. SINGH AS CHIEF MINISTER

Before the exit of Charan Singh, the five Rightist parties goaded by Gupta—Congress (O), BJS, BKD, SSP, and Swatantra—constituted the SVD alliance. Hence, it was of no surprise to anyone when an unholy alliance of the kind could not work satisfactorily.

It soon became clear that the SVD partners—Congress (O), BJS and the SSP—virtually working under the command of C.B. Gupta were pitted against the BKD and were trying to cut it to size. There arose a sharp difference on the question of implementing the earlier decisions of the government, especially the reduction of land ceiling and the abolition of land revenue, etc. The formation and working of the SVD ministry not only resulted in increased bad blood in these parties, but also created fissures in all of them. Sharp division developed in the SSP, which practically split into two halves. The Congress (O) faced a massive internal revolt. In BKD, there was widespread disgust, in a sizeable section against the party's participation in the ministry. Tensions developed in the BJS over the selection of partymen for ministerial posts. In the Swatantra Party, while the high command wanted B.P. Singh to be nominated as a minister, the legislators of the party selected Munshi Lal. The worst was the case of the SSP where the important national leaders now questioned the propriety of joining the ministry.

Chief Minister T.N. Singh continued in office in defiance of all laws of political gravity. He was badly defeated in the Vidhan Sabha election in early 1971 when he failed to fulfil the condition to become a member with in six months after becoming a Minister/Chief Minister. Even then he refused to resign. He remained clung to the office despite the fact that Charan Singh, whose party was his coalition partner, asked him in clear terms to resign. But the results of the Lok Sabha election in March 1971 turned the tide against the SVD parties.

The landslide victory of the Indira Congress in the mid-term Lok Sabha elections completely demoralized the entire 'grand alliance' leadership. The tremor caused intense convulsions in their ranks and dazed MLAs starting deserting their bosses in large numbers to join the Congress. The Syndicate, which had more than a hundred members in the Vidhan Sabha at the time of the split now had only 58, the BKD, which had entered the House with 98 members in 1969, was now left with just 36. The SSP strength was halved to 18, while the PSP become extinct with the desertion of all its three MLAs to the Congress. The BJS was left with 41 of 49 who had been elected on its tickets and the Swatantra lost 3 of its 5 MLAs. The Independents were reduced to 5 from 18. The deserters all joined the Congress whose strength now swelled to 229—an absolute majority in the House of 425. In the process, the T.N. Singh government was pulled down in the House in the last week of March.

With the disgraceful exit of the T.N. Singh government ended the era of hotch-potch coalitions that were brought about by strong anti-Congressism and sheer opportunism. Since 1967, the state had five short-lived governments that ruined the entire administrative machinery and caused such political upheavals that one thought the state had relapsed into the days of the Sultans. Now Kamlapati Tripathi formed the stable Congress government on 4 April 1971.

THE SECOND COALITION EXPERIMENTS, 1977

The Congress government under the leadership of Kamlapati Tripathi continued till 1974 when election to the Vidhan Sabha was due. In the 1974 elections, the Congress secured absolute majority. One of the reasons of that was that the working of the SVD government, though only for a short time, had utterly disappointed the people and they were disgusted with the unprincipled way in which the coalition partners quarrelled to further their selfish interests. However, the Congress could not improve its position in terms of its percentage of votes as the BKD manipulated large chunk of the votes of the backward class in its favour. The Congress did form the ministry but in spite of its majority could not continue in power for full term.

The Lok Sabha election of 1977 in the backdrop of Mrs Gandhi's Emergency was a kind of tornado against the Congress. Barring the ruling Congress, all other political parties had been disorganized during the Emergency rule and their leaders had been forced to remain non-functional. They were not prepared to face an election that was announced by Indira Gandhi all of a sudden. However, discerning the deep popular resentment against the Congress-sponsored Emergency and the governmental excesses during that period, the opposition leaders felt emboldened to give a fight despite their having disorganized parties and lack of resources. A nation-wide party merging Congress (O), Congress for Democracy, BJS, Swatantra, and the Socialist Party of India under the banner of the Janata Party was formed to defeat the Congress. The Congress was completely routed in the election especially in the north and Prime Minister, Indira Gandhi, too was defeated. After the election, the Janata Party formed the government at the centre. The Janata government took the position that the 1977 election showed that the Congress had lost the mandate to rule even in the states and therefore the Congress governments in nine Congress-ruled northern and eastern states were dismissed and fresh elections were held there. Uttar Pradesh also figured in that list of states. As was quite expected, the Congress once again was miserably defeated in the Assembly elections. The Congress secured an all-time low number of seats in the election, i.e. 47 out of 425. Curiously, there was no change in its percentage of votes polled. The reason for its defeat was that the opposition parties had fought together against the Congress. There was no difficulty in forming the government as the political alliance in the state was the replica of the one working at the national level. Hence, soon after the election Ram Naresh Yadav was appointed the Chief Minister of the state. As the fate of this government was tagged with the grand coalition at the national level, the repercussion of the growing trouble there was also felt at the state level. As such, Ram Naresh Yadav was replaced by Banarasi Das as the Chief Minister of the state in February 1979. Finally, the Janata government collapsed at the centre in 1979 and the Congress returned to power after the 1980 elections under the leadership of Mrs Gandhi. Mrs Gandhi now, on the logic of the Janata party, also dismissed the non-Congress government in the nine states as earlier done by the Janata party in 1977. The Congress returned to power in UP in two subsequent elections with a thumping majority by winning 306 of 425 seats in 1980 and 268 of 425 in 1985. Thus almost for a decade, the chances of coalition government and politics were sealed.

HEYDAY OF COALITION GOVERNMENTS AND POLITICS: 1989 ONWARDS

The election in 1989 marked the final end of the Congress rule in the state and the beginning of the phase of enduring coalition politics. The position of the Congress has dwindled since 1989 and now reached a point from where no redemption on its old dominance could be conceived. A number of new political parties representing different sectional interests have been formed and they have consolidated their support base. For instance, on the eve of 1989 election, V.P. Singh, a progressive Rajput, launched JD intending to protect and promote the interests of the backward castes. The party clicked and captured the largest number of seats, 204 in 1989 election, and its leader, Mulayam Singh Yadav, formed the government with the support of the Congress and the BSP. However, the coalition did not continue for long. In early April 1991, the Congress withdrew support to the JD government and on 4 April 1991, the Governor dissolved the Vidhan Sabha on the recommendations of the outgoing ministry. The fresh Vidhan Sabha election was also announced along with the Lok Sabha election as per the recommendation of the Mulayam Singh government and against the wishes of the Congress.

In the 1991 election, the BJP secured 211 seats in a house of 425 and formed its government led by Kalyan Singh as Chief Minister. It was a stable government though the party was short of a few seats. However, the drama of *Kamandal* politics, which had been launched by the BJP on all-India basis since 1990 by making an issue of construction of a temple in Ayodhya at the Ram Janmabhumi, where the Babri Masjid was allegedly constructed by Mir Baqi during Babur's rule, caused the sudden dismissal of the government. The supporters of the BJP who had been making all efforts since 1990 to remove the Babri Masjid and whose efforts had been foiled earlier by the Mulayam Singh government, now succeeded in demolishing the mosque on 6 December 1992 during the chief ministership of Kalyan Singh. This created a furore not only in the country but abroad to and consequently a great embarrassment to the union government. As such, the president sacked the Kalyan Singh ministry on the recommendation of the union cabinet, which held an emergency meeting on the night of 6 December 1992. Kalyan Singh, on his own, also submitted his resignation. The state was placed under President's rule.

In the election held in November 1993, the BJP came out as the largest single party by securing 177. However, in view of the bad name it had earned after demolition of the Babri Masjid, no other party agreed to give it support to form a government. The second largest party was the SP, which Mulayam Singh Yadav had launched on the eve of the 1993 election. It had won 109 seats. Therefore he managed to form the government with the support of the BSP, and others. But his government too did not last long. The BJP allured Mayawati, the leader of the BSP, to form an alternative government with its support. On 5 June 1995, the Governor dismissed the Mulayam Singh ministry and appointed Mayawati as the new Chief Minister. However, the unseemly acts of the supporters of the ruling party to remain in power following the BSP's withdrawal of support on 1 June, presented a sordid picture of the low level of coalition politics. Moreover, the unreliability of the BSP–BJP alliance for power was soon exposed. Barely four and a half months after the formation of the government, the BJP withdrew its support and Mayawati submitted her resignation. The Governor seeing no prospect of an alternative government imposed President's rule in the state on 18 October 1995, and the Assembly, initially under suspended animation was finally dissolved.

In the Assembly election in October 1996, no party secured absolute majority. The BJP emerged as the leader of the pack with 174 seats, but without crossing that crucial half-way mark. The other two political formations—the United Front and the BSP–Congress combine—were locked in a neck and neck race. All this made stable government much more of a difficult proposition.

Hence, the period of the President's rule, which expired on 17 October 1996, was extended on 18 October 1996 and the newly elected Assembly was not even formally constituted. Meanwhile, the parties continued their efforts to come together and wrest power. Ultimately the BJP, which had earlier caused the fall of the BSP government by withdrawing its support, persuaded the BSP to join hands for an innovative exercise in rotational power politics. As per this agreement, worked out initially for one year but renewable afterwards, the leader of the BSP, Mayawati, was to become Chief Minister for the first six months followed by BJP leader Kalyan Singh for the next six months. Accordingly, Mayawati was sworn in as Chief Minister on 20 March 1997. However, on the eve of the completion of her term a controversy was raised by the BSP to stall a smooth changeover. The BSP claimed that the Speaker of the Assembly (BJP) would also be changed as per its wishes. This, in fact, was not part of the agreement and the BSP wanted this apprehending that the BJP might encourage defection from its party. After many rounds of talks, the matter was finally settled and the BSP agreed to rotate the chief ministership without any precondition. Hence, Kalyan Singh became the Chief Minister on 21 September 1997.

The rotational politics of coalition failed to work. Kalyan Singh could hardly complete even a month of his six-month tenure as Chief Minister when on 19 October 1997, BSP withdrew its support and thereby the government was reduced to a minority. Following this, the Governor directed the Speaker that the trust vote should be decided by 'lobby division', that three observers from the Raj Bhawan, two independent observers, and a government official, would be present in the Assembly during the voting. He also directed that there would be only one agenda. The Speaker outrightly rejected the directives of the Governor as they were unprecedented and they also infringed on the authority and dignity of the office of the Speaker and the House.

On 21 October, the Assembly met for confidence vote amid violent exchanges resulting in injuries to several members including some cabinet ministers. However, Kalyan Singh won majority support for his government in the Assembly, securing 222 votes after the opposition had left the House. This he did by openly encouraging defections through promising ministerial berths to all such members. As such, twelve BSP rebels,[3] a majority of them of forward castes and OBCs, including the former minister, Markande Chand, defied the directive of Mayawati and sat with the BJP members. The others who voted for the government were twenty-two MLAs of the breakaway Congress led by Naresh Agrawal, three of seven-members JD legislature party and nine of the fourteen independents.

The way the confidence vote was managed prompted the UF government at the centre to recommend the imposition of President's rule in UP. The cabinet observed: 'We have taken note of the unprecedented acts of violence inside the Assembly on 21 October vitiating a fair trial of strength. Reports indicate brazen horse-trading and attempts at coercion, casting doubts on the validity of the process.'[4]

However, this move was opposed by Left leaders like Jyoti Basu and Indrajit Gupta and even the President sent back the cabinet's recommendation for reconsideration prompting the government to drop the proposal. The cabinet thus met twice on 22 October and was told by the Attorney General that the President's rule would be wrong. In addition, there was pressure from most Front constituents to renege, particularly after the President had sent back the recommendation. Thus on 22 October, the cabinet finally issued the statement: 'We took into account the views of *Rashtrapatiji* in the matter. Having carefully considered all relevant factors, the government feels that proceedings under Article 336 need not be undertaken.'[5]

Having thus survived, Kalyan Singh launched a huge ministry of ninety-six members in order to safeguard the continuance of his government in future. It was undoubtedly a questionable way of ensuring governmental stability in a coalition that others in similar situations would be tempted to ape.

Nevertheless, only after a few months, the Kalyan Singh government again faced a piquant situation. In a dramatic development, the Governor, Romesh Bhandari, dismissed the Kalyan Singh government on 21 February 1998 and installed a Loktantrik Congress-led government. A 17-member cabinet led by Jagdambika Pal and supported by the BSP, SP, Congress, and others was sworn in and it was asked to prove its majority by 24 February 1998. The Governor did this without giving Kalyan Singh any opportunity of a floor test. This infuriated the BJP national leader Atal Behari Vajpayee to being a fast unto death at his Lucknow residence. Meanwhile, division bench of the Allahabad High Court stayed the dismissal order of the Kalyan Singh government on 23 February and ordered to maintain the *status quo ante*. Further, the court rejected the application moved on behalf of Jagdambika Pal appealing to suspend the order for four days so that he could approach the Supreme Court against the interim order. The court also rejected the application, moved on behalf of the CPI, seeking impeachment in the writ petition and supporting the action of the Governor.

Meanwhile on 23 February, Jagdambika Pal urged the Supreme Court to stay the High Court's interim directive restoring power to Kalyan Singh. It was said in Pal's appeal: 'The said Kalyan Singh has already reached the secretariat and is forcibly trying to occupy the office of the Chief Minister and to sign papers as CM to show that he has already taken charge.' It was further maintained in the appeal that Pal and his council of ministers were constitutionally sworn in and without their dismissal the High Court order cannot be implemented. Finally, as directed by the Supreme Court, Kalyan Singh won the composite floor test in the Assembly on 26 February 1998. Supreme Court upheld the legitimacy of the Assembly's composite floor test and bestowed Chief Ministership on Kalyan Singh.

This coalition government of UP proved to be the most stable and remained in the office for the longest period than any other in the recent past, thanks to Kalyan Singh's inclusion in his ministry all possible defectors and trouble makers, without caring for its size and sinister impact on the finance and administration of the state. True, Kalyan Singh was later replaced by Ram Prakash Gupta as Chief Minister on BJP national party leadership and Gupta by Raj Nath Singh, in the run up to the approaching elections.

SUMMING UP

i. The coalition experiments in UP can be divided into distinct phases: the intermittent phase of 1967-70 and 1977-9, and the more enduring phase from 1989 onwards. Table 9.2 provides the details of these coalition governments:

TABLE 9.2: COALITION GOVERNMENTS IN UP

Sl. No.	Chief Minister	Period	Coalition Parties
Intermittent Phase			
1.	Charan Singh (Jan Congress) Bhartiya Kranti Dal	3 April 1967 to 24 February 1968 (11 months)	1. BJS 2. SSP 3. PSP 4. Swatantra Party 5. CPI (M) 6. Republican Party 7. Independents 8. Jan Congress (later BLD)
2.	Charan Singh (BKD)	17 February 1970 to 18 October 1970 (8 months)	1. Congress (I) 2. BKD
3.	T.N. Singh	28 October 1970 to 4 April 1971 (6 months)	1. Congress (O) 2. BKD 3. SSP 4. Swatantra Party
4.	Ram Naresh Yadav (Janata Party)	23 June 1977 to 28 February 1979 (20 months)	Janata Party government was a de facto coalition.*
5.	Banarasi Das	28 February 1979 to 17 February 1980 (11-1/2 months)	Janata Party
Enduring Phase			
6.	Mulayam Singh Yadav (JD)	5 December 1989 to 24 June 1991 (18 months)	1. SP 2. BSP 3. Congress
7.	Mulayam Singh Yadav (SP)	4 December 1933 to 3 June 1995 (18 months)	1. SP 2. BSP
8.	Mayawati (BSP)	3 June 1995 to 17 October 1995 (4-1/2 months)	1. BSP 2. BJP
9.	Mayawati (BSP)	21 March 1997 to 20 September 1997 (6 months)	1. BSP 2. BJP
10.	Kalyan Singh (BJP)	21 September 1997 to 21 October 1997	1. BJP 2. BSP
11.	Kalyan Singh/ Ram Prakash Gupta/ Raj Nath Singh (BJP)	22 October 1997 to the 2000	1. BJP 2. Jan BSP 3. Loktantrik Congress 4. Independents

Note: Congress (O), BJS, BLD, Socialists, and Congress for Democracy merged on the eve of the 1997 Lok Sabha elections but they never carried out the merger to its logical conclusion.

ii. In the intermittent phase, anti-Congressism was the propelling factor of coalition during 1967-9 and 1977-9. In 1967 and 1969 elections, the Congress was still the single largest party with 199 and 211 seats respectively and was only short of a few seats for majority. It could have managed to form the government and shelved the formation of any coalition. However, it could not do it on account of its internal conflicts and dissensions. In fact, the first coalition government was headed by the Jan Congress—a breakaway of the INC, led by Charan Singh. In 1977 elections, the people had defeated the Congress on account of its misdeeds rather than voted for the non-Congress parties on ideological or other considerations. The composite Congress lost its dominant influence but it had not yet lost the potentiality to return to power. The total period of coalition governments in the Intermittent phase was four years and eight months during 1967-80, with five governments coming and going. The resurgence of the Congress in 1980 marred the prospect of coalition governments for almost a decade.

iii. The election in 1989 marked the beginning of the enduring phase of coalition. Since then, except for a brief period, no single-party government has been formed and there seems to be no chance for it in the near future. The 1989 election finally put an end of the Congress rule in the state by reducing its strength to ninety-four seats. In subsequent elections in 1991, 1993 and 1996, the strength of the Congress further dwindled to 46, 28 and 33 respectively. As such, nobody can now think of its redemption. It has thus been relegated to a very low position in party politics in the state in recent years.

iv. The enduring phase of coalition government in the state is the result of the radical change in the nature of its party politics. The emergence of the party representing the interests of the backward castes and also another party representing the interests of the Scheduled Castes, having 22 per cent of the population of the state, are new political developments. The rise of these parties, viz., the SP and the BSP and also their spectacular success in the 1990s are quite significant. Along with this, the meteoric rise of the BJP in the country in recent years has special importance for this state. Based as it is on the ideology of *Hindutva*, UP is the main base of this party. Thus, in terms of the present party position, the four parties that matter most are the BJP, SP, BSP, and the Congress. The BJP and SP are evenly matched for the first position and the BSP and the Congress are placed in the ranks below them. All these four political parties now represent distinct and wide sectional interests and they have their solid support base. Hence, it seems difficult for one single party now to win enough seats in the Assembly for a single party rule. Even their fortunes in elections are contingent upon their intelligent strategies and mutual electrol adjustments. Thus coalition politics in the state has now come to stay.

v. Although it is a debatable question whether coalition politics *per se* is good or bad, the coalition experience of the state has not been a happy one and conducive to the health of the body politic. There have been eleven coalition governments in the state so far in nearly fifteen years of coalition experience. Thus the average life of the coalition government has been too short and that is not good for a state that badly needs faster development.

vi. Besides short-term governments, the coalition politics entails frequent elections, which put an unbearable burden on the exchequer of this poor country. In eleven years since 1989, UP has had five Assembly elections to date (monsoon 2002).

vii. The coalition experience of the state clearly shows that it has encouraged defections, brazen horse-trading, unprincipled and immoral alliances, individual adventurism, and indecency in public life. A celebrated journalist, Khushwant Singh, in his famous column 'With Malice Towards One and All' in *The Hindustan Times*, aptly summed up the ills of coalition politics thus:

> There are coalition, jumbo cabinets with howdahs not large enough to accommodate all aspirants to ministerial posts. Coalitions are always shaky. If not brought down by partners breaking away, they are toppled by legislators who do not get the loaves of office. Instability of governments have already demoralized our civil services; every change of government entails large-scale transfers from one post to another. If an IAS or an IPS official remains in the same post for more than a year he counts himself lucky. It is safer for them to do nothing except push files around, take no decisions and make as much money in their short postings as they can. If their ministers make money, what is wrong with them doing the same?

Although these ills are not unknown in one-party governments, they are magnified in coalitional dispensations. One may say that coalition has contributed in the past, is contributing today, and will also continue in the future to further increase and intensify four Cs of Indian democracy, viz., corruption, criminalization, communalism, and casteism.

viii. Notwithstanding all this, there is a silver lining. A good development has taken place in the context of the leadership of the state as a result of coalition politics. During nearly four decades of Congress rule in the state, there were eleven Chief Ministers but none was either from the Backward Castes or Scheduled Castes or a minority community. However, during nearly fifteen years of coalition governments, there were eleven Chief Ministers. Out of them, three were from the Backward Castes, one from the Scheduled Castes, one Jat, two Banias, and only two from the upper caste. Hence, the coalition politics had opened up the leadership for all sections including those who were deprived of this privilege earlier. But this sociological gain in representativeness cannot be sustained too long at the cost of good governance and economic development tempered by rule of law and equality.

NOTES

1. *Link*, 9 April 1967.
2. On 15 May 1967, Charan Singh formed Bharatiya Kranti Dal (BKD) and on 27 November 1967, Jan Congress merged with it.
3. Who later called themselves Jan BSP.
4. *The Times of India*, New Delhi, 22 October 1967.
5. Ibid.

PART III: DEEPER STRUCTURES AND COALITION GOVERNMENTS

CHAPTER 10

Reviewing the Federal Constitution: States' Rights and National Coalitions

Balveer Arora

The objective of this paper is to situate issues relating to federal institutions and processes in the context of the emergence of new coalitions, and to see to what extent they are relevant in the current debate on the review of the Constitution. It is important to recall at the outset that the perceived need for such a review arose in a specific situation arising from a series of hung parliaments and the repeated experience of coalitional instability. The presence and increased importance of state parties in these coalitions has added another dimension to the review exercise, because they have squarely posed the issue of the safeguard of states' rights in national policy-making processes. It is therefore necessary to simultaneously consider two issues arising from the close linkages between the agendas of state parties and the working of federal coalitions. First, we need to take a view on whether the federal principles and structures embodied in the Constitution are to be deemed as defining or basic features. Second, any review of the working of the Constitution during the past fifty years must necessarily include a reassessment of its federal provisions.

It is undeniable that the political system today is more federal than it was fifty years ago. The thesis we are putting forward here is that if India's democracy has survived this length of time, it is in no small measure due to the gradual strengthening and reinforcement of its federal character. Fifty years ago, there was a fear of federalism and an obsession with the requirements of unity and territorial integrity. This fear even led to a denial of federalism, where constitutional experts and jurists argued that India was not and was never intended to be federal.[1] Today, few constitutionalists would take this position, and yet, the three processes through which constitutional change takes place have really not helped in securing the federal idea in the Constitution and placing it on a firmer footing. First, constitutional amendments affecting federal structures and institutions have been few, if one sets aside those relating to territorial reorganization and the seventy-third and seventy-fourth amendments. Third, judicial interpretation has fluctuated, from an initial denial of the federal character of the Constitution to its acceptance with reservations in subsequent judgements.[2]

Finally, conventions, which can acquire the force of law and become binding if they are repeatedly followed, have not been favourable to the federal idea, because they reinforced practices which put a premium on centralization and central intervention. As we know, non-centralization is part of the essence of the federal idea, along with its search for a suitable combination of self-rule and shared rule. On both these fronts, conventions that were developed during the phase leading to the rupture of 1975-7. Emergency was not conducive to a framework of federal governance and led eventually to the emergence of alternative forces based on the assertion of states' rights and their articulation through national coalitions.

In the first section of this paper, I draw attention to the possibilities and limits of the ongoing review of the Constitution by situating it in the political context from which it arose.[3] In the second and third sections, the major areas of federal deficit and discontent arising from the concerns which were thrown up by the political process in the 1990s and looked into, which also saw the consolidation of the non-Congress alternative in the shape of state parties and gave rise to demands for a review of the federal component of the Constitution.[4] These demands can be clustered around two broad themes:

- Less intervention and dependence, involving not merely accrued devolution of financial resources but also administrative reforms. This also includes taking a fresh look at the changing role of the All India Services in the new framework of governance, which requires reconsideration of their capabilities as instruments of central intervention.
- More participation and empowerment, including a review of the third tier initiative and the halting progress towards multilevel

federalism. Here we argue that we need to go beyond the original obsessions of unity and integrity, and to rediscover the flexibility that was enshrined in the Constitution.

Finally, I conclude with some reflections on the continuing need for federal reform and the reasons for its perennial neglect. Tackling these issues is part and parcel of the imperative need to reconcile states' rights within the framework of national coalitions.

I

While the need for a review of the Constitution was undoubtedly a part of the election manifesto of the NDA, the scope and objectives of such a review were not clearly spelt out. One has to be mindful to the context in which it arose, namely the trauma of abruptly losing power in a few fateful days in April 1999. At that time two issues assumed salience. The first was the decision of the President to have a vote of confidence in the Lok Sabha after a major partner in the coalition withdrew support. This was undoubtedly necessary, given the fact that a major coalition partner had withdrawn support which had been a determining factor in the appointment of the Prime Minister in the first place. The second issue related to parliamentary functioning, notably the procedures that enabled governments to be overthrown without any assurance of being replaced by another government. Both these issues arose from the general recognition that state parties had carved out a durable niche for themselves in the system of governance, and that their aspirations would need to be incorporated in future efforts at building coalitions.

The hasty manner in which the first BJP-led coalition was cobbled together is reflected in the coexistence of two categories of allies, pre- and post-electoral (see Table 10.1). The collapse of this experiment exposed the inherent difficulties involved in the cohabitation of a national party committed to a centralist conception of governance with state parties seeking to assert their claims to federal power-sharing. At a more practical level, it underscored the need for devising effective methods for assuring intra-coalition harmony and coordination.

The April 1999 crisis also brought into sharp focus the delicate balance between the head of state and the head of government, which has been the object of quite a few tensions and controversies in the past.[5] It was therefore not unreasonable to conclude, when the NDA

TABLE 10.1: THE BHARATIYA JANATA PARTY-LED MAJORITY IN THE TWELVETH LOK SABHA

Parties	Type	Seats	Distribution
Pre Electoral Arrangements			
1. BJP	National	182	All states except Kerala & North East
2. AIADMK (O)	Single State	18	Tamil Nadu (AIADMK)
3. Samata Party (O)	Single State+	12	Bihar 10/UP 02 (Samata Party)
4. BJD (O)	Single State	09	Orissa (BJD)
5. SAD (R+)	Single State	08	Punjab (SAD)
6. Trinamool Congress (O)	Single State	07	West Bengal (TC)
7. Shiv Sena (R+)	Single State	06	Maharashtra (SS)
8. PMK (O)	Single State	04	Tamil Nadu (PMK)
9. MDMK (O)	Single State	03	Tamil Nadu (MDMK)
10. Lok Shakti (O)	Single State	03	Karnataka (LS)
11. HVP (R+)	Single State	01	Haryana (HVP)
12. Tamizhanga Rajiv Congress (O)	Single State	01	Tamil Nadu (V. Ramamurthy)
13. Independents		02	Maneka Gandhi (UP), Satnam Singh (Punjab)
Sub-total		256	
14. INLD (O)	Single State	04	Haryana (INLD)
15. Arunachal Congress (R)	Single State	02	Arunachal Pradesh (AC)
16. Sikkim Democratic Front (R)	Single State	01	Sikkim (SDF)
17. MSCP (R)	Single State	01	Manipur (MSCP)
18. Citizens Common Front (R)	Single State	01	Mizoram (Independent)
19. Bodoland State Movt. Cttee. (O)	Single State	01	Assam (Independent BSMC)
20. TDP (R)	Single State	11	Andhra (excludes Speaker)
21. JKNC (R)	Single State	03	Jammu & Kashmir (J&KNC)
22. Anglo-Indians	Nominated	02	
23. Unattached	Defection	01	Bihar (Anand Mohan Singh)
Sub-total		27	
Total		283	

Note: The Category of Single State + has been used to indicate parties whose electoral representation has marginally increased the confines of a single state. The sign 'O' is used for 'Opposition' and sign 'R+' for ruling in a state plus part of the ruling coalition at the Union level.

Source: Balveer Arora, 'Negotiating Differences: Federal Coalitions and National Cohesion', in *Transforming India: Socio-Political Dynamics of Democracy*, Francine R. Frankel et al., eds., New Delhi: Oxford University Press, 2000.

decided to include a review of the Constitution in its electoral agenda, that some restructuring of the political executive at the apex was being contemplated. This in turn gave rise to apprehensions that President K.R. Narayanan voiced for the first time while unveiling the bust of Dr Rajendra Prasad at Rajendra Bhavan. Referring to 'the talk about revising our Constitution', he recalled Rajendra Babu's definition of presidential functions so that it was 'remembered and followed by whoever tries to revise our Constitution today'.

> Whatever the strictly correct legal and constitutional position may be, there is no doubt that in the case of an elected President, people do look upon him also as a person having some authority in the governance of the country, and he can justify his position only by tending such advice and giving such suggestions as he considers necessary to the Cabinet before it takes any decisions. Once a decision has been taken, whether with or without his suggestions or even against his suggestions, he has to act according to that decision.[6]

In keeping with this conception of his functions, President Narayanan offered specific suggestions regarding the nature and scope of the proposed review in his address in the central hall of Parliament: 'Today when there is so much talk about revising the Constitution or even writing a new Constitution, we have to consider whether it is the Constitution that has failed us or whether it is we who have failed the Constitution.' He cited Dr Rajendra Prasad again in support of this view: 'If the people who are elected are capable men of character and integrity, they should be able to make the best of a defective Constitution. If they are lacking in these, the Constitution cannot help the country.'[7]

The terms of reference finally approved by the Cabinet for the Venkatachelliah Commission (CRC) appear to have heeded these suggestions as they stress the need to review the working of the Constitution thus:

> The Commission shall examine, in the light of the experience of the past 50 years, as to how best the Constitution can respond to the changing needs of efficient, smooth and effective system of governance and socio-economic development of modern India within the framework of parliamentary form of government and recommend changes, if any, that are required in the provisions of the Constitution without interfering tampering with its basic structure or features.[8]

This review needs to be further situated against the backdrop of the election results of October 1999 when, contrary to expectations, the relative strength of the BJP within the alliance actually declined as a result of its own tally remaining stagnant at 182 seats and a larger number of state parties joining or supporting the alliance. Over a third of the NDA majority in Parliament today is composed of state parties, which have long been clamouring for reforms in centre-state relations, and have therefore an alternative perspective and agenda. They argue that the persistent vote for regional parties reflects a popular mandate for federal reform. For instance, TDP leader, Yerran Naidu, analysed the results of the February 2000 state Assembly elections thus: 'People in these states want regional parties to rule and this also goes on to show that the spirit of federalism is here to prevail.'[9] On the other hand, the BJP has continued to maintain that the continued success of regional parties can only be interpreted as a mandate for governance through coalitions. Its efforts in this direction are reflected in the results of the 1999 Lok Sabha elections (Table 10.2).

It is worth recalling that an important portion of the Constitution, namely the provisions concerning centre-state relations, has already been reviewed very thoroughly by a previous commission chaired by Justice Sarkaria, who is also a member of the CRC. The recommendations of this Commission, which submitted its report twelve years ago, are yet to be implemented on many significant issues. To the extent that this is an area which is in dire need of review, the CRC is fortunate in having much of its federal reform agenda already chalked out. From another standpoint, this illustrates the limitations of such exercises, which must necessarily await the necessary political consensus to be forged in order to bear fruit in the shape of concrete changes.

The case for reviewing the federal component of the Constitution has been argued and squarely placed on the national agenda by state parties which have consistently championed reform on the twin themes of less intervention and more participation. I take up these two themes in the sections that follow.

II

Under the rubric of less intervention, the prime suspect is of course Article 356, which certainly needs a second look. It is today a liability rather than an asset for smooth and harmonious centre-state relations. After having been used one hundred times in fifty years, it is remarkable

TABLE 10.2: STATE-WISE DISTRIBUTION OF SEATS IN THE THIRTEENTH LOK SABHA 1999

Zones/States	Seats	INC	BJP	Other	Details of other parties
Zone I: 245 Seats: North and North-West (8 states + Delhi NCT + Chandigarh UT)					
1. Uttar Pradesh	85	10	29	46	SP 26 / BSP 14 / RLD 02 / Loktantrik Cong. 02 / Ind 01 (Maneka Gandhi) / SJPR 01 (Chandrashekhar)
2. Bihar	54	04	23	27	*JD(U)* 18 / RJD 07 / CPI(M) 01 / IND 01
3. Madhya Pradesh	40	11	29	00	00
4. Rajasthan	25	09	16	00	00
5. Punjab+Chandigarh	14	09	01	04	*SAD* 02 / CPI(M) 01 / SAD (Mann) 01
6. Haryana	10	00	05	05	*INLD* 05
7. Delhi NCT	07	00	07	00	00
8. Jammu & Kashmir	06	00	02	04	*JKNC* 04
9. Himachal Pradesh	04	00	03	01	*HVC* 01
Total North North-West	245	43	115	87	*NDA Members and Allies* 34
Zonal Percentage	100	17.6	46.9	35.5	*NDA Members and Allies* 13.9%
Zone II: 88 Seats: East and North-East (10 States)					
1. West Bengal	42	03	02	37	CPI(M) 21 / CPI 03 / RSP 03/ FB 02 / *Trinamool Cong.* 08
2. Orissa	21	02	09	10	*BJD* 10
3. Assam	14	10	02	02	CPI (ML) 01 / *BSMC* 01
4. Seven NE States	11	04	00	07	CPI(M) 02 / NCP 02 / *MSCP* 01 / *SDF* 01 / Indep. 01
Total East North-East	88	19	13	56	*NDA Members and Allies* 21
Zonal Percentage	100	21.6	14.8	63.6	*NDA Members and Allies* 23.9%
Zone III: 78 Seats: West (3 states + 2 UTs)					
1. Maharashtra	48	10	13	25	*Shiv Sena* 15 / NCP 06 / PWP 01 / JD(S) 01/ BBM 01 / Indep. 01
2. Gujarat + Daman and Diu Dadar and Nagar Haweli	28	07	20	01	Indep. 01
3. Goa	02	00	02	00	00
Total West	78	17	35	26	*NDA Members and Allies* 15
Zonal Percentage	100	21.8	44.9	33.3	*NDA Members and Allies* 19.2%

(contd.)

TABLE 10.2 (contd.)

Zone IV: 132 Seats: South (4 states + 3 UTs)					
1. Andhra Pradesh	42	05	07	30	*TDP* 29 / MIM 01
2. Tamil Nadu + Pondicherry	40	03	04	33	*DMK* 12 / *PMK* 05 / *MDMK* 03 / *MGRDMK* 01 / ADMK 11 / CPI(M) 01
3. Karnataka	28	18	07	03	*JD(U)* 03
4. Kerala	20	08	00	12	CPI(M) 08 / IUML 02 / KEC (M) 01 / KEC 01
5. Lakshadeep + Andaman Nicobar Island	02	01	01	00	00
Total South	132	35	19	78	*NDA Members & Allies* 53
Zonal Percentage	100	26.5	14.4	59.1	*NDA Members & Allies* 40.2%
Cumulative Totals					
Total Seats	543	114	182	247	*NDA Members & Allies* 123
Total Percentage	100	21.0	33.5	45.5	*NDA Members & Allies* 22.7%

Notes: (a) Members of the NDA and other BJP allies are indicated in italics.
(b) The states of the north-east are: Tripura, Manipur, Meghalaya and Arunachal (two seats each) and Nagaland, Mizoram, and Sikkim (one seat each).

Source: Compiled from Election Commission data available at www.eci.gov.in, supplemented by media reports for information on alliances and support details.

that there is no state under President's rule at this point of time. It would therefore be appropriate to seriously reconsider this provision, by deleting it in its present form and bringing into the fold of Article 352 its concern for territorial unity and integrity. Tackling this issue will also go a long way in resolving some of the problems that have arisen regarding the office of the state Governor, by virtue of its becoming an instrument of central intervention.

The role of the All India Services has been an issue of debate in many states: those like Gujarat, Goa, and Kashmir, which find themselves underrepresented, or those like Kerala and West Bengal, which initially objected to them on ideological grounds. Although the position of the All India Services was made secure by specific provisions in the Constitution, questions have been raised over the years about the appropriate role of national bureaucracies extending over the entire polity, particularly in the context of India's developing multiparty system and federal structure. These concerns have been voiced by scholars and state governments as well as official commissions. Responses to the Sarkaria Commission revealed that as many as five states would have preferred to govern exclusively through their own civil services and sought the freedom to opt out of the All India Services system while four others sought enhanced control over them.[10]

Recent changes in the polity and society have generated new and more intense debate on these issues. There are different interpretations of their role in the formative years of Indian democracy and a residual belief—at least for some—that the All India Services carry with them the baggage of foreign rule and colonial-style behaviours. While many view them as a foundational element of the Indian Union, others question their compatibility with the federal principle.

The argument that the All India Services as a 'steel frame' that allows the Indian system to maintain unity and integrity as a nation, transcending cleavages and differences that form the basis for states' identities, seems much less convincing today than it might have been at Independence. There are three major strands in the reasoning against this argument.

First, the increasingly frequent use of emergency provisions of the Constitution (Article 356) to impose direct central rule in the states for securing political objectives is cited as a factor in the growing politicization of the All India Services. Dual or joint control over these services by the central and state governments was instituted to enhance professional independence, while movement between the levels of government was seen as promoting integrated public policy perspectives. On both these counts, the evidence is unclear as to the extent these premises are currently applicable. While some see them as agents of political unity in a regionally fragmented polity, through informal integrative networks, others see problems of accountability. These arise from the expectation that they have to simultaneously secure local objectives and promote national agendas, in a federal polity where these are increasingly defined by different political parties wielding power at different levels of government.

Second, there is a growing perception that the All India Services infringe state autonomy. As noted earlier, states like Kerala and West Bengal, which had earlier opposed the deployment of these services in their states, have now become more comfortable with the system, as they have been able to adapt it to their needs. There is concurrently a view that state-based parties have wrecked the morale of civil servants, who enjoy too little protection from the central government when they resist unjustified demands of local leaders.

Third, they have to be viewed in the context of changes related to the composition of the services, as they move from being an elite administrative corps to a more sociologically representative bureaucracy. This has evidently affected the way they respond to castes and communities in civil society. Earlier, remoteness and distance were considered virtues necessary to secure good governance. This prompted the induction of, to cite Sarkaria, 'officers from outside whose vision and outlook transcend local horizons'. There is now evidence to suggest that this may have changed under the impact of new tensions generated by social transformation processes. Divisions in civil society have made their appearance in the Services as caste caucuses and communal lobbies in certain states.

It is not easy to make accurate assessments of levels of conflict between state bureaucrats and the All India Services officers, the level of differences between outsiders and insiders in the central services, and backgrounds of recent recruits to both state and central services. However, the demand for an increased representation of 'state subjects in the higher reaches of administration needs to be viewed in the light of these trends towards a more representative bureaucracy.

III

On the theme of more participation, the long-awaited Inter-State Council has proved to be a disappointment and the reasons for its non-performance need to be carefully analysed. Related to this is the reform of the Rajya Sabha, which again has belied expectations by its inability to function either as a chamber of mature.

Related to the quest for a more responsive and participatory federal democracy are two other issues which are relevant in this debate, namely asymmetrical federalism and multilevel federalism. In India, the inequality of states, and of regions within states, have commonly generated tensions and dissatisfactions. Asymmetrical federalism and special status provisions, including special fiscal regimes and incentives, have helped to some extent. Old regional identities have resurfaced, in search of official patronage and institutional recognition. At an intermediate level, some states have experimented with regional and district councils, with varying degrees of success.

Noted comparative federalist Ronald Watts distinguishes between two kinds of asymmetry: political and constitutional. The former 'arises from the impact of cultural, economic, social and political conditions affecting the relative power, influence and relations of different regional units with each other and with the federal government'. This is a characteristic that is found in all federations. However it is the second which is rarer, and which applies more specifically to the present analysis, viz., constitutional asymmetry. It 'relates specifically to the degree to which powers assigned to regional units by the constitution of the federation are nor uniform' (Watts 1999: 63).

It must be emphasized that special status and unique relationships to meet specific needs and requirement were a part of the original design of the Constitution right from the beginning. Exceptions and modifications to the general regime were regarded as legitimate, and non-uniformity was considered perfectly compatible with the overarching requirements of cohesion. Yet, with the passage of time, these attributes of the original design were partially obscured. Homogenizing forces intent on mainstreaming the peoples of India into a 'single, indivisible nation' continued to press for uniform dispensations. India's experimentation with asymmetry can be viewed as an extended discovery of the minimum degree of uniformity necessary for maintaining a coherent union.

Multilevel federalism, on the other hand, is to be conceptually distinguished from previous schemes of decentralization through devolution of administrative powers, schemes that failed largely because states could and did withdraw them at will. The seventy-third amendment mandates a framework of self-government institutions, which gives constitutional recognition to a multilevel federal structure. However, the mere fact of constitutional empowerment does not mean that multilevel federalism exists today already, or is likely to exist in the near future. It is more indicative of a direction in which movement is desirable, and a consensus on this direction would help in challenging all those tendencies which move in a different or even opposite directions. The reasons for the halting and uneven progress towards the objectives of the seventy-third and seventy-fourth amendments need to be carefully examined.

IV

Constitutions are living documents because each generation gives a contemporary content to the original intentions. While the core values and ideals of the Constitution in areas such as republicanism and secularism are widely accepted and endorsed, the federal idea remains insecurely founded. We have argued that while there was an initial reluctance regarding the quantum of federalism to be incorporated in the Constitution, yet there was a firm commitment to the federal idea itself. Flexibility was wrongly interpreted as ambivalence, even though there was some initial confusion and even judicial hesitation. There was at the outset a feeling that too much federalism might be inadvisable for the nascent union, in the hour of its integration and consolidation. The precise content to be given to the federal provisions was therefore left to future generations to define and flesh out, depending on changed needs and circumstances. What was provided was a basic framework capable of being utilized for both centralized and decentralized governance. Closing the centralized governance path and opting for a more federal reading of the Constitution is therefore in consonance with the original intentions.

It is also important to mention in conclusion the close link between the agenda for federal reform and the ongoing economic reforms. The success of the latter is largely premised on the development of a decentralized federal democracy capable of providing effective initiative and governance at the state and local levels. It is therefore important to dispel the notion that economic reforms require a return to centralized single-party rule for their success, as this would move the search for remedies away from power-sharing based on federal principles. There are three basic underpinnings of this approach:

The belief that the rise and consolidation of state parties means more inter-state tensions and loss of national cohesion, in turn premised on the assumption that the problems lie essentially in the relations between states, and not between the centre and the states.

- The idea that more federalism will spell more trouble, even disintegration; the creation of more states and even further decentralization of roles and functions are often opposed from this perspective.
- The conviction that only single-party rule can ensure effective central governance, based on the premise that coalition politics necessarily results in weak and ineffective governments at the Centre.

These propositions are tenacious even though they fly in the face of available evidence concerning the track record of governance in the 'Stable Eighties' as opposed to the 'Unstable Nineties'. We have on the contrary tried to demonstrate that these propositions are fallacious. The assertiveness of state parties and their often aggressive articulation of states' rights has contributed in no small measure to the transformations that we witness today in many sectors. Coalitions of the present and of the future will therefore need to constructively harness this energy by adapting the Constitution to the imperatives of more federal governance.

NOTES

1. H.M. Seervai has clearly demonstrated that the federal idea was not only present but also central to the understanding of the system of governance devised. *Constitutional Law of India* (1999, 3rd edn.). For judicial interpretations, see Fali S. Nariman, *The Supreme Court and Federalism.*
2. See *West Bengal* vs. *UOI*; *S.R. Bommai* vs. *UOI.*
3. There have been a number of precedents in the area of partial and comprehensive reviews of constitutional arrangements: the Swaran Singh committee spawned the forty-second amendment, which was largely negatived by the next Parliament, notably with regard to the restoration of the position of the judiciary. The Law Commission and the Election Commission have put forward recommendations on electoral reform. The Sarkaria Commission remains the most comprehensive review of the way in which the federal idea has been worked out in the Constitution.
4. Commission on Centre-State Relations, Report (Chair Justice R.S. Sarkaria), Nasik, Government of India Press, 1987-8.
5. See Singh (1998).
6. Speech of President K.R. Narayanan, Rajendra Bhavan, 3 December 1999.
7. Address to the Nation on the occasion of the 50th Anniversary of the Republic of India, K.R. Narayanan, 27 January 2000.

8. Notification of 22 February 2000. The National Commission to Review the Working of the Constitution had its first meeting on 23 March 2000 to chalk out procedures and schedules. It is expected to submit its report within one year.
9. Cited in *The Hindu*, 28 February 2000.
10. The argument developed here appear in a more detailed form in the Introduction to Balveer Arora and Beryl Radin, eds., *The Changing Role of the All India Services*, New Delhi: Centre for Policy Research, 2000.

REFERENCES

Anand, Adarsh Sein, *The Constitution of Jammu & Kashmir,* New Delhi, Universal Law Publishers, 3rd edn., 1998.

Arora, Balveer, 'Political Parties and the Party System: The Emergence of New Coalitions', in *Rethinking the Constitution of India,* ed. S.C. Kashyap, et al., New Delhi: Shilpa, in press.

———, 'Negotiating Differences: Federal Coalitions and National Cohesion', in *Transforming India: Socio-Political Dynamics of Democracy*, ed. Francine R. Frankel et al., New Delhi: Oxford University Press, 2000.

———, 'Multilevel Federalism', in *Third Survey of Research in Public Administration 1980-1990*, ed. V.A. Pai Parandiker, New Delhi: ICSSR/Konark, 1997.

———, 'Adapting Federalism to India: Multilevel and Asymmetrical Innovations', in *Multiple Identities in a Single State: Indian Federalism in Comparative Perspective*, ed. Balveer Arora and Douglas V. Verney, New Delhi: Centre for Policy Research/ Konark, 1995.

Arora, Balveer and Beryl Radin, eds., *The Changing Role of the All India Services*, New Delhi: Centre for Policy Research, 2000.

Austin, Granville, *Working a Democratic Constitution: The Indian Experience*, New Delhi: Oxford University Press, 2000.

Dhavan, Rajeev, *The Amendment: Conspiracy or Revolution?,* Allahabad: AH Wheeler, 1978.

Kashyap, Subhash C., 'Political and Constitutional Reforms', in *Principles, Power and Politics*, ed. D.D. Khanna and Gert W. Kueck, New Delhi: Macmillan, 1999.

Mukarji, Nirmal and Balveer Arora, eds., *Federalism in India: Origins and Development*, New Delhi: Centre for Policy Research / Vikas, 1992.

Seervai, H.M., *Constitutional Law of India,* Bombay: N.M. Tripathi, 1999.

Singh, M.P., 'The Union Executive', in M.P. Singh and Himanshu Roy, eds., *Indian Political System: Structure, Policies, Development*, New Delhi: Jnanada, 1998, 2nd edn.

Watts, Ronald L., *Comparing Federal Systems*, Kingston: Queens University, 2nd edn., 1999.

CHAPTER 11

Coalition Governments and Constitutional Reforms

Rekha Saxena

The purpose of this paper is to consider constitutional reforms aimed at promoting governmental stability in a coalition situation. A coalition situation is conceived as one in which no party has been able to obtain a clear majority in the parliamentary chamber to which the council of ministers is collectively responsible. A recurrent coalition situation in the Lok Sabha since the 1989 Lok Sabha elections has prompted this debate. Between the 1989 and 1999—a period of a decade—as many as five elections were held, all ending up in hung parliaments. During the same period as many as eight governments were formed, out of which only one could complete its full term by hook or by crook and the last one formed in 1999 is about to complete its five-year mandate. By any standard, this is a patently unstable coalition situation. The apprehended and prevailing uncertainties have given rise to two kinds of proposals over the years. Some have advocated a constitutional restructuring to replace the parliamentary federal system by a presidential federal system, while others do not go that far and instead propose piecemeal reforms in the existing Constitution.

The idea of switching over to the presidential system is in fact much older than the coalition situation in the 1990s. It was first debated in the late 1960s in the backdrop of declining electoral fortunes of the then dominant Congress party. The party actually lost in eight of the then existing sixteen states of the union and somehow scraped to a marginal victory at the centre, with a reduced majority in 1967. It was in this context that the Tamil Nadu Congress leader, R. Venkatraman (who later became the President of the republic), and a seminar at the India International Centre discussed a proposal to introduce the presidential system in India, an idea that was initially firmly rejected by the Constituent Assembly of India at the dawn of Independence.

The advocacy for the presidential system again made its appearance in a context different from the above. This was in the 1970s when Indira Gandhi had won a comfortable majority in 1971 on the populist electoral slogan of *Garibi Hatao*, but she found herself checkmated by the gathering clouds of an emerging extra-parliamentary mass movement led by Jayaprakash Narayan on the issue of corruption in high places and growing authoritarianism in the ruling party. Some Congress leaders supposed to be close to Indira Gandhi floated the idea of the presidential system covertly to strengthen her personal leadership but ostensibly rationalized in terms of a stabler executive and a cabinet of talent freed from the parliamentary pressures. The idea was first privately circulated by some Congress leaders before the Emergency and it fructified into the setting up of a 12-member committee chaired by Sardar Swaran Singh by the All India Congress Committee (AICC) during the Emergency in February 1976 to consider and report on this proposal. Besides the party circle, executive presidency was also supported by some legal luminaries like Nani A. Palkhivala, bureaucrats/ diplomats like B.K. Nehru, and some leading industrialists like J.R.D. Tata and G.D. Birla. The idea was, however, politically buried with the Swaran Singh Committee recommending in favour of the continuation of the parliamentary system which was declared to be best suited to Indian conditions in view of the parliamentary system's representative and responsive character (Granville Austin, 1999).

The Emergency regime was presumably deterred by the prospect of a direct confrontation with the judiciary which had already propounded the rudimentary doctrine of the unamendability of the 'basic structure' of the Constitution in the Keshavananda Bharati judgement of the Supreme Court in 1973, further elaborated in several landmark judgements. Mrs Gandhi was already under pressure of a mass movement that she had sought to suppress by clamping the Emergency. And the Constitution bench formed to review Keshavananda was abruptly adjourned by Chief Justice A.N. Ray never to be reconvened.

Despite the expressed views of the opposition parties against the presidential system, the idea continued to be discussed in the 1980s during the electorally restored Indira Gandhi regime and her successor, Rajiv Gandhi. Even some BJP leaders like L.K. Advani initially toyed with the idea though the BJP as a party never formally endorsed it. Nor did another leading light of the party, A.B. Vajpayee. With the increasing electoral prospects of the BJP by the late 1980s and early 1990s, the party formally took a position on the need of setting up the National Commission to Review the Working of the Constitution (NCRWC) but it remained silent on the specific issue of the presidential system. In the changing electoral context, the BJP may well have liked to promote this idea but it was presumably unable to persuade its coalition partners to support it. Thus in the National Agenda for Governance commonly agreed to by its allies in the aftermath of 1998 elections, it only proposed to set-up the NCRWC for the purpose. So also on the eve of the 1999 elections, the BJP-led NDA repeated the same promise. Besides its allies, the idea was also opposed by other parties, including the Congress and the Left. The NDA government finally did set-up the NCRWC chaired by M.N. Venkatchaliah in February 2000 but not without the anti-climax that its terms of reference included that the search for alternatives would have to be within the framework of the existing 'basic structure' of the Constitution. Additionally, the BJP was perhaps restrained in pursuing its hobby-horse of the presidential system by the Supreme Court's doctrine of the unamendability of the 'basic structure' of the Constitution enunciated in its judgements in the Keshavananda Bharati (1973) and the Minerva Mills (1980) cases.

In view of the recurrence of the idea of a presidential system for India, it would be still appropriate to join issue with the above debate. Much of this debate lacks conceptual clarity and theoretical depth as it is seldom made clear which presidential system is being talked about.

The American presidential system is not the only model around that goes by the name of the presidential executive. Besides it, there is the Swiss collegial executive with more than half a dozen Presidents with the one being elected by rotation as the Chief President.[1] More or less similar was the erstwhile Soviet presidium executive. Then there are the French (Fifth Republic) and the Russian (post-Soviet) models that combine the parliamentary system with the presidential one.

Any debate on constitutional restructuring in India cannot take place in a vacuum. We must not forget that we are dealing not only with an ancient civilization with a glorious past but also with one which has had half a century of practical experience with a fully democratic parliamentary federal system based on universal adult franchise. In view of the consideration that we have to contend with historical, social, and regional aspects, our options are rather limited—even more limited than what they were in 1947. That was a momentous and fateful Independence eve that rarely comes the way of a nation wishing to make a new beginning. India does not also have the kind of option that the Russians exercised in the wake of the disintegration of communism. Russia's was a totalitarian communist regime without the safety valve of democracy, so when the political and economic pressures started building up, the USSR completely disintegrated without offering much resistance. Hence, the facts of history limit the freedom of discarding a regime that has not become totally unworkable. John Kenneath Galbraith used to describe this country as a 'functioning anarchy' in the Nehru era. We have sunk deeper in the quicksand but the chaos has not become entirely dysfunctional. If some organs of the government have grown numb, there is compensatory activism on the part of others to rescue the system.

James Manor (1997) perceptively brings out the elements of decay as well as re-generation in formal and informal political institutions in the recent years. For example, he points out that while political parties, legislatures, executives and bureaucratic organs of the union and state governments have probably declined, some other institutions like the judiciary, independent federal agencies like the Election Commission, constitutional functionaries like the Governors/President, NGOs, the press have either held their own or have demonstrated a healthy trend of revival and regeneration. In a similar vein, Singh and Saxena (1996, 1997, 1998) have lamented the decline of some constitutional values and goals like secularism, social democracy, republicanism, and erosion of political institutions like parties, legislative and executive organs of the union and state governments. But at the same time, they have welcomed the new trends such as the growing federalization of the predominantly parliamentary regime, due mainly to the factors such as the transformation of the party system, judicial activism on the issues of constitutional and government performance, human rights and ecological protection; the emergence of new social movements and the NGOs.

Moreover, besides the legacies of history, there are other contemporary factors in the situation that cannot be easily wished away. In the words of V.S. Naipaul, the immense social and regional diversities of contemporary India manifested themselves in a 'million mutinies'. It is precisely due to these kinds of diversities that India as well as Canada have proved to be deviant cases where the parliamentary system and plurality/majoritarian representation have not produced the kind of two-party system that the political devices have in England and the White Commonwealth. Even in England, the emergence of the Scottish and Welsh nationalisms have tended to break the mould of the two-party system. As pointed out earlier, social diversities in India are engendering the effects of proportional representation without the latter being part of its Constitution. So these are the ground realities that no amount of statistical data from cross-national studies quoted out of context can conceal and confirm. Instead of uncritical comparison, one should settle for a close look at the Indian reality and compare the comparables, say India and Canada, that are more similar in some ways than any other two countries in the world. Given these ground realities of social diversities would leave the multiparty system unaltered as the experience of some Latin American presidential systems amply testify. Some fragmented societies in South America are known to have presidentialism and multiparty systems co-existing.

Even the US party system is only deceptively bi-partisan. For one thing, there is a presidential party system that differs radically from the congressional party system. Party organizations that get activated in the presidential campaign do not generally overlap. Also, presidential proposals are often shot down by his own party cohorts in the Congress. For another, the two American parties are largely state-based, with a tenuous national coordination. In this regard, the American parties are in certain respect similar to the JD in India in which until recently UP, Bihar, Orissa, and Karnataka units of the party practically functioned in their own separate ways. So those who count on the presidential system to produce a stable executive with broadly two-party systems may be miscalculating their predicted outcome. Thus, there can be no stable parliamentary system unless the parties are cohesive and disciplined with their centre of political gravities either in the Parliament or in a mass movement, generally the former.

It may be said that as far as the nation's constitutional choice is concerned there is need to exercise utmost caution because this in the ultimate analysis governs the historic destiny of the entire nation. One feels that the constitutional choice made by the Constituent Assembly at the time of freedom was wise and appropriate. We must stick to it tenaciously and not open a Pandora's box because not all avenues of making the present system workable have really been explored. Moreover, our familiarity with the parliamentary federal system for more than half a century should not be thrown to the transient winds. Unfortunately, electoral and party reforms have never been on serious agenda with our august Parliament. The proposals made in this direction by the Election Commission, the JP movement, and a number of parliamentary committees including the Dinesh Goswami Committee in 1993, the Indrajit Gupta Committee in 1988, and the Report of the Law Commission of India (1998) remain largely unimplemented. In this context, both the Congress and non-Congress governments are to be blamed.

The issue is serious enough to be probed into by a high-power commission like the Sarkaria Commission. It would be appropriate to point out here that Canada, which faced a lesser degree of electoral and party system failures as compared to India, appointed a Royal Commission on Electoral Reform and Party Financing chaired by Pierre Lortie and consisting of four other commissioners. This commission had submitted its four-volume report to the Government of Canada way back in 1993. Here the purpose is not to go into the details of the recommendations made by this commission. Suffice is to say that introduction of the parliamentary-federal system in India without at the same time ensuring a healthy and well-organized party system is like putting the cart before the horse. No wonder, the party system failure in India has landed us in the mess where parliamentary governance has become a nightmare with political parties extending support to the government from the parliamentary floor in an amoral exercise of power without responsibility. This practice of the so-called 'outside' support has been the immediate cause of premature collapse of all coalitional/minority governments in New Delhi since 1989, excepting that of P.V. Narasimha Rao that did not cover itself with glory on other accounts.

The NCRWC got prepared two consultation papers on electoral and party reforms, and its final report was submitted in the spring of 2002. These papers are largely academic in view of the practical importance of the NCRWC report itself.

The whole debate about changing the constitutional regime to usher in executive presidency today appears to be an escape from coalitional governance. For one thing, serious efforts to make coalitions work must be sincerely tried before the parliamentary system is condemned. For example, in a country of India's size and diversity, coalition governments in fact are a more democratic and federalizing experience.

To be sure, on an average, coalition governments are less stable than one-party governments. However, under certain specific conditions, coalition governments have been known to be stabler. The most important among such conditions is the ideological compatibility among the coalition partners. Also, oversized coalition governments in India have by and large remained stable under conditions of polarization of parties in a coalition with a dominant partner, either on the Left or the Right (for example, the LF in West Bengal, SAD–BJP coalition in Punjab, JKNC–Congress coalition in Jammu & Kashmir, and JD–BJP coalition in Haryana) or on either sides of ideological divide (e.g. the Congress-led UDF and CPM-led LF in West Bengal, and Congress–Tripura Upajati Juba Samiti (TUJS) coalition in Tripura). Even 'patchwork quilt coalitions' can be stable with parties having safe electoral seats or regions of influence. Good examples of such coalitions are the NF and UF governments at the centre, which were formed subsequent to the 1989 and 1996 Lok Sabha elections. And also, the BJP-led NDA.

Coalition governments at the centre in India have become a frequent occurrence since 1989. They have seldom displayed long-term pre-election parleys and organizations and very rarely extended to all levels of the political system—union, state, and local—and to all areas of politics—electoral, legislative, and executive. Some governing and opposition coalitions, as already mentioned, have, of course, been partial exceptions to this generalization. At the national level, only the Janata Party (a *de facto* coalition) and the NF can be counted as pre-election coalitions in the real sense. The cabinet coalition partners of the NF committed themselves to a joint manifesto that bore ample testimony to their programmatic compatibility. In the 1998 polls, though the alliance affected by the BJP with its allies was a pre-poll one, in the absence of a common election manifesto worked out in advance, doubts were raised, and rightly so, regarding the credibility of such alliances as could be seen from the attitude of the AIADMK, which had from the very beginning demanded certain conditions for according support to the BJP. Other allies in the BJP coalition too kept pestering the BJP with a variety of ad hoc demands on the government.

The examples of the Janata Party, the NF, the UF, the BJP–Shiv Sena combine represented a federal coalition in that these parties simultaneously held/hold power both in New Delhi and in some states. Most coalition governments in India have seen two types of coalitions—'executive' (parties joining the cabinet) as also 'legislative' (parties supporting the government from the parliamentary floor without joining the cabinet), depending upon the perceptions and objectives of the parties joining the coalition. An executive coalition demands a greater degree of ideological and programmatic cohesion than a legislative coalition, which invites parties to become a part of the coalition despite their glaring incompatible ideologies. But the flexibility comes at the high price of instability.

The coalition experiment in India has, of course, gradually been growing in complexity. Alongside the different layers of executive, legislative and federal coalitions, the coordinating or steering committees of the coalition are also becoming more complex. For example, in the wake of the fall of the Deve Gowda government and the installation of the Gujral government, a two-man apex committee consisting of the Prime Minister and Congress president Sitaram Kesari was formed to facilitate a smooth working relationship between the UF government and its legislative coalition partner, the Congress (I). Besides, there was the steering committee of the ruling UF itself whose core committee met more often. A coordination committee to deal with the Congress was also proposed but it never got off the ground. The CPI(M) did not join the cabinet but it was a part of the UF steering committee. The BJP coalition government formed a coordination committee, but it met infrequently. Moreover, some of the coalitional partners made it a point to absent themselves from subsequent meetings as part of their pressure tactics. Later, the Trinamool Congress resigned from the coordination committee, complaining about the reluctance on the part of the BJP leadership to convene its meetings and take the allies into confidence on important policy and emergent issues. In the post-1999 NDA government, the coordination committee is a defunct organization. These multi-layered coalitions and multiple committees to resolve the inherent contradictions of the coalitions nonetheless indicate India's endeavours to come to terms with the challenges of coalition-building in the world's most complex post-traditional society.

The ground realities in Indian politics also indicate that some sort of method needs to be evolved for affecting a harmony between political and social coalitions which refers to creative combination of culture and power within the broad multi-ethnic national matrix of India. It must, however, be admitted that any such permutation and combination of social groups in politics could not stand the test of durability, which is only natural in politics. For example, in UP, the SP–BSP alliance soon broke down and the Yadavs and Dalits fell apart; in the JD in Bihar too, before long, the Yadavs and Kurmis parted company, though the strategy of mobilization of putting together an OBC–Muslim–Dalit combination in this state proved to be comparatively more durable.

However, Mulayam Singh Yadav of SP and Laloo Prasad Yadav of RJD moved closer to form the Rashtriya Loktantrik Morcha but before long it fell apart. The social contradictions can be contained by making the entire process creative and non-exploitative rather than motivated by vested interests of the dominant castes and personal ambitions of the leaders. Political democracy in the long run can only be strengthened if, at the same time, the social democracy too is rejuvenated.

In the background of persisting instability of coalition governments, the much debated issue of constitutional restructuring gathered momentum with redoubled force. But the striking feature is that compared to the vast erudition and depth of the debate in the Constituent Assembly, the current debate appears deplorably shallow and misguided. Much of the discussion so far has almost completely over-looked the federal dimension of constitutional restructuring. If the form of the government at the centre becomes presidential in the American mode, will the state governments also become a replica of the states in the American federation under a directly elected Governor with similar quantum of autonomy? One is not sure if the Indian political system is prepared to do without Article 356. Besides, such a provision is alien to the grain of the American Constitution. Is the current phase of national integration in India adequate enough that the constitutional provisions relating to internal emergency can be dispensed with? If the French presidential system combining presidential and parliamentary features is adopted in India, the modalities of adding a federal component on it will have to be carefully worked out, the reason being that the

French system is unitary. These are the questions that have seldom been raised in the recent debate. It is an irony that in a country like India that takes pride in its glorious past and rich cultural heritage, no one has pondered over the question as to why our half-a-century plus of historical experience under the present Constitution should go down the drains. Also, little thought has been given to the question whether the uniquely exceptional American political experience could be replicated in India. The American style presidential system in countries other than America has tended to degenerate into an authoritarian regime. This is due mainly to the executive aggrandizement of power that the American constitutional system is prone to, thus resulting in authoritarianism in a society where the social and historical conditions supportive of democratic regimes are lacking. The point that even within the parliamentary-federal constitutional framework in India 'presidential' Prime Ministers like Nehru and Indira Gandhi appeared on the scene and even though the Emergency regime of Mrs Gandhi came to pass, it can never be lost sight of.

America is a country with uniquely homogeneous culture from coast to coast and with a national history without the legacy of feudalism. The separation of powers among the executive, legislature, and judiciary, even in America often leads to constitutional deadlocks, examples of which are too well known to be recounted. In any other system such a democratic reincarnation of the Tudor monarchy may lead to a stalemate, which is often resolved by usurpation of all powers by the executive under the pretext of national crisis. This is because in such societies, the institutions of the civil society that sustain a democratic regime are sadly lacking. Prominent examples of the failure of presidential systems dot the landscape of Latin America, Asia, and Africa. The experiences of Pakistan, Bangladesh, and Sri Lanka which experimented with presidential systems of some sorts are not very happy. While the former two went back to the parliamentary system,[2] a debate has been going on in Sri Lanka as well to reform the present system of executive presidency in the direction of a parliamentary executive (Kashyap, 2000).

If at all a constitutional restructuring becomes a necessity in India, the French and the Russian experiments in combining parliamentary and presidential system would appear to be much more desirable, mainly because this will allow India to build a presidential component on its existing parliamentary regime. Besides, this may introduce a balance of forces in the government represented by a directly or indirectly elected President on the one hand and a Prime Minister elected by the Parliament, on the other.

In the opinion of Chandan Mitra (1998), a major weakness of the method of electing the head of the parliamentary executive is that the voters 'are inhibited from thinking nationally while exercising their franchise, especially if anger against the state government is running deep'. He believes that a direct presidential election in the fifth Republication French mode would enable the voters to rise above the myriad social, regional, and local divisions and vote nationally. But I think this gain is not without a price. This is because the nationally aggregative process, which is a typical of the direct presidential election, does nothing to mitigate the prospects of constitutional deadlocks between a directly elected President with mass support and a Prime Minister with his seat of power in a directly elected Parliament. The news in the past from Russia of the tussles between President Yeltsin and subsequently the Communist-dominated Duma is too recent and well known to need a mention here. M.P. Singh (1996: 49) argues against the French system for India for two reasons: 'for one, the French President, apart from the challenge from the Prime Minister, is unrestrained even by the kind of the judicial and federal constraints that bridles the American President. For another, this system of government is even more likely to get into constitutional deadlocks and immobilism than the American system.'

In fact, the nationally aggregative process through direct presidential election that Mitra advocates could be achieved in India even without a constitutional restructuring by adopting the Canadian method of electing party leaders before each election in a national convention of the parties concerned. Canada in the last century elected its Prime Ministers in much the same way as in parties in Britain and India, i.e. by the elected members of Parliament belonging to the party. (In the Conservative Party in Britain, the choice of the leader is often left to the Queen whose preference is duly endorsed by the Conservative MPs.) Early in the twentieth century, Canada federalized its party leadership election process by adopting the American method of national party conventions where provincial delegates of a party from all over Canada elect the leader who leads that party in the ensuing House of Commons elections. This change was introduced with the objective of making leadership election more democratic and federally aggregative (Singh and Saxena, 1997 and 1998).

Douglas Verney (1997) who discusses at length the merits and demerits of the French and the Russian models of combining presidential and parliamentary systems for India, rightly concludes:

> Is it a risk (the switchover to the French or the Russian models) worth-taking?. . . (T)he regime established in 1950 has much to commend it. In fact, India has a right to be proud that the work of the framers has lasted so well as it has. And who knows? The next election might result in a new party system, one that introduces a new party regime which given stability and makes possible a 'reasonably durable constellation of policies'. India's search might be over.

This did not happen in 1998 nor in 1999. Yet in my opinion, even within the existing Constitution, constitutional and conventional ambiguities about the role of the President of India could be utilized to facilitate presidential activism.

The prospects hinted here were in fact at least partly manifested around the time of the Independence Day in 1998. Since the President was scheduled to address a special session of the Parliament on that day, the media did not carry his usual Independence Day address to the people. Instead there appeared an exclusive interview of the President earlier given to the editor of the *Frontline*, N. Ram, in which the President frankly expressed his views, some of which were obliquely at variance with the BJP coalition government. The conventional presidential addresses to the nation have seldom been so forthright and for that reason appeared not to be vetted by the government of the day.

In two other instances, President K.R. Narayanan returned the proposals of the Gujral government and the Vajpayee government for dismissal of the Kalyan Singh government in UP and the Rabri Devi government in Bihar respectively for reconsideration, following which the proclamation recommendations were quietly dropped. The UP instance was the first ever occasion when a President had publicly exercised this option. This may well herald a beginning of presidential activism. During the Kargil war and after the 1999 Lok Sabha elections in which the BJP-led NDA was voted back to power, President K.R. Narayanan continued to play an active role as a source of moral authority and sagely advice to the government. President A.P.J. Abdul Kalam appears to be less demanding in terms of substantive policy issues but continues to be forthright in expressing his personal views that may be unpalatable to the government, and at least in one instance here turned the electoral reforms legislations for reconsideration by the cabinet. But signed it after the cabinet struck to its views. In several matters, the President went to the extent of seeking information and explanation from ministers under Article 78 of the Constitution. And it is notable that governments of recently have been more responsive to the presidential sensitivities than in the 1970s and 1980s.

To conclude, no constitutional restructuring is required provided these suggestions and reforms in elections, political parties, and coalitional governance are seriously considered and carried out (M.P. Singh and Rekha Saxena, 2002, Chapter 9; Rekha Saxena, 1998). Legitimate constitutional change is possible by the amending power of the Parliament under Article 368 subject to judicial review. Had India been a purely parliamentary system, this smooth functioning would have been made possible by parliamentary supremacy as in England. Federal systems, however, have invariably produced some variant of supremacy of the Constitution as interpreted by the Supreme Court. India being a parliamentary federal system is species of this genre.

POSTSCRIPT

The eleven-member National Commission to Review the Working of the Constitution (NCRWC) chaired by Justice M.N. Venkatachelliah submitted its report in the spring of 2002.

As per its terms of reference, it was commissioned to examine 'in the light of the experience of past fifty years, as to how best the Constitution can respond to the changing needs of efficient, smooth and effective system of governance and socio-economic development of modern India within the framework of parliamentary democracy and to recommend changes, if any, that are required in the provisions of the Constitution without interfering with the basic structure or features' (NCRWC, 2002: Chapter 1, para 1: 3: 1). Thus any basic structural change was ruled out from the outset, presumably in deference to the jurisprudence of unamendability of the 'basic structure' of the

Constitution in a series of case laws laid down by the Supreme Court.

Since the Constitution went into effect in 1950, three Constitution Review Commissions have been set up: the five-member Administrative Reforms Commission (ARC) chaired by K. Hanumanthaiya, the two-member Commission on Center-State Relations chaired by Justice R.S. Sarkaria, and the NCRWC mentioned above. None of these commissions have considered it necessary to advise a structural change in the Constitution, the least indeed by the ARC. The ARC was in favour of some procedural changes in administrative and political decision-making. The Sarkaria panel was for a basic attitudinal re-orientation among the federal functionaries, with only marginal constitutional amendments. The NCRWC has gone beyond the preceding commissions in at least two respects. First, its scope was wide open to include all aspects of the Constitution and its working. Second, it has recommended piecemeal constitutional amendments relating to a variety of constitutional and legal provisions, besides a comprehensive set of laws in areas which were earlier left largely unregulated by law.

The recommendations of the NCRWC bearing on the question of reforming the working of coalition governments can be summarized and critically evaluated as follows. The main suggestion for stabilizing coalition governments relate to a more comprehensive legal ban on the politics of defection. In addition to individual defections banned in the 1985 Anti-Defection Act enshrined in the Tenth Schedule of the Constitution, the commission is now for prohibiting party splits and mergers as well during the pendency of the legislature. Any Act of defection by an individual or a group should entail the forfeiture of membership. A related recommendation is to limit the size of the cabinet to 10 per cent of the strength of the Lower House.

Another recommendation in this context is the introduction of what is called a 'constructive' vote of no-confidence by the changing the rules of business of the House whereby the Speaker would admit a motion of no-confidence only when it is accompanied by a proposal for an alternative government. Moreover, the commission recommends a comprehensive legislation regulating the structure, working, and financing of political parties.

A significant change in the electoral system is also recommended. Instead of the first-past-the-post or the plurality principle, the majority principle is suggested. It would mean that, if in the first round of balloting no party or candidate registers 50 plus 1 or above percentage of votes, a second vote would be taken with the candidates with the largest and the second largest plurality remaining in the field. This is indeed to check the extreme fragmentation of parties.

So far as the role of constitutional heads of the state at the union and state levels is concerned, the NCRWC, by and large, reiterates the recommendations of the Sarkaria Commission. The President and the Governors are expected to play a strictly constitutional and non-partisan role in the formation of governments and dissolution of the House. In case of a hung House where no party is voted back with clear majority, the commission advises the matter to be left with the members of Parliament and State Legislatures belonging to various coalitions of parties to elect a leader by majority.

For stability of party governments or coalition governments at the state level, the NCRWC report does not think it a good idea to delete Article 356 of the Constitution. Instead, its advice is to use the union's powers under this Article sparingly and only in cases of genuine emergencies. Besides, a state government against whom action is being contemplated must be given an opportunity to explain its own position. Normally, a state government should be dismissed on the Report of the Governor which should be a speaking document', spelling out the conditions and reasons that justify such an assessment.

Moreover, even if a state government is dismissed, the Assembly should not be dissolved until the Parliament had an opportunity to consider and approve the proclamation of President's rule in a state. These recommendations amount to constitutionally entrenching the case law regarding this matter in the Bommai judgement of the Supreme Court, which has virtually become the Constitution II for constitutional emergency in a state.

In view of the fact that the previous Anti-Defection Act largely failed in effectively curbing the politics of defection and political corruption, it is difficult to be very optimistic that these vices including criminalization of politics would be successfully checked, unless and until the recommendations of constitutional amendments as well as the comprehensive legislation regulating the organization and working of political parties are introduced simultaneously. Selective and patchy reforms would not do.

NOTES

1. It must be pointed out that there has recently been a major change in the Swiss Constitution. But this aspect remains largely unchanged.
2. An army coup in Pakistan overturned the parliamentary regime in 1999.

REFERENCES

Granville, Austin, *Working A Democratic Constitution: The Indian Experience*, New Delhi: Oxford University Press, 1999.

Kashyap, Subhash C., *Institutions of Governance in South Asia*, Delhi: Konark Publishers, 2000.

Manor, James, 'Political Institutions in India: Formal and Informal, Coercive and Non-Coercive', a paper delivered in the Conference on Democracy and Transformation: India Fifty Years After Independence, organized by the University of Pennsylvania, Institute for the Advanced Study of India (UPIASI), at India International Centre, 16-19 November 1997.

Mitra, Chandan, 'States vs. India', *The Pioneer*, 8 March 1998.

NCRWC, *Review of Election Law, Processes and Reform Options,* and *Review of the Working of Political Parties Specially in Relation to Elections and Reform Options*, available on the Government of India, Ministry of Law & Justice's website as vol. II of the NCRWC report. Volume is available in print in Delhi's Universal Law Publishing Release.

Noorani, A.G., *The Presidential System: The Indian Debate*, New Delhi: Sage, 1989.

Saxena, Rekha, 'Coalition Experiment: Problems and Prospects', *Mainstream*, vol. XXXVI, no. 18, 25 April 1998.

———, 'Need for Reforms', *The Pioneer*, 18 September 1998.

———, 'Viable Coalitions', *The Pioneer*, 1 April 1998.

Singh, M.P, 'After Congress What?', *Seminar,* 440, April 1996.

———, 'India: The Constitution and Consensus', in *The India-Canada Relationship*, ed. J.S. Grewal and Hugh Johnson, New Delhi: Sage, 1994.

Singh, M.P. and Rekha Saxena, *India At Polls: Parliamentary Elections in a Federal Phase,* New Delhi: Orient Longman, 2002, Chapter 9.

———, 'Introduction' in their edited book *India's Political Agenda: Perspectives on the Party System*, Delhi: Kalinga Publications, 1996.

———, 'Paradigm Shift in Canadian and Indian Party Systems', a paper presented to an International Seminar in Canadian Studies, University of Delhi, South Delhi Campus, January 1998.

———, 'India Independent: The First Half Century of Political Development and Decay', *The Indian Historical Review,* vol. XXVI, July 1999.

———, 'Prologue' in their edited book *Ideologies and Institutions in the Indian Politics*, New Delhi: Deep and Deep, 1998.

Verney, Douglas V., 'India in Search of a New Regime', in *Transforming India: Social and Political Dynamics of Democracy,* ed. Franncine Frankel et al., New Delhi: Oxford University Press, 2000.

CHAPTER 12

Consequences of Electoral Systems on Coalition Governments

Ravi P. Bhatia

INTRODUCTION

Coalition governments are the order of the day in India. At the centre, there is a coalition government of the NDA comprising twenty-four constituents. The earlier government in the twelfth Lok Sabha, was also a coalition government with the present Prime Minister Atal Behari Vajpayee also being at the helm then. At the state-level also, we have coalition governments in Haryana, Maharashtra, Orissa, Punjab, UP, etc.

In this article, some aspects of the structural basis of coalition governments in India, both at the centre and in the states, are discussed—how the coalition governments arise as a result of the plurality electoral system as well as due to socio-political conditions prevalent in our country. It will also be show, that the coalition governments at the centre and in most states are a manifestation of the social churning taking place in the country. They are inevitable in a large country with its diversity in terms of castes, classes, religions, and languages.

There is a general feeling that coalitions are always unstable. We argue that it is not always true. Since the phenomenon of coalition governments at the centre is relatively new, the coalition partners are learning the dynamics of coalition culture and are slowly adjusting to it. They are having a healthy and sobering effect on the functioning of coalition governments. There are signs that the present Vajpayee government will last a long time if not its full term.

As far as the situation in the states is concerned, some of the coalition governments formed by the LF are quite stable, and in fact have, in many cases, lasted longer than the single-party governments because of their ideological affinity and a common programme of governance. Those coalitions, which have come about because of opportunistic alliances and have no ideological affinities, however, are relatively unstable.

The results of the Lok Sabha elections in 1998 and 1999 as well as those of the Bihar Assembly election held in February 2000 under plurality electoral system are discussed in some detail. These results clearly bring out the role of the electoral system and how they affect the party system and through it the patterns of coalition governments in India. These results are also a clear reflection of the changing socio-political equations in the country. A schematic diagram depicting the relationship between the social and electoral systems and their effect on the party system, the electoral results and formation of coalition governments will be provided later.

The elections of the President and the Vice-President in the system of proportional representation are also discussed. We argue that if this system had been different, the results of the presidential elections could conceivably have been different.

ELECTORAL SYSTEMS

Before discussing the status of coalition governments in India, it would be appropriate to first consider the electoral systems of choosing representatives in democratic countries. Broadly speaking, there are three commonly practised systems:

- Majority System
- Plurality System
- Proportionality System

Majority System

In the majority system, only those candidates are elected who get the majority of votes polled. This is also called the system where a winning candidate has to get a minimum of 50 per cent + 1 votes. The candidates have usually to contest a second ballot to achieve this condition. This system is prevalent in France and Australia. In France, both for the presidential elections as well as the elections to the National Assembly, a restricted number of candidates have to run-off for the second ballot so that the successful candidates get a minimum of 50 per cent + 1 votes. However, there is a difference in these two elections—for the presidential election only the two candidates securing the highest number of votes in the first round of elections are allowed to contest in the second round, but in the national Assembly elections, any number of candidates getting more than 12.5 per cent of vote in the first round, are allowed to contest in the second round.

Plurality System

This system prevails in India, the UK, and most countries that were earlier British colonies. Here, as is commonly known, any number of candidates can contest from any constituency in the central or state level elections and the candidate who secures the highest number of votes is declared elected from that constituency. Obviously, there is no second or run-off ballot in this system. This is also called first-past-the-post system and has been the subject of some debate recently in India. Some well-known scholars and legal luminaries like the Supreme Court advocate, P.P. Rao, feel that if this system is changed to the majority system, many of the problems encountered in the recent years, defections and instability of the minority or coalition governments could be avoided. Simultaneously, the number of parties would be reduced, stability would increase and better governance would follow. These points will be discussed later in the article.

Proportionality System

Here, the seats won by different political parties in a particular election are based on the percentage of votes obtained by these different parties in an election. This system prevails in many countries of Europe and Israel. But even amongst these countries like Finland, Austria, etc., where the President is elected, the electoral system is similar to the French system. In India, we have the proportional system of elections with a single transferable vote for the post of the President and also for the Rajya Sabha elections. This makes the results largely deterministic since one knows the strength and composition of the Vidhan Sabhas of various states, which form the electoral college for the Rajya Sabha elections.

Significant differences in the election results arise in the second and the third systems regarding the number of seats won by different political parties. In the plurality system, a small swing towards or against a political party from one election to another, can lead to a large number of seats in favour or against that party. This often happens in most Indian elections and was more recently demonstrated in the 1999 Lok Sabha elections in Bihar when a small shift in the vote share obtained by the RJD led to its losing a large number of seats to the BJP candidates. In 1998 Lok Sabha elections, RJD won 17 seats but this number declined to 7 in the 1999 elections although its vote share marginally *increased* from 26.6 to 28.3 per cent. The corresponding numbers for BJP were 20 and 23 respectively despite the fact that its vote share marginally *declined.* But the same situation does not make a significant difference in the number of seats won by a political party in the proportional system of elections. It is for this reason that governments in those countries that have this system are relatively very stable and last their full terms. They are not afraid that a small change in their share of votes will lead to their decimation or marginalization. This helps them in making long-term coalitional bargains and arrangements.

MINORITY AND COALITION GOVERNMENTS

Governments, which do not have a majority of seats on the floor of the House, can be divided into minority governments and coalition ones. Minority governments can be formed by a single party (e.g. the Narasimha Rao government in 1991) or by a group of parties (e.g. the UF government in 1996, 1997). Coalition governments (Sridharan, 1997) can again be subdivided into oversized coalitions (which have redundant partners not necessary for a simple majority, e.g. the BJD government in Orissa or the INLD government in Haryana around the winter of 2000 or minority coalitions, which per force depend on one or more partners to acquire a majority (e.g. the Vajpayee government at the centre or the coalition government in Maharashtra, etc.). Even the minority coalitions, are of two types:

i. Those that are ideologically compatible like the left governments in West Bengal, and Tripura, which have provided effective government and implemented land reforms and other measures for the benefit of the poor.
ii. The incompatible ones like the one in Bihar where the government under the RJD has been formed with Congress and other parties supporting it. Obviously the character and stability of such coalition governments will depend on their ideological affinity, as well as the prevailing political situation and political leadership skills. As M.P. Singh has written: 'Coalition and minority governments not only require sophisticated reconciliatory political leadership skills, but are also supposed to be more unstable' (Singh, 1997).

India used to earlier have one-party majority governments, but since 1977, the political scenario has begun to change and from 1989, coalitions have become the norm rather than exceptions. The Janata Party was the first party (or a group of parties) that was able to form the first non-Congress government in 1977. In a sense it was also the first coalition government at the centre since it was composed of five different parties that hurriedly merged in 1977. Lacking in the experience required to keep the constituent partners into a cohesive whole, it quickly split and the splinter Charan Singh government, which followed, lasted a few months, courtesy the Congress party, but it never faced the Parliament. In 1989, the V.P. Singh government was swept to power but here also due to internal pulls and pressures, the government was forced to go. The Congress backed the splinter Chandrashekhar government, which was a minority one and lasted for a brief period of four months. The Congress government that followed in 1991 with Narasimha Rao as the Prime Minister was a minority government for half its term but acquired majority status through dubious means.

Since 1996, we have had three elections, all of which produced hung Lok Sabha and led to coalition governments. The first Vajpayee government lasted only thirteen days and was then followed by the Deve Gowda-led UF government. This was a minority government but it received outside support of the CPI(M) and the Congress until April 1997 when the Congress president, Sitaram Kesari, suddenly withdrew support paving the way for Inder Kumar Gujral to take over the reins of this government and become the second UF Prime Minister. However, this government also could not complete the remaining period of its term and stayed in power only for about ten months. The Congress again withdrew support to this government when the UF government refused to concede to its demand of dropping of the DMK ministers after the indictment of an earlier DMK government in Tamil Nadu for an alleged security lapse which resulted in the assassination of Rajiv Gandhi.

When elections were held after the fall of the Gujral government, the BJP obtained the largest number of seats and Vajpayee became the Prime Minister of a coalition government for the second time. This government lasted about thirteen months when the AIADMK pulled out of the coalition and the government lost the confidence vote by a mere one vote. Thus we see that coalition or minority governments are usually unstable and fall without completing their term because of internal contradictions and the various constituents jockeying for power and advantage in the ensuing elections.

The 1999 elections to the Lok Sabha have also produced an indecisive election result. But here there is a distinct difference in that the NDA, which was formed before the elections with a national agenda of governance, has acquired a comfortable majority in the Parliament and does not face any immediate threat of disintegration. There are, of course, contrary pulls and discordant voices among the coalition partners but the NDA government and the Prime Minister have learnt the skills of adjustment, compromise, and consensus to contain the centrifugal tendencies.

In a perceptive article written on the 1999 general elections in India, Roy Jenkins (Jenkins, 2000) argues that the NDA victory is not so much a result of the Pokharan II nuclear explosions, or even due to the Kargil factor (the Indian forces' victory over the intruders across the Line of Control in Kashmir in 1999), but rather due to tactical voting of the electorate and due to local factors. He writes:

> This is due to deepening rather than withering of India's democracy—in particular the tendency of marginalized groups to seek power on their own terms through parties explicitly established to represent them or for elections to be fought not as massive national referendum, but at levels much closer to people's own experience.

A tabular summary of the various types of governments in independent India, as adapted from M.P. Singh (Singh, 1997), is shown in Table 12.1.

TABLE 12.1: VARIOUS TYPES OF GOVERNMENTS

No. of parties	Type of government	Cases
One Party	Majority	Nehru, Shastri, Indira Gandhi, Rao (later part)
	Minority	Indira Gandhi (1967-9) Charan Singh, Chandrashekhar, Rao (early part)
Coalition of Parties	Oversized	BJD (Orissa, 2000), INLD (Haryana, 2000)
	Minority	V.P. Singh, A.B.Vajpayee Deve Gowda, I.K. Gujral

FEATURES OF COALITION GOVERNMENTS IN INDIA

Coalition governments have now become a regular feature of the Indian political scene both at the central and state levels. These governments can be analysed in terms of the following factors:

- Representation of the political, social and economic aspirations and demands of various regions and sections of society.
- Electoral systems and tactical voting of various social groups.
- Stability.

Representative Nature of Coalition Governments

Coalition governments are more representative of the electorate than the dominant one-party system or a two major party system. The greater the fragmentation of the party system, the greater is the probability of smaller social fragments as well as the larger ones entering the legislature through elections. Although two parties (e.g. BJP and Congress) may in the future play a dominant role at the central level, it is not unlikely that other groupings may emerge in the future, which may be more representative of important sections of society, e.g. the Dalits, Muslims, and Yadavs, etc. We see the BSP to be a representative of the Dalits in UP and to some extent in parts of Madhya Pradesh, Punjab, and elsewhere. Although the BSP has not won many seats except in UP, it has secured the fourth largest vote share in the 1998 and 1999 elections. Similarly, the SP is considered to be a party in which the OBCs and Muslims of UP repose their trust. The RJD has played a major role in Bihar for the last decade and is still considered a party of the Backward Castes and the Muslims. The DMK, the AIADMK, other Tamil parties, and the TDP have been receiving overwhelming support in their own states—in Tamil Nadu and Andhra Pradesh respectively. It is quite conceivable that some combinations of these parties may reach a broad understanding and come together to form a party, a group, a front, or an alliance and emerge as a third or possibly a fourth configuration at the national scene.

The Brahmins, the other upper castes and the ruling classes, threatened by the upsurge of the other segments of the society and the changing political equations, have decided to look towards leaders and parties other than the foregoing. This has led to the spectacular progress of the BJP from two Lok Sabha seats in the 1984 to 182 in the 1999 elections.

In a survey of the 1999 Lok Sabha elections carried out by the centre for the Study of Development Societies (CSDS), New Delhi, it was found that 50.5 per cent of the upper castes voted for the BJP whereas Congress received only 21.7 per cent vote from this section. However the majority of Muslims voted for the Congress. The scheduled classes have supported all the four political groupings although Congress received the largest share of 37 per cent. Table 12.2 gives the percentage of votes bagged by the Congress, BJP, the LF and BSP from different sections of the electorate in these elections.

It is only the left parties that have more or less maintained their vote share over the last few elections. Despite the fact that there has been some decline in their vote share in the urban areas of West Bengal, they have continued to maintain their stronghold over the

TABLE 12.2: CASTE/COMMUNITY-WISE VOTE RECEIVED BY DIFFERENT PARTIES IN 1999 LOK SABHA ELECTIONS

Caste/Community	% vote received by			
	Congress	BJP	LF	BSP
Upper Castes	21.7	50.5	5.9	0.5
Muslims	52.9	11.2	9.7	1.6
OBCs	30.9	38.5	4.7	1.3
SCs	37.C	20.6	9.7	11.0
STs	41.7	29.3	6.0	0.1

Source: CSDS Survey, 1999.

rural areas. But this is no accident. It is due to their pioneering efforts that empowerment of the rural masses, both in social and economic terms, has taken place in the state (Chakrabarty, 2000). The *panchayati raj* system and the land reforms that they have implemented in the rural regions have resulted in their support base remaining intact. Thus, the appearance of a large number of political parties in the centre as well as the states is a manifestation of the urge of various segments of society to assert their identity and interests. This is also a reflection of the support extended to these parties by the different sections/ communities of society. This was not possible under the umbrella-like Congress party in the 1960s and 1970s.

The February 2000 Bihar Assembly election results have brought out the changing socio-political equations unambiguously. In a post-election survey of the voting trends in the Bihar Assembly elections carried out by CSDS in *Frontline* (31 March 2000), Sanjay Kumar (Kumar, 2000) has shown that a sharp polarization along caste and religious lines is apparent. The region of north Bihar, which has a large concentration of Muslims, Yadavs, and OBCs, have continued to repose their faith in the RJD. However, in this region, the Brahmins and the Bhumihars have gone along primarily with the BJP and to a lesser extent with the Congress. In central Bihar, the Brahmins and other upper castes have by and large voted for the BJP, while the majority of Adivasis have continued to support the Congress. The Dalits have divided their support between the RJD and the BJP.

Table 12.3 gives the voting trends among different castes/communities for the Bihar Assembly elections held in February 2000. It can be clearly seen that the Brahmins and other upper castes have voted for the BJP and its allies. A significant portion of the Brahmins (33 per cent) has also voted for the Congress but not the Bhumihars. The MY (Muslim—Yadav) combination has continued to support the RJD as it has for the last ten years. But the Dalits in Bihar, unlike those in UP, have divided their vote almost equally between the RJD and the BJP. It may be observed that the voting pattern of different castes/ communities in the Bihar Assembly elections follow the pattern of the 1999 Lok Sabha elections, especially those of the upper castes and the Muslims. The Scheduled Caste (Dalit) vote is also not very different. The survey also found out the levels of satisfaction of various castes with the performance of the Laloo-Rabri government in the last ten years. About 77 per cent of the MY voters were either very much

TABLE 12.3: VOTING TRENDS OF DIFFERENT CASTES/COMMUNITIES IN THE BIHAR ASSEMBLY ELECTIONS, 2000

Caste/Community	% voting for different parties			
	RJD	BJP+	Congress	Others
Brahmin	3	55	33	9
Bhumihar	12	68	5	16
Rajput	19	56	11	15
Yadav	80	9	2	9
Kurmi	26	61	3	10
Koeri	23	61	9	14
Dalit	33	39	9	19
Adivasi	6	13	38	43
Muslim	61	8	7	24

Source: Adapted from Kumar (2000).

or partly satisfied with their governance. But among the upper castes, 58 per cent were not at all satisfied. Among the Adivasis, 40 per cent were not satisfied and the percentage of satisfied Adivasis was only 25 per cent. Among the Dalits, a larger proportion (48 per cent) was satisfied than not satisfied (31 per cent).

Stability of Coalition Governments

The other feature of coalition governments is that they are supposed to be unstable in the sense that they fail to complete their term of five years. This can be due to one or more constituents of the coalition threatening to withdraw support or speak in discordant voices and act at cross-purposes on key issues. This feature is true in a large number of cases, especially at the centre since the coalitions first came to be formed there. None of the coalition governments has so far been able to survive for its full term due to reasons cited. Interesting trends are discernable if one analyses the composition of the Lok Sabha and the results of the last three elections held in 1996, 1998 and 1999. These are:

(a) The decline of the Congress party.
(b) The emergence of the BJP as the largest party.
(c) The good showing of some regional parties like the TDP in Andhra Pradesh, the DMK and AIADMK in Tamil Nadu, the Trinamool

Congress in West Bengal, BJD in Orissa, the BSP and the SP in UP, etc.

(d) The *status quo* of the Left parties in terms of the areas of influence.

(e) The importance enjoyed by some other small parties like the JKNC and some Independents disproportionate to their strength.

Of course, the scenario is now more complex in that some other factors have also emerged—the breakup of the JD and the realignment of some parties. Whereas the AIADMK was aligned with the BJP in the 1998 election, it was the DMK that has become the alliance partner of the BJP in the NDA since 1999. Similarly the breakaway JD constituents like the JD(U) and the Samata Party aligned with this Alliance, although they were earlier opposed to the BJP.

But at the state level, the situation regarding stability is different. Sridharan (1999) has given the average life of various coalition governments from 1977 to 1997. Left party coalitions in West Bengal, Tripura, and Kerala, as well as the Shiv Sena and BJP alliance in Maharashtra have been largely stable and it is estimated that the fourteen governments in these states have lasted on an average for forty-one months. If we consider only the eight LF governments, these have lasted an average of fifty-two months, which is larger than the average for single party majority governments. Some governments, even though they have coalition partners, have a larger average lifetime. Why is this so? The reasons are that they are based on ideological similarities and have a common agenda for governance. There have also been seat adjustments before elections and consultation and other measures to ensure broad understanding on important issues. On the other hand, other coalitions, which are based on groupings of disparate partners who have formed alliances, whether pre-poll or post-poll, are basically opportunistic alliances and tend to fall apart easily due to opposing pulls and pressures. The eighty-six single-party majority governments in the period specified here, lasted on an average of forty-one months. This figure would be larger if one considers the fact that some of them were terminated before their full term. But the thirty-three coalition governments lasted only an average for twenty months and the fourteen minority governments lasted for about fourteen months. As indicated above, none of the coalition governments at the centre right from the Janata government in 1977 have lasted their full term—in fact the average of these has been only about twelve months. As a result of this, the country was forced to have premature elections in 1980, 1991, 1998 and 1999 because none of the previous governments could last their full term of five years. These governments have been unstable, mainly due to opportunistic politics, absence of any common policy or programme and parties trying to jockey for long-term electoral advantage in the next elections.

Vajpayee and the NDA government appear to be learning the dynamics of coalition politics, trying to accommodate the regional aspirations and demands with a national agenda for governance. In the process, some of BJP's own items on their agenda (building of a Ram Mandir in Ayodhya and a Common Civil Code) have been put in the background or altogether sidelined. Some of the NDA's allies have been given key portfolios in the ministry and the TDP, which chose not to be part of government, still has one of its MPs as the Speaker. It is also observed that the TDP and other constituents of the NDA have had a sobering effect on the governance—be it the RSS crisis in Gujarat, building of a consensus regarding the Kashmir policy, or the economic agenda in general.

One may mention in this regard the assertive role being played by the important constituents—the TDP and the Akali Dal, for example, to protect and promote their respective states' interests. Rangarajan (2000) has highlighted this factor in an interesting article in the governance of the present NDA government. In another article, Bhatia and Singh (2000) have discussed another aspect of the role of the central leadership or the High Command in the day-to-day functioning of the state governments and nominating Chief Ministers and other ministers, especially those that have coalition governments.

Coalitions and Electoral Systems

It would be appropriate to mention the Duverger's Law (Sridharan, 1997), which is concerned with the voting pattern of the electorate in different electoral systems. It states that the 'simple majority single ballot system favours the two-party system'. He suggested two main reasons why this system goes against smaller third parties:

i. A mechanical reason where parties exploit the electoral voting system to their advantage.

ii. A psychological reason where voters do not 'waste' their votes on candidates of those parties not likely to win.

The psychological reason is also sometimes known as tactical voting, where the voting pattern is conditioned by the knowledge of the candidate who is likely to win. For example, in Delhi it was either the BJP or the Congress candidates who were more likely to win from the seven constituencies. So, when a left candidate contested on the CPI(M-L) ticket from the outer Delhi constituency in the 1999 elections, sections of the electorate who would have otherwise supported this candidate, knowing that he had no chance of winning, voted for the Congress to reduce the possibility of the BJP candidate winning. Similarly, in these elections, those sections who were opposed to the BJP in UP, voted for that candidate from the BSP, the SP, or the Congress parties, who had the best chance of winning. In such cases, it was more a negative vote against the BJP than a positive vote for the candidate who ultimately won.

Duverger's law has been modified by Riker as follows: 'Plurality voting with a single ballot system favours a two-party system since the candidate with the most votes wins in such a system. . . .' He also adds that people tend to vote in a sophisticated manner so that only those candidates having a chance of winning in the prevalent electoral system, receive their votes. This, according to Riker, also explains how the plurality rule decimates third parties. (Riker, 1986).

However, in my experience this law does not seem to be applicable in a society that is heterogeneous. For example, in the Indian context, especially in the Lok Sabha elections, many candidates from a large number of parties have been elected due to local, regional, caste-based considerations and have become part of the central governments. Even at the state level, this law does not often seem to be true. The few states where it does seem to explain the voting trends are Delhi, Gujarat, Himachal Pradesh, Madhya Pradesh, and Rajasthan. These states have traditionally been supporting a two-party system and other regional parties have found it difficult to make their presence felt.

Bihar and UP, even though they are extremely economically backward, are politically highly polarized and so the preferences of the elite sections of society do not get superposed on the rest of the society. Hence, pluralist or multi-party systems there. But in other economically poor states like MP, Rajasthan and Gujarat, the political division of the elite classes gets superposed and leads to the emergence of the two-party system.

How even a small change in the percentage of votes polled drastically affects the number of seats won in the plurality electoral system is shown in Table 12.4. The Congress obtained 25.8 per cent of votes in the 1998 elections and won 141 seats. In 1999, although their vote share increased to 28.3 per cent, thc number of seats decreased to 114. Looking at the performance of various parties at the state level, a small increase from 20.9 per cent (in 1998) to 22.08 per cent (in 1999) lead to a jump from 4 seats to 14 won by BSP. In Rajasthan, although there was a small increase in the vote share of the Congress, the number of seats won by them were reduced to half—from 18 to 9. For BJP, the reverse phenomenon took place. Their seats increased from 5 to 16 with an increase in vote share from 41.6 per cent to 47.2 per cent. Again in Bihar and UP, small changes led to a substantial change in the fortunes of BJP—positive in Bihar but negative in UP.

The figures for Maharashtra are also revealing. The BJP won four seats with 22.4 per cent vote in 1998 but a similar vote share in 1999 led to their winning 13 seats. There are of course different reasons for such phenomenon. In Maharashtra, the Congress lost significantly because of the emergence of NCP in the state. In UP, the BJP lost because of the consolidation of the non-BJP vote and due to rebel candidates which cut their vote share in different constituencies.

Whatever may be the specific reasons, the indisputable fact is that this happens in the plural electoral system. This would not happen in a proportional system since the number of seats won by them would depend on their vote share. The nature of the coalition governments in the different electoral systems would also differ. There is an in-built instability in the plurality system because different constituents jockey for power for the ensuing elections.

The situation in West Bengal has not significantly changed from 1998 and 1999 elections despite a minor decrease from 24 to 21 seats. The Trinamool Congress won seven and eight seats respectively. BJP has also made a marginal progress from one to two seats. The situation in Tripura has also remained more or less the same with CPI(M) retaining its two seats won in 1998 as well as its vote share of about 50 per cent. In Bihar, RJD, which is recognized as a state or regional party, secured 17 seats with 26.29 per cent vote share in 1998 and seven seats with 28.29 per cent vote in 1999 elections. In UP, the SP is an

TABLE 12.4: PERFORMANCE OF NATIONAL PRTIES IN 1998 AND 1999 ELECTIONS.

State \ Party	1998										1999									
	BJP		INC		BSP		CPI		CPI(M)		BJP		INC		BSP		CPI		CPI(M)	
	A	B	A	B	A	B	A	B	A	B	A	B	A	B	A	B	A	B	A	B
Andhra Pradesh	4	18.30	22	38.46	0	0.21	2	2.56	0	2.89	7	9.90	5	42.79	-	-	0	1.33	0	1.4
Arunachal	0	21.75	0	23.90	-	-	-	-	-	-	0	16.30	2	56.92	-	-	-	-	-	-
Assam	1	24.47	10	38.97	-	-	0	0.95	0	3.27	2	29.84	10	38.42	-	-	0	0.58	0	1.77
Bihar	20	24.03	5	7.27	0	0.5	0	3.4	0	0.4	23	23.01	4	8.81	0	0.9	0	2.6	1	0.98
Goa	0	30.04	2	31.59	-	-	-	-	-	-	2	51.49	0	39.01	-	-	0	2.93	-	-
Gujarat	19	48.28	7	36.49	-	-	0	0.09	-	-	20	52.48	6	45.44	-	-	0	0.04	-	-
Haryana	1	18.89	3	26.02	1	7.68	0	0.15	0	0.34	5	29.21	0	34.93	0	1.96	-	-	0	0.15
Himachal	3	51.43	1	41.90	0	1.15	0	0.56	-	-	3	46.27	0	39.52	0	0.31	-	0.46	-	-
J&K	2	28.64	1	19.24	0	4.97	-	-	-	-	2	31.56	0	17.83	0	4.84	-	-	0	1.00
Karnataka	13	26.95	9	36.22	0	0.56	0	0.06	0	0.04	7	27.19	18	45.41	0	0.65	-	-	0	0.08
Kerala	0	8.02	8	38.67	0	0.13	2	8.32	6	21.0	0	6.56	8	39.35	0	0.09	0	7.57	8	27.90
Madhya Pradesh	30	45.7	10	39.4	0	8.7	0	0.6	0	0.11	29	46.5	11	43.9	0	5.2	0	0.2	0	0.05
Maharashtra	4	42.4	33	43.6	0	0.75	0	0.07	0	0.6	13	21.1	10	29.7	0	0.3	0	0.06	0	0.5
Manipur	0	12.61	0	18.6	-	-	1	20.47	-	-	0	1.02	0	25.29	-	-	0	3.95	-	-
Meghalaya	0	9.01	2	47.62	-	-	0	1.44	-	-	0	9.45	1	32.75	-	-	0	0.68	-	-
Nagaland	-	-	1	86.7	-	-	-	-	-	-	0	5.12	1	71.18	-	-	-	-	-	-
Orissa	7	21.19	5	41.04	0	0.32	0	0.99	0	0.41	9	24.63	2	36.94	0	0.33	0	1.18	0	0.20

(contd.)

TABLE 12.4 (contd.)

State \ Party	1998										1999									
	BJP		INC		BSP		CPI		CPI(M)		BJP		INC		BSP		CPI		CPI(M)	
	A	B	A	B	A	B	A	B	A	B	A	B	A	B	A	B	A	B	A	B
Punjab	3	11.67	0	28.85	0	12.65	0	3.4	0	1.06	1	9.16	8	38.44	0	3.84	1	3.74	0	2.18
Rajasthan	5	41.6	18	44.4	0	2.12	0	0.6	0	1.28	16	47.2	9	45.1	0	2.7	0	0.4	0	0.49
Tamil Nadu	3	6.86	0	4.78	0	0.23	1	2.45	0	0.63	4	7.14	2	11.10	-	-	0	2.56	1	2.35
Tripura	0	8.1	0	42.1	-	-	-	-	2	48.8	0	12.8	0	13.8	-	-	-	-	2	56.2
UP	57	36.4	0	6.02	4	20.9	0	0.18	0	0.23	29	27.6	10	14.7	14	22.08	0	0.28	0	0.03
West Bengal	1	10.2	1	15.2	0	0.2	3	3.64	24	35.4	2	11.1	3	13.2	0	0.24	3	3.4	21	35.5
Andaman & Nicobar	0	35.53	1	35.9	-	-	-	-	0	5.67	1	52.74	0	43.17	-	-	-	-	-	-
Chandigarh	1	42.36	0	38.7	-	-	-	-	-	-	0	45.07	1	47.00	0	2.75	-	-	-	-
Dadra &Nagar Haveli	1	53.73	0	4.13	-	-	-	-	-	-	0	20.83	0	14.74	-	-	-	-	-	-
Daman & Diu	1	41.96	0	1.98	-	-	-	-	-	-	0	43.13	1	49.48	-	-	-	-	-	-
NCR	6	50.73	1	42.64	0	2.34	-	-	-	-	7	51.75	0	41.96	0	2.24	-	-	-	-
Lakshadweep	-	-	1	51.55	-	-	-	-	-	-	-	-	1	53.96	-	-	-	-	-	-
Pondicherry	-	-	0	32.12	0	0.63	-	-	-	-	-	-	1	37.17	-	-	-	-	-	-
Total	182	33.21	141	23.56	5	1.99	9	15.92	32	45.07	182	23.75	114	28.30	14	4.16	4	1.48	33	5.40

Note: A: number of seats won, B: percentage of vote share.

Source: *Statistical Reports on General Elections, 1998 and 1999*, Election Commission of India.

important regional party. It secured 20 seats with 28.7 per cent vote share in the 1998 elections and 26 seats with 24.06 per cent vote share.

Elections of President and Vice-President

An electoral college consisting of the elected members of Lok Sabha and Rajya Sabha as well as the MLAs from various states elects the President. The election is according to the system of proportional representation by means of single transferable vote. However, if no candidate secures a majority in the first preference vote, the second preference votes are considered and the candidate with the lowest value in the first preference is eliminated and his votes are distributed among the other candidates. The procedure is continued till one candidate secures the requisite majority. Thus the procedure of selection of the President and the Vice-President is a mixture of proportional representation and a majority system. It would have been interesting to see the variegated results of this method but it has so happened that in all the elections held so far, one of the candidates has secured the requisite majority in the first round itself and hence the special procedure has never been invoked. This has occurred mainly because most of the political parties had in advance, decided to support a particular candidate, who ultimately won the election.

Because of this electoral system, the elections of the President right from 1952 to 1997 have been largely pre-determined, excepting in 1967 and 1969. The Congress which was in majority in the Lok Sabha and Rajya Sabha for most of this period and was also in power in most states had thus an unassailable advantage and their candidates invariably won the presidential elections. In fact, in 1957 and 1962, Rajendra Prasad and S. Radhakrishnan won over with 99 per cent and 98 per cent vote respectively (Butler et al., 1995, Election Commission of India, 1997).

The only occasions when there were close contests, were in 1967 when Zakir Hussain, secured 56.2 per cent against K. Subbarao with 43.4 per cent and in 1969 when V.V. Giri won by a whisker with 50.2 per cent against Neelam Sanjeeva Reddy who secured 48.5 per cent. In 1967, Congress dominance in the presidential electoral college was diluted because of its losing power in half of the state Assemblies. In 1969, Indira Gandhi rebelled against her party hierarchs and supported a rebel candidate—V.V. Giri against Neelam Sanjeeva Reddy. On both these occasions, the presidential party system became more competitive and a pluralist combination of parties was necessary to win. Thus in these elections the supposed effect of proportional representation on the presidential winning coalition was more clearly evident.

In 1992, even though the Congress under Narasimha Rao was reduced to a minority, its candidate S.D. Sharma won with 64.4 per cent against G.G. Swell with 33.8 per cent. In the 1997 presidential election, K.R. Narayanan swept the polls. He received 94.97 per cent of the votes against his opponent T.N. Seshan, who received the remaining 5.03 per cent. It was only the Shiv Sena that supported Seshan, otherwise a grand partnership of all the major parties—Congress, UF, BJP, and others, all voted for Narayanan. Thus we see that the voting pattern in the presidential election was quite different from the 1996 Lok Sabha elections in which no party received a majority. Had the electoral system for the post of President also been a plurality system, various non-Congress parties could perhaps have put up their own candidates with the hope that one of them would win. The actual results could conceivably have been quite different then.

The election of the Vice-President has also followed a similar pattern in the phase of one-party dominance with virtually no contest between the winner and the runner-up. The closest contest was in 1967 when V.V. Giri won with 483 votes against 193 by Prof. Habib (Butler et al., 1995). In the 1997 vice-presidential elections, Krishan Kant defeated S.S. Barnala in a straight contest. Krishan Kant received support of the Congress and the UF combine and secured 441 votes against the 273 votes of Barnala who received the support of BJP and its allies (Election Commission of India, 1997).

CONCLUSIONS

The electoral system of India for elections to the Lok Sabha and the Vidhan Sabha has continued to be the plurality system. However, the nature of the governments has changed over the years. In the beginning there were the single-party Congress majority governments (except during 1967-9) right up to 1977 when the coalitions started at the centre. We have argued that coalitions are inevitable in India with its diversity and the electoral system of voting. Then why is it that during the early phase of our independence, we had the dominant Congress party majority governments?

To answer this question, we must remember that Congress was inseparably linked with the independence struggle and consequently its candidates continued to win not only at the centre but also in the states. But once the aura of the independence struggle began to fade and new challenges and new aspirations began to surface, the people found other parties and leaders to voice their concerns and aspirations and in whom to repose their trust. At this time the plurality electoral system began to reflect the social and regional diversity in the country and as a consequence, coalition governments came into being. In 1980, the country again voted for the Congress party because the first Janata coalition government at the centre failed to act cohesively. In 1984, because of Rajiv Gandhi's assassination, there was a tremendous 'sympathy vote' for the Congress that returned to power with over two-thirds majority. So even though the same electoral laws were in operation, their supposed political consequences for the party system were submerged by other factors. The present situation indicates that coalition governments will continue in the country because of the factors outlined in the previous sections.

To improve the stability of governments—whether at the centre or in the states, some scholars and legal experts like P.P. Rao, advocate in the Supreme Court, have suggested electoral reforms and other measures. One of the most significant suggestions that has been made is that there should be the majority system of elections, i.e. a candidate must secure at least 50 per cent + 1 votes to be elected. Although this is a laudable suggestion with the desired objective of reducing the plethora of state and regional parties that have come into existence to possibly less than half a dozen, it is perhaps not a desirable goal in India with its size, diversity and different cultures, languages, castes, and communities.

Can two or three parties at the national level be able to faithfully represent this diversity and varied regional and sectional aspirations? Can any party truly represent the aspirations of educated affluent middle class and simultaneously those of tribes or illiterate, rural poor? How can a party be a party of the Muslims and Brahmins at the same time? Thus, we see that the division of votes and the consequential coalition politics is a result of the social churning and upheaval that is going on in the society. It is also due to the electoral system, which encourages candidates of smaller parties to put up their candidates and be able to win some seats.

The relationship between the social systems with its social, political, and economic diversity and the electoral system and consequential effect on the party system, electoral results and coalition governments can be represented by means of the following schematic diagram:

Social system ⇄ Electoral systems
↘ ↙
Party system and Electoral results
↓
Coalition governments

The social as well as the electoral system present in the country affect the party system as well as the electoral results which ultimately lead to coalition governments whenever one party or an alliance does not win an absolute majority. In addition, as one can see that the above, there is an inter-relationship between the social and electoral systems. When our founding fathers had debated in the Constituent Assembly about the type of electoral system for the country, with its large diversity in terms of religions, languages, castes, etc., it felt that the electoral system should be such that it allowed representation to these diverse groupings of our society. A proportional electoral system would not have fitted the bill because it would have fragmented the government on par with the fragmentation in the society. If on the other hand, we had had a majority electoral system, the government formed would not have given a chance to the smaller groups and sections of society to voice their concerns and seek partnership in the government. Only one or at most two dominant groups would have been represented at the cost of the smaller groups.

To avoid both these disadvantages, and also because the framers of the Constitution were influenced by the Anglo-Saxon model, the plurality electoral was finally decided upon for the country. As discussed earlier, this helps smaller parties to win some seats either independently, or in alliance with bigger parties.

As long as the society remains what it is, and the electoral system a plurality one, coalitions are bound to stay. And as can be seen from the example of LF governments, not all coalitions are unstable or have divergent policy framework. There is hope. As the political and social situation matures and the electorate gains in confidence, the coalition governments will acquire greater stability and resilience and also be faithful representatives of the aspirations of the different sections of Indian society.

REFERENCES

Bhatia, Ravi P. and M.P. Singh, 'Call off this Pilgrimage—The High Command Syndrome', *The Hindu*, New Delhi, 7 March 2000.

Butler, David, et al., *India Decides: Elections 1952-1995,* New Delhi: Books and Things, 1995.

Chakrabarty, Bidyut, 'The Prospect of Left Front in West Bengal', paper presented at *National Seminar on Coalition Politics*, Rajendra Prasad Academy, New Delhi, 24, 25 March 2000, and included in this volume.

Election Commission of India, *Election to the Office of President of India 1997,* New Delhi, 1997.

———, *Statistical Reports on General Elections, 1998 and 1999,* vol. I, New Delhi, 2000.

Jenkins, Rob, 'Appearance and Reality in Indian Politics—Making Sense of the 1999 Indian General Elections', *Government & Opposition,* vol. 35 (1), Winter 2000.

Khanna, D.D. and Gert W. Kueck (eds.), *Principles, Power, and Politics*, New Delhi: Macmillan, 1999.

Kumar, Sanjay, 'The Return of the RJD', *Frontline,* 31 March 2000, p. 27.

Rangarajan, Mahesh, 'Strength in Numbers', *The Times of India*, New Delhi, 22 March 2000.

Riker, William, 'Duverger's Law Revisited', in *Electoral Laws and Their Political Consequences*, ed. Arend Bernard and Grofman Lijpart, New York: Agathon Press, 1986.

Singh, M.P., 'Coalition And/Or Minority Governments in India', *Journal of Government and Political Studies,* vol. XVI, March 1997.

Sridharan, E., 'Coalition Politics in India—Lessons from Theory, Comparison and Recent History', *Occasional Papers*, New Delhi: Centre for Policy Research, May 1997.

———, 'Duverger's Law, its Reformulation, and the Evolution of the Indian Party System', *Occasional Papers*, New Delhi: Centre for Policy Research, May 1997.

CHAPTER 13

Pyramids of Coalitions: The Base *versus* the Apex

Ajit Kumar Jha

INTRODUCTION

Indian democracy has always been a paradox. As polities mature, its institutions consolidate. In India, it is the other way round. On 26 January 1950, when the Republic of India was created with a modern Constitution, the country was poor but appeared robust as far as its political institutions were concerned. For the next two decades, although its traditions seemed partly grafted from colonial foundations and partly the result of a national political movement, it continued to be the only beacon of hope for most democrats in the entire of the Third World. Still in its formative years, independent India reaped two full decades of political stability from 1947-67.

At the turn of the millennia as Indian Republic crosses fifty, its fragility becomes evident. As political competition increases, stable majorities become impossible to achieve. As political empowerment spreads, governance becomes a casualty. As the Leviathan of yester years, the Congress party, described as the one-party dominant system by the older generations of political scientists, gets marginalized by the electoral mechanism durability of governments shorten. In the last four years since 1996, India has had three general elections and five governments. In fact, the majority of coalition governments do not last its full term. Quite a few of the coalition attempts in the states are 'still' born, with President's rule as the only resort and suspended animation of the house the only alternative.

In the circumstances, with apprehensions of increasing instability, and the fear that the centre will not hold, and with even the possibility of eventual disintegration looming large, the phenomena of coalition politics appears as the great harbinger of new hope. At a time when the mood is full of pessimism, coalition arrangements seem like the new glue in the Indian tradition of party splittings and political sectarianism, the new cement in the Indian universe.

What is coalition politics? Former Prime Minister V.P. Singh's pithy phrase 'the nation is a coalition' although elegant and visionary makes it difficult to define. Former Agriculture Minister and former Chief Minister elect of Bihar, Nitish Kumar, provides a more tangible answer: 'Coalition politics is a form of seat-sharing arrangement among partners whereby the splitting of votes is prevented.' Nitish Kumar defined that as the purpose of NDA in Bihar. But that surely is coalition politics before an election. After elections, coalition politics represent lobbying and bargaining for distribution of loaves, the cabinet portfolios, the payoffs in game-theoretic language.

Central to coalition politics is a notion of sharing, seats and votes, lobbying and bargaining for payoffs and negotiating, mediating, and arbitrating for institutional arrangements for the sake of governance. In short, as Western theories of coalition emphasise, it is a power maximizing principle. Based on this central assumption, political scientists have modelled coalition behaviour. The formal theory on coalition making can be broadly classified into two divisions: power maximizing and ideology-based principle. Inspired by rational choice theory and game theory, the Western theoretical literature focuses on two main aspects of coalition government formation in democracies: one, the formation of a minimum winning coalition (MWC) (William Riker, 1962); and two, the stability of a minimum connected winning coalition (MCWC) (Robert Axelrod, 1982). In fact, the second aspect is more a rider to the first, an afterthought based on the realization that ideological proximity is crucial to the stability of a coalition.

I do find much of the positive theory developed in the West necessarily useful in understanding certain aspects of coalition formation in India, but it is surely not sufficient. India being federal, multi-cultural, multi-ethnic with the presence of a multiparty system (with multi-polarity) both at the centre and the states, its coalitional arrangement requires a new kind of theorizing. I have made some attempts in this paper to arrive at some generalizations based on empirical examples drawn from the various case studies of India and its states.

Although a detailed historical essay from the time the first coalitions arrived on the scene is the need of the hour, I venture to model the structure of the emerging coalition in India. Next, I try to locate the principal tension among coalition players, and unravel the central conflict between coalition layers. The coalition at the centre, particularly since 1996, is not only a result of the coalition among the various players at the state level, but the coalition at the apex holds only as long as the coalition players at the base support it. In other words, the mandate for the coalition at the apex is provided by the coalition players at the base of the pyramid.

The conflict, therefore, I argue, is less around issues of ideology and more around concerns of territoriality. In other words, the main conflict among the various levels of coalition in India is between the forces in the states and the countervailing forces at the centre. In short, the principal conflict between coalition players is between the base and the apex.

This paper is, therefore, divided into four parts. The first, as is evident, introduced the subject with a brief mention of the prevailing theories. Second, I begin with my case study of Bihar for two reasons—one, it challenges conventional coalition theory turning it on its head; two, it helps me build up the argument for the base *versus* apex model step-by-step. Third, I try to put forth a brief historical sketch of the various trends and patterns in coalition making in India. Since in this paper I attempt to build a model of coalitions suitable to the Indian context, the model has two aspects: micro foundations and a macro design provided by the two case studies. Finally, as a conclusion I draw generalizations from the Indian experience of coalition making and indicate towards some new areas where research should be carried out in coalition politics in India.

CASE STUDY OF BIHAR

Coalition politics began in Bihar in 1967, the same year when the Congress party lost for the first time in six other states in north India and Tamil Nadu. The SVD which assumed power, was an amalgamation of disparate group with enormous ideological divergences, from the Socialists to the conservatives. The result was extreme political instability and for a while governments fell every month or so. Political uncertainty was aggravated by the fact that President's rule was imposed on the state by Indira Gandhi under one pretext or another. Subrata Mitra's Ph.D. thesis on cabinet instability and Bruce Bueno de Mesquita's first book on political coalitions provide some interesting details of the ups and downs of this tumultous period. Bihar was rescued from extreme political instability by the revival of the Congress party by 1972.

The next phase of coalition governments began in Bihar in 1978 when the Janata Party under Karpoori Thakur formed the government in Bihar. The BJS controlled several important portfolios, including the important finance portfolio under Kailashpati Mishra. That was the first coalition arrangement that lasted a little over two years.

Since then Bihar has had several coalition arrangements that have been more or less stable and have lasted their full-term. Even the JD government under Laloo Prasad Yadav both in 1990 and 1995 were essentially coalition arrangements. Similarly, the RJD government of Rabri Devi (1998-2004) was also a coalitional arrangement until Laloo Yadav made forays into the enemy camp and weaned away thirteen JD legislators into the RJD fold. An abortive attempt was made at President's rule by the NDA government at the centre but the mission failed after a couple of months due to presidential intervention.

PARADOXES IN BIHAR's POLITICS OF COALITION

But the coalitions that have contested Assembly elections 2000 in Bihar are different from past coalitions in Bihar in two important respects. First, conventional coalition theory always started with the dictum: 'united we stand, divided we fall'. In other words, if two partners *A* and *B* are together in an alliance against the third player *C*, than both *A* and *B* stands to gain, while *C* stands to lose. It is commonly assumed that while the sharing of seats to prevent splitting of votes leads to gain for both, division of seats leads to splitting of votes. Therefore, division of seats between two possible partners leads to loss for both the players. The recent experience of coalition politics in Bihar disproves this otherwise intuitive assumption.

Consider this: While the Congress and the RJD contested the Lok Sabha elections 1999 in an alliance of sorts, the same two partners fought separately in Bihar Assembly elections 2000. The results:

While both the RJD and the Congress performed disastrously during the Lok Sabha (when they had the alliance), the two performed relatively better in the Assembly elections (when they had no alliance). The results were not only unexpected by the leaders themselves and proved to be counterintuitive for most people, they ended up falsifying all tall claims of predictions by pollsters and political pundits. The RJD, along with the Congress, the BSP, and some independents ended up forming a minimum winning coalition, thus swearing in the Rabri Devi government and winning the vote of confidence.

With the help of the alliance in Lok Sabha 1999, the RJD merely secured seven out of fifty-four Lok Sabha seats in Bihar, the Congress three. The RJD were leading in about eighty-five Assembly segments. In Assembly elections 2000 without the alliance, the RJD secured 124 Assembly seats, almost one and half times of their 1999 records. The Congress, which contested the Assembly elections alone in all 324 places, ended up wresting twenty-three seats.

What are the lessons from this empirical example?

1. United we fall, divided we stand; not always but in some cases.
2. A three-cornered contest is better than a two-cornered in a first-past-the-post-system, if and only if you have a threshold of close to one-third seats.

Since the time interval between the Lok Sabha elections held during Diwali 1999 and the Vidhan Sabha elections held right before Holi 2000 was less than six months, the Lok Sabha results were used by most political observers as indicators for predicting the Vidhan Sabha elections. They thus failed to predict the Vidhan Sabha outcome.[1]

Why such a paradox of performance? Why is it better to contest against your poll partner than ally with it, when challenging your principal opponent? A complete answer will only be available when all the data for both the election at the lowest unit, the polling station is available. But *prima facie* evidence suggests three ad hoc answers.

First, since both the Congress and the NDA stood on the same side of the main cleavage during the Assembly elections, i.e. they both contested on an anti-Laloo plank, they divided the anti-Laloo, anti-incumbency votes between themselves, thus providing an edge for the incumbent RJD government.

Second, the Congress and the NDA, other things being different, have one thing in common: both of them compete for more or less the same voters, the upper castes. The Congress by fielding a large proportion of Brahmin candidates in north Bihar, mainly in Mithilanchal and the Kosi region, rocked the NDA applecart, which had relied heavily on Rajput and Bhumihar bases. The consequences of this infighting: the RJD won by default in most of this region. Early estimates show that at least in fifty-eight constituencies of north Bihar, if the Congress' vote is subtracted from the margin of victory, the NDA would have won instead of the RJD.

Third, the anti-Laloo parties during elections ended up as pro-Laloo parties after elections more due to the compulsion of central politics than ideological proximity. The enemy's enemy is after all a friend. So while the state unit of the Congress party in Bihar is desirous of distancing itself from Laloo's RJD, the central high command finding the NDA a bigger enemy in the country, ends up imposing its fiat on the state level Congress party. Paranoid about a split within the state Congress, the central leadership not merely issued a chief whip but ended up permanently posting two central observers, Mohsina Kidwai and Ajit Jogi, in Patna.

This conflict between the central high command and the state unit of a party, here the Congress, is the kernel of what I consider the principal contradiction between the base and the apex of the pyramid of coalition in India. It is present in all coalitions, however, different the structure. It is precisely such hot points that lead to the demise of a particular coalition and the rise of an alternative coalition. More of this in the next section.

First, consider the conflicts within the NDA coalition in Bihar. While the BJP is the major player in the alliance, the minor players, viz. the Samata Party and the JD(U); even the Bihar People's Party (BPP), gained at the cost of the BJP. The minor players ended up being pivotal players both in terms of the choice of the chief ministerial candidate as well as in terms of garnering the major proportion during seat distribution.

For instance, while the BJP had contested twenty-nine seats in the Lok Sabha 1999, the Samata Party together with the JD(U) contested merely twenty-three seats. But consider the seat adjustment exercise among the NDA partners during the Assembly elections. While only 150 seats went to the BJP out of 354, Samata got 90, the JD(U) 64 and the BPP 20. Clearly, the share of the BJP allies went up compared to the BJP. Even the total of the Samata and JD(U) (154) was higher than the BJP's share of 150. Interestingly, while the Samata had fought for the JD(U)'s inclusion in the NDA alliance during the Lok Sabha elections, the two partners bargained separately for seats since they had split up. There is a parallel between this example and the RJD–Congress example disused earlier.

Two lessons from this example:

i. The pivotal player is invariably the minor partner in coalition since it has less stakes and can, therefore, bargain much more.
ii. It is better for allies to split up and bargain separately than unite and bargain together with the enemy.

HISTORY OF COALITIONS

India has, indeed, become a nation of coalitions, ever since the dominant party system, represented by the monopoly of the INC, ended in 1967. Coalition governments were formed in half the states (eight out of sixteen) for the first time, the Congress having lost in half of them. Gradually the turbulence in the Indian states began having affect at the centre, and almost a decade later Delhi witnessed a coalition government under the Janata Party experiment between 1977-80. The fact that the turbulence in 1967 was essentially in the northern states with the exception of Tamil Nadu was evident in 1977 since the Janata Party was essentially a northern phenomenon.

The entire 1980s witnessed a Congress revival at the centre, perhaps due to the apparent instability of the coalition experiment, which only lasted for three years but had two governments. However by 1989, the coalition experiment was back under V.P. Singh, his too remained more or less a northern phenomenon. It lasted for two years and the Congress revival began once more under Narasimha Rao's minority government. Like V.P. Singh, Narasimha Rao ran a minority Congress government with the help of some small partners.

Since 1996 all union governments have survived in Delhi because of coalitions. The two successive UF governments led by Deve Gowda and the next one led by I.K. Gujral were governments of over one dozen parties (both from the northern as well as the southern states) supported by the Congress and the CPI(M) from the outside. The two successive governments of the BJP, led by Prime Minister Atal Behari Vajpayee, have been coalition governments, the present NDA government supported by two dozen parties. (The first 13-day coalition ministry of Vajpayee could not win the vote of confidence and therefore resigned since it did not have the numbers.)

While the vacuum at the centre has been filled up by regional forces for a while, and of late by the BJP-led NDA, what is unmistakeable about the new pattern is the emergence of a new system—the coalition system. Since the decline of the one-party dominant system, the dominant party being the Congress, India has, indeed, become a nation that survives because of coalitions.

The important points to note are the following:

1. The 1996 coalitions were different from the earlier ones in that they were more broad based being from both the northern as well as the southern states.
2. Territorial and competition for votes were more important in terms of potential conflicts compared to ideology. For instance, the way the TDP switched loyalties in 1988 from the UF coalition to the BJP-led coalition. Reason: since Congress is the main rival for the TDP in Andhra Pradesh, they were averse to supporting the Congress-supported UF, as against supporting the BJP, which was hardly a rival in Andhra Pradesh.
3. Consider the CPI(M) shift as well. Earlier the CPI(M) was also averse to supporting the UF being rooted for by the Congress because the Congress was the main rival of the CPI(M) in West Bengal. But later, since after the rise of Mamata Banerjee and her siding with the BJP, the Congress became less of a enemy for the CPI(M), the Communists switched gear.
4. While the two UF governments were remote controlled by the Congress from the outside, therefore, they were unstable. As long as remote control is not allowed and each partner of the coalition allowed to join the council of ministers, the probability of stability becomes pretty high.

CONCLUSION

The discussion can be summarized in terms of propositions:

1. In all coalitional political arrangements, the minor player becomes the pivotal player. Additionally, the minor player that has less stakes

in the game ends up gaining more from the bargain than the major player, which has more stakes in the game.

2. The territorial conflicts dominate over the ideological contradictions. This usually becomes the reason for political instability and at times leads to formation of new coalitions.
3. Coalition governments are stable: if and only if all the players who form the coalition (thereby sharing the transaction costs) benefit from the resources at the disposal of the coalition. In short, coalition governments last longer if all the major and minor players join the cabinet or at least are provided with some payoffs.
4. Coalition governments are unstable if there are remote control players, for instance, the Congress in the two UF governments of Deve Gowda and I.K. Gujral.
5. Minimal winning coalitions end up with maximal distribution of state resources. To gain with the cabinets are usually large. The portfolio distribution does not follow any proportionately principle, viz., the Gamson hypothesis, or the Janata Party quota rule, but as is usual in coalition games the minor player is the pivotal player.
6. The volcanic faults lines of the various national coalitions—whether the UF or the NDA—lies along two dimensions: the ideological and the territorial. The ideological dimension will be the classic left-right split, or on both sides of a central agenda: say the Emergency or Ayodhya. But much more important is the territorial dimension: as among the various constituents of the national level alliances.

Since the Congress and the BJP (national level parties) have a presence in most states, unlike say the Communist parties, the probability of a conflict between the BJP and its allies over say the budget cuts or the RSS issue is as likely to flare up as that between the Congress and its allies. The example of the latter when in UP elections in 1996, the BSP–Congress alliance hurt the SP–JD alliance.

Additionally, in a hydraulic economy such as rural India where 70 per cent of the population is still dependent on agriculture, the tensions that have emerged among the various partners—whether of the UF or the NDA—not surprisingly have been around riparian states sharing irrigation water. The Cauvery water dispute between Karnataka and Tamil Nadu, the Almatti project controversy or the Krishna river between Karnataka and Andhra Pradesh, and the

Sardar Sarovar on the Narmada river between four states of Madhya Pradesh, Gujarat, Maharashtra and Rajasthan are cases in point.

7. Positive feature of coalition governments: President's rule 105 times in the past under Congress regime. It is rarely imposed now. The trend is towards greater devolution of power to the states. Political coalitions surface at two levels. At the institutional level of political parties, single-issue pressure groups or interest groups and lobbies. Political parties are essentially long-term coalitions of single-issue interest groups. The latter are short-term coalitions. Coalitions also surface at the level of deep structures such as castes, classes, regions and other cultural and ethic identities. The two levels are essentially related. And the purpose of further research in coalition politics should be to unravel the unwieldy knot in terms of the relationship between the two levels.

NOTE

1. Therefore, most psephological predictions gave the RJD anywhere between sixty to eighty-five seats, whereas the political analysts predicted about eighty to hundred seats for the RJD in the Assembly elections. While the RJD's disastrous performance, including the party supremo, Laloo Prasad Yadav's loss in Madhepura, stunned its top leadership in 1999, its relatively better show in 2000 equally surprised the top RJD leadership.

PART IV: COALITION GOVERNMENT AND PUBLIC POLICIES

CHAPTER 14

Coalition Politics and Economic Decision-making

Prem Shankar Jha

The article is being written at that awkward moment when the budget 2000 has not yet been presented, but will be out by the time it appears in print. This makes it possible that what I have to say below will be invalidated by its contents. However, for reasons explained below, that risk is small. For a month North Block has been leaking stories like a sieve that the coming budget is going to be a harsh one, because the government intends to make a serious dent in the huge fiscal deficit. It is now a safe bet that it will be nothing of the sort.

This became apparent when the NDA cabinet shot down two key recommendations of the Finance Minister last week. The first was to freeze all new recruitments to the central services except, for a few highly technical services, in order to bring down the size of the bureaucracy through superannuation. The second was to increase kerosene and cooking gas prices sharply in order to reduce the ten rupees per kilogramme subsidy on the former and the six and a half rupee per litre subsidy on the latter. The price hikes were, admittedly, only 'postponed' by 15 days. But it is a safe bet that when the measures are implemented they will bear only a remote resemblance to what the Finance Minister had originally proposed.

The reason is the wall of resistance that the measures have met from the BJP's partners in the NDA. The petroleum price hikes were allegedly put off to permit Chandrababu Naidu to complete the panchayat elections in Andhra Pradesh; but the most adamant opposition has come from Railway Minister Mamata Banerjee because her party,

Trinamool Congress, faces a state assembly election next year. Indeed Banerjee has just distinguished herself by presenting the most brazenly populist railway budget of the past two decades. Whatever little courage the BJP still retained after last week's setback has been leeched out of it by the resounding setback it, and the entire NDA, suffered in Bihar, where the RJD government dismissed by the union government was reinstated because the proclamation of President's rule in the state, approved by the Lok Sabha NDA majority, was rejected by the Rajya Sabha opposition majority, including the Congress.

The probable fate of the budgted forces us to ask ourselves a basic question. Is India a viable nation state? Is it ever likely to become one, or are we locked into a political system that must irreversibly lead to paralysis and eventual disintegration? There can be no definitive answer to these questions. Doom has been predicted for India more than once before, and India has shown an astounding capacity to confound the prophets. But the surest way to avert the risk is to face it squarely. And the risk is very real.

India is the only country in history to have successfully used democracy as a tool for nation building. In the whole of the Western world, the nation state had already been in existence for two hundred years before the advent of democracy. But today the very institution that India's leaders used to create the Indian nation state has become the greatest hurdle to its further consolidation and development. In the fifty years since the Constitution was enacted, the Indian political system has changed in three ways that were not foreseen by the founding fathers. The first is the separation of the parliamentary from the Vidhan Sabha elections. The second is the failure of the plurality voting system to prevent the proliferation of small but stable political parties at the national level. The third is the end of dominant party democracy and the emergence of coalition politics at the centre.

There is now not a single year in which at least three important states do not go to the polls. As a result there is not a single year in which the central government is not under severe pressure to postpone decisions that extract short-term costs from the people, no matter how beneficial these might prove in the medium and longer term. This did not incapacitate the central government when a single dominant party ruled India. But in 1989, dominant party democracy passed into history. Today almost the only thing anyone can be sure of is that all future governments will be coalition governments that will include several political parties with a vote base in only one state. To these the election in their home state is far more important than any election to the national Parliament. Members of any coalition government at the centre therefore hold a veto power on national policy but are taking decisions upon it on the basis of their parochial political concerns. This explains why some of the most development-minded and politically responsible political leaders, like Chandrababu Naidu and Mamata Banerjee, have opposed the subsidy reduction measures proposed by Yaswant Sinha, the Finance Minister.

Political competition makes it impossible for them to behave in any other way. For all Chief Ministers have learned that their political rivals will stop at nothing to oust them from power. A decade ago the BJP Chief Minister of Himachal Pradesh broke a state government employees' strike designed to push a demand for higher wages, on the grounds that the state budget simply could not bear the strain. In the 1993 state election, the BJP lost power with a 9 per cent decline in its vote, because the Congress promised the state employees everything they had asked for and more. The state was still reeling under that shock when the Fifth Pay Commission awards hit it in 1997. Today it is comprehensively bankrupt.

In Rajasthan, another BJP Chief Minister, Bhairon Singh Shekhawat, paid a similar price in 1998 for trying, among other things, to raise the price of electricity for its rural and urban consumers during the previous five years. In Andhra Pradesh, Naidu's predecessor and father-in-law, N.T. Rama Rao, promised two rupees a kilogramme rice ration and prohibition to oust the Congress. The TDP won the election, but when NTR died, Naidu was left to face the bankrupt Andhra treasury. In Haryana, Mr Bansi Lal also made his successful bid for power by promising prohibition. Both governments had to go back on this rash action but only after they had brought their states to bankruptcy.

Hard decisions are made next to impossible not only by competition within each state but between states. Haryana tried to raise power tariffs on the rural sector in 1992, but next door, Punjab, which was getting power for virtually nothing from the Bhakra Dam, also insisted on giving it away to the rural sector virtually free. The outrage of Haryana farmers forced the government to lower tariffs once more. Today the nation faces government by the lowest common factor. The factor is populism. Thus only one state has to succumb to the temptation to make populist promises for all the rest to feel compelled to follow. This explains why subsidies have gone out of control during the 1990s. The cause is not economic reform but the end of dominant party democracy and the institutionalization of government by coalition.

The only antidote to such parochialism and populism is the loss of power. In the cabinet system of government, this threat is created by a combination of the simple majority voting system and the prospect of dissolution of the legislature. The plurality voting system severely penalises smaller parties by giving them, proportionately, far fewer seats than votes. Thus a defecting group or alliance partner faces a complete rout in the next elections unless it can find a home in the rival coalition. This remorseless pressure results in the gradual absorption of smaller parties into larger ones till one is left with a two-party or two-coalition political system. In India this has happened in state politics, but the very process that has yielded stability in the states has institutionalized instability at the centre. For each state party, like the DMK, the Samata Party or the TDP now has a stable vote base that it can translate into a few seats in the Lok Sabha. This has resulted in there being no fewer than thirty-five parties at the centre, none of which is under any great pressure to minimise its differences with its alliance partners.

This cannot help but yield a weak coalition government at the centre, which stays together only so long as nothing it does threatens the vote base of its members in the home states. For a country facing the pressures of globalization on one hand, and fighting a war against a smaller but intensely determined neighbour on the other, this is a recipe for disaster.

The impact of the development of coalition politics on the economy is best reflected in the struggles the Vajpayee government is facing in cutting subsidies. The government has put off raising the price of petroleum products yet again. The first time it did so was two weeks before the announcement of the budget on 29 February 2004. The pretext then was that the TDP, one of the NDA's more important constituents, was facing panchayat (local government) elections in its home state of Andhra Pradesh. The Chief Minister of Andhra Pradesh, Chandrababu Naidu, feared that his party's prospects would be adversely affected by a rise in kerosene and LPG prices, and asked the centre to defer the rise till these elections were over.

This time, the government has decided to postpone the increase till after the meeting of the Organization of Petroleum Exporting Countries (OPEC) on 29 March. OPEC is expected to bring down the price of crude oil in response to pleas by the consumers, by raising its production quotas. The government's logic, that it is pointless to raise the prices of oil products only to lower them again a few days later, therefore sounds impeccable. That is, till one remembers that it never had any intention of raising prices sufficiently to eliminate the entire subsidy on cooking gas and kerosene. Newspaper reports had indicated after the first postponement that the government was planning to eliminate subsidies in three or more stages. Thus all that a fall in petroleum prices after 29 February would have done was to reduce the amount by which the price would have had to be raised in the future.

The truth is that the government is being forced, step-by-step, to renege on its promise to cut subsidies in order to reduce the fiscal deficit. Whatever Chandrababu Naidu's parochial concerns may have been, it is hardly coincidental that he is also the ring leader of a concerted move among the allies of the BJP in the NDA, to roll-back the cut in food grains and fertilizer subsidies that the Finance Minister announced in the budget. The cuts would together have totalled a measly Rs. 5,000 crore. Compared to the centre's fiscal deficit of Rs. 109,000 crore, and the estimated explicit subsidies of the centre and states of Rs. 150,000 crore, this is a peanut. But even this small fiscal correction was too much for Mr Naidu to stomach.

In much the same manner, the resistance within the NDA to the government's attempt to reduce the subsidy on petroleum products, especially on kerosene, is being led by Mamata Banerjee, the head of the Trinamool Congress. The fact that Mr Vajpayee has had to postpone the increase a second time shows that she too has found powerful supporters among the other partners in the NDA.

One can only hope that Mr Vajpayee and Mr Sinha will find the courage to resist the blackmail of their alliance partners and at least limit the roll-back that they are demanding. One is also tempted to blame Mr Sinha for not framing a strategy for reducing subsidies that took account from the outset of the fact that this was not an economic but a political problem. The key to its success would have been to tackle central and state subsidies together, to hammer out a strategy for doing so in meetings of the National Development Council, and to frame the reductions in such a way that there were at least as many gainers as losers. In India, the last would have been easy because four-fifths of the subsidies go to smugglers, inefficient or crooked manufacturers, and organized middle-income groups with the necessary political clout to feather their nests at the expense of the exchequer. Simply refocusing the existing subsidies would have benefited millions of poor people while cutting out the criminals and the more affluent recipients.

But in the final analysis, blaming the central government is an exercise in self-deception. It amounts to playing ostrich before the most frightening threat to its unity that India has yet faced. This is the fact that the impulse to prevent the reduction of central subsidies is coming not from populist or ideologically motivated national parties but from parochial parties that have strong and stable bases in a single ethno-national state.

This is self-evident when one examines how the two postponements of oil price hikes has actually taken place. The resistance to these, and other measures to reduce the fiscal deficit is not being spearheaded by a backwoods politician like Laloo Yadav of Bihar but by arguably the most forward looking Chief Minister in the country. Chandrababu Naidu of Andhra Pradesh has been dubbed India's cyber minister. He has already demonstrated his ability to take hard decisions in Andhra Pradesh by repealing the prohibition that was introduced as a populist gimmick by his late father-in-law, N.T. Rama Rao, and by reducing the scope of the rice-for-the-poor scheme to a level that the state budget can withstand. It is this same man, who did not shrink from reducing subsidies in his home state, who has emerged as the chief opponent of cuts in subsidies at the centre.

Had this been an isolated incident, one could have ascribed it to some quirk in his personality. But Naidu's behaviour is filling out a pattern that had already begun to emerge during the UF government. During the UF regime, it was not Mulayam Singh Yadav or even Laloo who emerged as the chief opponents of reform but the LF. Even while it was running a pragmatic, social democratic government in West Bengal that was ardently, and successfully wooing foreign direct investment into the state, the LF sent three of its most committed ideologues to man the steering committee of the UF in Delhi. These gentlemen sabotaged Mr Chidambaram's first effort to impose austerity on the central government by reducing not its plan but its revenue expenditures, stalled the increase in petroleum prices for a full ten months till the accumulated deficit on the oil account touched Rs. 20,000 crore, and finally sabotaged the effort of the government to reduce the impact of the pay hikes under the Fifth Pay Commission by raising the retirement age of central civil servants by two years.

Nor was the LF the only culprit. G.K. Moopanar, the leader of the forward looking TMC, peremptorily summoned the UF Finance Minister, Mr Chidambaram, to Chennai in the middle of talks with the central government employees' unions and ordered him not to go back till these had been concluded, on pain of expulsion from the party. Despite being a member of the cabinet sub-committee, which was negotiating the final pay package, Chidambaram complied. As a result, the remaining four members vied with each other in making populist concessions without any check from the finance ministry and ended by giving the employees 40 per cent more than the Pay Commission had recommended.

The pattern has persisted into the BJP-led second government, the NDA. Mamata Banerjee shares not one but two traits with the Andhra Chief Minister. She too is a forward looking and responsible politician with no dearth of courage, and she too is attempting to strengthen her base in just one state on the basis of an appeal to ethno-national sentiment.

The pattern that is emerging makes it necessary for every concerned Indian to ask himself the following question: If the very leaders who do not shrink from taking hard decisions in pursuit of economic growth in their own home states become the strongest opponents of similar hard decisions at the national level, then what is the future of the Indian union? The answer is truly grim. India's ethnic sub-states may prosper, but the Indian state will sink deeper and deeper into a crisis. The lack of resources will make it more and more difficult for it to meet essential common needs like defence, the strengthening of the economic infrastructure, and, the reduction of the gap between rich and poor states through differentiated investment. In short, all the functions that are essential for cementing the unity of the nation will atrophy. And this leads us to the next question: If India's centre continues to weaken but the states, or at least some states, continue to grow economically stronger, how long will it be before India starts to break up?

Chandrababu Naidu, Mamata Banerjee, G.K. Moopanar, Om Prakash Chautala and others of their ilk would do well to pause a moment and reflect on the consequences of their actions. They most certainly do not want India to break up. But that is where their attempt to have their cake and eat it at the same time will take the country.

CHAPTER 15

Coalition Governments and India's Foreign Policy

Nalini Kant Jha

With the gradual decline of the Congress and inability of any single party to occupy the space vacated by that party, coalition governments seem for the foreseeable future an inevitable part of India's democratic process. The inevitability of a coalition government at the union level is being more or less accepted not only by political pundits, but also by the prominent leaders of BJP and the Congress. This development in Indian politics has understandably generated debate about problems and prospects of coalition politics in the country.[1] The ongoing debate about the implications of the coalition era has, however, confined only to domestic field. In the process, a systematic effort has hardly been made to examine the relationships between the compulsions of coalition politics and foreign policy behaviour. This is especially surprising in view of the fact that Western scholars have increasingly emphasized the linkages between changes in political regimes and foreign policy restructuring in the Third World countries.[2] The present paper, therefore, intends to examine the implications of coalition politics for the making of foreign policy in India.[3]

II

It is generally argued that the foreign policy of a country is tailored to serve the national interest of that country. Implicit in this generalization is the belief that the nature of regime hardly makes a difference so far as the foreign policy making is involved, which is often marked by bipartisan approach. However, in order to understand foreign policy, the analyst has to go beyond this general level and break the concept into some specific components. The literature on foreign policy, analysis seems to emphasize three points, a sort of 'holy trinity': physical survival, economic well-being, and freedom of action or manoeuvrability at the international level.[4] But this is where the problem begins.

First, the concept of national interest is extremely vague because the components are not operationalized: for instance, does economic well-being mean economic self-sufficiency or does it rather follow the neo-classical trade theory of comparative trade advantage? Second, the components can be incompatible as some current debates clearly show: for example, 'guns *versus* butter'. The intense debate within India about the fallouts of the BJP-led government's decision to conduct nuclear tests vividly illustrates the subjectivity of the concept of national interest. Third, how does one integrate into the national interest trinity a foreign policy objective such as prestige, an objective that seems to be part and parcel of many countries' foreign policy? Fourth, there is also the ambiguity about immediate gains and long-term gains of a foreign policy move. While cooperating with the South Asian neighbours, the governments led by Indira Gandhi and Rajiv Gandhi, for example, insisted on reciprocity on their part, the non-Congress regimes of I.K. Gujral and Atal Behari Vajpayee attempted to improve ties with them without insisting on strict reciprocity to serve India's long-term interests.

At a less dramatic but equally basic level, the classical view about national interest ignores the question: whose national interest are we talking about within the state? Is it not possible that given the vagueness of the concept, each government or elite group may 'interpret' a country's national interest to promote its own interest? Such an interpretation may benefit the nation as a whole or—most probably the case—benefit one segment more than another. For example, a defence programme might find its effect trickling down to some of the unemployed, the rural population or the marginalized urban. However, the programme's primary benefit would go to the military within the country or to an external firm, in addition to speculators or commission-mongers.

But the classical view about national interest as the goal of foreign policy is based on the wishful thinking that though leaders accord priority to their own interest in domestic politics, they forget their interest to promote national interest once they turn their attention towards the making of foreign policy. In reality, however, leaders are often more concerned with their own survival or the interest of their regime rather than overall national interest in formulating and executing both domestic as well as foreign policies. It is a different matter that in certain circumstances such as in a stable democratic political system, the need of and room for using foreign policy for the sustenance and survival of a regime in power is much lesser as compared to an authoritarian and close political system.[5] As this writer has explained elsewhere, Mrs Indira Gandhi, for instance, used India's foreign policy during the Emergency to seek the legitimacy of her Emergency regime.[6] It is entirely a different matter that the regime interest need not necessarily clash with national interest. As I shall explain later, Indira Gandhi's interest of political survival as well as national interest dictated a friendly policy towards the erstwhile USSR after the Congress split in 1969.

The neglect of the conceptualization about the implications of the nature of regime for the foreign policy hits at the foundation of the classical approach to foreign policy analysis, which ignores the fact that in the name of national interest, a state's foreign policy is actually made by individuals in power. Such an approach also underestimates the human qualities such as fickleness and occasional mistakes of decision makers. As a result, this mental map excludes the various characteristics of regime, the complexity of state-society relations, and the different aspects of decision-making process. For, according to this model, each state has crystal clear concepts of its national objectives, their consequences, as well as the means-end trajectory to maximize gains and minimize losses. But if this rational approach were really applied by each and every decision maker, hardly any decision would fail. Obviously, this is not the case.

It is, therefore, necessary to go beyond the classical view about the national interest as the goal of foreign policy and rationality of foreign policy decision-making. Instead one must ask how many people are capable of viewing the world in a totally objective, unbiased manner? How many undertake the efforts to spell out goals and to come to grips with the often-agonizing choices between equally desired but mutually incompatible benefits? How many have the time to ponder all conceivable options, or possess the complete information to arrive at the very best solution? Pondering over these questions is especially essential in Third World countries like ours, which have weak institutions and where policy processes are usually personalized and regimes change without changing the type of government. The influence of the man at the top and the nature of regime should not then be overlooked in any worthwhile analysis of foreign policy.[7] This is, of course, not to argue that the nature of regime is the only or the most important factor in the making of foreign policy. Undoubtedly, however, out of several determinants of foreign policy behaviour such as the international milieu, domestic context, and personality factors, the nature of regime provides a significant clue to the understanding of foreign policy. The present paper therefore focuses at the implications of coalition governments for the making of India's foreign policy.

III

Coalition politics, and the consequent coalition government, can be perceived both in narrower political as well broader social senses. In its narrower political form, coalition government is a unique device of temporary political alliance between or amongst political parties in a parliamentary democracy. It comes into operation when an ambivalent electorate does not provide a clear mandate to any political party to form government. Political apathy of the ambivalent electorate in most cases reflects the failure of the political parties and leaders to carry conviction with the electorate regarding their ability to give an efficacious government. Coalition government is a response to this situation by the ad hoc coming together of two or more political parties for a temporary period with a specific objective of forming and running the government.

The formation of political coalition to form a government is, however, necessitated only at a later stage, when no single political party succeeds in forming a winnable social coalition. As many individuals tend to be politically influenced to make their electoral choices as a part of a group rather than in personal capacity, forging of a winning social coalition, is an integral part of the democratic process. In this broader social sense, coalition building implies initiation of measures to secure consensus among diverse social groups and communities in the pursuit of a common minimum programme. By this definition, in the competitive environment of democratic society, several agencies including broad mass movements, political parties, as well as the governments are constantly involved in building coalitions. It is only when attempts at forming a winnable social coalition by bringing together diverse interests under one roof of a single party fails, political coalition has to be created for the purpose of governance.

Viewed thus, Indian politics has often been coalitional. Those who believe that the era of coalition governments began in India in 1989, forget that the dominance of the Congress itself was an outcome of its evolution as a coalition. The INC before Independence was essentially a freedom movement under which people of diverse beliefs and background came together. The Swaraj Party, the Socialist Party, and, for a long time, even the Communist Party were within the Congress. It was a sort of what has been called an 'umbrella organization' with the all-embracing single aim of achieving the country's emancipation from foreign rule. Throughout the period of dominance, the real strength of the Congress was not its ideological or programme orientation or its performance in providing good governance, but its coalitional or consensual character. Not only was the single dominant Congress a social as well an ideological coalition, even the cabinet in the initial years was constituted on coalition principles. Thus, despite the commonly held understanding of the Indian political experience as a single-dominant party system transforming into a multiparty coalition, the modern Indian polity emerged as an example of coalition politics par excellence.[8]

With the accomplishment of the freedom and the consequent absence of the cementing national cause of independence, social coalition created during the course of national movement and sustained by the consensual politics of Jawaharlal Nehru began disintegrating by the mid-1960s leading to the emergence of several new parties and the formation of political coalition at the state level in 1967. The process of the erosion of consensual model reached its peak in 1969, when Mrs Indira Gandhi created a split in the grand old party. Following the Congress split, Mrs Gandhi's government was reduced to a minority and remained so for some time. As argued by Vernon Bagdonor, this kind of minority governments supported by one or more parties could also be constructed as coalition governments since such a support too is part of a temporary alliance between or amongst political parties.[9] Moreover, such a support, despite proclamations to the contrary, is never unconditional. I, therefore, an including the Nehruvian model of social coalition as well as Indira Gandhi's minority government during 1969-70 in this discussion of coalition governments and India's foreign policy.

The non-Congress governments at the union level during 1977-9 and 1989-91, too, in a sense were coalition governments of the Congress variety. Not only was the Prime Minister, Morarji Desai, a product of the Congress culture and a life-long Congressman, the JD itself was a coalition of several parties. Again, in 1989, the minority Janata Dal government headed by V.P. Singh, another former Congressman, was a coalition of several parties. Similarly, two coalitions headed by Deve Gowda (1996) and I.K. Gujral (1997) were also minority coalition governments formed by the JD and some regional parties such as DMK, TDP, AGP, and Congress (S). Both these governments could survive till the Congress party extended support to them without joining the government. The BJP has, however, been the first political party to understand the importance of creating a nation-wide political coalition. The expansion of the NDA led by the BJP from an eighteen-party coalition in 1998 to twenty-four-party broad-based coalition in 1999, consisting of some unexpected regional parties, manifested the flowering of the social as well as political coalition in the country. In the light of these preliminary introductory observations on coalition politics in India, this paper would attempt to examine the nature and tenor of India's foreign policy during the coalition governments.

IV

While legislative coalition of Congress, CPI, and some regional parties, notably DMK, came into existence only in 1969, in the social sense, Indian politics has been coalitional since the beginning. For, a vast country with an equally large population, India is almost a world in miniature.[10] It has a large variety of socio-religious, linguistic, regional groups and great amount of diversity in political opinion and economic interests.[11] It is not, therefore, surprising that both during the freedom struggle and thereafter Indian leaders had to develop ways and mechanism for accommodating diverse groups and interests. The Congress party that emerged as a grand social coalition under the leadership of Mahatma Gandhi and maintained its consensual character under the leadership of Nehru to respond to the challenges of nation and state building understandably opted for the centrist policies in domestic as well as foreign spheres. As explained by this writer elsewhere, Nehru opted for secularism and mixed economy in the domestic field and policy of non-alignment in the international sphere to facilitate the task of the building of the Indian nation.[12]

In addition to this imperative, one of the significant traits of Indian political culture that places a premium on *madhyam marg* (middle way) or rejection of any kind of extremism explains why Indian leaders attempted to refrain from embarking on radical shift in domestic as well foreign policies. In other words, Indian imperative of nation building and consequent socio-ideological coalition of the Nehruvian era when projected into foreign affairs inevitably led to a foreign policy, which could neither be pro-US nor pro-Russia, but only a policy of non-alignment.[13] While explaining the imperatives of India's policy of non-alignment in a course of speech at the Indian Council of World Affairs in New Delhi on 22 March 1949, Nehru clearly stated:

> Any attempt on our part, that is, the government of the day here, to go too far in one direction would create difficulties in our country. It would be resented and we would produce conflicts in our country, which would not be helpful to any other country.[14]

Nehru thus rightly thought that at a time when the informed public in India was bound to be sharply divided on the issue of Cold War, in view of the fact that it was advertised by both the blocs as a moral and intellectual conflict, and within India there were adherents of the ideologies advertised by both the blocs, non-alignment was the only consensus formula for foreign policy that could hold together the cross-sections of Indian public. Nehru therefore shunned both the political extremes of left and right in domestic as well as foreign policy to provide a viable government by building-up social coalition through accommodating various facets of opinion in a plural society and polity such as ours.

V

For the first time in the history of post-Independence India, the Congress suffered widespread electoral reverses in 1967 leading to fall of its governments in several states and substantial reduction in its majority in the Lok Sabha. This reflected not only a vote against widespread corruption prevailing in the Congress governments in states, but also an indication of the gradually disintegrating winning social coalition that had helped the Congress so far. As the rough and tumble of a highly competitive electoral politics and political expediency gradually reduced the social groups to vote banks, which could be wooed from election-to-election for success at the hustings, Indira Gandhi changed Congress's character from 'consensus' politics to plebiscitary politics. She reduced the social coalition into 'vote banks', approaching different sections of society individually and segmentally with sectional (even sectarian), limited and transient appeals.[15]

The Congress debacle in 1967 led to an intensive power struggle within the Congress in which Mrs Gandhi began to exert her independence from senior party leaders. This ultimately led to the Congress split in 1969. The split instead of ending the power struggle intensified and personalized it. As against the Nehruvian era, when the opposition attacked the party and not the personality, from 1969 onwards, the opposition concentrated its ire on Indira Gandhi and not on the Congress.[16] As struggle for power is nowhere naked, least of all in democracy, Mrs Gandhi wrapped her pursuit of power in the ideological garb of socialism and secularism. The articulation of party positions thus took the form of 'left' or 'right' of the centre. Not surprisingly, the socio-ideological coalition of the Nehruvian era that was already under strain since the Chinese aggression of 1962 now became a thing of the past. Notions that the time had come to 'fight a crucial battle against these forces of reaction'[17] blended easily into the new criterion for political morality. The split, moreover, reduced Mrs Gandhi's government into minority in Parliament. This compelled her to enter into alliance with the Communists for survival. The polarization of political forces was thus complete with the CPI, DMK, and PSP siding with the Congress (R) of Mrs Gandhi on the one hand and the right wing BJS, Swatantra Party, and BKD supporting the Congress (O) on other.[18]

The emergence of a new political coalition in the place of social coalition of the Nehruvian era had inevitable fallouts on India's foreign policy. As Mrs Gandhi's minority government needed the support of the Communists for survival at the union council, she had to cultivate the Soviet friendship. Besides, she needed the Communist support for enacting the Preventive Detention Act to curb the Naxalite menace in West Bengal. The CPI was, however, hesitant to extend its support on this issue for fear of inviting the charge of conniving with 'repressive measures', and Mrs Gandhi thus, also needed Soviet backing to persuade the CPI to cooperate with her government in this regard. Moreover, befriending the erstwhile USSR was necessary not only to serve India's international needs, but this was also likely to lend credibility to her 'progressive' image, which she had opted for in order to ensure her political survival. This was all the more necessary because her 'progressive' image was seriously compromised in the recent past due to her dependence on the USA for food aid and the Soviet lionizing of Kamraj Nadar, a critique of her US policy.

Mrs Gandhi was, therefore, under the compulsion to follow policies, both at home and abroad, that could provide her a 'progressive image', please Moscow and her so-called 'progressive' domestic supporters. This urge was reflected in the domestic sphere in the implementation of policies like the nationalization of banks in India and the withdrawal of privy purses and privileges of the princes. She epitomized her drive for socialism in the slogan of *Garibi Hatao* (eradicate poverty), which attracted favourable mass attention. In the foreign sphere, this compulsion found expression in an artificial tirade against the US and the playing up of CIA operations in India.[19] In both the domestic and foreign spheres, this compulsion was also reflected in Mrs Gandhi's growing reliance on her political adviser, P.N. Haksar, a civil servant, well known for his socialist and pro-Soviet inclinations.[20]

Not surprisingly, the Soviets enthusiastically welcomed the political changes in India, whereas the US appeared to give the impression of being uneasy and unenthusiastic. This further drove Mrs Gandhi closer to the erstwhile USSR. Though other factors such as India's defence and development imperatives as well as strategic divergences in India–US relations at that time were also important in this regard, yet Mrs Gandhi's domestic political considerations and her dependence on the Communists for the survival of her minority government were no less crucial in this respect.

VI

When the 1977 Lok Sabha elections brought the newly formed Janata Party—a combination of a number of political parties formerly in the opposition, together with some Congressmen, who had recently left their party because of their opposition to Indira Gandhi's Emergency rule—in power, there was a general expectation about changes in India's foreign policy especially with regard to its relations with the former USSR and Islamic countries. This was because several of the constituents of the Janata coalition (for, in essence, that was what it remained, despite the formal merger of the five groups) had, in the past, opposed aspects of foreign policy pursued by Nehru and his successors between 1947-76. The constituent parties had their own established positions on foreign issues and sanctified in their election manifestoes. These expectations about changes, of course, did not materialize. The then Foreign Minister, Atal Behari Vajpayee, was quick to declare that he would not act on the basis of his former views as a BJS leader; all the Janata constituents had subsumed their foreign policy positions in a more widely acceptable governmental consensus. Though the new government emphasized the need of a 'genuine' policy of non-alignment, it continued to maintain India's traditionally friendly ties with the erstwhile USSR and the Islamic countries of West Asia.[21]

With all its continuity, subtle yet significant shifts in India's foreign policy did occur during the Janata regime. Thus, although the policy of non-alignment and close, friendly relations with erstwhile Soviet Union continued, a greater keenness was discernible than before to improve ties with the US. American decision makers were quick to disavow assumptions of strategic incompatibility, evolved during the Indira era.[22] The newfound friendliness manifested itself in tangible terms, when in 1978, American direct developmental aid to India was resumed after a seven-year suspension. A series of significant visits of leaders of both the countries took place; the most important being President Carter's visit to India in January 1978 and Prime Minister Morarji Desai's return visit in June 1978. The Indo–US Joint Commission enjoyed some productive sessions. Though the initial euphoria about improvement in India–US ties could not sustain due to differences over nuclear issue and the expelling of American multinationals like Coca Cola and IBM from India, yet the climate of

Indo–US relations was better than any time during the last ten years of the Indira regime.

Similarly, though friendliness in Indo-Soviet relations continued and was manifested in a number of significant visits by leaders of each country and in conclusion of several agreements between them, yet the initial goodwill was certainly on a lower level than during the preceding decade. Janata made known its intention to look beyond Moscow's sales-lists for deep-penetration aircraft, and it turned to West German technology for a new steel process at the expense of existing arrangements with Soviets. The new government proved more effective in bargaining and it could settle Rupee–Ruble rate in India's favour after four years of debate. The Janata coalition's willingness to take the process of normalization of relations with China beyond the limited thaw secured by the Indira government was not too pleasing to the Soviets, which became apparent during Kosygin's visit to India in 1979.[23] Thus, even though the substance of Indo–Soviet relations did not undergo any major dilution, the Janata Party strove to avoid conveying the impression—prevalent under Indira Gandhi—that India's Soviet links obliged it to toe Moscow's line.

More significant changes could be noticed in India's policy towards the South Asian neighbours during the Janata coalition. Though the policy to improve relations with immediate neighbours had been a constant element of India's foreign policy especially after the 1962 Chinese aggression, the Janata Party showed more keenness in this regard than Mrs Gandhi. This policy exemplified not only by the series of visits made to the capitals of immediate neighbours, including Pakistan, in quick succession by the then Foreign Minister, Vajpayee, but also by the series of concessions made to these countries on such long-standing issues as the sharing of the Ganga water with Bangladesh, the construction of the Salal Dam in Pakistan, and the signing of two separate treaties—on trade and the other on transit—with Nepal. Indian diplomacy towards the immediate neighbours thus underwent significant changes. As against Indira Gandhi, who placed greater emphasis on the acceptance of India's dominant position in the region by the smaller neighbours, the Janata coalition went out of its way to show that it attached the highest priority to the establishment of a relationship with our South Asian neighbours based on mutual trust and cooperation.[24]

VII

These changes as well as continuity in foreign policy pursued by the Janata coalition were conditioned not only by international milieu as believed by some scholars,[25] but also by the compulsions of domestic politics in general and the working of coalition politics in particular. To begin with, if Mrs Gandhi's reign saw the fusion of all foreign policy-making authority in Prime Minister's hands, the Janata rule marked the diffusion of authority.[26] Having come to power on a strongly anti-authoritarian plank, the Janata government could hardly have reverted to Mrs Gandhi's style of functioning. In any case, the coalitional nature of the party precluded it. The locus of power no longer lay with the Prime Minister alone, but clustered around several factional leaders. Though the repercussions of this were more pronounced in domestic affairs, the ruling party spoke with more than one voice in foreign policy as well.

To cite only a few examples, while Prime Minister Desai declared foreclosing of India's nuclear option, Vajpayee stressed on retaining the option and thereby led the US to delay fuel shipments to Tarapur Power Plant. On China, Vajpayee spoke of improving the non-contentious aspects of India's relations with Peking, while Desai's early statements insisted on the need to resolve the border dispute before any other progress could be made. This promoted an international journal to 'wonder whether there is any point in sending Vajpayee to Peking at all'.[27] Desai got vocal support from the party General Secretary, Rabi Ray, and pro-Soviet Janata leader, Madhu Limaye. They regarded China as an imperialist power and stressed the need of maintaining traditional cordiality with erstwhile USSR to contain China.[28] A commentator, therefore, rightly observed that the government was not 'united enough to risk a border settlement with China'.[29] The Janata Defence Minister, Jagjivan Ram, was more vocal. His statements on military preparedness against Pakistan and China jeopardized Vajpayee's attempts to improve relations with these neighbours. His uncalled for criticisms of the Camp David Accord in the Middle East and support extended to this criticism by Madhu Limaye and Bahuguna obviously annoyed Egypt. The coalitional character of the Janata government thus led to pronouncements on foreign policy issues by cabinet ministers that were inconsistent with official positions.

The Lok Dal government led by Choudhry Charan Singh that came in power due to rank indiscipline in the Janata conglomeration, could not learn any thing from their past behaviours. Rather they elevated this to an art form. Charan Singh, whose authority, was already limited due the caretaker character of his government miserably failed to restrain his undisciplined colleagues like Raj Narain and C. Subramaniam. While Raj Narain's provocative statements on China and Tibet sent wrong signals to Peking, Subramaniam's call to the National Defence College for review of India's approach to the nuclear question seriously affected India's relations with the US, erstwhile USSR, China, and Pakistan. Nothing better could be expected from the Foreign Minister of such a government. An inexperienced, S.N. Mishra, represented India in the Commonwealth summit conference in Lusaka, where he embroiled India in a needless controversy by pursuing the Indian candidacy for the next Commonwealth Secretary-General—long after a consensus had already evolved for a second-term for the incumbent, Guyana.

Janata–Lok Dal coalition governments thus reflected the lack of planning and coordination at the foreign policy front. This could be explained more fruitfully by looking at the differences in terms of personality rather than in terms of factions or 'lobbies'. Even on the likely exception to this rule, the *kisan* lobby of Charan Singh did not truly act like a farmers' pressure group on foreign policy. It united on such issues as freedom for Tibet, opposition to compromise with China, and the condemnation of the *Jaguar* deal, none of which had any significant agrarian connection.

Whatever may be the intentions of these leaders, they and especially Raj Narain and Charan Singh introduced an element of unpredictability in India's external policy. The attacks in and out of Parliament on the *Jaguar* deal by these leaders against the Defence Minister, Jagjivan Ram, vividly manifested this fact.[30] The articulation of different viewpoints by the ruling party members—a tendency virtually non-existent under Mrs Indira Gandhi and her son, Rajiv Gandhi—however, enhanced the significance of Parliament and especially its consultative committee on foreign affairs, which benefited noticeably from the greater respect for pluralist institutions manifested by the Janata coalition.

VIII

After more than a decade of centralized and highly personalized foreign policy process under Indira and Rajiv,[31] India once again swung in the other direction: towards decentralization based on the inputs provided by various institutions that had originally been mandated to contribute to the framing of foreign policy. The NF government led by V.P. Singh in 1989 was a coalition of JD and several regional parties and it depended on 'outside' support of the right wing BJP and the LF. Accordingly, the Prime Minister was preoccupied with the problem of survival. He could therefore hardly spare time and energy for foreign affairs. He was also not very much interested in external affairs. Under the circumstances, other institutions concerned with the foreign policy process such as the Ministry of External Affairs (MEA), Cabinet, the Research and Analysis Wing (RAW), and Parliament began to re-assert their authority.

This change in the style of foreign policy process could be easily discerned in the manner in which some of the decisions were taken during the Gulf crisis that erupted due to Iraqi occupation of Kuwait. First, the NF government adopted a non-committal attitude towards the crisis. To avoid displeasing any one, it avoided taking a definite position and left the responsibility of handling Indian response in this regard to the MEA.[32] For the first time in the history of independent India, the Foreign Minister and his ministry got due autonomy to take a wide range of foreign policy decisions. Foreign Minister, I.K. Gujral, for instance, decided on his own to visit three capitals. He informed the Prime Minister just before he left. Such a decision under Indira and Rajiv would have been unheard of. As explained earlier, the Janata Foreign Minister, Vajpayee, too did not enjoy this autonomy.

Substantially, however, Gujral's policy towards the South Asian neighbours resembled the Janata policy of the abandoning of the 'big brotherly' attitude towards them. This was manifested in the withdrawal of the Indian Peace Keeping Force (IPKF) from Sri Lanka and normalization of relations with Nepal, which was disrupted due to Rajiv's clash of will with the king of Nepal. Though the emergence of democratic regime in Nepal also contributed to this normalization process, Gujral's contribution in this regard cannot be minimized.

The foreign policy making process continued to be decentralized during the premiership of Chandrashekhar, who manoeuvred to become

Prime Minister in the wake of the downfall of the V.P. Singh government. The position of this government was more precarious as the Prime Minister had only sixty-eight supporters in the Lok Sabha that consisted of 473 members. While the Prime Minister was preoccupied with the survival of his minority government with the support of Rajiv Gandhi, his Foreign Minister, V.C. Shukla, was concerned with his personal political survival, since he had been disqualified from continuing as a MP. Under the circumstances, neither the Prime Minister nor the Foreign Minister was in a position to devote due attention to foreign affairs. The officials in the MEA, therefore, continued to play a dominant role in the making of foreign policy. The Minister of State for External Affairs, Digvijay Singh, however, emerged as an additional significant player due to his interest in foreign affairs as he had studied the subject at the capital's Jawaharlal Nehru University. He tried to emulate the American system of interaction between the foreign policy establishment and academic experts.[33] The appointment of a leading expert on India's foreign policy, Professor Bimal Prasad, as India's Ambassador to Nepal was also a step in this direction. However, the Chandrashekhar regime was too short to sustain this innovative approach.

In Chandrashekhar's decision to unambiguously condemn Iraq's invasion on Kuwait, to send a delegation to China to discuss the resumption of border trade, to establish personal contacts with his Pakistani counterpart, Nawaz Sharif, and to visit Nepal to resolve bilateral issues, the input provided by the MEA was crucial.[34] Much to the annoyance of the MEA, however, the imperatives of survival of the coalition government obliged the Chandrashekhar government to allow Rajiv Gandhi to act as a Prime-Minister-in-waiting. This soon became apparent, when Rajiv Gandhi forced the government to withdraw transit and refuelling facilities to US Air Force transport planes during the Gulf crisis. New Delhi had granted this facility in accordance with its support to the UN Resolution 678, which authorized the use of force to free Kuwait from the Iraqi occupation. This government was also guided by India's traditional policy of opposing any aggression as well as by its desire to improve India's relations with the sole surviving super power, the US.[35] If the government nonetheless suddenly withdrew the refuelling facility, it was only due to pressures from Rajiv Gandhi, whose support was necessary for the government's survival. And

Rajiv was interested in mobilizing the anti-US and pro-Iraq sentiments of India's vast Muslim population (more than 100 million) to come back to power.[36]

Rajiv Gandhi's dream could not, however, materialize due to his assassination during the election campaign. The somewhat fractured electoral verdict forced his successor in the party, P.V. Narasimha Rao, to form the government only with the support of certain regional parties. He had to depend upon them for survival until he got his arithmetic right. Unlike Rajiv, he did not have firm control over his party; he received considerable challenge from his contenders within the party, who sought to dethrone him.[37] Not surprisingly, he could not centralize foreign policy decision-making despite his considerable knowledge of foreign affairs—much more than any other post-Rajiv Prime Ministers. The explosive internal situation generated by the Ayodhya movement compounded by the growing political uncertainty of his own political future as the head of his party could hardly enable him to shape a new global role for India in the post-Cold War era. India's foreign policy, therefore, remained tilted on the regional side, the basic underpinning of which was preserving India's pre-eminence in South Asia.[38]

IX

Inder Kumar Gujral's return to power after six years in 1996 first as Foreign Minister under the Deve Gowda government and then his elevation to premiership in 1997 brought a whiff of fresh air in the South Block. Given the composition of the thirteen-party UF government and Gowda's lack of interest in the area, Gujral got desired autonomy to respond to the post-Cold War global challenges. As if to announce this to the world, he displayed only one picture in his office, that of Jawaharlal Nehru, the architect of India's global role.

Unlike Nehru, however, he concentrated more on repairing the bridges of friendship with the South Asian neighbours rather than leading the Afro–Asian countries for improving the international system. He articulated his neighbourhood policy, known as the Gujral Doctrine, in London in August 1996. This policy was based on the principles of non-interference in the internal affairs of other countries, respect for each other's territorial integrity and sovereignty and settlement of dispute through peaceful methods. The most innovative aspect of the doctrine, however, was the recognition of India's responsibility as the most powerful country in maintaining peace by not expecting immediate reciprocity to this country's goodwill gestures towards smaller neighbours like Sri Lanka, Maldives, Bangladesh, Bhutan, and Nepal.[39]

As explained earlier, this policy was not altogether new. The Janata Foreign Minister, Vajpayee, and Gujral himself as the Foreign Minister in NF government had rejected the 'Indira Doctrine' that stressed on Indian dominance in the region. Vajpayee could not, however, get wide acceptability of that policy because of the existence of authoritarian regimes at that time in the South Asian periphery as also due to sharp criticisms of his policies by Indira Gandhi. Gujral, on the other hand, was luckier, as he had to deal with democratic regimes in these countries and more significantly with friendly governments in Bangladesh and Nepal. As against Indira Gandhi, Vajpayee, as opposition leader, also showed better understanding of the Gujral Doctrine. Besides, the support extended to Gujral by his coalition partners made his task easier. India's treaty with Bangladesh for the sharing of Ganga waters, for instance, could not have been concluded without much fuss in December 1996 without the key role played by West Bengal Chief Minister, Jyoti Basu, in finalization of the treaty. He brought a sense of empathy to the bargaining process, underpinned by an intimate knowledge of the interests of the West Bengal, an Indian riparian state having the most at stake. The Tamil Nadu Chief Minister, M. Karunanidhi, similarly helped Gujral in the task of working out a means of ensuring that *bona fide* fishing activity in the Palk Straits was not endangered by security worries in Sri Lanka.[40] Undoubtedly, these regional satraps wished to ensure the success of the union coalition government in which they participated through their nominees as key players.

These factors also helped Gujral to shape India's response to the challenges posed by the changing realities of the post-Cold War world. He could thus take a firm position on the Comprehensive Test Ban Treaty (CTBT), rejecting it first and vetoing it at Geneva later, when the treaty's sponsors tried to impose it on an unwilling India. He also took steps to gain support for this policy from the cabinet and from leaders of all political parties. It is indeed remarkable that while in the

Indian media quite a few questioned the government's policy in this regard, not a single member of either of the two houses of Parliament dissented from the official policy.

Gujral, however, had to face carping criticisms at home, when India lost to Japan badly in the contest for a non-permanent seat in the Security Council. But these critics forgot that the decision to seek this seat was taken by the Narasimha Rao government. Reversing this decision would have caused political problems for the UF government, which was dependent on the Congress support for survival.[41] This underscored the reality that if coalition politics facilitates the tasks of foreign policy makers, it also complicates their work. Thus if the coalition partners and solid domestic consensus partly contributed to the success of Gujral's efforts towards perceptible advance in India's relations with Bangladesh, Nepal, Sri Lanka, Russia, China, Iran, and Association of South East Asian Nations (ASEAN), his next agenda of improving ties with the US and Europe got a jolt because of uncertainties created by the Congress (I)'s withdrawal of support to the Deve Gowda government.

After elevation to premiership, Gujral retained External Affairs, his old love. This led to reassurance of continuity of the policies initiated by him and a promise of active engagement with the US and Europe. His pre-occupation with the new responsibilities and a host of problems associated with managing the coalition government, however, did not let foreign policy receive the attention it got the preceding ten months or so. As in a protocol-conscious world of diplomacy, the Foreign Ministers of other countries would not like to engage in a formal dialogue with the Minister of State here and the Prime Minister could not always spare time to talk to Foreign Ministers. Even if he wished to disregard protocol, he tried to partly address this problem by entrusting his coalition partners with foreign policy assignments. Examples are the Finance Minister P. Chidambaram's participation in the ASEAN and ARF meetings and the Industry Minister Murasoli Maran's contacts in London with the new government of Labour Party.

Prime Minister Gujral nonetheless failed to do justice with simultaneous responsibilities of managing the complex problems associated with heading a coalition government and responding to challenges of the fast changing world without a full-fledged Foreign Minister to assist him. The cancellation of his long overdue trip to Bonn and Paris in October 1997 due to his pre-occupation with the breakup of a coalition government in the largest Indian province of Uttar Pradesh was a logical outcome of his unmanageable dual responsibilities. The aborted trip was intended to fill a major gap in the Indian top-level diplomacy. Not surprisingly, the cancellation caused dismay not only among the top political leadership in the two capitals, including German Chancellor, Helmut Kohl, and French President, Jacques Chirac, but also among the top journalists and chief executives of industrial houses, who were to interact with the Prime Minister on possibilities of increased investment in India.[42]

X

Leaving aside the first government formed by the BJP in 1996 that could not last longer than thirteen days paving the way for the formation of the UF government headed by Deve Gowda, the next coalition government formed by the BJP in 1998 was better than preceding political coalitions, as it was formed after more sustained interaction between parties, which ultimately joined it. It had also a fuller and actual agenda and a coordination mechanism. But at the same time, the coalition suffered from a serious weakness because the BJP was too hasty in wooing partners; the temperament of AIADMK was not explored sufficiently leading to the fall of the government by one vote in April 1999. These plus and minus points of this coalition had significant implications for India's foreign policy.

To begin with, the formation of the BJP-led coalition government generated many apprehensions within India and abroad. For, the ruling parties had though changed, more than once, after the Congress monopoly of power at the centre had been broken in 1977, yet so far non-Congress Prime Ministers had been erstwhile Congress members. It was for the first time, that the leader at the helm was not a product of the Congress culture. He belonged to a party, which spelt out an assertive agenda in its 1998 election manifesto. The 18-point programme concerning foreign policy in the BJP election manifesto, for instance, not only expressed the party's determination to reject nuclear apartheid, but also to vigorously pursue India's case for a permanent membership of the UN Security Council, establish Indian sovereignty over the entire territory of Jammu & Kashmir including that which is now under Pakistan's occupation, and retrieve the territory ceded to China by Pakistan in 1962, etc.

When, however, the BJP formed the government with the help of its allies, the compulsions of coalition politics obliged it to drop some of its controversial agendas. The National Agenda for Governance formulated by BJP and its allies even while retaining programmes regarding reevaluation of nuclear policy and setting up a National Security Council, did not talk of retrieving Pakistan occupied Kashmir or territory ceded to China by Pakistan in 1962. Instead, the Agenda put stress on promoting regional and civilizational grouping on the lines of SAARC and ASEAN, and reorienting our diplomacy to pursue our economic and commercial goals.[43] The mixed complexion of the government made it easier for the BJP leadership to persuade the hard-liners within the party to be more pragmatic by simply pointing out that in view of the coalition arrangement, the government's policies can only be a product of a give and take.

The National Agenda nonetheless caused fears in the neighbourhood. It talked of promoting 'peaceful relationship with all neighbours on a reciprocal basis'. This generated apprehensions about departure from the policy of non-reciprocity, followed by Gujral, with good and beneficial results. Several BJP ideologues and foreign policy professionals had also been critical of Gujral for not seeking reciprocity in dealing with India's smaller neighbours in the last two years. Under the circumstances, a departure from the Gujral Doctrine appeared imminent. But the imperative of maintaining consensus in a coalition era apart, Vajpayee had the vision and sagacity to appreciate that the essence of the Gujral Doctrine was rooted in the political realism that India's aspirations for a larger global role cannot be realized so long as New Delhi was mired in conflicts within the subcontinent. Indeed, as indicated earlier, the so-called Gujral Doctrine was nothing but a culmination of the evolution of a positive approach to the neighbours over the years beginning with innovations made during Vajpayee's tenure as Foreign Minister in the Janata government.

Not surprisingly, the Vajpayee government acted in accordance with the broad consensus in the favour of deepening India's ties with the neighbours. The free trade agreement between India and Sri Lanka, for instance, was a major landmark not only in the bilateral era but, equally important, in the South Asian context. As such arrangements were already in place in regard to Nepal and Bhutan, this gave a boost to the move for the much talked-about South Asia Free Trade Area. Vajpayee's daring and innovative decision to visit Lahore for inaugurating the New Delhi–Lahore bus service and his acknowledgement of the reality of India's partition to rebuff his party hardliners was intended to move India's cooperative diplomacy beyond the river Sutlej, where the Gujral Doctrine had stopped. That Pakistan responded to his gesture by its Kargil misadventure and by masterminding the hijacking of the Indian aircraft are altogether different matters that need not detain us here. Fortunately, the inauguration of the Calcutta–Dhaka bus service during the height of the Kargil conflict to signal the government's determination to continue with India's peace initiatives has not met the same fate.

The BJP-led coalition also continued with the policy of 'extended neighbourhood'. The Rao government, to recall briefly, had taken a purposeful initiative towards South-East Asia, with its 'Look East' policy. He had also initiated interactions with newly independent republics of Central Asia and deepened relations with Iran. I.K. Gujral followed suit by looking beyond the narrow confines of South Asia. The BJP Foreign Minister, Jaswant Singh, too, reaffirmed India's large political and economic stakes in three regions by linking them to the concept of 'energy security'. Mr Singh especially identified the Gulf as part of India's neighbourhood and priority for Indian diplomacy. While India's diplomacy in the past was focused on business of extending solidarity with nations of Middle East against great power intervention, now it stressed on developing practical bilateral cooperation, particularly in the business sector. Partly due to this pragmatism and partly for fear of growing terrorism, several Islamic countries reciprocated by refusing to support Pakistan in its Kargil blitzkrieg and also by strongly condemning the hijacking of IC-814 in December 1999.

The conducting of nuclear tests on 11 May 1998 in accordance with militant nationalism of the BJP is regarded as a major departure in India's foreign policy during the BJP-led coalition. What, however, really marked the policy shift was India declaring herself a state with nuclear weapons and not the conducting of tests. After all, it was the Congress (I), which had built up India's nuclear weapon capabilities over the last five decades, with Jawaharlal Nehru laying the foundations for the nuclear weapon option. Mrs Gandhi conducted the first nuclear tests and Rajiv Gandhi initiated the missile programme and ordered the weaponization of the nuclear programme. And Narasimha Rao had come close to conducting nuclear tests in December 1995. In this sense, Pokhran-II merely represented the continuity and growth of the capability over the years.[44] The tests, however, jeopardized India's relations with developed countries, including the US, EU (except France), Japan, Australia, etc., and reinforced the image of the new government as 'a bunch of jingoistic Hindu nationalists'. Especially, the domestic opponents of the government complicated its image problem by sharp criticisms of the tests and thereby emboldened the foreign powers to exert more pressures on India. This punctured the myth about the bipartisan approach to foreign policy or consensus on what constitutes India's national interest.

The evolution of the post-Pokhran-II diplomacy towards greater maturity and responsibility after the initial mistakes, however, reversed to a considerable extent the negative international impression about the government. There is a shift away from punitive and containment policies to constructive engagement with India as manifested in continuing dialogue with the US, France, Russia, Japan, and China, etc. The Deputy Prime Ministers of UK and Australia visited India in March 1999, pulling back from an irrational initial condemnatory stance. An Indian delegation succeeded in ASEAN Regional Forum (ARF) meetings in forging consensus on regional security and non-proliferation. In particular, the sustained dialogue with the US considerably reduced Indo-US nuclear divide.[45] The government was not only able to maintain time-tested friendly ties with Russia, but could also deepen it by concluding a long-term Military-Technical Cooperation Agreement up to 2010 during the Russian Foreign Minister, Yevgeny Primakov's New Delhi trip in December 1998. The process of gradual appreciation of the Indian position ultimately culminated into unprecedented international diplomatic support to India during the Kargil conflict of 1999.[46]

XI

While the compulsions of coalition government, the moderation and vision of Prime Minister, Vajpayee, as well as the realities of international politics did not permit the BJP-led coalition to make foreign policy initiatives beyond the larger framework of continuity and consensus, the process and style of decision-making could not remain unaffected by the composition of the government. As against the Congress era, the foreign policy-making power is no longer concentrated in Prime Minister's secretariat even though the present Prime Minister has a keen interest and experience in the field. His trusted friend, Jaswant Singh, acted as one of the keyplayers and as the Prime Minister's emissary even before his formal elevation to the post of Foreign Minister in December 1998. In addition to Singh, the Principal Secretary to the Prime Minister, Brajesh Mishra, and the Samata Party leader and Defence Minister, George Fernandes, have also played notable role in the foreign affairs. After Pokhran-II, for instance, Singh, Fernandes, and Mishra made sustained dialogue with their counterparts in Britain, France, and Russia. Even the Human Resource Development Minister, Murli Manohar Joshi, the President, and some regional leaders were involved in the foreign policy process. Joshi, for instance, led an official delegation in April 2000 for attending the meeting of Group of 77 in Havana for South–South cooperation. President K.R. Narayanan visited Paris in April, where he discussed a wide range of international, regional and bilateral issues with his French counterpart, Jacques Chirac. To cap it all, coalition partners from Tamil Nadu deeply involved themselves in deciding India's response to the ethnic conflict in Sri Lanka.

If Singh, Mishra, and Joshi usually acted carefully, the JD(U) leader, George Fernandes, President Narayanan, and some Tamil coalition partners, apart from the irresponsible opposition, have embarrassed the government on several occasions. Farnandes, for example, declared China as the prime target of the Pokhran-II nuclear tests. This avoidable comment obviously jeopardized the ongoing process of normalization in India–China relations. It was left to Jaswant Singh to utilize the ASEAN Ministerial Conference in Manila in July 1998 to meet the Chinese Foreign Minister, Tang Jiaxuan, to begin the process of controlling the damage to bilateral relations from the then Defence Minister's statement and the Prime Minister's leaked letter to the US President, Bill Clinton, naming China as the threat leading to nuclear weaponization.[47] Mishra too made specific statement to assuage the Chinese.

Farnandes again embarrassed the government during the Kargil conflict by virtually giving a clean chit to the Nawaz Sharif government by stating that the Pakistani Army had conspired to intrude into Kargil without his knowledge. Fernandes and his party spokespersons may have the satisfaction in pointing out that later developments and especially the military takeover in Pakistan vindicated his stand. It was, however, not at all necessary for the Defence Minister to publicly express his views and stir unnecessary controversy. But the compulsion of coalition politics, especially the clout of Fernandes in the politically significant state of Bihar, did not allow the Prime Minister to restrain his then Defence Minister. The clout of Fernandes became apparent when the Prime Minister preferred to lose his government rather than to concede the demand of another coalition partner, J. Jayalalitha, to remove Farnandes from the Defence Ministry and reinstall the former Navy chief, Admiral Vishnu Bhagwat, who was sacked on disciplinary grounds by the then Defence Minister.

It is surprising to note that though Farnandes acted as one of the main troubleshooters for the beleaguered Prime Minister, yet he forgot to notice that utmost carefulness on his part was necessary in view of the fact that unlike the past, the opposition was determined to anyhow find fault with the government even in the midst of the Kargil conflict without caring for morale of the fighting soldiers. While distinguishing between the political leadership and the defence forces, the opposition forgot that the latter were working only under the direction of the former and an attack on the political leadership in the midst of the intense fighting could only demoralize the brave soldiers.[48] Earlier, while criticizing the government for not taking the opposition into confidence before conducting nuclear tests, they missed the point that such sensitive matters required utmost secrecy, though the government too was guilty of provoking them by trying to pocket the entire credit for this move for itself.[49] It may also be recalled that at one stage, the Congress (I) leaders had decided to send their delegation to South Africa and China to 'contain the damage done by the government' to relations with these countries. Had they gone ahead with this decision, India would have become a laughing stock in the world. Though good sense prevailed and the Congress dropped this plan, yet opposition's constant attempts to fish in the troubled waters of the evolving coalition governance only created an image of a soft state about India. The constant display of disunity at crucial occasions gradually culminated into a situation where the hijackers could force the government to liberate the hardcore master-minds of terrorism.[50] The allegations by a news portal called Tehelka against top functionaries of the government as well as the BJP and Samata parties (including George Fernandes) concerning their involvement in corrupt defence deals at the cost of national security leading to resignations of Fernandes and others not only tarnished the image of the ruling NDA in India and abroad, but also displayed the gross irresponsibility of the opposition, which is indefinitely blocking parliamentary proceedings instead of debating the issue within the house.

The coalition partners and opposition apart, the President of the country, too, has not spared the government from embarrassing situations. As the first citizen, the President has, of course, the right and even a duty to raise contentious domestic issues that make one pause and think. But should he be flying solo in the complex area of foreign relations? It is really regrettable that the President misjudged the time and timing of the speech he made at the banquet he threw for the US President Bill Clinton at the Rashtrapati Bhawan. Elements of courtesy in general and Indian culture in particular dictated that a civilized person organizing a dinner in his own house for a visiting Head of State should not have sternly lectured him or made vaguely insulting remarks. Even if President Narayanan wished to dissociate himself from the euphoria that greeted President Clinton's visit to India, he could have done so by using subtlety and elegance of phrase to put his message across. But it appears that the Rashtrapati Bhawan saw no need to clear the speech with the Foreign Ministry, which was shocked and horrified by its tone when it was finally delivered. Considering that the Americans were clearly offended by K.R. Narayanan's remarks—judging by briefings given to reporters accompanying the presidential entourage—a degree of consultation may well have worked to India's advantage.[51]

XII

While the intervention of President and coalition partners like George Fernandes and others merely shows the shift in the style of foreign policy decision-making under the present NDA government in New Delhi, its coalition partners hailing from Tamil Nadu have conditioned the substance of foreign policy, namely, Indian response to the ethnic conflict in Sri Lanka. The government's first reaction to the defeat of the Sri Lankan Army (SLA) at Elephant Pass in the summer of 2000 and the subsequent run of LTTE victories in attacks on other army camps north of it was both correct and measured. Though it ruled out sending Indian troops to Sri Lanka, yet immediately offered humanitarian aid, and said that it would consider the dispatch of arms if Colombo made the request. But it took just one visit from a team of Tamil politicians headed by the Tamil Nadu Chief Minister, M. Karunanidhi, for the NDA government to start backing away. The reason, put succinctly by the Chief Minister, was that the Tamil parties could not afford to allow any government of which they were a part to do anything that would directly or indirectly take Tamil lives.

The Tamil leaders' fears are understandable. Once word of India's involvement in Sri Lanka on the government's side spreads, they would all face public anger and erosion of support. Worse still, they would all be forced to respond by taking more Tamil chauvinist postures and that would destabilize both the NDA and the Indian polity. Faced with the Tamil leaders' implied threat, therefore, the Vajpayee government chose to beat a retreat.[52] In the process, however, one carefully and steadfastly followed policy towards neighbours since 1971, namely, to minimize the impact of destabilizing changes in them, was challenged as never before in Sri Lanka.[53]

Though prominent leaders like Karunanidhi deny any intention to bind the hands of the coalition government in New Delhi in deciding about Indian response to the Sri Lankan conflict, yet their statements in support of the creation of a Tamil *Eelam* go against New Delhi's declared policy of finding the solution of the problem within the united framework of Sri Lanka. While the MDMK and DMK carefully couch their Sri Lanka stance in subtle pro-*Eelam* sentiments, the PMK has been rather overt in its support for the LTTE. Its appeal to New Delhi to recognize the Tamil *Eelam* liberation struggle and poster campaign in the cities of Tamil Nadu in favour of the LTTE are emboldening that outfit.[54] Obviously, the joining of these polltical parties with an avowed pro-*Eelam* stance the ruling DMK camp in the state and the NDA at the union came as a shot in the arm for these pro-LTTE groups. Though the PMK has now left the NDA boat to join the front consisting of AIADMK, TMC, and Congress in Tamil Nadu and Pondicherry, the Congress party's willingness to join hands with the PMK despite its alleged sympathy for the killers of Rajiv Gandhi shows the clout of this outfit in this region.

It was therfore not surprising that Prime Minister Vajpayee convened a meeting of all opposition parties on 8 May 2000 for evolving a consensus on India's approach to the crisis in Sri Lanka to bypass the pro-LTTE voices within the union cabinet. The Prime Minister rightly consulted first the allies from Tamil Nadu, then the Chief Minister, and finally all the political parties to build consensus on the formulation of a new approach to the Sri Lankan crisis. Unfortunately, however, the clash of views among the constituents of the NDA struck a jarring note at this all-party meeting. Apart from the TMC, which is in the opposition, even the TDP, an ally of the NDA, raised questions on public support for the LTTE by the NDA constituents from Tamil Nadu. It is one thing for these parties to adopt political resolution on the *Eelam* issue at their conferences, but quite another to be in government and advocate secession in another country. NDA's coalition partners cannot be immune to the problems faced in Kashmir and elsewhere in India. New Delhi cannot adopt double standards either in combating terrorism or supporting secession. In any case, foreign policy can be kept hostage to chauvinistic voices from Tamil Nadu only at the cost of jeopardizing national security.

XIII

The preceding pages, it is hoped, explain the implications of coalition governments for the conduct of foreign policy in India. This linkage is, of course, more visible in the realm of the style of foreign policy making leading to a shift from centralized decision-making process during the single party rule of Congress to decentralized process of foreign policy formulation during the coalition era. Yet, the substance of foreign policy has also not remained unaffected by the exigencies of coalition politics. While the imperative of social coalition partly motivated Nehru to opt for non-alignment, Indira Gandhi's dependence on the CPI for survival of her minority government and her compulsion to cultivate a 'progressive' image after the Congress split partly contributed to her moving closer to the erstwhile USSR. Though the Janata–Lok Dal conglomeration tried to accommodate the neighbours, it could not pursue an effective foreign policy due to the lack of discipline among the government stalwarts.

Again, Prime Minster Chandrashekhar had to withdraw the refuelling facility granted to the UN forces led by the US during the Gulf crisis in 1991, as his government was dependent for survival on the support of Rajiv Gandhi. On the other hand, the West Bengal Chief Minister, Jyoti Basu, who was an ally of the UF government, helped I.K. Gujral to strike a deal with Dhaka to solve the long-standing problem of the sharing of Ganga waters at Farakka. But Gujral too suffered from the handicap of coalition politics on several occasions.

In the case of the BJP-led government, while the compulsions of coalition politics forced the party to drop its controversial agendas in foreign (also in domestic) policy, its allies from Tamil Nadu have limited its options in Sri Lanka. The weak position of the government has also emboldened her other allies as well as the President to embarrass the government on numersous occasions. Not surprisingly, the opposition does not leave a single occasion to find fault with the government. This shatters the myth about bipartisan approach to foreign policy or consensus on national interest. As the perception of national interest is not always objective, as believed by naïve observers, the nature of regime in general and the compulsion of coalition politics in particular influence the process as well as the substance of foreign policy.

As India continues to experiment with coalition politics, the conduct of foreign policy is likely to be increasingly vulnerable to the vicissitudes of domestic politics. In fact, as the preceding pages show, in circumstances where a coalition government's sustenance in power depends upon its response to foreign policy demands of those political entities or interest groups, on whose support its survival depends, the influence of domestic constraints become more important in the shaping of foreign policy of such a government. It follows that all that India can do under the circumstances is to minimize the likely damage by devoting greater efforts towards building a domestic consensus on key-foreign policy issues. This must necessarily involve far more frequent and intensive consultations on national security issues both among the partners of the coalition and between the government and the opposition. The UF government was able to build up consensus on the CTBT and sharing of Ganga waters. It is satisfying to note that after the departure of the turbulent AIADMK partner, the present coalition partners are showing more maturity and cohesiveness. This should enable the government to develop consensus with the opposition and act more boldly in international politics for the promotion of national interest.

NOTES

1. See, for instance, Subhash C. Kashyap, ed., *Coalition Governments and Politics in India*, New Delhi, 1997; also his, 'A Case for Review: Constitution in the Coalition Age'; E. Sridharan, 'Principles, Power and Coalition Politics in India: Lessons from Theory, Comparison and Recent History', in *Principles, Power and Politics*, eds. D.D. Khanna and Gert W. Kueek, New Delhi, 1999; and papers presented at the National Workshop on 'Making A Success of Coalitions' sponsored by K.A. Stiftung Foundation, Madras Management Association and Stayamurthi Center for Democratic Studies in Madras on 7 and 8 December 1999. Also, see S.K. Chatterjee, ed., *The Coalition Government*, Madras, 1974.
2. Stephen Andriole and Gerald Hopple, 'The Process, Outcome, and Impact of Regime Change in the Third World, 1959-1981', *International Interactions*, vol. 12, 1986, pp. 363-92; Joe D. Hagan, 'Regimes, Political Opposition, and Comparative Analysis of Foreign Policy', in *New Directions in the Study of Foreign Policy*, ed. Charles F. Hermann, et al., Boston, 1987, pp. 339-65; and his, 'Political Regime Changes and Foreign Policy Restructuring in the Third World', paper presented at the annual meeting of the American Political Science Associations, 3-6 September 1987; K.J. Holsti, 'Restructuring Foreign Policy: A Neglected Phenomenon in Foreign Policy', in his, ed., *Why Nations Realign: Foreign Policy Restructuring in the Post War World*, London, 1982, pp. 1-20; Kjell Goldmann, *Change and Stability in Foreign Policy: The Problems and Possibility of Détente*, Princeton, 1988; Charles F. Hermann, 'Changing Course: When Governments Chose to Redirect Foreign Policy', *International Studies Quarterly*, vol. 34, 1990, pp. 3-21; Ted R. Gurr, 'Persistence and Change in Political Systems, 1800-1971', *American Political Science Review*, vol. 68, 1974, pp. 1482-1504; Jonathan Wilkenfeld, et al., *Foreign Policy Behaviour: The Interstate Analysis Model*, Beverly Hills, 1980; Bruce E. Moon, 'Consensus or Compliance? Foreign Policy Change and External Dependence', *International Studies Quarterly,* vol. 27, 1985, pp. 297-329; Zeev Maoz, 'Joining the Club of Nations: Political Development and International Conflicts, 1816-1976', *International Studies Quarterly*, vol. 33, 1989, pp. 131-99; Thomas J. Volgy and John E. Schwarz, 'Does Politics Stops at Water's Edge? Domestic Political Factors and Foreign Policy Restructuring in the Cases of Great Britain, France and West Germany', *Journal of Politics*, vol. 53, 1991, pp. 615-43; Randolph M. Siverson and Harvey Starr, 'Regime Change and Restructuring of Alliances', *American Journal of Political Science*, vol. 38, 1994, pp. 145-61.

3. For a detailed treatment of coalition theories, see William H. Riker, *Theory of Political Coalitions*, New Haven, 1962; Abraham de Swaan, *Coalition Theory and Cabinet Formation*, Amsterdam, 1973; Bruce Bueno de Mesquita, *Strategy, Risk and Personality in Coalition Politics*, Cambridge, 1975; E. Sridharan, 'Coalition Politics', *Seminar* (New Delhi), no. 437, January 1996; E. Sridharan, 'Principles, Power and Coalition Politics in India: Lessons from Theory, Comparison and Recent History', in Khanna, et al., eds., n. 1; and Ajay K. Mehra, 'Coalition Making in India: Imperatives, Disincentives and Pitfalls', paper presented at the National Workshop on 'Making a Success of Coalitions, no. 1, pp. 5-8.
4. F. Pearson and J. Rochester, *International Relations*, Mass.: Addison-Wesley, 1984, pp. 145-41.
5. Nalini Kant Jha, *Domestic Imperatives in India's Foreign Policy*, New Delhi: South Asian Publishers, forthcoming, Chapter I.
6. Nalini Kant Jha, *Internal Crisis and Indira Gandhi's Foreign Policy*, Patna/New Delhi: Janki Prakashan, 1985.
7. Bhagat Korany, 'When and How Do Personality Factors Influence Foreign Policy?', *Journal of South and Middle Eastern Studies,* vol. 9, no. 3, 1986, pp. 35-60.
8. For an elaboration of this view, see Ajay K. Mehra, 'The Cabinet System in a Coalition Situation', in Kashyap, ed., n. 1, pp. 91-9.
9. Vernon Bogdanor, *Multiparty Politics and the Constitution*, Cambridge, 1983, pp. 170-95. Scholars like E. Sridharan and S.R. Maheshwari also treat minority government as a variant of coalition. See E. Sridharan, 'Principles, Power and Coalition Politics in India', ibid; and S.R. Maheshwari, 'Coalition Governments, 1946-1996', in Kashyap, ed., n. 1, p. 57. But Subhash C. Kashyap believes that minority and coalition governments cannot be equated. See Subhash C. Kashyap, 'Coalition in Indian Politics', paper presented at the National Workshop on 'Making a Success of Coalitions', n. 1, p. 3.
10. G.A. Grierson's survey of the Indian languages early last century had listed 179 languages and 544 dialects in India. See his, *Linguistic Survey of India, 1903-1928*, Calcutta, vols. I-XI. This list, however, has been contested on the ground that dialects too are languages and this kind of distinction is not possible. See, S.K. Chatterjee and S.M. Katre, 'Languages', *The Gazetteer of India*, ibid, pp. 367-412. These differences of opinion notwithstanding, one cannot detract from the point that the lingual variety of India is mind-boggling.
11. See M.N. Srinavas, 'Social Structure', *The Gazetteer of India: Country and People*, New Delhi, vol. 1, 1965, p. 501.
12. Nalini Kant Jha, 'Foreign Policy and National Integration: The Indian Experience', *Journal of Integration Studies*, Annamalai Nagar, vols. 2, 3 and 4, January 1998, pp. 1-15.
13. Nalini Kant Jha, 'Cultural and Philosophical Roots of India's Foreign Policy',

International Studies, New Delhi, vol. 26, no. 1, January-March 1989, pp. 45-67.

14. Jawaharlal Nehru, *India's Foreign Policy: Selected Speeches, 1946-April 1961*, New Delhi, 1961, p. 41.
15. For discussion on transformation within the Congress Party, see Paul R. Brass, *The Politics of India since Independence*, Cambridge, 1992, 2nd edn., p. 72; and Ajay K. Mehra, 'Political parties and Party System in India', in Khanna et al., n. 1, pp. 238-69.
16. See Girilal Jain, 'The Image and Reality', *Times of India*, New Delhi, 19 September 1979; and Iqbal Narian, 'Democratic Politics in India', *Asian Survey,* Berkeley, Calif., vol. 10, no. 2, February 1970, p. 88.
17. The text of the resolution on political and economic situation adopted at the Patna AICC meeting, 13-14 October 1970, was published in AICC, *Congress Marches Ahead-III*, New Delhi, 1970, p. 147.
18. See, for details, M.P. Singh, *Split in a Predominant Party: The Indian National Congress in 1969*, New Delhi, 1981; Nalini Kant Jha, *Domestic Imperatives in India's Foreign Policy*, New Delhi: South Asian Publishers, 2000; and Basant Chatterji, *The Congress Split*, New Delhi, n.d.
19. The fact that Mrs Gandhi's tirade against the CIA was a political ploy was evident from the fact that the trade between India and the US continued to grow as usual and the assets of the top twenty business houses in India, which had substantive dealings with the US rose from approximately Rs. 24 billion in 1969 to Rs. 44 billion in 1975. See S.K. Goyal, *Monopoly Capital and Public Policy,* New Delhi, 1979.
20. For an elaboration of this view, see Sashi Tharoor, *Reasons of State: Political Development and Foreign Policy under Indira Gandhi, 1966-77*, New Delhi, 1982, pp. 144-55.
21. For a brief overview of continuity and changes in India's foreign policy during the Janata regime, see Bimal Prasad, 'An Overview', *International Studies*, vol. 17, nos. 3-4, July-December 1978, pp. 889-93.
22. See, for instance, the US Secretary of State, Cyrus Vance's interview with M.V. Kamath, *The Illustrated Weekly of India*, Bombay, 11 June 1978, pp. 8, 11.
23. See, Inder Malhotra, 'Relations with Russia: The Kosygin Visit and After', *Times of India*, 15 March 1979.
24. Bimal Prasad, n. 21, pp. 891-2. The then Foreign Minister, Vajpayee, declared: 'India does not desire a position of pre-eminence. The big brother attitudes have proved counter-productive in the past.' See his interview in *Sunday*, Calcutta, 18 March 1979, p. 19.
25. For a representative view on the continuity in Janata's foreign policy due to the influence of international system, see Vijay Sen Budhraj, 'India and the Soviet Union', ibid, pp. 739-58.
26. Jha, n. 6, and Tharoor, n. 20, pp. 396-403.

27. *The Economist*, London, 4 November 1978, p. 61.
28. Madhu Limaye, 'We have ho China Policy', *Sunday*, 22 April 1979, pp. 22-6.
29. Kuldip Nayar, 'Vajpayee's Mission to China', *Indian Express,* 28 October 1978.
30. For a brief review of domestic criticism on the Jaguar, see Richard Wigg, 'Jaguar Deal Raises Outcry in India', *The Times*, London, 23 November 1978.
31. During this period, Foreign Minister, Foreign Secretary, and the Foreign Service got progressively marginalized and the conduct of foreign policy got centralized in the Prime Minister's office. This led to establishment of direct links between the PMO and foreign governments bypassing the MEA in India and out missions abroad. See K. Subrahmanyam, 'Removing the Irritants', *Hindustan Times*, Patna, 28 December 1989.
32. Gautam Adhikari, 'A Time for Hard Realism: India's Foreign Policy', *Times of India*, 9 October 1990. See also, J. Mohan Malik, 'India's Response to the Gulf Crisis', *Asian Survey,* vol. 31, no. 9, September 1991, pp. 847-56; and J.K. Baral and I.N. Mohanty, 'India and the Gulf Crisis: The Response of the Minority Government', *Pacific Affairs*, Vancouver, BC, vol. 66, no. 3, 1992.
33. I attended the first meeting of academic experts convened by Mr Singh at the MEA in New Delhi in December 1990.
34. *India Today*, New Delhi, 31 March 1991.
35. US officials reportedly met senior MEA officials and succeeded in persuading them to grant the facility; Chandrashekhar accepted the proposal. See *Times of India*, 29 January 1991.
36. Malik, n. 32, p. 856.
37. Contrary to popular impression, coalition politics did not take rest at the national level during the tenure of the Rao government. His minority government survived on the support of several small groups till he got his arithmetic right.
38. Harish Kapur, *India's Foreign Policy, 1947-92: Shadows and Substance*, New Delhi, 1994, pp. 146, 201-3.
39. For details, see Padmaja Murthy, 'Gujral Doctrine and Beyond', in *India's Foreign Policy in a Changing World: Essays in the Honour of Professor Bimal Prasad*, ed. Nalini Kant Jha, New Delhi: South Asian Publishers, 2000; and John Cherian, 'Clear and Coherent: Indian Foreign Policy Under I.K. Gujral', *Frontline*, Madras, vol. 14, no. 6, April 1997, pp. 4-7.
40. Sukumar Muralidharan, 'The Political Context of Policy Doctrine', *Frontline*, ibid., pp. 16-17. Also see, Nalini Kant Jha, 'Foreign Policy Making in Federal States: The Indian and Canadian Experiences', *India Quarterly*, New Delhi, vol. 55, nos. 3-4, July-December 1999, pp. 1-16.
41. As reported by a noted columnist, Pran Chopra, Gujral revealed that the former Congress Foreign Minister, Pranab Mukherji, had requested him not to withdraw from the contest for the UN seat. See Pran Chopra, 'Lessons from Votes in the UN', *The Hindu*, Madras, 26 November 1996.

42. K.K. Katyal's dispatch from Bonn, 'Cancellation of PM's Visit to Germany Causes Dismay', *The Hindu*, 23 October 1997.
43. For the full text of the National Agenda for Governance released by Prime Minister, Atal Behari Vajpayee, see *The Hindu*, 19 March 1999.
44. As early as 1946, in response to a question about the possibility of Indian deployment of nuclear weapons, Prime Minister, Jawaharlal Nehru, had warned, 'As long as the world was constituted as it was, every country has to develop and use the latest scientific device for its protection.' Cited in Lorne J. Kevic, *India's Quest for Security: Defence Policies, 1947-65*, Berkeley, 1967, pp. 27-8; See also, Jasjit Singh, "India's Nuclear Policy after Pokhran-II', in *Peace and Cooperative Security in South Asia*, ed. N.K. Jha, et al., New Delhi, Poonrani Pub., 2000, pp. 109-34.
45. Nalini Kant Jha, 'The US, Pokhran-II and South Asia', *India Quarterly*, vol. 55, nos. 1-2, January-June, 1999, pp. 1-18; and Nalini Kant Jha, 'The US Response to Nuclear India: From Containment to Realism', in *Nuclear India: Problems and Perspectives*, ed. A. Subramanyam Raju, New Delhi: South Asian Publishers, 2000, pp. 115-26.
46. Nalini Kant Jha, 'Roads that Lead to Kargil', *Trishul*, Willington, Autumn, 1999, pp. 1-7.
47. J.N. Dixit, 'Reactive to Pro-Active', *Indian Express*, New Delhi, 18 March 1999.
48. As against the Kargil conflict, the entire country supported Indira Gandhi during the India–Pakistan conflict in 1971. The then leader of opposition, Atal Behari Vajpayee's hailing of Mrs Gandhi as an incarnation of Goddess Durga cost him dearly in the 1972 general elections. See, for details, Nalini Kant Jha, 'Pakistan, India and the Creation of Bangladesh', *International Studies*, New Delhi, vol. 29, no. 1, January-March 1992, pp. 79-94.
49. Two surveys on public opinion and nuclear options found substantive support for overt nuclearization in India and Pakistan. See Samina Ahmed et al., 'Public Opinion and Nuclear Options for South Asia', *Asian Survey*, Berkeley, vol. 38, no. 8, August 1999, pp. 727-44.
50. When the government convened an all-party meeting to evolve a consensus on dealing with the hijacking crisis, the opposition instead of advising to act tough with the hijackers, simply demanded to secure the safe release of the hostages without compromising with terrorists, knowing fully well that under the circumstances it was virtually impossible to guarantee that both the demands could be met at the same time.
51. 'Dangers of Monologue', *Hindustan Times*, New Delhi, 24 March 2000.
52. Prem Shankar Jha, 'Dire Threat to India', *The Hindu*, 10 May 2000.
53. There are two compelling reasons for India to ensure the unity and integrity of Sri Lanka: The disintegration of that country will send a powerful fillip to numerous secessionist movements within India. Second, once the Tamils will get their *Eelam* in Sri Lanka, their next target would be to integrate Indian

Tamil Nadu with the new *Eelam* (nation). For an analysis of India's paramount interest in maintaining the unity and integrity of Sri Lanka, see Nalini Kant Jha, 'Opposition to Indo-Sri Lanka Accord: Failure to Understand a Complex Reality', *Third Concept*, New Delhi, vol. 2, no. 1, March 1988, pp.19-20.

54. When media persons questioned the propriety of the PMK as one of the constituents of NDA adopting a contradictory approach when the union has set its face against Tamil *Eelam*, the PMK leader Dr Ramdoss said that his party has the right to voice its views. See *The Hindu*, Madras, 11 May 2000.

Contributors

BALVEER ARORA, Professor of Political Science and Rector, Jawaharlal Nehru University, New Delhi.

C.P. BHAMBHRI, distinguished scholar, Centre for Political Studies, Jawaharlal Nehru University, New Delhi.

RAVI P. BHATIA, Director of Publications, University of Delhi, Delhi.

BIDYUT CHAKRABARTY, Professor of Political Science, University of Delhi, Delhi.

AJIT KUMAR JHA, *India Today*, New Delhi.

NALINI KANT JHA, Professor of Political Science, Pondicherry University, Pondicherry.

PREM SHANKAR JHA, senior journalist, New Delhi.

S.K. JHA, former Director, Gandhian Institute of Studies, Varanasi, Uttar Pradesh.

ANIL MISHRA, Department of Political Science, PG-DAV College, New Delhi.

KAMALA PRASAD, former Chief Secretary, Government of Bihar.

HIMANSHU ROY, Reader, Department of Political Science, Deen Dayal Upadhyaya College, New Delhi.

REKHA SAXENA, Lecturer, Department of Political Science, Janaki Devi Memorial College, New Delhi.

MAHENDRA PRASAD SINGH, Professor of Political Science, University of Delhi, Delhi.

E. SRIDHARAM, Academic Director, University of Pennsylvania Institute of Advanced Study of India, India Habitat Centre, New Delhi.

Index

Abdullah, Sheikh 58
Administrative Reforms Commission (1969) 36, 246
adult franchise 22; launching of 124
Advani, L.K. as Deputy Prime Minister 33
AGP of Assam 60-1
AIADMK 57; ally with Congress 46-7; and Congress alliance 57; and MDMK, PMK, BJP alliance 58
Akali Dal and splits 59
All Assam Students Union 60
All India Anna Dravida Munnetra Kazhagam (AIADMK)–Congress alliance 13
All India Forward Bloc (AIFB) 56
All India Services 224-6
alliances, types of 71-3
Ambedkar, B.R. on democracy 36
Anjaiya, T. as Andhra Pradesh Chief Minister 132
Andhra Pradesh and two-party system 14-15
Annadurai, C.N. and cultural and linguistic autonomy 132; as DMK first Chief Minister 57
anti-Congressism propagated by Ram Manohar Lohia 49
anti-BJPism 79
anti-Defection Act (1985) 246-7
anti-high caste Arajak Sangh 199
anti-Hindi agitation 132
Apang, Gegong and Arunachal Congress 47
Article 356 222-4
ASEAN Regional Forum (ARF) 314
Asom Gana Parishad (AGP) of Assam 57
Association of South East Asian Nations (ASEAN) 310
Ayodhya, temple issue 207

Babri Masjid demolition (1992) 14, 80; and Congress' loss of UP 108
Backward and Minority Communities Employees Federation (BAMCEF) 63
Bahuguna, H.N. 51
Bahujan Samaj Party (BSP) 63-4
Bajrang Dal 66, 134
Balayogi, G.M. 31
Banerjee, Mamata and Trinamool Congress, formation 147, 168; as challenge to CPI(M)-led coalition 158; as Trinamool Congress supremo 164
Bangla Congress in West Bengal, formation of 45
Bhagalpur riot 108
Bharatiya Jana Sangh (BJS) 12, 59, 189-90, 203-4; formed in 104; and RSS 197; and Swatantra Party as alternative to Congress 189

Bharatiya Janata Party (BJP) 16, 48-9; allured Mayawati , the leader of the BSP 207; and coalitional partners 130-2; and 1993 election 207; and electoral failures 32; and Hindu communalism 109; and *Hindutva* ideology 134; and *Hindutva* revivalism 93; and its *Hindutva* agenda 66-7; and its organization 134; and Muslim MPs 134; and NDA allies 30-1; and non-Congressism 13-14; and secular forces 131; and splits in 48; government in 88; government, Common Civil Code and Article 356 93; *Hindutva* and Indian nationalism 85; its charge of minority communalism 93; its Somnath to Ayodhya *rathayatra* 84; its thirteen-day government and way for UF 311; led coalition and foreign policy 314-15; led coalition government and 'extended neighbourhood' 313; led coalition government and communalization 14; led coalition government, fall of 70; led coalition rule 30; led government and nuclear tests 294; led National Democratic Alliance (NDA) 13, 66; rise of 212; *Sangh Parivar* and the minorities 133-4
Bharatiya Kranti Dal (BKD) 50, 203; and Congress coalition government 200-3
Bharatiya Lok Dal (BLD) 12, 50; faction, government formation and Congress support 83
Bharti, Maharaj Singh 199
Bhujbal, Chhagan and joining Congress 62
bi-coalitional system 139-42
Bihar and coalition politics, case study of 275-9; and Lok Sabha election 131
bi-party system 139
Birla, G.D. 234
Brahmananda Reddi, K. 46
BSP minority government, fall of 81; and Congress combination 208
Butler, David, Ashok Kumar Lahiri, Prannoy Roy and study on elections 126

Calcutta–Dhaka bus service 313
Camp David Accord 304
Canada and method of electing party leaders 243-4
Carter, U.S. President, and his Indian visit 302
Caste/Community-wise vote 258-60
caste-based parties 64-6
Central Vigilance Commission (CVC) 35
Centre for Indian Trade Union (CITU) 176
Centre-State relations and Constitution review 222
Chakraborty, Swadesh of CPI(M) and victory 163
Chandrababu Naidu as TDP leader 60
Chandrashekhar 50-1, 125; his government 129, 255; fall of his government 69
Chandraswami, P.V. Narasimha Rao and Lakhubhai Pathak cheating case 81
Chatterjee, Somnath as CPI(M) MP 172
Chautala, Om Prakash 46
Chidambaram, P. as UF Finance

Minister 290-1; ASEAN and ARF meetings
Chinese aggression 303
class parties 65
coalition government 16-17; and electoral alliance 67-73; and minority 254-7; and politics 206-10; as representative nature of 257-60; as stable 239; at the centre 239-40; beginning of 297; definition of 296-7; features of 257-68; in Kerala 76; phases of 75-6; role of 77; stability of 260-2
coalition idea, growth of 103-8; prospect of 173-4
coalition politics 114-16; definition of 274
coalitional and federal government, consequences of 33-5
coalition and electoral systems 262-7; history of 279-80; situation and government formation 88-9; social bases and impact of 64-7
Coca Cola, expelling of 302
Commission on Centre-State Relations 246
Communist Party of India (CPI) 55, 104; and Congress 297
community organization 25; Tirupati Devasthanam Trust as 25; Shiromani Gurudwara Prabandhak Committee as 25
Congress–CPI coalition governments 76
Congress (I) 45
Congress (O) 82, 203-4
Congress (Socialist) 46
Congress (U) 46
Congress 16, 104-8; and BKD 200-3; and non-BJPism 13-14; as one-party dominant system 273; dominance, end of 33; its defeat of Assembly elections 205; its loss as Trinamool Congress' gain 159; led UDF 76
Congress government formation and Tripathi, Kamalapati 204-5; its return to power 206
Congress party 45-8; ADMK, JKNC alliance 81-2; and Vidhan Sabha elections defeats 124; and 1984 general election 44; as alternatives for 108; its split in West Bengal and emergence of Trinamool Congress 70; led government 200-10; led United Democratic Front 23; party and 1996 elections 108; return of (1980) 21; splits in 45; system and its crisis 137-8
Constitution (Article 356) 225
Constitutions 228
CPI(M) 109, 159-64; and split in 55; led LF governments 23
CPI (Marxist-Leninist), or CPI (ML) 55

Dange, S.A. 196
democracy 174-5
Desai, Morarji 12, 125; and Congress (O) representation 82; as Prime Minister 50
Deshmukh, Nanaji 200
Devi, Rabri, RJD government of 276
Dinesh Goswami Committee (1993) 138
DMK, and BJP alliance 58; as breakaway from the Dravida Kazhagam (1949) 57; MDMK and stand on Sri Lanka 318; splits in 57;–TMC alliance 91
Dravidian parties of Tamil Nadu 56-7
Dunkal draft proposals and Sharad Joshi 24

economic liberalization and bureaucratic control 35
election 1991 and formation of BJP government 207
electoral alliances and coalitions and pattern evolution 70-3
electoral systems 252; and coalitions 262-7
Electricity Regulatory Authority of India (ERAI) 35
eleventh Lok Sabha elections 1996
Emergency 58, 68, 82, 107, 128, 205, 234
'Ethnic' parties 64-5

fascism, Hindu variants of 134
Federal Front, formation of 92
federalism 228-9
Fernandes, George 125, 131; and Indo–China relations 315; and Kargil conflict 315-16; as Defence Minister and foreign affairs 315; as NDA convener 30; of Samata Party 112
first Vajpayee government 255
Forward Block 157
French and Russian presidential systems 242-3

ganasanghas 76
Gandhi, Indira 12; and Congress party domination 125; and CPI support 301; and her economics 148; and her *Garibi Hatao* slogan 301; and her minority government 301; and power struggle 300; and USSR 301; as Information and Broadcasting Minister and anti-Hindi agitation 132-3; as Prime Minister 23-4; Congress returned to power 51; Emergency and India's foreign policy 295
Gandhi, Rajiv as successor of Indira Gandhi 235; Bofors scandal and public votes 128-9; his leadership of the Congress 51
Gandhi, Sonia and decision to lead 156; as leader of Congress 46
general elections and hung parliaments 43
Giri, V.V. 267-8
Gowda, H.D. Deve and coalition government 279; and formation of government 126; and I.K. Gujral, as UF Prime Ministers 29; and Janata Dal (Secular) 52; as Prime Minister 26; government and inter-state water disputes 130; led UF government 255; replacement of 69
Gujarat riot 31
Gujral Doctrine 308-9, 312
Gujral, Inder Kumar 255; and Comprehensive Test Ban Treaty (CTBT) 309; and government 279; and H.D. Deve Gowda as UF Prime Ministers 29; as Prime Minister 26; as Prime Minister and resignation of 69; his foreign policy 310; his return to power 308
Gupta, C.B. 191, 199-200
Gupta, Indrajit as first Communist Home Minister 79
Gupta, Ram Prakash 48, 196

Hanumanthaiya, K. as Chairman of ARC 246
Haryana Lok Dal (Rashtriya) 52
Haskar, P.N. as Indira's political adviser 301
Hegde, Ramakrishna of JD (U) and BJP 52, 132
Hindi as all-India language and *Sangh Parivar* 133; its imposition 133

Hindu leaders, and central government control of 134
Hindu militant nationalism, rise of 29
Hindu *Sangh Parivar* 29-30
Hindu–Muslim communal carnage 31
Hindutva and coalition government 130-2; and Indian State 124
Hussain, Zakir 267

IBM, expelling of 302
INC *see* Indian National Congress
India, ties with Russia 314
India's first coalition government (1946) 11
Indian National Congress (INC) as freedom movement 297; Jawaharlal Nehru as its founder of 11
Indian Peace Keeping Force (IPKF), withdrawal of 306
Indian political system, changes in 286
Indian Union Muslim League and CPI(M) 124
Indo–Soviet relations 301-3
Indo–US Joint Commission 302
Indo–US relations 302-3; and nuclear divide 314
Indrajit Gupta Committee (1988) 238
Inter-State Council 226

Jain Commission Report and Congress drops DMK 96
Jain, A.P. 191
Janata Dal (Secular) 52
Janata family of parties 49-54, 85
Janata government and foreign policy 303; collapsed 206
Janata *parivar see* Janata family
Janata Party/JD and NF as pre-election coalition 239; and non-Congress coalitional alternative 82; as first non-Congress government 12; first coalition government 255; formation and Congress 205; its formation of 107; its government 125; its victory of 50
Janata–Lok Dal coalition government and foreign policy 305
Jayalalitha, J. and BJP, breach with 112; as AIADMK supremo 30; as M.G. Ramachandran's successor 82; with NF and BJP 91
JD-led NF coalition 71; alliance 68-9; Congress withdrawal of support 206; in Karnataka, splits in 70; led NF government 83; led UF government, formation of 85
Jharkhand Party 62
JKNC of Jammu & Kashmir 57-8
JMM 62
Jogi, Ajit as Congress observer 278
Joshi, Manohar of Shiv Sena 31
Joshi, Murli Manohar and foreign policy process 315
JP movement 12
Justice Party 57

Kalam, A.P.J. Abdul 245; as successor of K.R. Narayanan 32
Kanshi Ram 63
Kargil war as vote gaining 112-13
Karunanidhi, M. of DMK and BJP 132; and Gujral 309
Kerala and coalition government 12
Kerala Congress (Mani) 45
Kerala Congress 45
Kesri, Sitaram 46; as Congress president 96, 255
Khanna, Dau Dayal 191
Kidwai, Mohsina as Congress observer 278
Kisan Mazdoor Praja Party (KMPP) 104

Kriplani, J.B. as Congress president 103
Kumar, Nitish 131

Lahiri, Ashok Kumar on study on elections *see under* Butler, David
Lal, Bansi and Haryana Vikas Party (HVP) 46; and prohibition in Haryana 287
Lal, Devi of Janata Party 83
land revenue, abolition of 196
Left Democratic Front (LDF) 13
Left Front (LF) 13; and panchayati institutions 165-6; government and Sarkaria Commission (1980) 166; in WB and decline in popular votes 158; its government, diminish in popularity 168-72; its partners 157; its policy of eliminating English 171-2
left parties 55-6
Limaye, Madhu 125
Lohia, Ram Manohar 78; and anti-Congressism 67, 188; and ideological rationalism 14
Lok Sabha election in 1971 23-4; and Gandhi, Indira 77; in 1977, impact of 205; in 1996 80, 85; in 1999 155; in 1991 and hung Parliament 25
Lok Sabha mid-term election 1998 28; in 1999 28
Lok Shakti 52
Lokayuktas (ombudsmen) 35
Loktantrik Congress Party (LCP) 47

Maharashtrawadi Gomantak Party of Goa 62
Majority systems 252-3
Mandal Commission recommendations, implementation 83-4; and internal conflict in JD 69; and V.P. Singh 129-30
Mandal OBC 29
Maran, Murasoli, Labour Party in London, contact with 310
Mayawati as the new Chief Minister 207-8
MDMK 57
Military-Technical Cooperation Agreement with Russia 314
minimum connected winning coalition (MCWC) 274
minimum winning coalition (MWC) 274
Ministry of External Affairs (MEA) 306, 307
MLA's Syndicate, joining Congress 204
MNF of Mizoram 62
Modi, Narendra, his government and INC agitation 31-2
Moopanar, G.K. as TMC leader 291
MPVC 91
multiparty coalitional system 139, 142-5
multiparty system 15; emergence of 22
Muslims 148

Nadar, Kamaraj and Indira's U.S. Policy 301
Naidu, N. Chandrababu 90; as India's cyber minister 288, 290; as ring leader of NDA 289; of TDP and BJP 132
Narayan, Jayaprakash (JP) 12; and anti-corruption movement 78; and ideological nationalism 14; and movement against Congress misrule 107-8
Narayan, K.R., and return of proposal 244-5; as President 244; on review of Constitution 221

nation building 299
National Commission for Review of the Working of the Constitution (NCRWC), report of 17, 37, 235, 238-9, 245; recommendations of 246-7
National Democratic Alliance (NDA) 29, 108-14
National Development Council 289
National Front (NF) 13
National Human Rights Commission (NHRC) 35
National Women and Child Welfare Commissions 35
Nationalist Congress Party 48-9
NDA and AIADMK withdrawal of support 112; and *Hindutva* forces 31; as political opportunism 134; coalition 66; Tamil Nadu and foreign policy on Sri Lanka 317-18
Nehru, B.K. 234
Nehru, Jawaharlal and foreign policy 299; and nuclear weapon 314; as one party leadership 104; his centrist policies 299
New Delhi–Lahore bus service 313
new politics, idioms in 116-19
NF minority coalition governments 69
ninth Lok Sabha elections and governance in India 125-6
non-Congress coalition governments, formation of 50
non-Congress parties, evolution of 43-4
'non-Congressism' 78 -9

one party *vs* alliance or coalitional system 139, 146
Other Backward Classes (OBCs) 146-7; and Congress 15, 147

Palkhivala, Nani A. 234
parliamentary parties in government, role of 89-94
party system 23; study of 27-8; types of 138-46
Parvathi, Lakshmi, NTR'S widow 90
Paswan, Ram Vilas 131
Patel , J.H. of JD(U) and BJP 53, 132; and Lok Shakti merger 70
Pawar, Sharad 47; led NCP 62
plurality system 253
PMK 57-8; and support to LTTE 318
political system, structure of 119-20
politics, and society relationship 123; centralization *vs* federalization 24; transitions of 126-30
populism 288-9
Praja Socialist Party (PSP) 49, 78; 104; and Congress coalition governments 76
Prakash, Kailash 191
Prasad, Rajendra, 267
President's rule 1995 207-8
presidential election 267-8
presidential system advocacy for 234-7; and coalition situation 233; failure of 242
Prime Minister at federal centre, role of 34
proportionality system 253-4
Pudhiya Tamizhagam a new Dalit party 58

Radhakrishnan, S. 267
Rai, Gauri Shankar as Congress nominee 198
Ram, Jagjivan 125; as a Scheduled Caste leader and Congress for Democracy; merged with Janata Party 45; as Janata Defence Minister 304
Ramachandran, M.G. (MGR) 57
Rao, N.T. Rama (NTR) and TDP 132; formation (1983) 60; as TDP Chief Minister 83

Rao, P.V. Narasimha, and government formation of 308; and 'Look East' policy 313; and coalition government 279; and foreign policy 308; and formation of Congress government 126; and his government 46; as Prime Minister 26; as the Congress president and Deve Gowda 95-6; his minority government in 1991 94
Rashtriya Janata Dal 52
Rashtriya Janata Party 48-9
Reddy, Neelam Sanjeeva 88, 268
Regional Parties 24, 56-63; and bourgeoisie favouritism 24; its existence of 298
regionalism, growth of 149-51
Report of the Law Commission of India (1988) 238
Research and Analysis Wing (RAW) 306
review of the Constitution 219
revolt of 1994 80
Revolutionary Socialist Party (RSP) 56-7
roll-back factors in NDA 289
Roy, Prannoy and study on elections *see under* Butler, David
RSS 134; and splits in 48
rural capitalism 152
ryotwari system 146-8, 150

SAD of Punjab 57-8; and alliances 59-60; and BJP alliance 64; as party of Sikh community 59
Samajwadi Janata Party 51
Sampurnanand's exit and UP 191
Samyukta Socialist Party 49, 104; Raj Narain faction 50
Samyukta Vidhayak Dals 106
Sangh Parivar 66
Sangma, P.A. 47; as Congress Speaker 94
Sarkaria Commission on Centre–State Relations (1987-8) 36, 238
Sarkaria, R.S. as chairman of Commission on Centre-State Relations 246
Sayeed, Mufti Mohammad, and People's Democratic Party 59
Scindia, Madhavrao and Digvijay Singh 91; and Madhya Pradesh Vikas Congress (MPVC) 91
Security and Exchange Board of India (SEBI) 35
Sengupta, Nitish, victory of 163
Seshan, T.N. 268
Sharma, Shankar Dayal 88, 268
Shekhawat, Bhairon Singh as Rajasthan Chief Minister 287
Shishu Mandirs established by RSS 196
Shiv Sena of Maharashtra 57, 61; and BJP alliance 61-2
Shukla, V.C. as Foreign Minister 307
Sikkim Democratic Front 62
Sikkim Sangram Parishad of Sikkim 62
Singh, Ajit 51
Singh, Charan 125; and his government 255; as Chief Minister in UP 50, 200; Jan Congress 212; resignation of as Chief Minister and imposition of the President's rule 198-9
Singh, Choudhary Charan and Lok Dal government 305
Singh, Digvijay and Madhavrao Scindia 91; as Minister of State for External Affairs 307
Singh, Jaswant as BJP's Foreign Minister 313
Singh, Kalyan and his government 209-10; as Chief Minister 207; dismissal of government 209; expelled from 48-9; his ministry

sacked by President 207
Singh, T.N. 202; as Chief Minister and rightist coalition 203-4
Singh, V.P. (JD) and coalition government 279; and his government 125-6, 129, 255; and interests of Backward Castes 206; as Prime Minister 25, 51; his resignation from Congress 29
Sinha, Ramesh (CPI) 198
social movements 25
Somnath to Ayodhya *rathayatra* 14
sons-of-the-soil movement as anti-Communist 61; as anti-Muslim mobilization 61
South Asia Free Trade Areas, tasks of 313
South Indian Liberal Federation 57
South–South cooperation 315
Sri Lankan crisis and NDA stand 318-19
Srikrishna Commission 88
SSP 204; and Tripathi meeting 202
state parties *see* regional parties 24
Subramaniam, C. and National Defence College, call to 305
SVD coalition government 68, 199-200; failure of 195-9
Swaraj Party (SP) 207; and Congress 297; in Uttar Pradesh led by Mulayam Singh Yadav 84
Swaran Singh Committee 234
Swatantra Party 50; as a protector of cow and Hindu *dharma* 189

Tamil Maanila Congress (TMC) 46-7, 58; and DMK alliance 58
Tamil parties and elimination of Congress rule 57
Tata, J.R.D. 234
TDP of Andhra Pradesh 30, 57, 60; its leader, Yerran Naidu on federalism 222; and BJP alliance 132
Telecom Regulatory Authority of India (TRAI) 35
tenth Lok Sabha elections and Congress' government formation 126
Thackeray, Bal as authoritarian leader 62
Thakur, Karpoori and Bihar Janata Party government 276
Trinamool Congress and BJP electoral pact 16; as alliance 176
Tripathi, Kamalapati 191; and formation of Congress government 204-5
two-party system 21

'umbrella' organization 297
United Front (UF) 13-14, 208; and caste sentiments 109; and Common Approach and Minimum Programme (CAMP) 94; as Left Front 110-11; in the eleventh Lok Sabha 94-6; its formation of 89-90; its coalition 66; its government, fall of 69; its rule 29
United Liberation Front of Assam (ULFA) 61
Utkal Congress in Orissa 45, 50
Uttar Pradesh, and 1967 Election Scenario 188-91; Assembly, violence inside 209; coalition governance in 17; government, formation of 191-5; its political profile of 187-8

Vajpayee, Atal Behari 125; and coalition government 279-80; as Foreign Minister 302, 303, 309, 312; as Prime Minister for two weeks 91
Venkatachelliah Commission 221-2

Venkatachelliah Constitution Review Commission (2002) 36
Venkatachelliah, M.N. as chairman of NCWRC 245-6
Venkataraman, R. 88, 233
VHP 66, 134
Vice-President, election of 267-8
Vidhan Sabha election 1971 23-4

West Bengal and thirteenth Lok Sabha and BJP, growth in 160; and coalition government 12; coalition governance in 16; and Local Committees (LCs) 173-4; its poll outcome and Left Front 164-7
West Bengal Industrial Development Corporation (WBIDC) 172
WTO Treaty 1995 24

Yadav, Laloo Prasad 131; and coalition government in Bihar 276; and RJD formation 52; as possible Prime Minister 91
Yadav, Mulayam Singh 51, 207
Yadav, Ram Naresh as Chief Minister 206
Yadav, Sharad 131; and Samata Party in Bihar 52

Zaheer, Ali 191
zamindari system 148-50